Regionalists on the Left

Regionalists on the Left
Radical Voices from the American West

Edited by

MICHAEL C. STEINER

UNIVERSITY OF OKLAHOMA PRESS : NORMAN

Publication of this book is made possible through
the generosity of Edith Kinney Gaylord.

Library of Congress Cataloging-in-Publication Data

Regionalists on the left : radical voices from the American West / edited by
Michael C. Steiner.
    pages cm
Includes index.
ISBN 978-0-8061-4340-8 (hardcover)
ISBN 978-0-8061-9462-2 (paper)
1. Regionalism—West (U.S.)—History—20th century. 2. Right and left (Political science)—West (U.S.)—History—20th century. 3. West (U.S.)—Intellectual life—20th century. 4. West (U.S.)—Politics and government—20th century. 5. West (U.S.)—Biography. I. Steiner, Michael (Michael C.), author, editor of compilation.
F595.R375 2013
978'.033—dc23

2012041366

The paper in this book meets the guidelines for permanence and durability of the Committee on Production Guidelines for Book Longevity of the Council on Library Resources, Inc. ∞

The manufacturer's authorized representative in the EU for product safety is Mare Nostrum Group B.V., Mauritskade 21D, GC Amsterdam, The Netherlands, email: gpsr@mare-nostrum.co.uk

Copyright © 2013 by the University of Oklahoma Press, Norman, Publishing Division of the University. Paperback published 2025. Manufactured in the U.S.A.

All rights reserved. No part of this publication may be reproduced, stored in a retrieval system, or transmitted, in any form or by any means, electronic, mechanical, photocopying, recording, or otherwise—except as permitted under Section 107 or 108 of the United States Copyright Act—without the prior written permission of the University of Oklahoma Press. To request permission to reproduce selections from this book, write to Permissions, University of Oklahoma Press, 2800 Venture Drive, Norman OK 73069, or email rights.oupress@ou.edu.

To the memory of Carey McWilliams (1905–1980),
egalitarian dreamer and dissident

Contents

List of Illustrations	ix
Preface	xi
Acknowledgments	xiii

Introduction: Varieties of Western American Regionalism,   1
    by Michael C. Steiner

PART I. THE MIDWEST   21

1. "Revolution can spring up from the windy prairie as naturally as wheat": Meridel Le Sueur and the Making of a Radical Regional Tradition   25
    by Julia Mickenberg

2. Feet in the Grassroots: Josephine Herbst's Midwest   47
    by Sara Kosiba

3. Radical Regionalism in American Art: The Case of Joe Jones   65
    by Bryna R. Campbell

PART II. THE GREAT PLAINS AND TEXAS   87

4. Blowout Grass: Mari Sandoz, Historical Pessimism, and Great Plains Regionalism   93
    by Robert L. Dorman

5. Radical by Nature: Sanora Babb and Ecological Disaster on the High Plains, 1900–1940   111
    by Douglas Wixson

6. Theorizing Regionalism and Folklore from the Left: B. A. Botkin, the Oklahoma Years, 1921–1939   135
    by Jerrold Hirsch

7. Discover the Truth and Publish It: Angie Elbertha Debo and the Roots of America's "Real Imperialism"   157
    by Shirley A. Leckie Reed

8. Texas, the Transnational, and Regionalism: J. Frank Dobie and Américo Paredes 184
   by José E. Limón

PART III. THE NORTHERN WEST 205

9. Wrong Side Up: Joseph Kinsey Howard and the Wisdom of the Dispossessed 209
   by Timothy Lehman

10. Bad Medicine: D'Arcy McNickle Locates Liberalism and the Left from a Tribal Perspective 229
    by William W. Bevis

11. Robert Cantwell and Northwest Left Literary Labors 253
    by T. V. Reed

PART IV. CALIFORNIA 277

12. John Sanford's Radical Regionalism: The Universal of the Particular 283
    by Jack Mearns

13. Toward a Transnational Liberalism of the Left: Positive Liberties and the West in Carlos Bulosan's "America" 303
    by Stephen J. Mexal

14. Regionalism and Social Protest during John Steinbeck's "Years of Greatness," 1936–1939 327
    by David Wrobel

15. Carey McWilliams, California, and the Education of a Radical Regionalist 353
    by Michael C. Steiner

Contributors 377
Index 383

Illustrations

Meridel Le Sueur	24
Josephine Herbst	48
Joe Jones	66
Roustabouts (1934), by Joe Jones	75
Mari Sandoz	92
Sanora Babb	110
B. A. Botkin	134
Angie Debo	158
J. Frank Dobie	185
Américo Paredes	186
Joseph Kinsey Howard	208
D'Arcy McNickle	228
Robert Cantwell	252
John Sanford	282
Carlos Bulosan	302
John Steinbeck	328
Carey McWilliams	352

Preface

Thoughts about *Regionalists on the Left* have been gathering in my mind for decades, but two fairly recent events brought the book's purpose and title into focus. In May 2004, while giving a talk at the University of Lodz in Poland, I was startled by the audience's reaction when I used the words "region" and "regionalism." "That's fascism!" a number of people protested when they heard these troubling words. After my talk, several thoughtful young professors came up to explain their response, and our conversation continued over beer. "We didn't mean *you're* a fascist," they insisted. "It's just the whole idea of regionalism that's dangerous."

The ingrained notion that regionalism is dangerous has cropped up throughout my career, but I've never heard it more bluntly expressed than that afternoon in Poland. Quick dismissal of regionalism and even of the study of regions as being inherently reactionary or hopelessly outdated had colored many conversations over the years. I knew that regionalism in its largest sense—the basic fact that culture varies over space and that people identify with portions of the earth that they inhabit—is a fundamental human variable that transcends any ideological label. I also knew that in the United States and elsewhere there have been self-conscious regionalists of every ideological persuasion and from every part of the political spectrum. Yet snap judgments and blanket condemnations of regionalism as a retrograde impulse remain standard fare, and it was this sharp reaction in a distant country that planted the seed to set the record straight by writing a book with a more balanced view of this complex, many-sided aspect of culture.

If the outburst in Poland helped launch this book, a memorable conversation three years later in California gave it sharper focus and a title. In May 2007 my good friend and colleague Leila Zenderland and I had been at a social event in San Diego, and while driving back to Fullerton along the Pacific Coast, I described one of my earliest trips down the coast to San Diego, soon after I arrived in California from Minnesota. I had driven there in 1976 for an academic conference where I first met Carey McWilliams, one of my intellectual heroes and a regionalist with strong progressive values. To Leila's predictable remark that McWilliams's leftist regionalism must have been extremely rare, I listed a whole batting order of left-leaning regionalists, most of them from the Midwest and West and active during the 1930s and early 1940s. I mentioned the incident in Lodz and several similar moments, and Leila simply said, "You need to write a book about regionalists on the left."

Leila's suggestion, with its echo of Daniel Aaron's notable *Writers on the Left* (1961), captured my purpose perfectly. The title *Regionalists on the Left* would be simple, straightforward, and doubly meaningful. It would refer to people on the left politically, but also to people on the left geographically—to a significant number of women and men who were progressive intellectuals and activists from the western, or left-hand, side of the map. That *Regionalists on the Left* as a title would surprise people was borne out by expressions of dismay when I mentioned it to friends and colleagues: "I didn't know there were any." "That doesn't make much sense." "That's a contradiction." "Isn't that an oxymoron?" These were a few of the responses that simply reaffirmed the need for a less distorted, more open-minded understanding of regionalists and regionalism.

There were many steps between these events and the book that was finished five years later. After giving several conference papers on radical western regionalism late in 2007 and early in 2008 and receiving positive responses from a surprising number of scholars, it seemed that a collective effort would be the most fitting way to draw attention to a collection of people representing a largely hidden side of regionalism. A chorus of many voices, no matter how different and sometimes dissonant, seemed more effective and appropriate than my single perspective in reflecting the multivocal nature of radical western regionalism in the 1930s and early 1940s.

It has been truly gratifying that so many talented people from so many disciplines accepted my invitation, threw themselves into this project, and stuck with me through its many versions and revisions. It is my hope that our collaboration has uncovered an important but surprisingly neglected gathering of egalitarian dreamers and dissidents from the American West and that we have cleared the way for a wider view of regions and regionalism in general.

Acknowledgments

Many people and places have shaped this book. Looking back at this project and beyond, I realize how lucky I've been with the company I've kept and the places where I've lived. For more than forty years, a host of teachers, colleagues, students, friends, and family members have cheered me on in countless ways, and they've been especially helpful with two major interests—love of the land and the politics of place—that weave their way throughout these chapters. I know that I have relied on the active kindness and simple presence of a multitude of people, and although it's impossible to fully thank every one of them, this acknowledgment is a long-overdue beginning.

I am immediately indebted to the fourteen talented scholars who generously agreed to join a project that promised to be finished in two years but took more than twice that long. *Regionalists on the Left* is truly a collective effort, and it has been an honor to work with this sometimes unruly but always colorful company. I value the intellectual depth and multiple perspectives these scholars have given the book you're now reading, and I treasure the friendships we've forged along the way.

From the beginning, I was heartened by Doug Wixson's keen interest, vast knowledge, and shrewd suggestions, and José Limón's early endorsement was a crucial catalyst. From start to finish, Chuck Rankin has been a tireless advocate and patient sounding board. Chuck's formidable grasp of western history, astute editorial and conversational skills, and high good humor lifted my spirits and kept the book alive. His positive influence can be felt throughout these pages. I am grateful to other gracious people at the University of Oklahoma Press, especially Managing Editor Steven Baker and copy editor Laura Oaks, who helped push the book through to the finish. The book also benefited from the comments of four anonymous outside readers who reviewed the manuscript at several stages along the way.

Like every book, this one has deep and far-reaching sources. I am forever thankful to my remarkable parents, Paul and Sheila Steiner, for their steadfast love of learning and sense of social justice. As an undergraduate in the late 1960s at Carleton College, I was fortunate to have dedicated teachers like Carlton Qualey, Erling Larsen, and Wayne Carver, whose grasp of intellectual history, literary sensibility, and love of place are with me today. My teachers in the American Studies Program at the University of Minnesota promoted the study of region, regionalism, and place as respectable topics for a graduate student and as themes that have possessed me ever since. Hy Berman, John Berryman, Bernard Bowron, Art Geffen, John Fraser Hart, Karal Ann Marling, David Noble, Mulford Sibley, Mary Turpie, Donald Torbert, and Yi-Fu Tuan have all shaped the way I think, teach, and write. Three of them have had particularly lasting impacts. Mulford Sibley introduced me to the significance of radicalism, utopianism, and the value of nonviolent protest; Yi-Fu Tuan opened my eyes to the myriad meanings of space and place; and more than anyone, my advisor and primary mentor, Mary Turpie, believed that regionalism was an important and understudied part of American Studies.

I'm also deeply grateful to early support of number of veteran regionalists from the interwar decades. Deeply encouraging letters from Jack Conroy, H. G. Merriam, and especially from Lewis Mumford fired my conviction that such work was needed. Interviews with Meridel Le Sueur in Minneapolis and Rupert Vance, W. T. Couch, and Paul Green in Chapel Hill in the early 1970s, as well as conversations a few years later with Carey McWilliams in San Diego and Henry Nash Smith in Berkeley—these personal exchanges gave me a more immediate sense of the regionalist movement, and as Brenda Ueland, another Minnesota radical regionalist, would say, they gave strength to my sword arm.

When I came to California in 1975, I was fortunate to find similar strength and support from a number of scholars who wrote with verve and wisdom about frontier and region and about California and the American West. I met many of them at the Huntington Library in San Marino, where I was fortunate to talk about western regionalism with Ray Allen Billington, Martin Ridge, Wilbur Jacobs, Dick Etulain, Bill Deverell, David Wrobel, and Chuck Rankin. I am forever grateful to two brilliant thinkers and writers—historian Robert Hine and environmental philosopher Paul Shepard—whose conversations and guidance profoundly shaped my understanding of regionalism and sense of place. Like my Minnesota mentors, Californians Bob Hine, Paul Shepard, Martin Ridge, and later

Lawrence Levine and George Lipsitz supported these ideas and added insights of their own. My friendship with these generous souls and heroic American scholars has been a pivotal experience in my life.

Most of all, I am forever indebted to the vibrant academic community at California State University, Fullerton, that has been the center of my professional life since 1975. For nearly forty years, my colleagues and dear friends in the American Studies Department—Allan Axelrad, Erica Ball, Jesse Battan, Adam Golub, Wayne Hobson, John Ibson, Carrie Lane, Elaine Lewinnek, Karen Lystra, Terri Snyder, Pam Steinle, the late Jim Weaver, and Leila Zenderland—have embraced my ideas, accepted my imperfections, and nurtured my enthusiasms. Within this remarkably generous group, Allan, Karen, and Leila deserve extra praise for their steadfast intellectual, emotional, and editorial support as this book came to life. I have also been cheered on by colleagues beyond my department, especially by our splendid former dean Tom Klammer and by Stan Breckenridge in Afro-Ethnic Studies, John Carroll in Geography, Nancy Fitch in History, Merrill Ring in Philosophy, and Mark Stohs in Finance. Many wonderful students have helped me think about this book over the years, but one outstanding graduate student deserves infinite praise for being my indispensible right-hand man as *Regionalists on the Left* moved toward publication. John Carlos Marquez's powerful research and editorial skills, sharp intellect, and enthusiasm have enhanced every part of the book and brought it to completion.

This book has benefited greatly from the long-standing support of the larger American Studies profession, especially from friends and fellow regional scholars Eric Sandeen, Simon Bronner, Jay Mechling, Pamela Mittlefehldt, and Elizabeth Raymond. I am deeply indebted to my three past co-authors and editors: Clarence Mondale, Wayne Franklin, and David Wrobel. I have learned about regionalism in a global context from my remarkable Fulbright colleagues in Eastern Europe: Tibor Glant and Judit Molnár at the University of Debrecen in Hungary and Jurek and Joanna Durczak at Marie Curie Sklodowska University in Lublin, Poland.

Finally, I send my everlasting gratitude to my loving life-long partner, Lucy Lefren Steiner, my wisest, most affectionate critic and companion, who has been a steadfast source of strength and support for more than forty years.

Introduction

VARIETIES OF WESTERN AMERICAN REGIONALISM

Michael C. Steiner

"Regionalism is a forever agenda."
—Archie Green, 1982

"There are healthy forms of regionalism but rigid, ideological regionalism is usually dangerous. Nothing is more anathema to a serious radical than regionalism."
—Henry Nash Smith, 1980

In the early 1980s two veteran regionalists living on opposite sides of San Francisco Bay looked back on the 1930s and reached dramatically different conclusions about their youthful hopes for a progressive regionalism based in the American West. Henry Nash Smith, an eminent Berkeley English professor who had once championed a folk and working-class renewal in his native Texas, regretted that regionalism almost always succumbs to reactionary impulses. Archie Green, a San Francisco–based labor historian and folklorist who had been radicalized in the Bay Area shipyards of the 1930s, continued to believe in regionalism as a progressive force for working-class concerns.

These opposing viewpoints—Smith's rueful skepticism and Green's undying optimism—frame the boundaries of this book and evoke a host of questions that are raised and examined in every chapter. What are the political implications of regionalism in the American West in the past and the present? Is western regionalism essentially a backward-looking impulse, as Smith laments? Or can a progressive, even left-leaning, regionalism thrive in the West and elsewhere, as Green believes? Can westerners express deep pride of place without turning to the right? Are there "healthy forms" of inclusive, pluralistic western regionalism from the past that might help us answer these questions in the present?

Informed with such questions, *Regionalists on the Left: Radical Voices from the American West* explores the political, aesthetic, and ideological dimensions of western American regionalism during its heyday in the 1930s and early 1940s to provide a deeper grasp of this protean impulse in general and its significance today. This book examines the lives and work of sixteen artists and intellectuals whose critical affection for their particular portions of the American West deserves a chapter in the ongoing history of American regionalism. Deeply engaged with critical as well as elegiac love of their native and adopted grounds, these men and women were "radical" in the deepest sense of the term: their passionate sense of injustice done to the land and the people who live upon it drove them to seek the roots of social problems and demanded thorough social change. As succeeding chapters here will reveal, many of these regionalists on the left were moved by what has been termed "the radicalism of tradition": they found inspiration for progressive concerns in the present by recovering deeply rooted egalitarian traditions in the past.[1]

These radical regionalists were firmly planted on "the left" in what historian Michael Kazin describes as the classical sense of the term. Emphasizing that the label emerged from the French Revolution and retained a foreign ring for Americans until it entered their vocabulary in the 1930s, Kazin defines the left as "that social movement, or congeries of mutually sympathetic social movements, that are dedicated to a radically egalitarian transformation of society." Employing "a broad spectrum of ways to attempt such a transformation—from quietly distributing anti-capitalist leaflets on street corners to organizing a revolutionary army to smash the state," a host of "egalitarian dreamers" have had a profound if indirect impact on American society from the 1820s to the present.[2] In almost every instance, the radical regionalists in this present book were egalitarian dreamers with a critical affection for the land and people of their native portions of the American West.

While never constituting a unified movement replete with manifestos and specific goals, these novelists, poets, painters, historians, folklorists, and journalists often knew one anther, and they raised voices of protest against racial, environmental, and working-class injustices in the 1930s and 1940s that reverberate in the twenty-first century. Their radical voices and visions—ranging from fierce indignation to biting humor to tragic irony—constitute a significant but neglected strain of western regionalist expression.

A basic purpose of this book is to expand our understanding of western regionalism and American regionalism in general by uncovering a woefully neglected intellectual tradition—what Michael Denning has identified as a "proletarian regionalism" concentrated in the West and Midwest. In a larger sense, the left-wing regionalists of the 1930s and 1940s were part of what historian Robert Hine has described as "a cultural voice as strong and dominant as a prairie wind" that has blown across the West from the Populist movement of the 1890s to the present.[3] Although western regionalists have ventured all over the political map and have often staunchly opposed anything proletarian or urban, this book illuminates a largely hidden, often urban and working-class, multicultural regionalism in the West. Far from being rough-hewn allies of the Southern Agrarians in the 1930s or range-riding precursors of right-wing libertarian or Tea Party fundamentalism, the radical regionalists in this book paved the way for the pluralist, cosmopolitan versions of western regionalism that are increasingly possible in the present.

To lay the groundwork for this book and present its cast of characters, this introduction traces the larger contours of western American regionalism in the 1930s and 1940s, briefly surveys critical interpretations of that impulse both then and now, and weighs the significance of western regionalists on the left in light of recent scholarship.

REGIONALISTS AND REGIONALISMS ALL OVER THE MAP

"Regionalism" in its most basic sense is a noun describing the fact that culture varies over space. It includes both the study of spatial variations within a national culture and various groups' and individuals' sense of belonging to the portion of the earth they inhabit. In this fundamental sense, regionalism recognizes the irrepressible diversities of culture and nature, and it reflects how people and places interact to create an ever-changing mosaic of cultural landscapes. Seen in this large context, regionalism is an essential variable of human experience, and to judge it as good or bad, laudable or lamentable, would be like imagining work or leisure, race or gender, or any other basic cultural category as a completely positive or negative force.

Like all basic human variables, however, regionalism and regional identity easily evolve into an array of social causes and ideologies. The fact that culture varies over space and that people identify with places and patches of territory means that regionalism easily becomes a self-conscious and heightened concern, especially during periods of personal and collective transition and trauma. This was particularly true during the interwar decades, when the slippery and all-purpose terms "region" and "regionalism" became key words and signposts for deeper anxieties and impulses. They became prolific catchall words, generating myriad associations and implications: they were "yeasty" concepts evoking "admiration, hostility, embarrassment, and study."[4]

Beginning in the 1920s and burgeoning during the Great Depression, "regionalism" became an intellectual buzzword. Remindful of the late-eighteenth-century French origins of the political term "left," the word "regionalism" was coined by French decentralists in the late nineteenth century and first used in the United States in the wake of World War I as substitute for the more fractious term "sectionalism."[5] As a transplanted word for an appealing impulse, "regionalism" and associated concepts spread rapidly across the continent, first among city planners and social critics. As an ism, it became the seedbed for frequently conflicting schools of thought and partisan ideologies, and it captured the imaginations of a spectrum of artists and intellectuals, policy makers and politicians.

By 1920, when many Americans seemed weary of war and wary of international involvement, John Dewey could wryly observe that "the wider the formal, the legal unity, the more intense becomes the local life" and that "the only things that seem to be nation-wide are the high cost of living, prohibition, and devotion to localism," while Mary Austin declared that "decentralization is the only way to accomplish the release of the American genius." In 1922 Frederick Jackson Turner noted, in a resonant comment regarding political conditions, "We are so large and diversified a nation that it is impossible to see the situation except through sectional glasses."[6] At the very end of the 1920s Benjamin Botkin, Carey McWilliams, and others detected a "New Regionalism" across the American landscape, a "new feeling for locality . . . growing out of world unrest and conflict during and since the War."[7]

By the early 1930s sectionalism rehabilitated as regionalism had become a patriotic duty. In 1932 Franklin Roosevelt announced his devotion to regional principles as "the way of the future" and championed policies over the next sixteen years that made him "one of the great regionalists of the age."[8] By the late 1930s regionalism was a fixture of mass media and advertising with regional writers and painters working for such powerful culture brokers as Time-Life, Walt Disney Studios, and Twentieth Century–Fox. The movie version of *The Wizard of Oz*, for example, was steeped in regionalist imagery, from the John Steuart Curry–like farmstead in Kansas to the Grant Wood–inspired cornfields and hillsides of Munchkinland. Regional motifs were used to sell products ranging from Lucky Strike cigarettes to Westinghouse appliances. "When business needed to appeal to public good will," a critic has observed, "it relied on the Americana flavor and blissful futurism of Regionalism." The "Boom in Regionalism" that the *Saturday Review of Literature* touted in 1934 had swollen into a torrent of words and images by the eve of World War II.[9]

The title of Botkin's essay "We Talk about Regionalism—North, East, South, and West" (1933) gives a glimpse of this widespread concern, and his observation in 1937 that "there are as many cults as there are regional cultures" was especially true of the trans-Mississippi West.[10] This was neither the first nor the last time westerners would declare their pride of place in a variety of ways. Like American regionalism in general, western regionalism has had an episodic history with a sharp political edge.[11] Regional consciousness emerged in the trans-Mississippi West at the end of the nineteenth century in many forms—including local-color writing, architecture, and arts and crafts in parts of the West—but regional identity was most powerfully expressed in fierce populist protest against the moneyed powers of the East. One hundred years later, at the dawn of the twenty-first century, self-conscious western regionalism was riding high once again as a complicated tangle of New Right and New Left politics, environmental protest, local food movements, transnational migrations, racial and ethnic awareness, and cultural criticism touting a "New West," a "New Western History," and a western "critical regionalism" in academic and public arenas.[12]

To gain a deeper perspective on western regionalism in general and its myriad manifestations in the present, it is essential to look to the past and spotlight the era when the topic was most widely and explicitly debated.

To describe every regionalism that sprouted across the West during the 1930s and early 1940s would fill a large volume. Several insightful books and many of the chapters in this volume map much of this territory, and this introduction simply provides a broad overview and representative samples of this protean impulse—how it was expressed and how it has been interpreted.[13]

Cropping up all over the western map, self-proclaimed regionalists ranged from cliques of English professors and folklorists in Texas, Oklahoma, Nebraska, New Mexico, and Montana to groups of New Deal planners in the Columbia, Colorado, and Missouri River basins. Western-flavored regionalism motivated intellectuals as different as Carey McWilliams and Walter Prescott Webb, writers as varied as Mary Austin and Meridel Le Sueur, painters as disparate as Grant Wood and Joe Jones. Scores of "little magazines" trumpeted the spirit of western place, and footloose journalists, novelists, and photographers—stirred by the racial, economic, and environmental tumult in the West—scoured the landscape to discover, in Alfred Kazin's words, "a whole world of marvels on the continent to possess—a world of rivers and scenes, of folklore and regional culture, of a heroic tradition to reclaim and of forgotten heroes to follow."[14]

This Whitmanesque urge to "study out the land" and folk of the West took many shapes, from Mary Austin's yearning for "the feel of the purposeful earth" in the Native American landscapes of New Mexico to Dorothea Lange's stinging images of earth-scarred migrant workers in California. A search for a more grounded and authentic America beneath the veneer of mass civilization—for what Iowa writer Ruth Suckow described as "something that underlies the mechanical America of skyscrapers, filling-stations, and bungalows"—motivated regionalists of all political persuasions.[15]

Three examples from a myriad of possibilities reflect conservative, liberal, and radical versions of this impulse. On a train trip to Santa Fe in the early 1930s the Southern Agrarian poet and polemicist John Crowe Ransom glanced through his window at seemingly happy Pueblo Indians who laughed and praised their gods as they threshed wheat on ancient threshing floors. "So this was regionalism; flourishing on the meanest capital, surviving stubbornly, and brilliant," he concluded. "Their culture persists, though most of it goes back to the Stone Age, and they live as they always have lived." On another train trip across the West a few years later Hallie

Flanagan, director of the Federal Theatre Project, was moved by the drama of the sprawling landscape and reached a different conclusion: "The great plains, the cactus and sage brush, the vast cattle ranges, the rivers blazing with reflections of red and yellow trees, the sheer precipices of brilliantly colored rocks—where were the plays which made you feel the vastness and might of this land?" In 1935 the Minnesota writer Meridel Le Sueur addressed a congress of left-wing artists and intellectuals in New York City extolling the wide terrain and brave workers of the Midwest. "There is only one class that has begun to produce a mid-Western culture," she proclaimed, "and that is the growing yeast of the revolutionary working class arising on the Mesaba range, the wheat belt, the coal fields of Illinois, the blown and ravaged land of the Dakotas, the flour mills, the granaries." She concluded: "Revolution can spring up from the windy prairie as naturally as wheat."[16]

These three intellectuals epitomize the ideological sweep of 1930s regionalism: from Ransom's nostalgic primitivism to Flanagan's New Deal folk-regional nationalism to Le Sueur's working-class revolution. A host of fellow regionalists across the West voiced similar and distinctly different sentiments about their home grounds during that era. Many cultural critics—both during and after the interwar decades—have analyzed this regional resurgence, yet most have offered predictable, one-dimensional interpretations blind to the wide range and full significance of that impulse.

THE CRITICAL RESPONSE

Most cultural observers have interpreted 1930s regionalists as cranky reactionaries building foolish barriers against the acids of modernity and tides of pluralism and progress. John Crowe Ransom would be their representative regionalist rather than Meridel Le Sueur, a nostalgic Mary Austin would typify this impulse in their minds rather than an indignant Dorothea Lange. There is *some* truth to this conclusion. Witnesses across the political spectrum in the 1930s voiced doubts about regionalism in general. Lewis Mumford, one of the nation's most thoughtful regional theorists, for example, cautioned in 1934 that regionalism easily degenerated into a "neurotic retreat" and charged, "The besetting sin of regionalism lies in the fact that it is part of a blind reaction . . . an attempt to find refuge within an old shell against the turbulent invasions of the outside world."[17] Echoing Mumford's warnings, Marxist critic V. F. Calverton dismissed the typical 1930s regionalist as "a modern Don Quixote stabbing at steel windmills," and sociologist Louis Wirth scorned regionalists as crackpots who would "squeeze life into a rigid mold . . . and retard the integration of life into a wider and more inclusive scale."[18]

The Southern Agrarians, with their neo-Confederate manifesto *I'll Take My Stand* (1930), bore the brunt of these attacks, but western regionalists seemed equally guilty of antimodernist excesses. Many of the most ardent western regionalists, including Walter Prescott Webb, James C. Malin, Vardis Fisher, Grant Wood, and Mary Austin, seem to fit a reactionary, backward-looking mold that troubled their contemporaries. A few examples will suffice. To listen, for example, to Idaho regionalist Fisher rant against eastern urban writing and "the tiresome trivia of Jewish family life," the "proliferating lunacies of their cities, the robotized togetherness of their feverish lives, and their dull, inbred, and over praised books" would arouse indignation. To hear Austin advocate the bracing tonic of "the aboriginal poetic orgy" or to read Webb's paean to the noble Texas Rangers and condemnation of "ditch water" Mexican blood and the "cruel streak in the Mexican nature" would provoke even harsher indictments.[19]

Western regionalism in the 1930s seemed full of such narrow, provincial barbs, and liberal and radical observers were especially wary of regionalist excesses. In 1935, for example, *New Masses* columnist Kyle Crichton, firmly established in New York City, lambasted southwestern regionalists as urban refugees filled with "mystical nonsense of God, the Indian, and the good dark earth" and driven by the foolish notion that "machine civilization could be evaded by retreating into the kiva." Dudley Wynn, a southwesterner himself, bluntly condemned regionalism there as "a petty patchwork carried on by misfits."[20] Until the Popular Front movement of the mid-1930s brought official Communist Party approval of American folk material, urban-based radicals tended to dismiss anything that smacked of regionalism. They reserved special scorn for left-wing regionalists like Le Sueur, Sanora Babb, and Jack Conroy, who despite their proletarian and Marxist credentials were condemned as sentimental lovers of the land and advocates of a counterrevolutionary Tolstoyan back-to-the land movement. Looking back on the early 1930s, Babb recalled, "'Regional' was the stinging word used by certain influential New York groups to try to keep writers outside NY in their places. It was a patronizing put-down."[21]

In several piercing attacks beginning in 1936, Bernard DeVoto—a truculent westerner himself—ridiculed regionalism as a mere "coterie manifesto" and lambasted the surge of regionalist fiction "reeking of the soil." Mocking grim prairie regionalists who "import the novel of the middle-Minnesota period in which soup dribbles down the paralyzed side of grandma's face," DeVoto then derided New Mexico sojourners Mary Austin, D. H. Lawrence, Mabel Dodge Luhan, and their disciples: "Preciosities about the mythical awareness that neolithic savages are supposed to have ... are going to remain preciosities ... fiction that wears a squash blossom in its hair or talks about the plumed serpent is just silly." In a sweeping attack, the art historian H. W. Janson detected deeper, more menacing tendencies, warning that "almost every one of the ideas of the regionalist credo could be matched more or less verbatim from the writings of Nazi experts on art."[22]

Variants of such attacks continue today. Contemporary western regionalists—whether expressing themselves as "new regional" historians, bioregionalists, or new localists—are often dismissed as backward-yearning traditionalists longing for organic purity and fearful of the new world order with its flux and fusion of cultures. Western regionalism is often scorned, in the words of a recent observer, as a form of "boosterism, a fatuous puffing of merely local talent—a kind of literary chamber of commerce juxtaposed to the three national congresses of race, class, and gender." Condemning regionalism as a misguided rejection of modernity, others argue that it "concocts for us a pacifying, relaxing, New Age image of organic traditions and communities" stone deaf to the "multicultural Babel" of contemporary life.[23] In a free-floating world where, as Karl Marx famously remarked, "all that is solid melts into thin air," concerns for place and regional identity seem archaic, moribund, and potentially oppressive.

The surge of global capitalism, permeability of national boundaries, ubiquitous digital communication, and massive global migrations—such present-day conditions seem to erase any earnest discussion of "roots," "region," "regionalism," and "sense of place." Yet these words continue to spark critical firestorms, for they are cast as tribal, potentially tyrannical responses to the messy vitality of the all-inclusive, ever-expanding world order. The antagonists of this global battle are bluntly opposed in the title of Benjamin Barber's *Jihad vs. McWorld* (1995), and the fury surrounding Salman Rushdie's *Satanic Verses* (1988) can be seen as a case study of this struggle. Stressing that his novel "celebrates hybridity, impurity, intermingling.... It rejoices in ... the great possibility that mass migration gives to the world.... It is a love-song to our mongrel selves," Rushdie warns against the "apostles of purity" who crusade against mixed-up, migratory, impure people across the earth.[24]

American regionalists too have been condemned as apostles of purity. The cultural critics Werner Sollors and Roberto Dainotto, for example, denounce regionalism as a bogus form of cultural diversity—as an inherently reactionary urge that encourages differences *between* regions and nations at the same time that it smothers differences *within* them. For Sollors, regionalism represents a destructive "vision of America as a structured society composed of neatly defined 'ethnic regions'": it is a dangerous pipe dream of "homogenous components" within which ordered and orderly cultures can grow.[25]

For Dainotto, regionalism is "a pastoral sensibility" that yearns to recreate a cozy world where "all things have their place, and all places their own traditions." "The literature of place and region," he warns, "will transform the entire planet into a happy coexistence of different regional traditions, each valid in its 'place,'" and the connections between such literary hankerings and fascist appeals to racial purity for land and folk are obvious. Summoning the ghost of Martin Heidegger, whose blood-and-soil philosophy of roots in the region and suspicion of rootless foreigners made him a Nazi spokesperson, Dainotto concludes that regionalism with its repressive vision of "imaginary communities, happy and beautiful in their orthodox and pristine purity" is a clear menace in the postmodern world.[26]

Many critics allude to Heidegger and fellow fascist place theorist Mircea Eliade, warning of the dark, tribal tendencies of regional and place-related ideologies. Voicing concern about the "recrudescence ... of problematical senses of place, from reactionary nationalism to competitive localisms to sanitized obsessions with 'heritage,'" geographer Doreen Massey typifies this criticism. Commenting on the alluring dream of dwelling in a regional homeland, architectural historian Neal Leach, for example, warns that "it is precisely in this dream—the fantasy of the homeland—that the repressed may be unleashed" and that outsiders and transient folk, whether Jews, Gypsies, or migrant workers, fall victim to a "single totalizing vision" of homeland purity.[27]

Historian Wolfgang Schivelbusch echoes the common "regionalism equals fascism" equation by detecting close links between American regionalism in the 1930s and regional impulses in Mussolini's Italy and Hitler's Germany. Deeply critical of "the cult of the soil, land, and 'organic' society" that gripped a cross-section of politicians, writers, and intellectuals at the end of the nineteenth century, Schivelbusch traces how, by the 1930s, an "emphasis on soil in all its forms, from the farmer's field to the regional landscape, now took on quasi-religious, magical, 'primordial' significance" and inspired three New Deals in the United States, Italy, and Germany. Such dangerous primal appeals to land and folk, he implies, shape regionalism in Europe and America today.[28]

Bringing the regionalists-as-fascists story to the contemporary American West, the historian Gerald Nash, to give a final example, has accused the New Western historians of the 1990s of having direct links with totalitarian intellectuals and apologists of the 1930s. Deeply suspicious of these new historians, with their focus on region, their "special passion for the 'folk,' the common people at the grass roots," and the background for many of them at Yale, where one-time Nazi apologist Paul de Man taught, Nash argues that their methods "bore striking similarity to the modus operandi of Nazi, Fascist, and Communist academicians in their heyday." These brash radical regionalists, he concludes, "are attempting proselytization for what in essence are totalitarian ideologies. . . . Their goals are not the stuff of scholarship but of propaganda."[29]

Such blunt and sweeping criticisms bring back the quotations that began this Introduction—and hence this book. In light of this ongoing critical salvo, was Henry Nash Smith ultimately correct in declaring that "there is nothing more anathema to a serious radical than regionalism"? Or is a progressive, even leftist regionalism possible, as Archie Green asserted? What is it about the words "place," "region," and "regionalism" that draw such ire from critics, that seems to unleash such dark and sinister forces? Can one have a deep-seated love of the land and the people who live upon it without being reactionary?

The contributors to *Regionalists on the Left* provide answers to these and other pressing questions by unearthing a tradition of left-wing regionalism in the West that defied reactionary stereotypes. Each author demonstrates how blanket condemnations of regionalism miss the mark by ignoring the full spectrum and rich complexity of regional thought; each clearly reveals how critics of regionalism usually commit the logical fallacy of condemning a complex whole on the basis of one of its parts. Deeply aware of this critical misperception, our collective project illuminates how a cross-section of largely left-wing radicals—from acclaimed to nearly forgotten figures—promoted varieties of progressive regionalism across the landscape of the American West in the past that are increasingly relevant today. Before spotlighting each of our sixteen regionalists on the old left, clustered in four regions across the West, it is important to mention other scholars who have caught glimpses of this alternative tradition.

DISCOVERING A RADICAL REGIONAL COUNTERCURRENT

Although *Regionalists on the Left* is the first book to give this radical countercurrent the full attention it deserves, several critics have recently lent their voices to this discovery. As we have seen, regionalism is a basic, irrepressible feature of human experience that transcends judgments of being completely good or bad, entirely admirable or regrettable. As the famed Supreme Court jurist Felix Frankfurter argued, "Regionalism is a recognition of the intractable diversities among men." Stressing regionalism's positive potentials among its negative possibilities, Frankfurter concluded that "at bottom, the problems of American regionalism are the problems of American civilization: the continuous process of bringing to fruition the best of which American men and women are capable."[30]

Recognizing the "intractable diversities" of land and life across the West in the interwar decades, a wide variety of writers, artists, and intellectuals—especially those featured in this book—have rediscovered their home regions both as sources of protest and as seedbeds of promise. As early as 1933 the cultural historian Constance Rourke detected a revolutionary regionalism on the land and argued, "we have a deeply rooted, widespread folk expression—regional in character, some explicitly proletarian in sentiment." She concluded: "Even if the revolution starts in a tenth floor loft in New York or in the textiles mills of a southern village or in the River Rouge, a knowledge of these regional differences would seem essential for the enterprise of initiating the class struggle on any broad scale."[31]

Reviving Rourke's insight many decades later, several recent historians of the 1930s, including Michael Denning, Lary May, and Morris Dickstein, have portrayed radical western regionalists as central figures of the era. For Denning, groups of proletarian regionalists expressed "their iconoclastic communisms with a militant regionalism" on the pages of little magazines in the Midwest and Far West. In cities and rural regions across the West these regionalists provided a distinctive twist to the pluralistic nationalism of Roosevelt's New Deal and the Communist Party's Popular Front movement. Proletarian regionalists like Rourke, Botkin, Le Sueur, Tillie Olsen, Kenneth Rexroth, Carey McWilliams, and Sanora Babb produced work "on the popular arts, industrial folklore, and regional cultures" that were "not the sentimental invocations of a people without race or ethnicity, nor were they the 'politics of patriotism,' resolving all conflicts in the harmony of 'Americanism.' Rather they were attempts to imagine a new culture, a new way of life, a revolution."[32]

For Lary May, West-based film directors, novelists, and commentators like John Ford, Frank Capra, Edna Ferber, and Will Rogers drew upon radical western traditions of a frontier democracy and a "'republican' creed hostile to monopoly capitalism and class inequality" to create a left-leaning and forward-looking vision of America. Will Rogers, a popular entertainer and homespun intellectual, with his Oklahoma Cherokee and cowboy background, embodied this western-rooted "radicalism of tradition" and populist evocation of a pluralist past as a model for an egalitarian renewal. Through widely distributed films and radio commentary this rope-twirling pundit became the most admired figure in Depression America. Combining left-wing populist rhetoric with down-home humor and drawing upon his mixed-race roots in Oklahoma and recollections of a "mestizo republic" there, Rogers called for the redistribution of wealth and the creation of a regionally diverse and racially inclusive nation.[33]

Morris Dickstein also highlights radical regionalism, much of it rooted in the West, as a key feature of the 1930s. A left-leaning and progressive "fascination with America itself—its history and geography, its diverse population, the songs and legends of its folk culture, its heroes and social myths" was at the heart of the decade and motivated scores of western writers, folksingers, composers, and documentarians, among them John Steinbeck, Carey McWilliams, Woody Guthrie, Aaron Copland, Paul Taylor, and Dorothea Lange. Like Rogers, Capra, Ford, and Ferber, they were moved by a love of the land and folk and a sharp sense of the betrayal of democratic hopes by capitalist greed and inequality. Such regionally rooted artists and intellectuals, Dickstein concludes, "created a left-wing populism that could be urban as well as rural, that lent dignity to common people, recaptured lost elements of America's lost history and folk heritage, instilled energy and hope into people who were suffering from fear and privation, and tried to bridge gaps of sympathy and understanding between different races, classes, and regions."[34]

Scholars have not only begun the task of reinterpreting regionalism in the West during the 1930s, they have also started using it as a framework for cultural criticism and analysis. As early as 1976, the western radical historian William Appleman Williams called for "replacing the American empire with a federation of regional communities," and in subsequent articles he advocated a West-based "regional socialism" as the most effective bulwark against empire and centralized authority.[35]

Emerging in the 1980s and taking a less volatile political stance, the New Western historians unearthed the grubby reality of western conquest, environmental exploitation, and racial conflict. In this process they were often excavating the work of earlier radical regionalists. As we have seen, like their predecessors in the 1930s, these new regionalists have also been stigmatized as propagandists and extremists. The American West, as Patricia Limerick, William Cronon, Richard White, Donald Worster, and others tell us, is an infinitely complex constellation of places and people, not just a big safe place for a few white folks, as the Marlboro Man ads pretend. Like their radical regionalist forebears of the 1930s, they see a cultural kaleidoscope of many Wests, where Native American, Mexican, Asian, African, and European cultures, diverse in themselves, continue to collide and interact. The down-to-earth clarity of the region as the locus of cultural pluralism now appeals to a wide variety of western historians and critical regionalists who see themselves as the opposite of backwater antiquarians and protofascists. John Sayles's film "*Lone Star* (1996), with its tangled tale of cultural conflict and cross-fertilization between Anglos, Latinos, and African and Native Americans on the Texas-Mexico border, may be a cinematic model of this new regionalism that owes so much to the earlier work of J. Frank Dobie, Américo Paredes, Carlos Bulosan, Carey McWilliams, and others.[36]

Patricia Limerick, in many ways the unofficial spokesperson for this movement, has described the awakening of her belief that "regional identity could provide the cultural and social loom to knit a fragmented society together" and has outlined her hope for "a regionalism in which environmental history provides a foundation for an interwoven ethnic history." She relates how in writing her now classic *Legacy of Conquest* (1987) she discovered that adopting a regional framework was the best way to develop a coherent narrative of the lived experience of cultural diversity. "If one tried to reckon with the whole of American history at once," she realized, "one saw only an uninstructive blur, a jangle of unrelated parts. But region permitted one to adjust and train one's vision in a way that uncovered connections, ties, relations. With particular people in particular places ... one could build one's units of generalization outward, from place to subregion to region to hemisphere to planet."[37]

For Limerick and others a regional focus is the foundation for wider, interconnected levels of meaning. Far from being narrowly provincial, regional scholarship, in Limerick's words, "can inhabit at one and the same time, regional, national, and planetary levels of significance. Without the regional level of meaning, the more general levels are unrooted, ungrounded, abstract, and unconvincing." The title of her article "Going West and Ending up Global" (2001) aptly conveys how western regions function within a whole-world context, and her sense of the links between global and local, between the universal and the particular, echoes insights of any number of earlier progressive regionalists.[38] John Dewey's succinct statement in 1920, for example, that "the locality is the only universal" and Lewis Mumford's observation in 1941 that "every regional culture necessarily has a universal side to it" prefigure the contemporary rediscovery of the region as the common ground of human experience where everything takes place.[39]

A regional perspective, furthermore, can be anchored in the lived experience of people interacting in particular places. For Limerick, this vantage point enabled her to gather "the disparate stories of Indian tribes, Hispanic villages, Anglo-American pioneer settlements, and Asian immigrant communities and [pull] them into one story, as these various groups interacted in the big process of the invasion and conquest of the region." "Region," she concludes, "permitted ... a way to find, quite literally, common ground in seemingly detached and separate narratives."[40]

Although Limerick presented regionalism as a promising approach still in the making in the mid-1990s, it is clear that a variety of new regionalisms have transformed western American studies since then. It should be equally clear that these "new" progressive movements have deep historical roots. Though largely forgotten by contemporary regionalists, these roots reach back, not only to the radical regionalists of the 1930s featured in this book, but even deeper, into the early-twentieth-century work of Frederick Jackson Turner and Josiah Royce, whose notions of a healthy sectionalism and a "wise provincialism" laid the groundwork for many strains of progressive regionalist thought that would follow.[41] It is also important to recognize that progressive and left-leaning regionalism grew and often flourished in other parts of the country.

Regionalists on the Left is devoted to uncovering a radical regionalist tradition from the past that has surprising relevance in the present. The radical regionalism that found its strongest voices in the West in the 1930s can inspire us today. "The fires that burned so brightly—if briefly—in the best days of the 1930s," a prominent radical Westerner has observed, "will never be wholly extinguished."[42] Responding to the tumult of their times, the sixteen writers, artists, and intellectuals whose voices you will soon hear, used their passionate sense of place and critical affection for their native grounds to pioneer the way for pluralist, cosmopolitan versions of western regionalism that have become increasingly possible in our own time. By answering Walt Whitman's famous call to "study out the land" and by descending into the earthly realities of regional experiences, these women and men, in various ways, discovered both the "intractable diversities" and insistent commonalities of human experience. Their egalitarian dreams and devotion to environmental, economic, and racial justice can inspire us today. It is now time to settle in and learn as much as we can about these largely unsung pioneers.

NOTES

Epigraphs: Archie Green, "Regionalism Is a Forever Agenda," *Appalachian Journal* 9 (1982): 172–80. Henry Nash Smith, interviewed by Michael C. Steiner, Berkeley, California, July 18, 1980.

1. Craig Jackson Calhoun, "The Radicalism of Tradition: Community Strength or Venerable Disguise and Borrowed Language?" *American Journal of Sociology* 88 (1983): 886–914.

2. Michael Kazin, *American Dreamers: How the Left Changed a Nation* (New York: Knopf, 2011), xiv.

3. Michael Denning, *The Cultural Front: The Laboring of American Culture in the Twentieth Century* (New York: Verso, 1997), 132–34, 219–21, 445–54; Robert V. Hine, *The*

American West: An Interpretive History (Boston: Little, Brown, 1984), 358. Denning uses the alternate terms "radical regionalism" and "left-wing regionalism" throughout.

4. See Raymond Williams, *Keywords: A Vocabulary of Culture and Society* (New York: Oxford University Press, 1976). The quotation is from Simon Bronner, *American Folklore Studies: An Intellectual History* (Lawrence: University Press of Kansas, 1986), xii.

5. Hedwig Hintze, "Regionalism," in *Encyclopaedia of the Social Sciences* (New York: Macmillan, 1934), 13:217; Fulmer Mood, "The Origin, Evolution, and Application of the Sectional Concept," in Merrill Jensen, ed., *Regionalism in America* (Madison: University of Wisconsin Press, 1951), 7–9; Michael Steiner, "Regionalism," in John Mack Faragher, ed., *American Heritage Encyclopedia of American History* (New York: Henry Holt, 1998), 774–76.

6. John Dewey, "Americanism and Localism," *Dial* 68 (June 1920): 686, 685; Mary Austin, "New York: Dictator of American Criticism," *The Nation* 111 (July 31, 1920); Frederick Jackson Turner, "Sections and Nation" (1922), in Turner, *The Significance of Sections in American History* (New York: Henry Holt, 1923), 326.

7. Benjamin A. Botkin, "The Folk in Literature: An Introduction to the New Regionalism," in *Folk-Say: A Regional Miscellany* (Norman: Oklahoma Folklore Society, 1929), 14. See also Carey McWilliams, *The New Regionalism in American Literature* (Seattle: University of Washington Press, 1930); and Lowry Charles Wimberly, "The New Regionalism," *Prairie Schooner* 6 (Summer 1932): 214–21.

8. Franklin D. Roosevelt, "Growing Up by Plan," *Survey* 67 (February 1, 1932): 483; and Roosevelt, "Extemporaneous Address on Regional Planning," December 11, 1931, in Samuel I. Rosenman, ed., *The Public Papers and Addresses of Franklin D. Roosevelt* (New York: Random House, 1938), 1:498. The evaluation of Roosevelt's regionalism is by Richard Maxwell Brown, "The New Regionalism in America," in *Regionalism in the Pacific Northwest*, ed. William G. Robins et al. (Corvallis: Oregon State University Press, 1983), 40.

9. Erica L. Doss, "Borrowing Regionalism: Advertising's Use of American Art in the 1930s and 40s," *Journal of American Culture* 5 (Winter 1982): 16, 15; "The Boom in Regionalism," *Saturday Review of Literature* 10 (April 1934): 606.

10. B. A. Botkin, "We Talk about Regionalism—North, East, South, and West," *The Frontier* 13 (May 1933): 286–96; Botkin, "Regionalism: Cult or Culture?" *English Journal* 15 (June 1937): 181.

11. For greater detail see Michael Steiner and Clarence Mondale, *Region and Regionalism in the United States: A Sourcebook for the Humanities and Social Sciences* (New York: Garland, 1989).

12. The literature surrounding the recent rise of the "New Western History," "New Western" regionalism, and western "critical regionalism" alone is immense. The best summary of the New Western regionalism since the 1980s appears in Patricia Nelson Limerick, "The Realization of the American West," in Charles Reagan Wilson, ed., *The New Regionalism* (Jackson: University Press of Mississippi, 1998), 71–98. A few representative texts of this movement in history include Patricia Limerick, Clyde Milner, and Charles Rankin, eds., *Trails: Toward a New Western History* (Lawrence: University Press of Kansas, 1991); William Cronon, George Miles, and Jay Gitlin, eds., *Under an Open Sky: Rethinking America's Western Past* (New York: Norton, 1992); David Wrobel and Michael Steiner, eds., *Many Wests: Place, Culture, and Regional Identity* (Lawrence: University Press of Kansas, 1997); and Patricia Nelson Limerick, *Something in the Soil: Legacies and Reckonings in the New West* (New York: Norton, 2000). Representative sources on the New West and new

localism include William Riebsame, gen. ed., *Atlas of the New West: Portrait of a Changing Region* (New York: Norton, 1997); Michael L. Johnson, *New Westers: The West in Contemporary American Culture* (Lawrence: University Press of Kansas, 1996); Krista Comer, *Landscapes of the New West: Gender and Geography in Contemporary Women's Writing* (Chapel Hill: University of North Carolina Press, 1999); Jeff Roche, ed., *The Political Culture of the New West* (Lawrence: University Press of Kansas, 2008); Daniel Kemmis, *Community and the Politics of Place* (Norman: University of Oklahoma Press, 1990); and Lucy Lippard, *The Lure of the Local: Senses of Place in a Multicentered Society* (New York: The New Press, 1997). For a taste of the recent western "critical regionalism" see José Limón, "Border Literary Histories, Globalization, and Critical Regionalism," *American Literary History* 20 (2008): 160–82; Neil Campbell, *The Rhizomatic West: Representing the American West in a Transnational, Global, Media Age* (Lincoln: University of Nebraska Press, 2008); and critical-regionalism.com, an elaborate website devoted to the topic.

13. The most thoughtful and thorough surveys of western regionalism in the interwar decades are Robert L. Dorman, *Revolt of the Provinces: The Regionalists Movement in America, 1920–1945* (Chapel Hill: University of North Carolina Press, 1993) and Richard Etulain, *Re-Imagining the Modern American West: A Century of Fiction, History, and Art* (Tucson: University of Arizona Press, 1996).

14. Alfred Kazin, *On Native Grounds* (New York: Doubleday, 1942), 394.

15. The phrase "study out the land" is from Whitman's "By Blue Ontario's Shore," stanza 12. H. N. Smith, "The Feel of the Purposeful Earth: Mary Austin's Prophecy," *New Mexico Quarterly* 1 (February 1931): 17–18; Anne Whiston Spirn, *Daring to look: Dorothea Lange's Photographs and Reports from the Field* (Chicago: University of Chicago Press, 2008); Ruth Suckow, "The Folk Idea in American Life," *Scribners* 88 (September 1930): 246.

16. John Crowe Ransom, "The Aesthetic of Regionalism" (1934), in *Selected Essays of John Crowe Ransom*, ed. Thomas Daniel Young and John Hindle (Baton Rouge: Louisiana State University Press, 1984), 45–58, originally published in the *American Review* 2 (January 1934): 290–310; Hallie Flanagan, *Arena* (New York: Duell, Sloan & Pearce, 1940), 283; Meridel Le Sueur, "Proletarian Literature and the Middle West," in Henry Hart, ed. *American Writers' Congress* (New York: International, 1935), 136, 138.

17. Lewis Mumford, *Technics and Civilization* (New York: Harcourt & Brace, 1934), 292. Mumford developed a highly sophisticated and thoroughly cosmopolitan regionalism during the 1930s, one that intertwines the local and the global.

> It would be useful "if we formed the habit of never using the word regional without mentally adding it to the idea of the universal—remembering the constant contact and interchange between the local scene and the wider world that lies beyond it. . . . The drama of human development centers in part on this tension between the regional and the universal. As with every human being, every culture must be both itself and transcend itself; it must make the most of its limitations and must pass beyond them; it must be open to fresh experience and yet it must maintain its own integrity.

Mumford, *The South in American Architecture* (New York: Harcourt, Brace & World, 1941), 30–32.

18. V. F. Calverton, *American Literature at the Crossroads* University of Washington Chapbooks, no. 48 (Seattle, 1931), 39; Louis Wirth, "The Limitations of Regionalism," in

Merrill Jensen, ed., *Regionalism in America* (Madison: University of Wisconsin Press, 1951), 392–93.

19. Vardis Fisher, "The Western Writer and the Eastern Establishment," *Western American Literature* 1 (Winter 1967): 245, 253; Mary Austin, *The American Rhythm: Studies and Reexpressions of Amerindian Songs* (Boston: Houghton-Mifflin, 1930), 37; Walter Prescott Webb, *The Great Plains* (New York: Ginn, 1931), 126; and Webb, *The Texas Rangers: A Century of Frontier Defense* (New York: Houghton-Mifflin, 1935), 14.

20. Kyle Crichton, "Cease Not Living," *New Mexico Quarterly* 5 (May 1935): 71, 74; Dudley Wynn to Carey McWilliams, July 2, 1937, Carey McWilliams Papers, Special Collections, University of California, Los Angeles.

21. Sanora Babb to Douglas Wixson, September 18, 1983, in Douglas Wixson, *Worker-Writer in America: Jack Conroy and the Tradition of Midwestern Literary Radicalism, 1898–1990* (Urbana: University of Illinois Press, 1994), 377. See Wixson's account of the Communist Party's pre-Popular Front rejection of regionalism, *Worker-Writer*, 377–81.

22. Bernard DeVoto, "Regionalism, or the Coterie Manifesto," *Saturday Review of Literature* 15 (November 28, 1936): 8; DeVoto, "Horizonland," *Saturday Review of Literature* 15 (April 24, 1937): 8; H. W. Janson, "Benton and Wood, Champions of Regionalism," *Magazine of Art* 39 (May 1946): 186.

23. Michael Kowalewski, "Writing in Place: The New American Regionalism," *American Literary History* 6 (Spring 1994): 175; Roberto M. Dainotto *Place in Literature: Regions, Cultures, Communities* (Ithaca: Cornell University Press, 2000), 23.

24. Benjamin Barber, *Jihad vs. McWorld: How Globalism and Tribalism Are Reshaping the World* (New York: Ballantine, 1995); Salman Rushdie, *Imaginary Homelands: Essays and Criticism 1981–1991* (London: Granta, 1991), 394. "To be a migrant," Rushdie writes elsewhere in the book, "is, perhaps, to be the only species of human being free of the shackles of nationalism (to say nothing of its ugly sister, patriotism)." 124.

25. Werner Sollors, *Beyond Ethnicity* (New York: Oxford University Press, 1986), 178, 185. Others who see regionalism as a false form of pluralism include Susan Armitage, "From the Inside Out: Rewriting Regional History," *Frontiers* 22 (2001): 32–48; and Richard Jensen, "On Modernizing Frederick Jackson Turner," *Western Historical Quarterly* 11 (1980): 307–22.

26. Dainotto, *Place in Literature*, 9, 15, 17, 170–73.

27. Doreen Massey, "Power-Geometry and a Progressive Sense of Place," in *Mapping the Futures*, ed. Jon Bird et al. (London: Routledge, 1993), 64; Neal Leach, "The Dark Side of *Domus*," in Neal Leach, ed. *Architecture and Revolution: Contemporary Perspectives on Central and Eastern Europe* (New York: Routledge, 1999), 158–59, 160.

28. Wolfgang Schivelbusch, *Three New Deals: Reflections on Roosevelt's America, Mussolini's Italy, and Hitler's Germany, 1933–1939* (New York: Henry Holt, 2004), 112, 115.

29. Gerald D. Nash, "Point of View: One Hundred Years of Western History," *Journal of the West* 32 (January 1993): 4. For another example of hostility toward this new regionalism, see: William Savage, Jr., "The New Western History: Youngest Whore on the Block," *AB Bookman's Weekly*, (October 4, 1993): 1242–47.

30. Felix Frankfurter, "Foreword," in Merrill Jensen, ed., *Regionalism in America* (Madison: University of Wisconsin Press, 1951), xvi.

31. Constance Rourke, "The Significance of Sections," *New Republic*, 76 (September 20, 1933): 148, 149.

32. Denning, *The Cultural Front*, 219, 134.

33. Lary May, *The Big Tomorrow: Hollywood and the Politics of the American Way* (Chicago: University of Chicago Press, 2000), 3, 14, 19.

34. Morris Dickstein, *Dancing in the Dark: A Cultural History of the Great Depression* (New York: Norton, 2009), xxii, 462.

35. William Appleman Williams, *America Confronts a Revolutionary World, 1776–1976* (New York: Morrow, 1976), 193–94; Williams, "Radicals and Regionalism, *Democracy* 1 (July 1981): 87–98; Williams, "Regional Resistance: Backyard Autonomy," *Nation* 233 (September 5, 1981): 161, 178–80. Even earlier, in his *Roots of Modern American Empire* (New York: Random House, 1969), Williams had called for decentralization and the creation of "autonomous interacting political economies that will function as communities" (452). For an echo of Williams's argument see Robert Goodman, "Regional Socialism: An American Alternative," in Goodman, *The Last Entrepreneurs: America's Regional Wars for Jobs and Dollars* (New York: Simon & Schuster, 1979), 171–205.

36. See note 12 for a survey of the new western history as well as critical regionalism based in the West.

37. Patricia Nelson Limerick, "Region and Reason," in *All Over the Map: Rethinking American Regions*. ed. Edward I. Ayers et al. (Baltimore: The Johns Hopkins University Press, 1996), 85, 88, 84.

38. Limerick, "Region and Reason," 93; Limerick, "Going West and Ending Up Global," *Western Historical Quarterly* 32 (Spring 2001): 5–23.

39. John Dewey, "Americanism and Localism," 687; Lewis Mumford, *The South in American Architecture* (New York: Harcourt & Brace, 1941), 30. See also J. Frank Dobie, "Out of Regionalism, a Larger View," *Saturday Review* 60 (May 21, 1960): 17–18.

40. Limerick, "Region and Reason," 94, 95.

41. See Michael Steiner, "The Significance of Turner's Sectional Thesis," *Western Historical Quarterly* 10 (October 1979): 437–66; Steiner, "Frederick Jackson Turner and Western Regionalism," in Richard W. Etulain, ed., *Writing Western History: Essays on Major Western Historians* (Albuquerque: University of New Mexica Press, 1991), 103–35; and Steiner, "From Frontier to Region: Frederick Jackson Turner and the New Western History," *Pacific Historical Review*, 64 (1995): 479–501.

42. Carey McWilliams, "Steinbeck & the Thirties" (1970), 32-page typescript, Carey McWilliams Papers (Collection 1319) Department of Special Collections, Charles E. Young Research Library, University of California, Los Angeles.

PART I
THE MIDWEST

Meridel Le Sueur (1900–1996), Josephine Herbst (1892–1969), and Joe Jones (1909–1963), from Minnesota, Iowa, and Missouri, respectively, were part of a long-standing tradition of radical protest in their native region, the Midwest. Through their writing, painting, and political activism, they tapped into memories of the late-nineteenth-century "Lincoln Republic" with its homegrown (non-Marxist) egalitarian ideals and its distrust of monopoly capitalism and class exploitation. This heartland tradition had imbued a generation of turn-of-the-century midwestern progressives and radicals, including politicians (John T. Altgeld, Victor Berger, and Robert La Follette), historians (Frederick Jackson Turner and Charles Beard), writers (Hamlin Garland, Carl Sandberg, and Theodore Dreiser), and social critics ("Mother" Mary Harris Jones, Eugene Debs, Clarence Darrow, and Jane Addams). These progressive and radical midwesterners with their sense of injustice and vision of an "alternative America" paved the way for the more self-conscious left-wing regionalists of the 1930s.[1]

The Great Depression brought this earlier tradition to a boil. Labor wars gripped the region, with farmers, teamsters, steel and auto workers, and iron and coal miners on strike and left-leaning politicians like Minnesota's Floyd B. Olson and Iowa's Henry Wallace rising to national prominence. Many midwestern writers coming of age during the 1930s forged an indignant, often militant regionalism. Urban and rural regionalists ranged from nationally recognized authors like Nelson Algren, James T. Farrell, Josephine Johnson, Ruth Suckow, Langston Hughes, Jack Conroy, Le Sueur, and Herbst to obscure figures like Dale Kramer, Karlton Kelms, H. H. Lewis, Ben Hagglund, Joseph Kalar, Raymond Kresensky, and Orrick Johns. As in other western regions, these radical writers gathered at John Reed Club meetings, Federal Writers' and Theatre Project offices, and strike and picket lines, and they published their views in a constellation of short-lived little magazines including *The Anvil, The Rebel Poet, Midwest, Left Front, Hinterland,* and *Dubuque Dial.*

Conroy and Le Sueur were prominent members of this movement and its most insistent and ardent advocates. Like B. A. Botkin in Oklahoma and Carey McWilliams in California, they proselytized the regionalist cause throughout the 1930s by dashing off manifestos, organizing writers' conferences, and launching scores of proletarian regionalist magazines. Conroy's role as the quintessential proletarian regionalist has been carefully covered in Douglas Wixson's richly textured biography *Worker-Writer in America: Jack Conroy and the Tradition of Midwestern Literary Radicalism 1898–1990* (1994). Le Sueur's contribution to radical regionalism has been largely neglected.

Our opening chapter, by Julia Mickenberg, admirably fills that gap. In addition to restoring Le Sueur's significance as a regionalist on the left, Mickenberg also contributes a path-breaking perspective on the political dynamics of regionalism by introducing sociologist Craig Calhoun's notion of the "radicalism of tradition." Among other things she traces how Le Sueur, beginning with a speech to the American Writer's Congress in 1935 and culminating a decade later with the publication of her powerful folk history of the Upper Midwest, *North Star Country* (1945), used her fierce loyalty for her native ground and her personal knowledge of the long tradition of left-leaning protest there to write passionate, politically charged prose that stands as a model of radical regional literature.

Le Sueur's work grew from intimate ties to a wellspring of radical traditions, and she was proud of staying rooted in her native Midwest, unlike so many of her contemporaries who fled to cosmopolitan centers in the East or abroad. Following a different path than Le Sueur's, Herbst and Jones did indeed leave the Midwest in order to gain a fuller understanding of it. In large and small ways, they followed the pattern, traced in Malcolm Cowley's *Exile's Return: A Literary Odyssey of the 1920s* (1951), of abandoning home and then returning to rediscover and fully appreciate the place for the first time. Sara Kosiba's insightful chapter demonstrates that although Herbst caught fleeting glimpses of a heroic radical past as she grew up in Sioux City, she first embraced revolutionary politics once away from the Midwest, as a student at Berkeley in 1917 and as a participant in the New York and Paris radical intellectual circles of the early 1920s. A return to Depression-ravaged Iowa as a reporter for *The New Masses* deepened her respect for her native region and inspired her finest work, the Trexler/Wendel trilogy of politically indignant novels comparable to Robert Cantwell's acclaimed northwestern proletarian novel *Land of Plenty* (1934) (discussed in chapter 11).

Joe Jones, an artist, also had to leave the Midwest to gain critical appreciation of it. As skillfully described by Bryna Campbell, his working-class background in St. Louis was a starting point for proletarian art, but it required a stay among left-wing East Coast artists for him to discover class consciousness, become a communist, and apply this vision to the Midwest. Among other issues, Campbell contributes to the rehabilitation of Jones's reputation as a leftist artist whose stark images of contemporary racial, economic, and environmental injustice stand in sharp contrast to the nostalgia-steeped midwestern regionalism of Thomas Hart Benton, Grant Wood, and John Steuart Curry. Leading the way for other leftist painters like Aaron Bohrod and James Turnbull, Jones taught confrontational art to interracial groups of unemployed workers, painted murals depicting African Americans as labor agitators and lynching victims, and had his work censored and whitewashed like fellow radical muralists Diego Rivera and David Alfaro Siqueiros. Campbell's evocative conclusion that Jones's art was motivated by the transience and rootlessness of the Midwest and the feeling that it was "a blank slate . . . a template upon which history was made" adds a distinctive twist to the neglected story of radical regionalism in the Midwest.

NOTES

1. For a classic account of the enduring ideals of the Lincoln Republic, rooted in the Midwest, see John L. Thomas, *Alternative America: Henry George, Edward Bellamy, Henry Demarest Lloyd, and the Adversary Tradition* (Cambridge, Mass.: Harvard University Press, 1983). Ray Ginger's *Altgeld's America: The Lincoln Ideal versus Changing Realities* (New York: Funk & Wagnalls, 1958) and Dale Kramer's *Wild Jackasses: The American Farmer in Revolt* (New York: Hastings House, 1956) are vivid accounts of heartland radicalism and progressivism in the late nineteenth and early twentieth centuries.

Meridel Le Sueur. Courtesy of Minnesota Historical Society, St. Paul.

CHAPTER ONE

"Revolution can spring up from the windy prairie as naturally as wheat"

MERIDEL LE SUEUR AND THE MAKING OF

A RADICAL REGIONAL TRADITION

Julia Mickenberg

In the spring of 1935 Meridel Le Sueur (1900–1996) traveled from Minneapolis to New York City to present a speech to the newly formed League of American Writers.[1] Hundreds of writers from around the United States (but disproportionately from New York City) had joined forces "to unite on a general program for the defense of culture against the threat of fascism and war."[2] Le Sueur, the only woman among twenty-eight speakers, was not on the platform to advocate the inclusion of "women's concerns" on the league's agenda. Her topic, rather, was "Proletarian Literature in the Middle West," both a reminder that American writing, proletarian or otherwise, did not begin and end in New York and a call to recognize the revolutionary potential simmering on the prairies of the Middle West. Her speech emphasized two points: midwestern traditions of popular protest against eastern monopoly, and the democratic heritage of the early American frontier.

Her focus on the midwestern landscape as central to a national transformation hinted at a politically committed regionalism. Among the roster of radical and progressive writers invited to speak, only Le Sueur addressed this theme. Her brand of regionalism linked a broader interest in region in the interwar years to the radicalization of many artists, writers, and intellectuals in the 1930s, a connection that scholars have not yet adequately explored. Studies of Le Sueur's life and career share this artificial separation: she has become relatively well known as a feminist with radical political leanings, but her rootedness in the midwestern landscape has not often been read as integral to those commitments.[3]

Reading Le Sueur through a regionalist lens requires both a reassessment of the course of her work as a writer and a reconsideration of established definitions of regionalism and regionalist writing. People I have spoken with who read radical "little magazines" like *New Masses* in the 1930s and 1940s remembered her as a "midwestern" writer. However, contemporary scholars hesitate to discuss her as a "regional" writer. This is perhaps because her concerns with class and gender seem, by today's scholarly standards of primacy, more significant axes of analysis, as though the regional label would minimize the importance of her work.[4]

Le Sueur joined the Communist Party in the second half of the 1920s. She became well known in leftist literary circles in the 1930s for her short stories and reportage, published in journals and little magazines such as *New Masses, Partisan Review,* and the Midwest's own *Anvil,* as well as in less explicitly political periodicals like *American Mercury* and *Scribner's.* She was blacklisted during the McCarthy era, followed by the FBI, and cited repeatedly in hearings by the House Committee on Un-American Activities (HUAC), during a wave of repression that effectively rendered writers like Le Sueur invisible on the American literary scene for several decades. Not only were her political commitments deemed subversive, but the paradigms of Americanism that she propagated through her writings also threatened the "consensus" view of a classless nation, and her regionalist emphasis seemed out of place in an era that emphasized national homogeneity and called for international hegemony of the "American way of life." In the 1970s second-wave feminists seeking a "usable past" rediscovered her work, finding a thinker and artist whose feminist standpoint made her seem ahead of her time to women of this new generation. Le Sueur's life and work proved that women could actively participate in class-based political struggles without sublimating feminist concerns.

Few people have read Le Sueur as a regionalist, because they fail to recognize the way this framework both deepens our understanding of her work and complicates existing interpretations. A look at one of her major projects of the 1930s, the period of focus for most studies, and at selections from work through the late 1950s, the "dark time," reveals that she firmly grounded her class consciousness in a powerful regional tradition of grassroots radical protest. This work suggests an "alternative Americanism" that goes beyond Popular Front strategies and brings to light a deeply personalized attachment to place and history. Examination of these neglected texts also enriches and expands feminist categories of analysis by demonstrating that the political (or public) can also be personal.

Cary Nelson's work with American poetry offers a model for the recovery of works and authors that have been neglected because of a sexist, racist, and elitist process of canonization that creates arbitrary standards of literary excellence. Nelson makes the bold assertion that "we should always read what people assure us is no good."[5] But in this process of "recovery" of those texts once deemed "minor" or unliterary, we should not be content to resurrect the "repressed" text by reading it along a single axis. Recent years have witnessed the rediscovery of "minority" texts, "feminist" texts, "radical" texts, and even some "regional" texts, but the fixation on a single axis of analysis has constricted the interpretation of Le Sueur and others like her. Le Sueur's regionalism coincided with a wider interest in regional culture in the interwar years that was part of the "Re-Discovery and Re-Evaluation of America."[6] The cultural programs of the New Deal, which paid artists, writers, and folklorists to collect and document examples of the nation's regional diversity fed this rediscovery and reevaluation. Interwar regionalism is often understood as a reaction to modernization and economic devastation: these phenomena generated "a desire for stable communal identity and a reverence for the past—especially the memories that could bring a sense of order and certainty to a tumultuous present."[7] This logic bolsters the common scholarly perception of regionalism as backward-looking and retrogressive and adds credence to Warren Susman's arguably outworn assessments of 1930s culture: he maintained that beyond its initial impulses, the "search for the 'real' America" in the 1930s served ultimately to validate the existing system.[8] But this interpretation fails to take into account what Craig Calhoun has called the "radicalism of tradition," or the ways in which an exploration of national and regional traditions could actually fuel change.[9]

The appeal of Marxism in the 1930s has tended to be viewed as completely separate from the regionalist impulse. In their exploration of American civic traditions, folk cultures, and landscape, regionalists, according to Robert Dorman, "diverg[ed] from the Marxists and Communists." He says regionalists "look[ed] to 'native American' ideologies—such as republicanism, populism, or liberalism—rather than to 'imported creeds' to find their values and agendas, because, to their minds, such alien internationalist doctrines ignored the saving diversifying and decentering graces of place."[10]

The move to distinguish regionalism from Marxism ignores the potential ideological links between the two that propelled writers like Le Sueur. Calhoun provides us with a way of understanding the ways in which a strong grounding in locale and tradition can support a commitment to broader changes. He argues that most people become radicalized when they have something specific to defend, noting that "traditional communities provide the social foundations for widespread popular mobilizations and . . . traditional values provide their radicalism."[11] This, of course, goes directly against Marx's contention, put forth in *Eighteenth Brumaire*, that "the tradition of the dead generations weighs like a nightmare on the minds of the living."[12] Marx believed that traditions were in the realm of religion, that is, mere distractions. The strategic use of American traditions by the Communist Party during its Popular Front period was thus condemned by anti-Stalinist Marxists as counterrevolutionary. But the interest in American traditions—and this had regional dimensions as well—provided a way for American radicals to express their discontent with current conditions but still assert their commitment to American promise.[13]

In its U.S. incarnation, the Popular Front was an informal alliance between Communists, independent radicals, and New Deal liberals that put the revolutionary rhetoric of third-period Communism on hold in favor of a common stance celebrating "the people" and condemning fascism. Its unofficial motto was Earl Browder's slogan as the Communist Party candidate for President: "Communism is Twentieth-Century Americanism." Although the Popular Front grew out of a 1935 directive from Moscow, it brought the Communist Party an unprecedented "measure of acceptance, respectability and power within ordinary American life."[14] Popular front icons such as Tom Paine, Thomas Jefferson, and, more than anyone else, Abraham Lincoln, spoke to a genuine desire among left-wing American radicals to prove their dedication to America's revolutionary ideals, of democracy, egalitarianism, community virtue, and the right to reject a government that fails to represent the will of the people. The Popular Front was shaken by the Nazi–Soviet Nonagression Pact in 1939 but rehabilitated after the Nazi invasion of Russia in 1941; however, by the election of 1948, the dismal failure of Progressive Party candidate Henry Wallace showed that the Popular Front coalition was unsustainable.

Yet radicals like Le Sueur continued to explore the oppositional elements in American and regional history throughout their writing careers. Working from a philosophy of "progressive regionalism," which she articulated in the magazine *Midwest* in the 1930s, Le Sueur explored the popular heritage of the Midwest throughout her life. She published *North Star Country,* a folk history of Minnesota and Wisconsin, in 1945, and *Crusaders,* a tribute to her parents and their role in midwestern farm and labor movements, in 1956. Between these two histories, she wrote books for children on Johnny Appleseed, Black Hawk, Abraham Lincoln, Davy Crockett, and Lincoln's mother, Nancy Hanks. She also wrote essays, short stories, and poetry about "forgotten" men and women in the midwestern landscapes.[15]

Le Sueur's work points to a radical regionalist heritage within American traditions. The folklorist Constance Rourke had pointed out in 1933 that regional folklore, customs, and traditions, the "explicitly proletarian" sentiment in localized folk cultures, could serve as a viable basis for revolution. In forging a new meaning of Americanism, a range of Popular Front cultural workers sought to give "regional" literature new credence among radicals as well as the literary establishment. This move ran counter to the thinking of radical critics like V. F. Calverton and Granville Hicks, who saw regionalism as a backward "return to the soil."[16] Le Sueur was at the forefront of an effort, spurred in part by works of folklorist B. A. Botkin, to build a "progressive regionalism" among midwestern writers.[17] Their goal was to create a strong, localized basis for the Popular Front against fascism, grounded in native democratic traditions. Botkin called for a regionalism that would use "the local and the past" as "material for the present and the future, to give both explanation and power to the whole social fabric as well as to the separate regional units." He asserted that a regionalism that resists parochialism and backward-looking isolation, a regionalism that includes the industrial and the metropolitan, "can serve both society and literature. It can give first-hand data on the people and on their living and working conditions. It can help make the masses articulate by letting them tell their own story, in their own words. And it does not simply provide source material—it can create new forms, styles and modes of literature by drawing upon place, work, and folk for motifs, images, symbols, slogans and idioms."[18]

In the Midwest a storehouse of radical traditions served as fuel to a cadre of left-wing writers who sought to build a rooted American working-class literature. Douglas Wixson's groundbreaking study of Jack Conroy and his milieu, *Worker-Writer in America,* demonstrates how a group of midwestern literary radicals combined rootedness in place with class consciousness. He contends that these writers fostered a "democratic myth of concern" as the basis of a new society: "regional difference, social content and 'labor lore' were elements of a new democratic myth of concern constructed by the radicals, who resurrected traditional values such as community and cooperation and reasserted others such as the right to take exception in an open assembly."[19]

The way in which midwestern literary radicals recognized the "radicalism of tradition" is key to their articulation of an alternative Americanism. This group shared certain tendencies with the strands of interwar regionalism that have received the most attention from scholars: namely, the sense that republican virtue and the other founding creeds of the nation were being neglected by those who held the reins of the nation and that the interests of the Northeast were being served at the expense of people in other regions of the country. Midwestern regional identity stemmed in part from a pervasive current of opposition to the hegemonic rule of a putative eastern establishment (Le Sueur certainly felt this) but also from a shared sense of history and geographical conditions. The Midwest was the early western frontier that Frederick Jackson Turner had characterized as the basis for American democracy, which stressed "the rights of man, while the statesman who voiced the interests of the East stressed the rights of property."[20]

The midwestern literary radicals with whom Le Sueur was associated sought a socially and politically conscious regional cultural tradition, a usable past in their own region's history. That is, they tried to build upon the democratic traditions of their locale without replicating a naive jingoism, although some did suggest that those in the heartland represented the "real America." Some were associated with the Communist Party, but they were notorious for not following the party line. As Wixson argues, their version of Marxism was one firmly rooted in midwestern insurgent traditions:

If Marxism can be said to have had any important appeal to the Midwestern literary radicals, then it was an "Americanized" version adapted to local circumstances rather than a European transplant.... An anti-ideological current runs through the various radicalisms, as if the Midwestern mind functions on contingency and not principle. The ideological sources of Midwestern literary radicals... derive from indigenous traditions of protest, expressed in earlier manifestations such as the Farmer's Alliance, the People's Party, the Non-Partisan League, the IWW, certain unions, and various infusions of immigrant liberalism such as the freethinking forty-eighters. Their legacy was grass-roots democratic expression, a spirit of egalitarianism and individualism that seemed at times at odds with the demand for revolutionary change.[21]

But what, then, defined these writers as midwestern? They were largely self-defined, although their deference to that label did not necessarily imply that their work was regionalist. Rather, it signaled a feeling of common interest with other radical writers of the area by virtue of geography. The magazine *Midwest*, edited by a consortium of writers from Minnesota, Iowa, Illinois, South Dakota, Nebraska, Ohio, Wisconsin, Michigan, and Missouri, concerned itself less with putting lines around the Midwest as a region than with exploring and fostering a sense of regional identity.[22] That a group of writers defined themselves as midwestern, whether they were from Iowa, Kansas, or South Dakota, makes them part of a "vernacular region," or what the geographer Wilbur Zelinsky calls "the shared, spontaneous image of a territorial reality."[23] As writers, their sense of place as "midwestern" was not just a product of birth but a kind of half-resentful, half-self-righteous knowledge that they were among those who did not go east or west to make their fortune. In this context there is a certain attraction in Jules Chametzky's claim that regional identity is "an image, created by what you read," but his notion that it "ain't what you do or what you are" seems to close the topic too abruptly.[24] Midwestern radicals played upon the long-standing image of their region as "the most American part of America"—egalitarian, progressive, and exemplifying the traits of the yeoman farmer.[25] Trying to succeed as a writer without going to New York (or sometimes to California) might indicate a lack of means, but it just as often demonstrated a rootedness and dedication to place. Such was the case with Le Sueur, who never felt "at home" or accepted anywhere but in the Midwest.

She felt a deeply personal call to foster a progressive midwestern regional community of writers and artists and to promote a socially and politically conscious literature of place. One way she did this was by building a cooperative network for regional publications. In June 1936 she was an instrumental figure in the organizing and execution of a Midwest Writers Conference, held in Chicago and representing a kind of regional arm of the national American Writers Congress held by the League of American Writers. (Similar regional conferences were organized in Cleveland, Minneapolis, San Francisco, and other cities across the United States.) Beyond the larger goals of opposing war and fascism at home and abroad, the group aimed to foster regional publication networks to build a local audience for the work of midwestern writers, so that these writers would no longer be "forced to leave the Middlewest for lack of audience and publishers."[26] The conference generated the Midwest Federation of Arts and Professions, a confederation of artists, writers, actors, musicians, and various other professionals, "united against fascist attacks, against war, and for the creation of a true historical and progressive regionalism, which can be a carrier of the vital traditions of mid-American life, and serve as a unifying factor against the old regionalism which breeds reaction, which was retrogressive, seeking impossible reversions of the past, returns to the soil, and values tradition not as a self continuing and growing force but as a restrictive element only."[27]

The Midwest Federation sponsored the little magazine *Midwest*, of which Le Sueur and Dale Kramer became editors. Kramer had started the magazine *Hinterland* in Iowa two years earlier, later turning its editorship over to the Midwest Literary League, comprised primarily of the WPA Iowa Writers' Project's editorial staff and allied with the Midwest Federation of Arts and Professions.[28] Other short-lived little magazines with a leftist bent appeared in the Midwest *(Left, Dubuque Dial, Hub, New Quarterly,* and, most importantly, Jack Conroy's *Anvil)*, but no centralized vehicle had yet emerged to combine efforts of writers across the region. This gap in regional coverage became especially pronounced when the New York–based *Partisan Review* merged with *Anvil* in 1935 and disbanded the *Anvil* altogether the following year. *Midwest* was also explicitly designed to be a voice of progressive regionalism and, in true Popular Front fashion, was to build upon the region's revolutionary traditions as a bulwark against fascism.

"We needed a magazine," Le Sueur said later, looking back on that time. "We needed it badly. We needed a pathway."[29] In the 1920s and 1930s, little magazines were important outlets for writers and artists whose work was political or experimental and thus had limited commercial appeal. Beyond providing an outlet for work that might otherwise not be published, regional little magazines were also important community-building devices. Le Sueur saw *Midwest* as a means of rallying progressive thinkers across the region, especially as the Midwest's population was becoming increasingly conservative. Her attempt to construct a community through *Midwest* magazine served as a 1930s precedent for the kinds of issues and the genres of writing that would be characteristic of her writing in the late 1940s and 1950s, when government repression of writers, artists, performers, and scholars who espoused leftist ideas would redefine dissent as "un-American" and would greatly marginalize any calls for an alternative (i.e., anticapitalist) Americanism.

To build *Midwest's* base, Le Sueur wrote letters and sent flyers to writers and artists who might have similar concerns. To Iowa writer Karlton Kelm she wrote:

> We need material from established Midwestern writers and artists. We need short stories, poetry. We need essays and reportage. We want to poetically recreate the mid American history, fable, myth, not in the old regional sense of deifying history merely, but making of it a dynamics of present movement. Some proposed essays would be the Haymarket Riots. Racial migrations in the villages.... Lindsay, Johnny Appleseed, Lincoln and possibly portraits of anonymous but typical Midwestern people.... there will of course be reportage on the present fascistic trends here, the third party and so on. In other words, this will be a creative review of the Midwest, handling these things in a way that eastern publications seldom do.[30]

An eight-page preview and three full-length issues of *Midwest* were published between August 1936 and January 1937 before the magazine went the way of so many little magazines of that era and folded for lack of funds. In that time it published both relatively well-known and little-known progressive midwestern fiction and nonfiction prose writers, poets, "correspondents," artists, and photographers, including Sherwood Anderson, Jesse Stuart, Frank Lloyd Wright, Archibald Motley, Syd Fossum, Kerker Quinn, Norman Macleod, Opal Shannon, Jay Sigmund, H. H. Lewis, Ruth Suckow, Alfred Morang, Raymond Kresensky, and Weldon Kees. The final page of magazine's last issue offered a complete list of the contributors, presented under the statement "MIDWEST—A *Review* draws on the living root of American culture." The list of authors gives a sense of the community of writers and artists Le Sueur seemed to be successfully building.

Rather than offering any in-depth analysis of the magazine, discussion here is most concerned with how the idea behind the magazine and the contributions of Le Sueur herself connected to a particular ideology of regionalism and Americanism that carried through her work into later decades. That ideology must also be understood in connection with her working-class and feminist perspective.[31] This cultivated perspective (Le Sueur was of middle-class origins) is evident in her work that deals with national themes, but often her feminism seems somewhat muted in these texts: the very language of Americanism, particularly in working-class manifestations, stresses the manliness of the ideal citizen-worker. (So too is the proletarian worker-hero the embodiment of masculinity).[32] This accounts for the difficulty of integrating women into a drama of nation or even region. As geographer Jeanne Kay has pointed out, "women do not normally appear as protagonists in national epics"—and, furthermore, "if they appear at all in national epics, they typically do so as camp followers, titillating distractions, rewards for male heroism, or answers to male loneliness."[33]

In works dealing with regional and national identity, Le Sueur's "feminist" standpoint is most evident in two ways. First, she peoples the midwestern landscape with women as well as men, although almost all of these figures are more static and idealized "types" than complex human beings. Second, she conceived of, and illustrated, abstract concepts like region and nation in personalized terms of place and community, in a sense domesticating them. Because of this, *Midwest* magazine took on great importance for her as a vehicle for combating a sense of isolation and as a possible solution to her longing for connection and community. She expressed this sense in her private journal during the time she was trying to pull together the magazine:

> It seems we must be together. That is the strong feeling behind the magazine, we must be together it may all fail it may come to nothing but there must be some sense of being together again, this is the great psychic element behind a resurrection. I feel this so strongly because my own life has perhaps exaggerated the sense of isolation.... there is the effort to see myself standing in a corn field, to see myself standing in front of wooden houses, standing on streets... trying to have some personal emotion.[34]

The image of Le Sueur or her protagonist in a cornfield is a recurring motif in her work, and it represents a deliberate act of placing herself in a landscape, of searching for an organic rootedness. Her will to show the richness of a landscape she often described as "ruined and desolate," like a "strong raped virgin," demonstrates a regional identity that is framed by an inner struggle. In her short story "Corn Village" (part of her 1940 collection *Salute to Spring*), she wrote of Kansas villages and farmlands in these terms, as if pleading with the landscape itself: "the mind struggling to get into your meaning, trying to get you alive with significance and myth." This urgent need for a mythic history of place was central to her commitments as a writer: "not going to Paris or Morocco or Venice, instead staying with you, trying to be in love with you, bent upon understanding you, bringing you to life. For your death is mine also."[35]

The article in *Midwest* that best translates this personalized political position while demonstrating as well the magazine's progressive regionalism and alternative Americanism is Le Sueur's piece "The American Way," published in the first full-length issue (November 1936). Significantly, the article followed a reprint of B. A. Botkin's article from the *English Journal*, "Regionalism: Cult or Culture?" in which he eloquently articulated the theory of a progressive, cosmopolitan regionalism, upon which Le Sueur seems to have modeled the magazine. She opened her essay with a quotation from Whitman's "Democratic Vistas" (which would become an epigraph in *North Star Country*, her folk history of the upper Midwest), calling for a genuine American literature that draws upon both local landscapes and native traditions of equality and brotherhood: "Did you too,

O Friend, suppose Democracy was only for election, for politics? I say Democracy is only for use, that it may pass on and come to its flower and fruit in the highest form of interaction between men and their beliefs." The Whitman quotation represents a kind of civic call to arms, insisting that Americans who forsake political involvements fail to recognize the dangerous potential of those who would use democracy as a tool to gain power and suppress the will of the people.[36] Whitman's call for active efforts to build a national literature and a democratic public sphere points to an older tradition within American literature, but in 1936 his words could be read as an outcry against the possibility of fascism if the urges of those in power were not checked. The text of Le Sueur's piece is sandwiched between the Whitman epigraph and a full copy of the U.S. Constitution's Bill of Rights, grounding her project in classic republican traditions.

The essay itself uses a trip through depressed areas in Kansas as a moment to reflect upon the failure of America's democratic promise and to demonstrate that those who built the nation's riches were its rightful inheritors. Le Sueur begins with the ravages to the landscape and people of the Midwest and cites this destruction as evidence that the men in power have taken America from the people who rightfully own it. "You can drive through prairie states for hours," she explained. "The middle west is familiar to me. I was born on these prairies in the winter solstice. There are Iowa, Kansas, the Dakotas, Minnesota, Indiana, Illinois. These were for a long time frontier states. There is still the tension of pioneering in these villages and fear on the streets, and now hunger." Her journey reveals the disastrous effects of droughts and of "misuse and plundering," creating not just a wasted landscape but also "ruined people in mine, in factory, in village, and farm."[37]

The great villains in this story are Mr. Landon (the governor of Kansas) and Mr. Hearst (the newspaper magnate), who "say a great deal about this being their country, about the American way of life. But it is doubtful," Le Sueur makes clear, "if by virtue of care, good usage, or love, America belongs to these." Her bemused critique of Alfred Landon's call for "the American Way," "for maple syrup, for men and women together in homes, 'traveling from the cradle to the grave without ever feeling the coercive or directing hand of government except in so far as they may have transgressed the rights of others,'" may, for the present-day reader, evoke Tea

Party activists' rhetoric of the early 2000s, but even today it remains difficult for the left to lay claim to American patriotism.[38] Read in our current moment, her arguments remind us that she raised enduring questions and issues, pointing to the contradictions embedded within the very discourse of the nation's founding creeds. In answer to Landon's assertion that "'our people have been free to develop their own lives as they saw fit and cooperate with one another on a voluntary basis,'" Le Sueur asked,

> What else did the lead and zinc miners of Kansas think, were they not following the American way when they banded together to strike for improved conditions and a living wage? And Mr. Landon, as governor of the sunflower state, called out troops, used violence against the miners and broke the strike. And called out troops also against relief protests in Fort Scott where the American way of life provided $1.08 a week for a family of three to live on.[39]

She points to Landon's support from the Morgans, Rockefellers, and Duponts, as well as from William Randolph Hearst, support that would make a mockery of his calls for free competition. She condemns these so-called captains of industry, placing them on par with reactionary demagogues of the day, who deceive the people and who must be checked by "writers, artists, professionals, those who care for the traditions by which America has always stood."[40]

Here Le Sueur called for a regionalism that was no mere literary trope but rather an urgent attempt to resurrect a history of struggle that could sustain people against attacks to their fundamental belief system and to the way of life that was their birthright as American citizens:

> The regionalism which can now be effective is one not of isolation but of contact. In the middle west the historical movement of pioneering, of the Populist movement, the great agrarian revolts against the piracy of eastern capital, against the looting of the prairies, and the forests, against the wanton destruction that has destroyed now the land, high bred herds, and has started upon the people themselves, taking toll of their rich, obscure and anonymous lives. These things must come alive.[41]

She sees history in "the bulk of our people, not in the gentry who import, as Whitman says, the effete and dying culture of the old world." And this history, "obscure, like a lost one below the obvious one, recorded and known, . . . would be the source for future action."[42]

Her heroes in this story are nameless, voiceless, "anonymous" men and women, pioneers, "lumberjacks, the whistlepunks, the gandy dancers who laid the railroads, the immigrant women." She finds written "in the face of a prairie woman . . . history and economics and also the future." Her idealized "prairie woman" was the timeless, human equivalent of the ravaged and yet somehow enduring landscape, the qualities of the landscape that cannot be recorded or mapped, "as this map of such a woman, dried like the soil, these hands over the husked stomach that has born children in a locked shanty alone, the veins showing the course also of an unmarked history, the course of the blood, and the prairie eye that looks without seeing, that adjusts to distances to ward off madness."[43]

The anonymous maternal prairie woman represents Le Sueur's effort to people the midwestern landscape with women and to demonstrate the way in which women are central to the region's history. Her conception of midwestern people in general, and the way in which place has shaped their identity, is, like the prairie woman, idealized as well, echoing a Turnerian sense of sectional "types." These idealized portrayals arguably fall prey to a pitfall that Botkin identified as common to regionalist expression, "the tendency of the provinces to substitute their local myths for the national myth of Americanism."[44] In celebrating the "unknown people" of the Midwest, Le Sueur very definitely played upon the midwestern mythos marked by a "deep Lincolnian suffering": "There has always been something about the Midwestern prairies, perhaps by remoteness, which has thrown up a peculiar new totality of individual. . . . Then there is the prodigality and amplitude, the strange mixture of delicacy and power and continence here untouched by the Atlantic bringing European memories, that creates our prairie men and women."[45]

Le Sueur intended this myth of place, constructed as it may seem, to serve as a rallying point to inspire others to reclaim their place and their history and to recognize that *their* American way was being rejected:

> The artist, writer, audience will rouse from the same root, the wide plains and prairies, the wheat belt, the corn belt . . . the factories,

mills and mines, the small towns and the industrial cities.... These men and energies that have looted America, who dangerously want to scrap certain American institutions such as freedom of speech, press and assembly, guaranteed by the Constitution, and the right, embodied in the Declaration of Independence of the people to throw off the yoke of any government which becomes oppressive, these are the real and certain enemies.[46]

This extended tribute to the midwestern landscape, its people and its hidden history, marks a pattern in her writing that sustained discourses of regionalism and republicanism well into the 1950s. This pattern runs counter to the scholarly consensus that both of these impulses had fallen flat by the 1940s, as both the Depression and World War II demonstrated the need for centralized, national action.[47]

Even in the 1930s Le Sueur never felt that many people shared her passions for place and history. Few of the writings that others submitted to *Midwest* seemed like adequate testaments to her vision as the magazine's editor, and yet this lack never caused her to doubt or question that vision. "What I miss in these writings I get," she wrote in her journal, "is a sense of wonder, it is the mystical and mid American sense—o they are all so sensuously dry and so limited and so clever. Not one with that sense of longing, that sense of the future. Time... is a thing that rests upon the moment and history a thing you can feel and it makes you feel good. It makes you feel rich and propels you to action."[48] Many people with whom she corresponded, especially those who had gone away from the region, could only see the limitations of the Midwest, associating it, as one letter writer put it, with "a kind of nasty bitterness" and with "God fearing people."[49]

The mythic midwesterner Le Sueur put forth in some of her published writings paralleled her private musings and hopes for the future latent in the midwestern prairie and in "the blank sheet of the men and women upon whom nothing is written" with their "great mystical purity."[50] The vision grew out of her sense of rootedness in a landscape where, as she noted in her speech to the American Writers Congress (mentioned at the opening of this chapter) few things were rooted.

In 1945 Le Sueur's *North Star Country* was published as part of Erskine Caldwell's American Folkways series, which was designed to "describe and interpret the indigenous quality of life in America ... the cultural influences implanted by the original settlers and their descendants... [and so] reveal the ingrained character of America."[51] Caldwell's series seems to have been a haven for radical writers like Le Sueur and Carey McWilliams, whose *Southern California Country* (1946) abounds with regional protest. *North Star Country* presents a tribute during wartime to the strength of the American people and yet suggests resistance by renarrating regional history from below. In an introduction to the book's 1984 reprint edition, Le Sueur described the book as a legacy of the WPA Writers' Project—thereby attempting to validate and perpetuate a program about which she had mixed feelings while she was actually involved in it.[52] She also had more freedom in *North Star Country* to connect the region's folk with a tradition of radicalism than she had had as a writer for a federal government that was under scrutiny for alleged radical influences.

North Star Country portrays the Midwest as the cradle of democracy; it is the story of the creation of a new culture "from the blend of diverse strands, sharing strengths, confidence, and myth." The history Le Sueur reconstructed is one where public expression grew naturally out of the prairie: "expression grew like corn," she wrote. "Newspapers sprang up like whiskey stills. Democratic man wished not to die, but to be perpetuated, to speak in meeting, to write to the papers."[53] In telling this story of the Midwest, she quoted pioneers, Whitman, Lenin, Thoreau, the Bible, Frederick Jackson Turner, a Swedish immigrant woman, a village poem spelled in corn kernels, Carl Sandburg, the Kensington runestone, a Negro rebellion song of the Civil War, Black Hawk, frontier newspapers, Floyd Olson, farmers, a Finnish poet, missionaries, traders, Indian songs, folkways, and the Congress of Industrial Organizations (CIO). With this cacophony of voices she told a story rife with contradictions, at one point celebrating the subjugation of the land and the pioneers' bravery against the Indians, at other moments bemoaning the destruction of the prairies and the pioneers' treachery and betrayal of the Indians. Her portrait of the Midwest at moments seems simplistic and blindly celebratory, an odd praising of individualism from a woman whose credo was collectivism. But the celebration in *North Star Country* was meant to speak to the people of the Midwest, to validate their experience and remind them of movements, organizations, and events in the region that were central to the making of American democracy—cooperatives, the Industrial Workers of the World, the Farmers Alliance, the Minneapolis Truckers' Strike, and the Populist movement, which became "a vast university of the common people."⁵⁴ The dual projects of celebration and critique, this problem of being in love with a place and people while being fully cognizant of their flaws, may well account for the book's many contradictions.

History, for Le Sueur, was as essential to community—in this context, the regional, or even the national community—as memory is to the individual. And in the true spirit of "history from below," she saw it as her task to chart the unrecorded and unmapped contours of life on the midwestern landscape, the names that had not been signed to the important documents, the details not marked on maps like the one La Salle sent to Louis XIV, "showing the crawl of the Mississippi, marking the tin, iron and coal mines."⁵⁵ She also hoped to create a model for other working-class writers to emulate. *North Star Country* did, in fact, carry on her own WPA legacy, putting into practice the paradigm she laid out in her manual for writers that was published in 1937 through the WPA workers' education project, *Worker Writers*:

> More and more we need words to write the true history of the past so we can create a true history in the future. History is a thing that everyone feels and some of us make it and many of us are living it right now. It is only you who are making this history and can write the true story of it. No matter what you are a part of history. If you buy an orange or ride in a car or decide to have a baby, you are making history.⁵⁶

Le Sueur continued to explore regional history in *Crusaders* (1955), a paean to her parents and to the midwestern populist tradition in general. At the time of that book's writing, she had been blacklisted from most publishing venues; she was being followed by the FBI and was viewed as a threat to "the American way."⁵⁷ But even though her brand of "Americanism" no longer fell within acceptable limits in the dominant political culture, *Crusaders* demonstrates that she, like others whose voices were so actively repressed, never abandoned her principles.

Crusaders tells the story of Arthur and Marian Le Sueur. (Arthur was Meridel's stepfather, but her own father was part of a past she was not interested in claiming.) The story of their struggles is contextualized within the wider movements of workers and farmers throughout the Midwest.

The book's themes echo those of earlier works by Le Sueur that emphasize the unwritten history of popular struggles. Most interesting is the way in which she considers the place of individual lives within larger movements, and, perhaps more importantly, how in the act of writing about her mother she found a way to write about women as historical actors. *Crusaders* calls for exhuming women's histories along with those of other groups that are often erased from the historical record. She explained that "it is hard to write about Marian Le Sueur, not because she was my mother, but because like myself she was a woman. In many ways her history is suppressed within the history of the man, the history of an oppressed people is hidden in the lies and the agreed-upon myth of its conquerors."[58]

Space constraints do not permit writing about full-length works like *North Star Country* and *Crusaders* in any depth here, except to suggest the way in which they sustain earlier (and previously overlooked) themes in Le Sueur's work, demonstrating that, as Alan Wald has insisted, "thirties" writing did not begin in 1930 and end in 1939. Even in the darkest years of Cold War repression in the 1950s and 1960s and during her rediscovery as a pioneering feminist in the 1980s and 1990s, Le Sueur maintained her radical regionalist faith in the struggle to build a "people's" culture in the region she knew so well. The effort to keep history and a communal sense of place remained alive, central to her being, throughout her life. In 1982 she told an interviewer: "I'm a passionate, partisan Midwest lover.... I've been made by the Midwest, by the people in the Midwest, by the struggles in the Midwest . . . I believe in that, for creative artists to belong. . . . That doesn't mean that they become small . . . but I don't think you can belong to the entire world unless you live somewhere or *are* someplace. . . . The people of the Midwest are to me a great source of strength and beauty. I think I was created by them."[59]

NOTES

1. The chapter's title is from Le Sueur's address to the conference "Proletarian Literature in the Middle West" (1935), in *American Writers' Congress*, ed. Henry Hart (New York: International, 1935), 138. An earlier version of this essay was published as "Writing the Midwest: Meridel Le Sueur and the Making of a Radical Regional Tradition," in *Breaking Boundaries: New Perspectives on Women's Regional Writing*, ed. Sherrie A. Inness and Diana Royer (Iowa City: University of Iowa Press, 1997), 143–61. Permission from the University of Iowa Press to reprint that material is gratefully acknowledged.

2. Waldo Frank, Foreword, in Hart, *American Writers' Congress*, 12.

3. Most studies of Le Sueur and her work have tended to focus on her feminism or her radicalism, in part due to her rediscovery by second-wave feminists. See, for example, Linda Ray Pratt, "Woman Writer in the CP: The Case of Meridel Le Sueur," *Women's Studies: An Interdisciplinary Journal* 14, no. 3 (1988): 247–64. The closest thing to a book-length study of Le Sueur can also be understood as operating in this vein; see Constance Coiner, *Better Red: The Writing and Resistance of Meridel Le Sueur and Tillie Olsen* (New York: Oxford University Press, 1996). A number of studies have appeared regarding other aspects of her work, such as her use of language, the place of the body in her work, and her children's literature; on the latter, see my own "Communist in a Coonskin Cap? Meridel Le Sueur's Books for Children and the Reformulation of America's Cold War Frontier Epic," *The Lion and the Unicorn* 21, no. 1 January 1997: 59–85. For other work dealing with the midwestern dimensions of Le Sueur's radicalism see Sara Kosiba, "The Strength of the Midwestern Proletariat: Meridel Le Sueur and the Ideal Proletarian Literature," *MidAmerica: The Yearbook of the Society for the Study of Midwestern Literature* 31 (2004): 80–90.

4. Raymond Williams says that regional novels are thought to be regional because they explore local rather than universal themes; see his "Region and Class in the Novel," in *The Uses of Fiction*, ed. Douglas Jefferson and Graham Martin (Milton Keynes, England: Open University Press, 1982), 59–68. Michael Kowalewski claims that identifying an author or a work with the label "regional" has historically been a kiss of death; see "Writing in Place: The New American Regionalism," *American Literary History* 6, no. 1 (1994): 171–83.

5. See Cary Nelson, *Repression and Recovery: Modern American Poetry and the Politics of Cultural Memory 1910–1945* (Madison: University of Wisconsin Press, 1989), 37, 51, 7.

6. Earl Rovit, "The Regions versus the Nation: Critical Battle of the Thirties," *Mississippi Quarterly* 13, no.2 (1960): 90.

7. Michael Steiner, "Regionalism in the Great Depression," *Geographical Review* 73 (1983): 443–46.

8. Warren Susman, "The Culture of the Thirties," in *Culture as History* (New York: Pantheon, 1984), 164.

9. Craig Calhoun, "The Radicalism of Tradition," *American Journal of Sociology* 88, no. 5 (March 1983): 886–914.

10. Dorman, *Revolt of the Provinces: The Regionalist Movement in America, 1920–1945* (Chapel Hill: University of North Carolina Press, 1993), 22. For an assessment of the reasons why the regionalist painter Thomas Hart Benton ultimately rejected Marxism see Erika Doss, *Benton, Pollock, and the Politics of Modernism: From Regionalism to Abstract Expressionism* (Chicago: University of Chicago Press, 1991), 124. Recent years have seen increasing recognition of regionalism's radical possibilities, as this collection attests. For instance, in his landmark study of the Popular Front's cultural dimensions, *The Cultural Front: The Laboring of American Culture in the Twentieth Century* (New York: Verso), 132–34, Michael Denning identifies a strand of "proletarian regionalism" in American writing.

11. Calhoun, "The Radicalism of Tradition," 888.

12. Karl Marx, *The Eighteenth Brumaire of Louis Bonaparte*, quoted in Calhoun, "The Radicalism of Tradition," 887.

13. For more on this interpretation of the Popular Front see Maurice Isserman, *Which Side Were You On? The American Communist Party during the Second World War* (Middletown, Conn.: Weslyan University Press, 1982); Mark Naison, "Remaking America:

Communists and Liberals in the Popular Front," in *New Studies in the Politics and Culture of U.S. Communism*, ed. Michael E. Brown (New York: Monthly Review Press, 1993), 45–73; and Robbie Lieberman, *"My Song is My Weapon": People's Songs, American Communism, and the Politics of Culture, 1930–1950* (Urbana: University of Illinois Press, 1989). On the anti-Stalinist left see Alan M. Wald, *The New York Intellectuals: The Rise and Decline of the Anti-Stalinist Left from the 1930s to the 1980s* (Chapel Hill: University of North Carolina Press, 1987); and Judy Kutulas, *The Long War: The Intellectual People's Front and Anti-Stalinism, 1930–1940* (Durham, N.C.: Duke University Press, 1994).

14. The quoted phrase is from Irving Howe and Lewis Coser, *The American Communist Party: A Critical History* (New York: Da Capo, 1974), as given in Lieberman, *"My Song Is My Weapon,"* 4.

15. On Le Sueur's children's books see Julia Mickenberg, "Communist in a Coonskin Cap" and *Learning from the Left: Children's Literature, the Cold War, and Radical Politics in the United States* (New York: Oxford University Press, 2006).

16. Constance Rourke, "The Significance of Sections," *New Republic* 20 (September 1933): 146. The opposite sentiment is expressed in V. F. Calverton, *The Awakening of America* (New York: John Day, 1939), and Granville Hicks, *The Great Tradition* (New York: Macmillan, 1935).

17. For more on this tradition see Julia Mickenberg, "Left at Home in Iowa: 'Progressive Regionalists' and the WPA Guide to 1930s Iowa." *Annals of Iowa* 56 (Summer 1997): 233–56.

18. B. A. Botkin, "Regionalism: Cult or Culture?" *English Journal* 25 (March 1936): 181–85, reprinted in *Midwest* 1, no. 1 (November 1936): 4, 32; and Botkin, "Regionalism and Culture," in *The Writer in a Changing World*, ed. Henry Hart (New York: International, 1937), 157. For more on Botkin and on progressive regionalism see Jerrold Hirsch, "Folklore in the Making: B. A. Botkin," *Journal of American Folklore* 100, no. 395 (1987), 3–37; David Ryan Moore, "Exiled America: Sherwood Anderson, Thomas Hart Benton, Benjamin A. Botkin, Constance Rourke, Arthur Raper, and the Great Depression," Ph.D. thesis, Brown University, 1992, 158–98; Paul Sporn, *Federal Theater and Writers' Projects in the Midwest* (Detroit: Wayne State University Press, 1995), 52; and Jerrold Hirsch and Lawrence Rodgers, eds., *B. A. Botkin: Folklore in the Making* (Norman: University of Oklahoma Press, 2010).

19. Douglas Wixson, *Worker-Writer in America: Jack Conroy and the Tradition of Midwestern Literary Radicalism* (Urbana: University of Illinois Press, 1994), 224.

20. Frederick Jackson Turner, "The Significance of the Section in American History," *Wisconsin Magazine of History* 8 (March 1925):255–80, reprinted in *Frontier and Section: Selected Essays of Frederick Jackson Turner*, ed. William Leuchtenberg and Bernard Wishy (Engelwood Cliffs, N.J. Prentice Hall, 1961), 116.

21. Wixson, *Worker-Writer*, 248.

22. Geographer John Fraser Hart notes that "the purpose of regional geography is to understand areas, not to draw lines around them" ("The Highest Form of the Geographer's Art," *Annals of the American Association of Geographers* 72 [1982]: 8).

23. Wilbur Zelinsky, "America's Vernacular Regions," *Annals of the American Association of Geographers* 70, no. 1 (March 1980): 1.

24. Chametzky, quoted in Werner Sollors, "Region, Ethnic Group, and American Writers," *Prospects* 9 (1984): 458.

25. James R. Shortridge, "The Vernacular Middle West," *Annals of the American Association of Geographers* 75, no. 1 (1985): 48.

26. Meridel Le Sueur, "No War, Say Midwest Writers and Artists," *Midwest* 1 (August 1936): 1.

27. Le Sueur, "No War."

28. On *Hinterland* see Julia Mickenberg, "Left at Home in Iowa."

29. Le Sueur, interview with author, January 27, 1995.

30. Le Sueur, letter to Karlton Kelm, Kelm papers, University of Iowa Special Collections, Iowa City.

31. Douglas Wixson recognized the way in which Le Sueur was both central to the midwestern literary radical group and yet differentiated by the feminist perspective that she brought to her writing: "One who articulated eloquently the differences felt by Midwestern radicals, the uniqueness of their place, culture and history, was Meridel Le Sueur.... Le Sueur's depictions of working-class women, appearing in *Anvil, The Dial, American Mercury, New Masses* and elsewhere, wed a feminist consciousness to progressive ideals in midwest settings" (*Worker-Writer in America*, 358). Constance Coiner, writing in *Better Red* on Le Sueur and Tillie Olsen, suggests ties between these writers' communism and their feminism. For more on working-class women's writing see Deborah Rosenfelt, "Getting into the Game: American Women Writers and the Radical Tradition," *Women's Studies International Forum* 9, no. 4 (1986): 363-72.

32. See Christine Stansell, *City of Women: Sex and Class in New York, 1789-1860* (Urbana: University of Illinois Press, 1987 [1982]), 21-23; Paula Rabinowitz, *Labor and Desire: Women's Revolutionary Fiction in Depression America* (Chapel Hill: University of North Carolina Press, 1991); Gary Gerstle, *Working-Class Americanism: The Politics of Labor in a Textile City, 1914-1960* (Princeton: Princeton University Press, 2002); Elizabeth Faue, *Community of Suffering and Struggle: Women, Men, and the Labor Movement in Minneapolis, 1915-1945* (Chapel Hill: University of North Carolina Press, 1991).

33. Jeanne Kay, "Landscapes of Women and Men: Rethinking the Regional Historical Geography of the United States and Canada," *Journal of Historical Geography* 17, no, 4 (1991): 442.

34. Le Sueur, journal entry, Journals, Le Sueur papers, Minnesota Historical Society, St. Paul.

35. Le Sueur, "Corn Village," in *Salute to Spring* (New York: International, 1940), 24-25.

36. Ironically, this accusation was leveled against the Communist Party, whose Popular Front rhetoric of democracy belied an organization whose workings were far from democratic. For commentary on this contradiction see Lieberman, "*My Song Is Weapon.*" Whitman quotation in *North Star Country*, 316.

37. Le Sueur, "The American Way," *Midwest* 1 (November 1936): 5.

38. Le Sueur, "The American Way," 5.

39. Le Sueur, "The American Way," 5.

40. Le Sueur, "The American Way," 6.

41. Le Sueur, "The American Way," 6.

42. Le Sueur, "The American Way," 6.

43. Le Sueur, "The American Way," 6.

44. Botkin, "Cult or Culture?" 4.

45. Le Sueur, "The American Way," 6.
46. Le Sueur, "The American Way," 6.
47. John L. Thomas, "The Uses of Catastrophism: Lewis Mumford, Vernon Parrington, Van Wyck Brooks and the End of American Regionalism," *American Quarterly* 42, no, 2 (1990): 245–49.
48. Le Sueur, Journals. Le Sueur papers, Minnesota Historical Society.
49. Letter to Le Sueur, Le Sueur papers, Minnesota Historical Society.
50. Le Sueur, Journals, Minnesota Historical Society.
51. Erskine Caldwell, quoted in Blance Gelfant, Foreword, *North Star Country* (Lincoln: University of Nebraska Press, 1984 [1945]), vii.
52. Le Sueur had a mixed history with the WPA, having had difficulty obtaining a job with the Federal Writers' Project because of her "radical" past (WPA correspondence, National Archives, Washington, D.C.). Yet she did gain national notoriety for winning second prize, behind Richard Wright, in a short story contest for Federal Writers' Project workers.
53. Le Sueur, *North Star Country*, 5.
54. Le Sueur, *North Star Country*, 219.
55. Le Sueur, *North Star Country*, 15–16.
56. Le Sueur, *Worker-Writers* (Boston: West End Press, 1980 [1939]), n.p.
57. In her introduction to *Ripening: Selected Work of Meridel Le Sueur*, 2d ed. (New York: The Feminist Press at CUNY, 1993), Elaine Hedges states that HUAC "issued a subpoena" for Le Sueur, "but process servers were unable to find her" (16). *Crusaders* was originally published by Howard Fast's independent Blue Heron Press, which Fast launched when he was blacklisted as well.
58. *Crusaders: The Radical Legacy of Arthur and Marian Le Sueur* (St. Paul: Minnesota Historical Society Press, 1984 [1955]), 38.
59. Meridel Le Sueur, sound recording (St Paul, Minn.: Minnesota Public Radio, 1982).

CHAPTER TWO

Feet in the Grassroots

JOSEPHINE HERBST'S MIDWEST

Sara Kosiba

The writer Josephine Herbst (1892–1969) holds a complicated place in American literary and cultural history. Although her friendships with writers such as John Dos Passos and Ernest Hemingway link her with eminent figures in American literature, her novels were not as widely circulated or applauded at the time, nor do they command the same status and respect today. She does not clearly fit the mold of a proletarian writer, either, due to her ambivalence concerning that label and its associations.[1] Raised in Iowa, Herbst left when she was in her twenties, spending the majority of her life in Pennsylvania and places in the East, making it problematic to define her clearly as a regional writer. Yet continued reference to the Midwest in much of her literature and reporting suggests a lingering and complicated regional attachment. The difficulty of placing her clearly into a recognized literary-critical framework has led to much of her marginalization.

If Herbst is a writer who defies easy categorization, her focus on the radical and the regional clearly aligns her with much of the proletarian or working-class literature and reporting produced in the early twentieth century, particularly in the 1930s. In articles such as "Feet in the Grass Roots" (*Scribner's*, 1933), detailing activities of the Iowa "farmer's holiday" organized to improve prices for agricultural products; "The Farmers Form a United Front" (*New Masses*, 1934), reporting on the Farmers' Second National Conference in Chicago; and "The Farmer Looks Ahead" (*American Mercury*, 1935), focusing on conditions for farmers in the Dakotas and the Midwest, Herbst recorded the lives of midwestern individuals who often resorted to radical or unorthodox means to better the political

Josephine Herbst. Courtesy of Archives & Special Collections, University of Nebraska–Lincoln Libraries.

and economic systems they were facing. Her trilogy of novels, *Pity Is Not Enough* (1933), *The Executioner Waits* (1934), and *Rope of Gold* (1939), dealt with the broad changes taking place in American culture, much as did Dos Passos's *USA* trilogy, but with a far more autobiographical and often midwestern orientation. Her dedicated effort in traveling to the region in the 1930s—assessing the conditions there firsthand while taking copious notes, and then writing about those situations in her journalism and prose—reveals compassion and an interest in the defiant voices for change emerging from a place that many, including Herbst herself, had often dismissed as conservative or insignificant. Still relevant amid the debate over regional significance often found in political and economic forums today, Herbst's work continues to resonate within American culture by demonstrating that even in the smallest local context there are voices that strive to be heard and people who can reveal a great deal about who we are as Americans and where we are going as a society.

Rural Iowa and the bucolic stereotypes depicting the region would not seem to typify a location where radical political ideas originate and grow, yet Herbst's rural upbringing nonetheless provided her with a strong foundation for her later progressive ideas. She was raised on her mother's embellished tales of the family history, which provided her with a vision of pioneering and heroic American identity, particularly when added to her firsthand observations as her hometown, Sioux City, grew and expanded. This view of history and change influenced the novels and articles she wrote later in life. During her adolescence and early years of college and work, both in Iowa and elsewhere, she slowly became more aware of differing political ideas. Her biographer, Elinor Langer, has vividly described the changing dynamics of the small town that would begin to influence a larger worldview: "The Wobblies [Industrial Workers of the World (IWW)] had come to town, organizing seasonal workers on the ice harvest, and for a time two or three men were dropping off every passing freight to add their bodies to the war of labor against capital. In the streets there was marching and singing. In the library *The Masses* and *The Little Review*."[2] Small pockets of radicalism existed in the Midwest, but Herbst wanted to be on the front lines of the larger struggles that she was hearing and reading about.

Her first real interactions with individuals engaged in ideas of change and revolution would not occur until she was outside the Midwest. Langer cites Herbst's brother-in-law, Andrew Bernhard, as saying, "Do not look too hard for the origins of her radicalism. She simply *was* radical"—and her behavior and writing during the course of her life demonstrated this.[3] Her choices and beliefs were less associated with specific political agendas (she maintained only a tenuous association with the Communist Party) and more motivated by personal opinions and convictions free of party doctrine, ideas often classified as "radical" for their progressive slant. Her views toward revolution and politics can be seen in later commentary, such as her written response to "What is Americanism?: A Symposium on Marxism and the American Tradition," published in *Partisan Review and Anvil* in April 1936. Rather than simply spouting Marxist dogma (although she does comment on Marxism as being a positive influence on

American culture), the reply is entirely influenced by an organic sense of American identity:

> I see no conflict between a truly revolutionary literature and what I have termed "Americanism." Our revolutionary literature has been too confined in its beginnings to isolated substances. It seems to me, the pattern is too tight. All of the qualities that we term "American" are rich and useful—the marvelous idiom, the variegated pattern of events almost overpowering in their diversity. America is to me a country that has never fulfilled itself; it will only do so through the processes of revolution.[4]

Despite her distrust of party politics, Herbst did take comfort in forming friendships with others who believed in many of the same ideas. During her time at the University of California, Berkeley, in 1917, when she was finishing her undergraduate degree, she first encountered a group of people who shared many of her own principles and embraced radical ideas. She found more intellectually sympathetic friends when she moved to New York in October 1919 and became part of literary and radical circles there, beginning friendships with Genevieve Taggard, Mike Gold, Max Eastman, Floyd Dell, and other writers often associated with radical publications like *The Masses* and *The Liberator*.[5]

Throughout the 1920s she further established herself as a talented writer and critic, broadening her perspectives through time spent in Germany, France, and other European countries and interacting with many in the expatriate literary establishment. Meeting John Herrmann in Paris in 1924 also significantly shaped her life; they found a shared interest in radical ideas and events, eventually married, and ultimately settled in Pennsylvania. By the fall of 1930 they were more engaged in the American radical movement than ever and were invited by Mike Gold to be unofficial attendants at the International Congress of Revolutionary Writers in Kharkov, Russia.[6]

Although Herbst was an active participant in and prominent figure at many radical events, she still maintained her distance. Even in the early 1930s, "Josie identified with the radical movement, she made her contributions freely, and as her work took more of a radical direction the lines between her literary and personal interests were at times obscured. But her overwhelming intention, right from the beginning of the decade, was to keep her agenda her own."[7] A variety of experiences influenced her perspectives and commentary. In 1935 she traveled to Germany and viewed the rise of Hitler's regime, and also to Cuba to observe the people's struggle under Batista. She reported on an automobile strike in Flint, Michigan, in 1937 and viewed aspects of the Spanish Civil War from the front lines.[8] In every case where she interacted with people seeking change and revolution, she was always interested in the humanity of that moment and the principles of the fight, not the often convoluted politics that surrounded the movement.

Her concerns paralleled those of other writers and reporters during the 1930s. William Stott, who has examined the nature of documentary reportage during that decade, comments that the radical writing "describes the lives of specific individuals who represent a group of common people overlooked in the society. Like all documentary of the early thirties, [the writing] used a specific case to sabotage the general claims, the proud boasts, of those in power."[9] Herbst's own reporting adhered to these ideas, focusing on individuals and their surroundings. She used the stories to evoke sympathy and interest from her readers. The lives of the people themselves drove her work more than the politics.

She returned to the Midwest a few times after leaving the region, mostly for obligatory family visits such as funerals. Like many former midwesterners, she appeared to enjoy the freedom and sense of escape from the conservative world of her origins, which she felt she had left behind. In a piece published in *The American Mercury* in 1926, she captured some of her contempt for the region in an "Iowa Takes to Literature," discussing Iowa literary life and the prominence of women's book clubs. "Half-baked knowledge has dulled rather than sharpened the Iowa female brain," she wrote. "The old pioneer types are gone. The shrill squeak of radios is in the land; automobiles race over perfect roads; new fangled lamps sprout up from the floor. Everywhere the home is up-to-date, and everywhere the inhabitants are making the fight of the modern pioneers—a burlesqued, impoverished fight against nothing more exciting than futility, meaninglessness, ennui."[10] Clearly she shied away from becoming one of these women, through her desire to leave the region. Rather than experiencing the world through the safety of a women's club or local town meeting, places—where, she explained, "returned travelers from Europe are still looked upon with respect and invited to lecture before the Rotarians on the economic situation in Austria after two days in Vienna"—she chose instead to be an active participant and observer of events and determined that leaving the region was the only way to gain that accurate picture.[11]

This strong sense of independence, often in contrast to larger political or governmental agendas, harkens back to the pioneering spirit inherent in American identity and characteristic of many depictions of midwestern life. Although in her earlier writing Herbst would disparage the Midwest as conservative and small-minded, the social and economic changes occurring during the 1930s would reignite her sense of connection to the region. She returned to Sioux City in 1933 to report on the striking farmers there, turning her observations into an article for *Scribner's Magazine* titled "Feet in the Grass Roots." The area farmers were engaged in a "farmer's holiday," protesting the low prices for their products by blocking roads and picketing in towns that engaged in pricing that undermined their ability to earn a living. Farmers had experienced a boom in prices and production before and during World War I; in the decade following, the market had become oversaturated with agricultural products due to the wartime increase in production, ultimately lowering prices. When this development combined with the economic collapse of the country as a whole in 1929, many farmers were left vulnerable and increasingly unable to turn a profit.

Her time away from the Midwest and the circumstances of this particular return trip encouraged Herbst to see Iowa in new ways. In several typed pages of notes prepared for "Feet in the Grassroots," she commented on her increased nostalgia for the past: "This is the farm country, this is the way of life, [that] made me change my life six years gol [sic] leave the city, sit down in the country, in Pennsylvania, find a spot where could get some feel of the soil."[12] In many ways this reaction toward the Midwest after so long an absence was characteristic of many midwestern writers, particularly those who settled permanently outside the region or even abroad, who found value in the place by reflecting on it from a distance. One of the strongest descriptions of this reaction is found in Ernest Hemingway's posthumously published memoir *A Moveable Feast*: "Maybe away from Paris I could write about Paris as in Paris I could write about Michigan. I did not know it was too early for that because I did not know Paris well enough. But that was how it worked out eventually."[13] Herbst admitted to sharing the sentiment: "I was never satisfied with my home town, and the beautiful Iowa land never came alive to me until years in Europe had taught me to see it."[14]

"Feet in the Grassroots" presents a more militant side of the Midwest than the idyllic rural landscapes and farms that often come to mind when thinking of the region. This is particularly striking as the region enjoyed a rather radical or progressive political history in the late nineteenth and early twentieth centuries.[15] Geographer James R. Shortridge, who has made an extensive analysis of the term "Midwest" and examined definitions of the region, has noted that regardless of realities the Midwest has maintained an idealized pastoral image since the late nineteenth century: "The vision of independent farmers creating a rural, egalitarian culture came to focus on the Middle West. The region became America's middle ground, located literally and figuratively between the urbanized East and the western wilderness."[16] This strain between the idealized, pastoral Midwest and the changing realities of the region characterized many literary and cultural debates in the early twentieth century.[17] Topical articles such as those written by Herbst further emphasized a more accurate and complex view of the region.

She reported firsthand on the struggles of farmers during the Depression, using their own words and incorporating details from her many interviews to portray the long-standing difficulties farmers faced, even in the era of her childhood:

> My father sold farm implements to these men in northwest Iowa, Nebraska, and the Dakotas. He was a kind of family doctor to their machinery too when it began limping into threshing season. As a child I drove all over this country with my father, eating fried chicken and chewing corn on the cob, and when the crops were in I would take the team and drive around to see what cash we could pick up on old debts. They put him off oftener than not. . . . My father lost his business trusting farmers who could not pay their debts.[18]

Despite the impact the economics of farming had on her own family, Herbst was sympathetic to the plight of the farmer. In her notes for the article, she commented, "These not the bellyaching farmers of my childhood, ceaselessly but philosophically complaining, they are awake, determined, desperate, leaving their chores in desperation, because they must and because doing chores is no longer of any use. *Why feed a dying cow.*"[19] Throughout her notes she included statistics that also would serve to inspire sympathy, such as a handwritten marginal note "89% in trouble with debts" and, among other comments, "*Land values decreased 34% since 1920. During 5 year period 24% farms foreclosed.*"[20]

Many critics, both then and now, take issue with the idea that the plight of the farmers was as bad as that of other laborers during the Depression. Herbst seems to have seen no significant difference, for she further comments in her notes to "Feet in the Grassroots" that "farmers holiday the rural adaptation of labor union strike."[21] While these farmers had the luxury of owning their own land and dictating their own routines, they were faced with various conditions, mainly economic, that undermined their ability to achieve success. She had listened carefully to the discussions of the farmers in Sioux City: "The talk goes back to their woes and unequal struggle. To the hogs that ought to go to market, but what's the use with the price at two cents?"[22] Although no one forced debt upon them, many farmers had found themselves in deep financial trouble in their pursuit of a decent living because of the ease with which the banks were willing to lend money: "During the evening, one of the committee men tells me he could see this coming ten years ago. The banks were after you then to take bigger loans. If you asked for $500 they urged you to take $1000. They were always suggesting new barns or silos."[23] Whereas the farmers ultimately made the choice of borrowing the money, driven by a desire to achieve success more than outright greed, the easy extension of credit made reaching for greater profit and prominent reputation seem a more attainable reality, a mistaken assumption that has led many, from other occupations and in other generations, into financial difficulty even until today.

"Feet in the Grassroots" gives a more personal voice to the farmers caught up in these economic struggles. Appearing in the press when the nation's economy was in turmoil from the Depression and a number of New Deal programs had been rushed into action to help alleviate the strain on all Americans, the article injected more realism and humanity into a political situation covered with professional detachment by most major news outlets. Herbst continued to follow the politics and issues related to the farmers' conditions even after the publication of the article, as attested by a clipping file among her collected papers, now at Yale. She had saved several articles from the *New York Times* dealing with the farmers' conditions, including one comprehensive piece (Sunday magazine section, February 12, 1933) bearing the headline "The Farmer in a Fighting Mood." A clipping from later that year ominously titled "Farmers 'Arming,' Roosevelt is Told" notes that despite the debates and attempts at federal intervention, the situation was far from resolved: "While five governors sought to effect an immediate price-lifting program through the Federal administration, renewed bombings in Wisconsin, fisticuffs in Iowa, and violence in other states were reported. The intensified picketing brought from Representative F. H. Shoemaker at Minneapolis the assertion that 'It may be impossible to quell demonstrations' unless farm prices are raised immediately."[24] News outlets were competent at reporting facts but failed to give a more personal voice to the frustrations that instigated the bombings and violence. Herbst's reporting provided a more intimate point of view.

Her continued interest in farming conditions led to her attending the Farmers' Second National Congress in Chicago, November 15–18, 1933. Her resulting article, "The Farmers Form a United Front," published in *New Masses* in January 1934, "emphasized," says Langer, "what different elements of the farm population had in common, and had in common with workers ... and she stressed the farmers' opposition to the New Deal's proposed destruction of crops."[25] Herbst wrote of the farmers: "They are not yet, as a whole, politically minded. But they are not afraid to have visions of a new social order. That auditorium was as spirited a place as I've ever been in, with a kind of contagious belief in the rights of farmers rather than merely needs."[26] Her reporting emphasized the participating farmers as people, speaking of their frustrations and realities rather than merely examining them as statistics. The article was first submitted to *New Republic*, whose editor, Bruce Blivin, rejected it. Herbst took issue with many of Bliven's assertions about the piece, in correspondence printed alongside the article as it ultimately appeared in *New Masses*. To Bliven's accusation at one point that Herbst had editorialized rather than reported facts, she responded angrily, "I have very carefully looked over the article and can nowhere find an expression of personal opinion about the 'deplorable' conditions of the farmer. ... The article is packed with figures, the farmers' figures, not mine, as these figures were the basis of the conclusions of the convention and of the demands."[27] In view of the care with which Herbst recorded so many individual perspectives in her notes and drafts, now accessible in her collected papers, it is clear that capturing the reality and authenticity of the moment concerned her more than editorializing on the issues.

In September 1934 Herbst embarked on a final survey of midwestern farm conditions (sponsored by Farm Research and *New Masses*), with the object of examining the "present status of rural protest" in Iowa, Nebraska, North Dakota, and South Dakota.[28] Her observations formed the substance of her article for *American Mercury*, "The Farmer Looks Ahead" (1935). The article synthesized her observations and argued for a continued interest in the struggles of the farmer, emphasizing the inadequacy of the state and federal attempts at relief, particularly in the federally adopted policy of paying farmers not to produce: "The tendency seems to be to force farmers who must apply for relief, either for themselves or their cattle, to a smaller unit of production. These small farmers are saying that they are being forced out of commercial production."[29] She offers more detail in some of her pronouncements in this article, highlighting her firsthand knowledge or discussions with various farmers and officials, though not always citing them by name. As with "Feet in the Grassroots," the specific examples here provide a more substantive view of the struggles of actual people and make a strong argument for why the larger blanket solutions being proposed by national and regional authorities did not address individual needs.

"The Farmer Looks Ahead" provides a strong depiction of farm conditions in the region during that era, but the greatest value to present-day students and scholars of agricultural conditions during the 1930s, and to those interested in the social and cultural dynamics of the Midwest, lies in the notations Herbst made during her travels. The nearly eighty unpublished pages of typed notes among her papers at Yale record conversations she had with farmers and officials, in locales ranging from various small towns and counties to cities such as Pierre, South Dakota. Quite often in these notes she manages to convey a sense of the individual's voice or personality. Nora Ruth Roberts's analysis of Herbst's writing points out that "the genius of her reportage was to be her eye for the responses of ordinary people in extraordinary circumstances and the inclusion of the doings of women and children in her accounts."[30] Although the notes are at times fragmentary, repetitive, or cursory, records of her experiences, together they capture a moment of midwestern rural life relatively free from embellishment or editorializing. Herbst does present her own thoughts and contrasting views regarding many of the comments and details she compiles, but she is careful to note these personal observations separately, leaving the reader of her notes with a rather unbiased view of the individuals she interviews.

The notes present the voices of the farmers themselves alongside the statistics and opinions of officials. In South Dakota, she describes a random encounter near Pierre: "FERDIE KOOP: Found him cutting cane fodder in a field with two horses. Says he has nothing but skampy roughage, thistles, foxtails, and no grain. Traded cattle for corn at 80 cents a bushel from Minn. Gets a feed loan for his cattle."[31] Heading north from Pierre, she found similarly dire conditions: "Dugout and dilapidated shack on route 83. High wind blowing. Dirt and confusion. Old stove, chips, dirty dishes on table, broken furniture. Cheerful middle aged man kneeding big batch of dough in breadpan. Says this is the first he has made in some time, flour very dear."[32] Notations such as these paint a vivid picture of the personal struggles these individuals were weathering, the frustrations over their living conditions, and the happiness that could still come with small pleasures like bread.

While many of her comments highlight the ordinary, everyday aspects of farm life, Herbst's interest in the revolutionary aspects of the midwestern experience also manifests in the notes. She came across several individuals who considered themselves Communist or radical and recorded their opinions on the farming situation as well. She describes Carson Anderson as a "town worker" in Mitchell, South Dakota, and reports, "This man comes from a radical background, all his 6 brothers, his sister, his parents 'hellraisers,' old Populists, socialists, saw the light when C P party came in. Had brother who went to school in Vermillion and wrote songs for a populist songbook. One verse goes 'Come ye weary toilers, we'll not cease our labor, Until victory is won.' Family of rebels, sister 'a fighting fool.'"[33] Fred Keller, near Foster, Nebraska, "says he has not been working with Holiday [the Farmer's Holiday Association], says its been busted. Says nothing can be started now while relief has quieted people. The burst they were in has died down. They've stopped foreclosures. Thinks Charley Taylor and Harry Lux too far ahead. *Can't alienate the mob.*"[34] In some places she observed that the drive for change seemed to have diminished, but for several of the ordinary individuals she spoke with, in locations throughout the Midwest, dissatisfaction continued to invoke radical considerations.

Her notes also provide a valuable depiction of the midwestern landscape that she observed as she was traveling to various cities and farms. Periodically she transitions between interviews with commentary on surroundings themselves. For example: "On the road from White Lake [South Dakota] to south, to Bijou Hills country: Dilapidated falling to pieces houses and shcaks [shacks], huge mounds of Russian thistle, cornfields with corn withered down to couple of inches, tiny tassels. Handsome grantie [sic] monument in family burying ground in midst of once prosperous fields, now desolate and gray with tumble down shacks in distance."[35] In another passage, she writes, "Winner [in Tripp County, South Dakota] toward Pierre: Buttes toward Rosebud county, black pasty soil, drifts in sandlike mounds, tar paper shacks, unpainted houses, great grey unbroken sky, flock of turkies picking in a Russian thistle field."[36] Most references to the landscape in Herbst's notes show bleak or difficult conditions, in line with the rough conditions of the farmers, but the focus on the landscape shows an additional dimension of the social and economic struggle not always captured in commentary by other observers of the region. Readers of the notes can see the landscape as she herself saw it, with an immediacy that brings the historical moment to life.

Herbst's politics, while subtle, and the firsthand observations of her reportage both had a large impact on her fiction, particularly the three notable books that comprise the Trexler/Wendel trilogy: *Pity Is Not Enough* (1933), *The Executioner Waits* (1934), and *Rope of Gold* (1939). Much of what takes place within this fictional trilogy is based on aspects of Herbst's own family history and her own life. The first book of the three, *Pity Is Not Enough*, takes on the ambitious task of tracing the Trexler family history from just after the Civil War until World War I, following the lives of various family members. Interspersed within this history are vignettes set in Oxtail, Iowa, several years after much of the narrative occurs, explaining the reactions and experiences of Anne Wendel (formerly Trexler) and her daughters to those earlier memories and stories. The novel opens with a scene in Oxtail during cyclone season, dated 1905. Later on, in another Oxtail vignette, the reader is told:

If Amos Wendel had made a go at his business Anne Wendel, who was a Trexler, might not have dug so deeply in her past, fishing up stories for her children. She was only one of many women not acclimated to the Iowa town that never lost its frontier flavor. Even when the hot winds did not blow, the streets seemed hard and bare, the buildings squat and cut short in their growth. But in the spring when the lilacs bloomed it was easy to feel at home, even in Oxtail.[37]

The descriptions of Iowa often mirror much of Herbst's own ambivalence toward the region. The radical influences are subtle in this first novel and appear mostly near its end, where the narrator mentions that anarchists were executed in Chicago (the result of the Haymarket Riot in 1886), vaguely referencing the politically subversive thoughts that were emerging throughout the country.

The next novel in the trilogy, *The Executioner Waits*, continues with the evolution of the family, focusing mostly on David Trexler's success in Oregon and his sister Anne's struggle to maintain solvency in Iowa. The main story line details the lives of their children, as David's and Anne's sons and daughters start to venture out into the world, marking the shift to a new generation. *The Executioner Waits* also assumes a much more political orientation. In one passage near the beginning of the novel, Anne has traveled to the East to take care of her sick brother Aaron and two of her daughters, Victoria (Vicky) and Rosamond, return home for a visit. Their father, Amos, discusses taking them to his friend Gus's house, where Gus's brother, an IWW member, is visiting. Later, while they attend a dinner at their sister Clara's house, her husband disputes the value in the IWW and cites the resistance in town to a rally the group has scheduled.[38] Ultimately Amos, Vicky, and Rosamond disagree with these comments and side with the rights of the worker, echoing Herbst's own sympathies. A secondary story line concerns Jonathan Chance (modeled on Herbst's husband, John Herrmann), a boy from a rich family in Michigan who crosses paths with some of the other characters in the novel and eventually becomes involved with Anne's daughter Vicky (who bears similarities to Herbst).

The relationship between Vicky and Jonathan becomes the focus of *Rope of Gold*, the last and most radical novel in the trilogy. Herbst's various reporting experiences are clearly evident throughout the novel. As Jonathan and Vicky's marriage falls apart, Jonathan becomes increasingly radical and advocates for the working class, participating in fundraising and marches, while Vicky begins to look at various working-class cultures, covering the issues through journalism. Almost all the characters in this novel are in some way affected by the economic and political situation of the 1930s. One of the narrative threads follows the Carson family in the Midwest, who have a photo of Eugene Debs hanging above their kitchen table. The son, Steve, is described as growing up hearing about "Gene Debs and our martyred brothers and during the big steel strike he put all his pennies in a little box to send to the strike fund."[39] Into the narrative are interpolated italicized vignettes that express different radical voices and experiences, spanning worker protests in the United States to conditions of the migrant workers in sugar and coffee fields in Cuba, to European aspects of the struggle, including the death of the noted Italian socialist and antifascist Carlos Rosselli, as well as the efforts of the international Abraham Lincoln and George Washington brigades in the Spanish Civil War.

Although *Rope of Gold* never arrives at a resolution of these diverse radical vignettes, it does end on the idea that the struggle will continue. The very last scene presents a group of workers who have shut down a factory to protest their treatment and to argue for union rights. As readers, we never find out what happens to them, but as they are as ardent in their beliefs at the end of the novel as they are indignant at their treatment or conditions throughout, it is clear that the author believes in their cause and is hopeful. A review of *Rope of Gold* in the *New York Herald Tribune* by Alfred Kazin commented on Herbst's dedication to her subject:

> Of all the crusading novelists who started out so bravely a decade ago to create a lean, hard social fiction fit for the 1930s, Josephine Herbst has not weakened. . . . she wrote carefully and with a quiet grace of that shambling portion of the middle class which she knew. . . . Her books are the latest in that long line of Mid-west chronicles of failure which have joylessly hacked the Valley of Democracy.[40]

Her trilogy puts into an epic American form the individual struggles she witnessed firsthand (along with regional struggles within the Midwest) and argues for a view of the country that contrasts personal hopes and dreams with the divisive issues and the reality of the 1930s.

Herbst never felt she achieved the full effect of what she intended through her trilogy; she was particularly distressed that all three volumes were never published as one continuous set. The trilogy did encapsulate much of what she was trying to convey through her reporting and from insights gained from her travels and interviews. She reflected on her intentions for the trilogy in an interview with Daniel Madden as he was composing his *Proletarian Writers of the Thirties*: "the books contain some first hand documentation, for I never wrote about anything I hadn't some understanding of first hand. . . . The urgency of the times crumpled much that would have made the works more valid but there was never time or space. The whole business of that kind of world view and type of writing needed room for development which never came."[41] Herbst made a dedicated effort in her writing, both fiction and nonfiction, to give further voice to the obstacles facing individuals as they addressed the political and economic forces unique to that time.

Kazin's review and Herbst's own reflections place her work in a similar context with many midwestern writers of that era, and indeed her writing bears similarities to what other authors in the region were producing at the time. Yet her actual interactions with other radical midwestern writers were sporadic, although they did cross paths in their similar literary circles and in their work with the radical establishment. She was present at the same 1935 League of American Writers' Congress that Jack Conroy, Meridel Le Sueur, and James T. Farrell attended, although her friendship with Farrell was more developed than her interactions with the other writers.[42] A leaflet for the Midwest Literary League is among Herbst's papers at Yale, bearing endorsements from Le Sueur and Conroy, although there is no evidence that Herbst herself contributed to the League or made a contribution to their journal, *The Hinterland*.

Despite her tenuous personal connections to many of these midwestern writers, the philosophies behind their creative work show shared sympathies. Conroy's *The Disinherited* (1933), with its fictional portrayal of Larry Donovan's working-class life in the Midwest, was based on his firsthand knowledge of working-class conditions in places like the mines of Missouri and the factories of Detroit. Le Sueur's short story "Salute to Spring" (1940) attempts to capture the struggle of rural farmers in the midst of economic hardship. A man and woman desperate to improve their lives leave their sick child at home in order to attend a meeting meant to organize the area farmers. Despite the positive emotions inspired by the meeting, they return home to find their child dead. This destroys their new hopes, making the conditions they are living in seem even more insurmountable. All of these writers sought to convey the voice and real experience of the ordinary individual in their writing, rather than creating characters to serve as stereotypes. This faithful adherence to realism rather than to blind optimism or fictional idealism bridges the work of writers like Herbst, Conroy, and Le Sueur and provides valuable detailed commentary on individual experiences in the Midwest.

Herbst's writing is especially important for showing us a more outspoken, proletarian Midwest than most histories, as well as the social expectations of the time, would have revealed. If she was often ambivalent in her allegiance to the region, as were many other native midwestern writers of the era, her coverage of the farmers' struggles, as well as her fiction characterizing midwesterners caught up in working-class struggles, reveals an awareness that the region serves as a symbol or point of contrast for ideas of American identity as a whole. The "heartland," "America's breadbasket," and similar other metaphors attached to the Midwest call attention to the region's central importance to American identity and culture. Herbst's analyses and depictions of this region, which contrast so strongly with the prevailing social and political ideas affecting the country, provide a descriptive example of that role. And many of her comments and observations about the economic struggles and foreclosures afflicting farmers during the 1930s resonate all too clearly with the recurring financial difficulties facing the United States and other countries around the globe in later decades and even today. Just as the governmental solutions to larger social and economic problems, such as the conditions faced by rural farmers, often proved inadequate for many individuals in the 1930s, broadscale legislative solutions to current economic conditions seem unable to address the varying needs of individuals in every region of the United States. Reading Herbst's work provides insight into a historic past that may also teach us much about our present struggles as well.

NOTES

1. In a letter to David Madden, responding to his request for a contribution to his collection *Proletarian Writers of the Thirties* (Carbondale: Southern Illinois University Press,

1968) and excerpted in his introduction to the volume, Herbst comments that "when I was writing my trilogy I never thought of it as 'proletarian'—in fact I hated the term, and thought it never comprehensive enough. Actually the Soviet Union gave it up in the thirties for the equally ambivalent and never defined term of social realism. Still, there is more sense to that than to proletarian" (xix).

2. Elinor Langer, *Josephine Herbst* (Boston: Little, Brown, 1983), 38.

3. Langer, *Josephine Herbst*, 44, italics in original.

4. Josephine Herbst, "What Is Americanism? A Symposium on Marxism and the American Tradition," *Partisan Review and Anvil* 3 (1936): 6.

5. Langer, *Josephine Herbst*, 53–54.

6. Langer, *Josephine Herbst*, 115.

7. Langer, *Josephine Herbst*, 118.

8. Her experiences and comments about Germany were published in a series of six articles as "Behind the Swastika" (*New York Post*, 1935), later collected into a pamphlet of the same name published by the Anti-Nazi Federation in 1936 (with permission of the *Post*). Her responses to the situation in Cuba were published as "The Soviet in Cuba" (*New Masses*, March 19, 1933: 9–12), "Cuba—Sick for Freedom" (*New Masses*, April 2, 1935: 17–18), and "A Passport from Realengo 18" (*New Masses*, July 16, 1935: 10–11). Her experiences in Spain are characterized most comprehensively in "The Starched Blue Sky of Spain" (*The Noble Savage*, 1, 1960: 76–117).

9. William Stott, *Documentary Expression and Thirties America* (New York: Oxford University Press, 1973), 172.

10. Josephine Herbst, "Iowa Takes to Literature" *American Mercury,* April 1926, 470.

11. "Iowa Takes to Literature," 467.

12. Folder "Notes for 'Feet in the Grassroots,'" Box 24, Josephine Herbst Papers, Beinecke Library, Yale University.

13. *A Moveable Feast: The Restored Edition* (New York: Scribner, 2009), 19. Malcolm Cowley notes similar tendencies in his book *Exile's Return* (1934).

14. Quoted in "Josephine Herbst." *Twentieth Century Authors: A Biographical Dictionary of Modern Literature.* ed. Stanley J. Kunitz and Howard Haycraft (New York: Wilson, 1942), 641.

15. For a detailed summary of midwestern political movements see the sections "Labor Movements and Working Class Culture" and "Politics" in *The American Midwest: An Interpretive Encyclopedia*, ed. Richard Sisson, Christian Zacher, and Andrew Cayton (Bloomington: Indiana University Press, 2007). These sections define the various political and social movements in the Midwest from the rise of populism, socialism, and communism to the influence of various social and labor movements throughout the region's history.

16. James R. Shortridge, "The Emergence of the 'Middle West' as an American Regional Label," *Annals of the Association of American Geographers* 74 (1984): 241.

17. Much of this cultural conflict between a dull, conservative Midwest and a more dynamic depiction of the region can be seen in (among many examples) novels such as Sinclair Lewis's *Main Street* (1920), articles such as Carl Van Doren's "The Revolt from the Village: 1920" (*Nation*, October 11, 1921, 407–12), and later critical works such as Anthony Hilfer's *Revolt from the Village, 1915–1930* (Chapel Hill: University of North Carolina Press, 1969).

18. "Feet in the Grassroots," *Scribner's Magazine, January* 1933, 46–51; quoted, 46.

19. Folder "Notes for 'Feet in the Grassroots,'" Box 24, Herbst Papers, Beinecke Library, emphasis (underscored) in original.
20. Emphasis (underscored) in original. She does not cite her sources.
21. "Notes for 'Feet in the Grassroots.'"
22. "Feet in the Grassroots," 48.
23. "Feet in the Grassroots," 49.
24. *New York Times,* November 4, 1933, 2.
25. Langer, *Josephine Herbst,* 150–51.
26. "The Farmers Form a United Front," *New Masses,* January 2, 1934, 21–22.
27. "The Farmers Form a United Front," 22.
28. Langer, *Josephine Herbst,* 158. Farm Research, Inc. was an organization founded by Harold (Hal) Ware to focus on the problem of the farmer-worker; it was affiliated with the Communist Party.
29. Herbst, "The Farmer Looks Ahead," *American Mercury,* February 1935, 217.
30. Nora Ruth Roberts, *Three Radical Women Writers: Class and Gender in Meridel Le Sueur, Tillie Olsen, and Josephine Herbst* (New York: Garland, 1996), 158.
31. Folder "Midwest Drought Trip 1934, Notes p. 1–10," 2, Box 24, Herbst Papers, Beinecke Library.
32. Folder "Midwest Drought Trip 1934, Notes, pp. 11–19," 18, Box 24, Herbst Papers.
33. Folder "Midwest Drought Trip 1934, Notes p. 1–10," 4.
34. Folder "Midwest Drought Trip 1934, Notes p. 65–70," 66, emphasis (underscored) in original, Box 24, Herbst Papers. "Charley Taylor" refers to Charles E. Taylor, a prominent figure in the Nonpartisan League and radical organizer and legislator. Harry Lux was a Nonpartisan League member and prominent Communist Party organizer in Nebraska. Their participation in the Communist and radical aspects of the farm movement is well documented in Lowell K. Dyson's *Red Harvest: The Communist Party and American Farmers* (Lincoln: University of Nebraska Press, 1982).
35. Folder "Midwest Drought Trip 1934, Notes p. 1–10," 9.
36. Folder "Midwest Drought Trip 1934, Notes p. 11–19," 15.
37. *Pity Is Not Enough* (New York: Harcourt, Brace, 1933), 136.
38. *The Executioner Waits* (New York: Harcourt, Brace, 1934), 120–22.
39. *Rope of Gold* (New York: Harcourt, Brace, 1939), 132. Debs was a prominent union leader, one of the founders of the International Labor Union and the Industrial Workers of the World (IWW) and ran several times as a Socialist candidate for president of the United States.
40. Alfred Kazin, "Flies in the Mid-West Kitchen" (review of *Rope of Gold*), *New York Herald Tribune Books,* March 5, 1939, 7.
41. Quoted in Madden, *Proletarian Writers of the Thirties,* xxi.
42. Langer, *Josephine Herbst,* 184.

CHAPTER THREE

Radical Regionalism in American Art

THE CASE OF JOE JONES

Bryna R. Campbell

Although art history has favored another Missourian, Thomas Hart Benton, in the canon of regionalist art during the 1930s, leftist critics looked not to Benton but to Joe Jones as the artist who best expressed the experiences and struggles of midwesterners of the day. A painter and printmaker from St. Louis, Jones came into national prominence in the spring of 1935 with a critically acclaimed solo exhibition at the American Contemporary Art (ACA) Gallery in New York City. Featuring dynamic images of St. Louis workers and striking drought-ravaged farm scenes, this exhibition was so well received that the gallery reopened it later that summer with additional lithographs.[1] Jones would continue to engage with leftist themes throughout the rest of the decade, taking up such subjects as urban poverty, lynching, and the psychological effects of the Dust Bowl. He became a fixture in the art world during these years, holding four more solo exhibitions in New York, speaking at the First American Artists' Congress in 1936, and working for the federal government—first as an artist for the Resettlement Administration and then as a post office muralist for the Section of Fine Arts—before turning his attention to commercial art commissions in the 1940s.

Jones's interests shifted from project to project over the course of the decade, but his commitment to the Midwest endured as he searched for a visual language and subject matter that would best express both the vitality and the turmoil of the region he considered home. His political and artistic engagement with the Midwest, the subject of this chapter, had the

Joe Jones. Courtesy of Bryna R. Campbell.

effect of invigorating regionalist art discourse of the period with a radical political energy. Like his more conservative colleagues, he found inspiration in the rural countryside and in the farmers who committed their lives to the land. But he also engaged with explicitly urban issues, turning his attention to economic and social problems within the city of St. Louis. His outlook differed dramatically from that of his better-known peers in several important respects. Whereas both Benton and his Iowa colleague Grant Wood, for instance, imbued the region with a sense of nostalgia, Jones constructed the Midwest as a site of struggle and change. In contrast to Benton especially—a New Deal liberal who depicted "aesthetic affirmations of a democratic society"—Jones concentrated on political upheaval, drawing from a more radical, communistic ethos.[2] For leftist critics in the period, his work represented a refreshing departure from the folksy midwestern imagery created by Benton and Wood. His art imagined the region as a space constantly under transition, and his oeuvre became one of the most vibrant examples of a counter-construction of regionalism forged not just by him, but also by like-minded artists such as his St. Louis colleague James Turnbull and the Chicago-based painter Aaron Bohrod.

This chapter takes up Jones's career as a case study of this vital, yet largely overlooked, leftist regional art tradition. It explores his engagement with the place he considered home through his professional relationships, his art, and his activism. And it situates his work within the broader political and social context of the Great Depression in the Midwest. His career in the 1930s can be divided into three overlapping periods, each marked by key events that illuminate his role within this radical tradition. The focus here is particularly upon his early body of work and activism in St. Louis; his first exhibition and subsequent commission at the politically radical Commonwealth College, in Mena, Arkansas; and his engagement with Dust Bowl themes in the second half of the 1930s. By the end of the decade, he would settle down with his family, have his first child (in 1941), and subsequently turn his attention inward toward family life. And like many of his peers, during the Cold War he would downplay his once vital engagement with radical politics.[3] Despite his departure from the ethos displayed in his works from the 1930s, available sources enable us to recover his role within the tradition of radical regionalism, in the process expanding our very conception of regionalist art history.

BECOMING A RADICAL REGIONALIST

More than any other American visual artist in the period, Jones was what might be called a radical regionalist, or "proletarian regionalist," as folklorist B. A. Botkin put it in 1937.[4] In his art and actions Jones had more in common with his radical literary colleagues than with the regionalist artists who would later come to dominate the art-historical narrative. This leftist sensibility was shaped in large part by his membership in the Communist Party, which seems to have given him a sense of social purpose throughout much of the 1930s. But it also derived in part from his working-class roots. Born in 1909 in North St. Louis, he was the youngest of six children, all supported by the meager income of their father, Frank, a struggling housepainter who had lost his arm early in life. After completing grade school, Joe made ends meet by working as an apprentice for his father, and he continued to take on housepainting jobs early on in his career.[5] This background not only brought him firsthand experience with painting—albeit in an industrial form—but it also provided him with a sense of empathy for others struggling during the economic downturn in the 1930s. This time in the workplace became an integral part of Jones's autobiography once he became a better-known entity in the art world, and for leftist art critics it made him uniquely suited to depict proletarian themes within his art.

Jones did not begin his career a leftist artist, however, nor did he initially craft his public persona in this way. Rather, like many of his peers in the interwar period, when he began working as a professional artist around 1930, he was attracted to the liberating expression of artistic modernism. He applied this pictorial language to traditional subjects—still lifes, landscapes, nudes—to explore the limits of those conventions through the use of simplified forms and a reduced color palette. This accessible version of modernism is exemplified in *Landscape* (1932), a wooded scene whose mauve and green color scheme and undulating lines provocatively suggest fabric or bodily forms.[6]

These modernist experimentations were extremely marketable even in the sluggish economic environment, and by 1931 Jones, though still young, had already shown his first work, a nude study, at the prestigious City Art Museum (now the Saint Louis Art Museum) and had held his first solo exhibition at the studio of Lisbeth Ebers Hoops, a dance instructor who shared his passion for aesthetic modernism.[7] By 1933 he had made connections with several art patrons in the city, notably Elizabeth Green, a politically liberal local arts enthusiast who had secured financial independence through her father, a physician who had died a few years earlier. Green saw in Jones an artist who had the potential to make St. Louis a more vibrant cultural center, and she became the most important financial supporter of his career. The two would become close confidants over the years, despite disagreements over Jones's political radicalism; their extensive correspondence serves as the most important documentation of his activities over the course of the decade.[8]

Jones was attracted to formal modernism not only for its palatability within the art market but also because it countered more academic forms of expression found in the Midwest. He found such modes inauthentic and overburdened with historical tradition.[9] He publicly confirmed this point of view in 1931 by becoming a charter member of the New Hats, an organization of like-minded bohemians explicitly devoted to promoting more "liberal" tendencies within the arts. Through this affiliation he was able to show his art beyond St. Louis for the first time, in the Illinois cities of Quincy and Springfield. Although his connection with the New Hats would also mark his first experience as a civic activist, the organization's activities were limited primarily to concerns relevant within artistic circles.[10] Any hint of the tremendous social problems in St. Louis, a city hit hard by the Depression—as evidenced by a mile-long Hooverville along the banks of the Mississippi—remained largely absent in his work and activism during these initial years of his career.[11]

All of this would abruptly change in the fall of 1933, after Jones returned from his first trip to the East Coast that summer. It was there, while spending two months in an art colony in Provincetown, Massachusetts, that he first began to engage with leftist ideologies through a group of painters, teachers, and workers in the area who, as the *St. Louis Post-Dispatch* would later report, "chose to spend their time studying and discussing the economics of Karl Marx."[12] Still quite young (he was twenty-three years old), he had likely encountered such political ideologies earlier, through bohemian circles in St. Louis, and had even cited the desire to "paint things that will knock holes in the walls" in an interview earlier that winter.[13] But it seems he needed to be away from his hometown to become more fully receptive to these political views. Elizabeth Green, who had funded the eastern stay and had joined him during the initial road trip through Washington, D.C., and New York City, had hoped Jones would make important artistic connections on the East Coast.[14] Instead he discovered class consciousness and returned to St. Louis that fall a Communist. From that point until the end of the decade, he worked as a radical regionalist. His art brought attention to social justice and labor issues specific to the Midwest and focused on St. Louis, especially, as a site of political agitation.

Nowhere was this newfound sense of political purpose better expressed than in first major project executed upon his return, a large-scale mural titled *Social Protest in Old St. Louis*, completed early in 1934. This work, which garnered national attention in the radical press when it sparked controversy in St. Louis, exemplifies his early engagement with proletarian regionalism. The events surrounding the creation and reception of the mural—which no longer survives; it was censored and fell into disrepair—also demonstrate the opposition he faced in the city once he publicly declared his allegiance to the Communist Party. After returning from Provincetown he began to teach the Unemployed Art Class, which offered free instruction to a small group of unemployed artists on the premises of the Old Courthouse, which had been vacated. The mural became their first group project, conceived by Jones but executed collectively by seven of the students. This work was thus intimately tied to the Unemployed Art Class and must be understood within that context.

The Unemployed Art Class was the conception, it seems, of both Jones and Green, his closest supporter. Or at the very least, Green was financially responsible for its materialization; as the chief supporter of this work, she utilized her connections to help raise money from many of the city's more liberal patrons of the arts and used it to purchase supplies and to help pay rental fees for the group's workspace.[15] Meanwhile Jones himself was supported by federal government funds he obtained through the Public Works of Art Project.[16] Green likely had a hand in securing the site at the Old Courthouse as well, which was already in use at the time by the local Art League, which held paid classes in the building.

The Unemployed Art Class was designed in part to counter those very classes—to provide the unemployed students with training for no fee—and in a more modern style than the Art League offered. Jones also hoped to use the class to develop an "art in St. Louis that will express the regional characteristics of the city and the Middle West." But he defined this art as one of free expression, "regardless of whether [the students'] work is a protest against the social, economic or political conditions of the day."[17] This radical redefinition of regional art became one of the most contentious aspects of the class. The interracial composition of the group, about half of whom were African American, was also controversial. From the very beginning, Jones faced resistance from members of the Art League, who felt personally affronted by his decision to teach where they had been working. However, it was the city's public safety director, George Chadsey, who condemned the the group's actions most heavily. When Jones and his class unveiled their large-scale work, a 37-by-16-foot chalk pastel mural that spanned the entire width of an old courtroom, tensions between city officials and the class reached fever pitch.

Social Protest in Old Saint Louis focused especially on the role of African Americans as labor agitators and featured episodes emphasizing the Communist Party's importance within the city. The program of the work centered on a group of black riverboat dockworkers whose solid bodies and steady poses formed a dynamic compositional anchor. To their left was a group of unemployed men standing before a pawnshop, and to their right was depicted an African American baptismal gathering, which, according to Jones, represented "the conception of religion as an opiate."[18] A blue eagle, symbol of the New Deal's National Recovery Administration (NRA), appeared on the pawnshop window, a symbolic barb suggesting that the program did little more than create "pawns" of its workers.[19] The baptismal group, meanwhile, blended into a band of agitators bearing signs that, the artist explained, represented "the natural evolution of discontent which cannot be appeased by religion."[20] The demonstration scene was likely a reference to the 1933 Nut Pickers Strike, involving employees of the Funsten Nut Company. This motif was highly significant to the Communist Party, which had been instrumental in organizing the strike, as well as to African American women, who had played the central role in its success.[21] The mural also depicted a group of men clinging to freight cars bound for a demonstration in Washington, D.C., which had the effect of linking local activists to a larger network of political activism.

Taken as a whole, the mural was a work that constituted an entire reordering of race and class within St. Louis. The work was purposefully provocative and, at its unveiling, was accompanied by posters from the Soviet Union that further incited anger among Jones's most ardent critics. About one month after the unveiling, a group that claimed affiliation with the American Fascist League vandalized the classroom, tearing down the posters. They left a note warning that they intended to destroy the mural. It included the following threat: "This is a public building, a building of the American people. We, as Americans, will not tolerate its use for the worship of any foreign idols or fetishes because it is un-American. It destroys homes and separates families, it destroys men as God meant them to be. We say it must stop. Do you understand? We say it must stop."[22]

This incident had the effect of rallying a number of key regional activists around the mural, including the poet Orrick Johns, who publicized the art class and mural in the leftist weekly *New Masses*, and the writer Jack Conroy, who had personally contributed to the success of the Nut Pickers' Strike.[23] Letters indicate these two figures also forged a close friendship with Jones during this period, and Conroy even briefly shared an apartment with Jones in 1936.[24] Jones himself, meanwhile, continued to teach the class throughout the spring and summer and presented a public lecture, "The Art of Soviet Russia," that March. This seemed to further agitate his critics, especially Chadsey, who continued to critique his activities in the press. In December, Chadsey, as a public safety official, took the extraordinary step of ordering Jones to vacate the premises immediately, claiming that the classroom was being used as a Communist meeting place. Jones ignored this order, arguing that the classes were legitimate, and on December 14, 1934, Chadsey forced an eviction and had the doors to the classroom padlocked.[25]

Although Chadsey used Jones's Communist Party ties as justification for shutting down the class, racial elements were undoubtedly in play as well.[26] Jones's decision to teach an interracial class in this period would have been remarkable, and the symbolism of encouraging African American protest in the Old Courthouse—the site where slaves were once sold and where the Dredd Scott case was heard—would not have been lost on local officials. Although Jones and his students would petition to reopen the class, they were ultimately unsuccessful, and the mural, which had been produced with cheap materials (chalk and beaverboard), quickly fell into permanent disrepair. The Unemployed Art Class dissolved.

Despite the defeat of the censorship battle, *Social Protest in Old St. Louis* and the Unemployed Art Class represented one of Jones's most successful endeavors to bridge artists and workers in the class struggle.[27] The controversy around the art class served as a rallying point that brought together other leftist activists in the region and also drew national attention in the radical press to social and artistic issues important to St. Louis. As the decade wore on, the mural controversy would come to serve as a symbol of artistic struggle against fascist forces within American society. It became associated with Diego Rivera's Rockefeller Center mural *Man at the Crossroads* (1933), destroyed the same month that Jones unveiled his work in St. Louis: Rivera had refused to remove from it a portrait of Vladimir Lenin.[28] Jones no doubt had the art of Rivera and his colleague José Clemente Orozco in mind when he produced his own work that winter. He had seen Orozco's monumental mural, *A Call for Revolution and Universal Brotherhood* (1932), at the New School of Social Research in New York and had visited Rivera's *Detroit Industry Murals* on his way back to St. Louis from Provincetown.[29] Like these Mexican artists, Jones sought to use mural art as a highly visible and monumental public art form that could serve as an effective political weapon.

Ultimately, however, he seems to have found the experience disappointing and later recounted his frustration in a speech, "Repression of Art in America," presented at the First American Artists' Congress against War and Fascism, in 1936.[30] He had left for New York shortly after the Unemployed Art Class was shut down, in search of a more sympathetic audience, and he secured his first East Coast exhibition that spring. From that point on he exhibited his work primarily in New York City, even though he still spent most of his time in the Midwest. The scope of his activism also broadened in the following years, as he became increasingly interested in the social problems experienced by people struggling in rural areas in both the Midwest and the South.

FROM NEW YORK CITY TO MENA, ARKANSAS

The years between 1935 and 1937 proved to be some of the most productive and politically active in Jones's career. He gained a foothold in the New York art world during these years and began showing works in several key socially progressive exhibitions. Among these was the landmark exhibition *Struggle for Negro Rights* in 1935, a show organized in support of radical anti-lynching legislation, to which he contributed a work entitled *Lynching* (now lost).[31] In the Midwest, meanwhile, he utilized his connections with friends and colleagues to further encourage a more radical regionalist style of expression. From the end of 1934 to November 1935 he served as the art editor for the midwestern proletarian journal *Anvil*, run by his friend Jack Conroy.[32] He also worked with Green and the local artist Donald McKenzie to open a new art venue in St. Louis, the Vanguard Gallery, a "non-sectarian organization devoted to exhibitions of contemporary art having social significance."[33] This nonprofit space, which opened in 1936, served a key role in providing a venue to display more progressive local and national works. Exhibits included prints by the well-known leftist cartoonist William Gropper and the politically themed show "Graphic Art against War and Fascism." In the spring of 1936 the Vanguard Gallery group also worked with the director of the New York–based ACA Gallery, Herman Baron, to organize a traveling exhibition of paintings by midwestern artists working in a progressive mode.[34] The implicit goal of this exhibition was to provide an example of a very different construction of regionalism than that which had been popularized by Wood and Benton.

By far the most important events in these years were Jones's first solo exhibition in New York and his mural commission at Commonwealth College, in Mena, Arkansas. The former represented the first major venue outside the Midwest to display numerous works of his; the latter constituted some of the most difficult subject matter in his body of work.[35] Both played a vital role not only in his career but also within the larger discourse on leftist regionalism. His experience at Commonwealth was also important because it marked his first major trip to the South. His visit to the Arkansas Delta and the state's mining region would become a vital source of artistic and political inspiration.

Almost immediately after the Unemployed Art Class dissolved in early 1935, Jones set off for New York with the goal of finding gallery representation. This was his first time east since he had joined the Communist Party, and the first time he had been in New York for more than a couple of days. Initially he hoped to connect with a mainstream gallery there, perhaps because he imagined it would be the most advantageous path for him financially; but in the end he was turned down by these institutions and thus began working with the ACA Gallery.[36] Although this was not his first choice, it was a site that suited him well. The director, Herman Baron, held a particular interest in leftist artists like Jones and had created his gallery as a space for radical art to be shown freely. Through Baron, Jones was able to make important connections with other leftist artists, including William Gropper, and to become politically involved through such organizations as the American Artists' Congress. Meanwhile, Baron saw Jones as the real deal—a more authentic, proletarian representative of the Midwest than the well-known artists Wood and Benton.[37] These two regionalists, as well as the Kansas artist John Steuart Curry, had each held exhibitions earlier that season.[38] Baron no doubt had these artists in mind when he organized Jones's exhibition, and perhaps he even constructed the show, which included paintings of labor agitation, landscape scenes, and anti-lynching imagery, to invite comparisons.

When the exhibition opened in May 1935, it received rave reviews from both mainstream and leftist critics. Lewis Mumford, writing for the *New Yorker*, cited Jones as one of the "season's most promising artists," while the *New York Times* critic Edward Allen Jewell praised the newcomer for his "very auspicious" beginnings.[39] The *New Masses* critic, Stephen Alexander, focused specifically on the proletarian character is his work. He especially praised Jones's most political paintings, like *We Demand* (1934), as "powerful canvases" that gave "effective expression of the increasingly militant fight of the organized working class."[40] Such paintings as *We Demand*, which depicted black marchers protesting on behalf of the Communist-supported Unemployment Insurance Bill, HR 7598 (a radical alternative to the Social Security Act), were especially appealing because they seemed

Roustabouts (1934), by Joe Jones (1909–1963); oil on canvas, 25 × 30 inches. Courtesy of Worcester Art Museum, Worcester, Massachusetts (Gift of Aldus C. Higgins; © Heirs of Joe Jones).

honest and direct. "His art is a living expression of his participation in this struggle," Alexander wrote, "and grows organically out of the environment and the people he knows."[41]

Alexander was the critic who drew the sharpest comparisons between Jones and other regionalist artists. He described Wood's depictions as "slick waxen lies" and "prettying up." Benton's paintings, meanwhile, represented stylistic "chaos."[42] Although Alexander was certainly polemical in his critique, the difference between these artists' works and Jones's is indeed striking. A closer look at one of Jones's most highly praised paintings from the exhibition, *Roustabouts* (1934), is particularly instructive. *Roustabouts* depicts a white supervisor surrounded by nine African American boatyard laborers, or "roustabouts," unloading a barge at St. Louis's Mississippi riverfront. Like *We Demand*, the work focuses thematically on the subject of labor, although here the racial autonomy of the marching protestors is replaced with a social order of oppression, as embodied in the boss's relationship with his black employees. Upon closer inspection, however, we find signs of resistance in the poses and expressions of the workers. None of the laborers acknowledges the supervisor, and several actively turn their heads and bodies away from him. The figure in the far right foreground, whose red bandana forms a visual link with the boss's red tie, is particularly striking in this regard: his body stands in counterpose to his boss's, while his downturned face signals his defiance. It is as if Jones has depicted the entire social order in the very process of transformation.

Alexander singled out this work, especially, as a representation that sharply contrasted with what he described as the "patronizing attitude" toward African Americans in Benton's paintings.[43] The critic likely had Benton's *Arts of the South,* from his 1932 series *The Arts and Life in America,* in mind, a work that had been widely criticized for its use of stereotypical images. Recent opinion has viewed the depiction of rural black folksingers in this work as representing "folk art's value as a socially regenerative force."[44] Perhaps, but as many critics in the period noted, they are also reductive and condescending. In *Roustabouts,* by contrast, Jones ties his figures to a specific social issue and imbues them with an aura of dignity. In addition, these strong and forceful black figures can also be read as a response the work of another, earlier Missouri artist, George Caleb Bingham. They especially stand in dramatic contrast to the caricatured black workers in the Bingham's *The Jolly Flatboatmen in Port* (1857). The two works share the same waterside setting, and notably, the City Art Museum in St. Louis had held a Bingham retrospective in 1934.[45] Through such imagery, Jones was thus addressing an entire tradition of Missouri art and replacing it with a radical alternative.

Jones's solo exhibition in 1935 provided him with an opportunity to introduce the larger arts community to a more socially engaged representation of the Midwest. Through paintings like *Roustabouts,* he was able to reimagine the Midwest as a site of continual struggle and social change. Having secured a reputation as one of the most important leftist artists coming out of that region, he continued to hold solo exhibitions in New York on an annual basis for the next several years. He also forged a strong friendship with Baron, who would remain a constant supporter.

A few months after the exhibition closed, Jones was afforded a very different kind of opportunity in Mena, Arkansas, at the left-leaning Commonwealth College. Founded on socialist principles in 1923, the school was considered the foremost labor college in the region, with a curriculum that included classes on proletarian literature and union organizing.[46] The college administration had probably learned about Jones through reviews like Alexander's and decided to invite the artist as a guest lecturer in the summer of 1935. The school commissioned him to paint a mural focusing on social discord for their main dining area. This resulted in some of the most expressive and difficult imagery produced in his career. Although fragments of the work still survive at the University of Arkansas Library in Little Rock, they are in severely damaged condition. Commonwealth College was shut down in the 1940s for suspicious activities, and the mural disappeared into a private collection, surfacing only recently.[47]

The Commonwealth College mural was originally displayed as a multi-panel work that lined the entire circumference of the college's circular dining room. It was comprised of three separate scenes united by their focus on key social issues in the South. These episodes, which centered on tenant farming, mining labor conditions, and lynch crimes, also came together to form a powerful meditation on social and racial injustice. In preparation for the mural, Jones traveled around the state by car, taking photographs that served as the basis for his mining and tenant scenes.[48] He may have also consulted his summer colleagues. The Southern Tenant Farmers' Union (hereafter STFU) organizer Ward Rodgers and the well-known farm labor organizer "Mother" Ella Reeve Bloor were among the other guest lecturers that summer, and judging from his correspondence with Green, Jones was profoundly inspired by his conversations with Bloor.[49]

The school itself probably also collaborated with Jones, as his work focused especially on themes important to the college. For example, the scene of miners on the verge of striking (mural, at right), would have been especially meaningful to student activists who had become increasingly engaged with labor protests at the mining communities around nearby Paris and Jinny Lind.[50] The scene showing a tenant family's eviction (at left), on the other hand, tied to efforts by the school to become increasingly involved with the STFU, which had been working in the eastern part of the state to insure fairer treatment for tenant farmers and to advocate possible property redistribution.[51] The anti-lynching theme, treated at the center of the mural, was one of the most important issues for Communists like Jones during this period—and would have resonated especially in Arkansas, where more than three hundred lynchings had occurred between 1890 and 1930.[52] The Communist Party had acted as a major force against lynchings in the South since the beginning of the Great Depression, linking the violence to other social injustices believed to be similarly produced within the class-based structure of capitalism. Two years before Jones joined, the party had brought national attention to the cause through its involvement in the notorious Scottsboro case (named for the town in Alabama where it was first tried), in which eight black teenagers had been unjustly accused of raping two white girls who were riding with them on a freight train. The boys, who had almost been lynched by a mob upon their arrest, had been spared execution thanks in part to the efforts of the legal arm of the Communist Party.[53]

Jones may have had this event in mind as he constructed the important anti-lynching scene on his mural. He made it the centerpiece of his work, the most powerful and dramatic aspect of its conceptual program, and chose as its focus the brutal portrayal of a group of white men murdering two African American men—one a haunting silhouette against a fiery inferno, the other in the process of being hanged. Through the use of caricature and grotesquery, he vilifies the lynchers and makes somatically visible the victims' psychological and physical terror.

Jones had already tackled this subject in other works, including *Lynching* (now lost) and *American Justice* (1933), but here he connects the theme with the mural's larger program of class injustice—thereby suggesting, in conformity with Communist principles, that these specific problems all emerge from the same social construct. Most notably in this work, he builds outward from his focus on the victims of various injustices to construct a complex narrative of agency and agitation. Entering from one side of the lynching scene, a sturdy black woman, a strong maternal figure with a child clinging to her leg, strides toward the violent action in angry protest. Her expression, executed in careful and sympathetic detail, stands in contrast to the caricatured faces of the lynchers. Her arrival, as if from another scene in the mural, enhances the viewer's impression of overall interconnection of the themes that are portrayed.

What Jones also does in the Commonwealth College mural, as with his Old Courthouse mural, is promote a vision of social and racial protest rooted squarely within the region in which the work and its themes originated. He transcends familiar stereotypes of African Americans and takes the bold step of representing a black woman—a figural type that had historically suffered great abuse under slavery—as the primary agent of agitation. At the same time, his brutal expression of the lynching also brings into dramatic relief the horrendous nature of a crime committed widely and repetitively, with virtual impunity, into his own time. He would continue to create scenes that focused on themes of social and racial justice, but never with the same dramatic intensity. In works like *Bottle Dancer* (1936), for example, portraying an East St. Louis prostitute whose body is battered and bruised, he used pictorial realism to create a sympathetic portrayal that captures the woman's sense of isolation. The melancholic quality of the scene would be a cornerstone of his Dust Bowl imagery, as well, which he produced in the second half of the 1930s.

THE DUST BOWL

Discussion thus far has focused almost exclusively on Jones's artistic engagement with subjects relating to industrial labor and racial justice. These two themes held his attention throughout the Great Depression and provide a vital framework for distinguishing his thought and work from that of other regional artists. But such themes only represent one facet of his artistic production in the 1930s. From the beginning of his career onward, he maintained a steadfast interest in agricultural subjects as well, returning repeatedly to the rural Midwest as a source of inspiration. His solo exhibition at the Walker Gallery in New York in 1936, for instance, was comprised almost exclusively of scenes of farmers harvesting wheat.[54] He had produced these fertile scenes while spending the summer of 1935 in St. Charles (near St. Louis), sketching the fields that lined the Missouri River. After his Commonwealth College commission—and likely owing in part to his experiences there—he became increasingly interested in more critical aspects of American agriculture. From 1936 to 1938 he turned his focus especially to the problems of the Dust Bowl. This large-scale economic and ecological disaster in the Great Plains and the Midwest, which had been caused by severe drought and bad land management practices, became one of the most sustained themes within his oeuvre. Even though relatively few of his works on this subject survive, those that do speak in poetic ways to the his ongoing commitment to the rural people of the Midwest.

Jones first became engaged with the problems of the Dust Bowl in the summer of 1936, when he joined the Special Skills Division of the Resettlement Administration (RA), an agency formed in 1935 under the leadership of Rexford Tugwell with an explicit goal of alleviating rural poverty caused by the Dust Bowl. Jones, who secured his position in the government with the help of Elizabeth Green, was likely attracted to the agency for its particularly progressive initiatives.[55] Among Tugwell's more controversial ideas were the resettlement of tenant farmers and the establishment of rural cooperatives that would function in part by collectively sharing modern equipment. These initiatives, which helped earn Tugwell the label "Rexford the Red" and ultimately contributed to the agency's demise in 1936, fit well with Jones's Communist belief system. Although the goal for artists in the Special Skills Division was to produce posters, pamphlets, and other images that advertised the importance of this agency, the feature that most interested Jones was the possibility of working directly with local communities.[56] "Our subject matter will be the social aspect of these people portrayed honestly," he explained enthusiastically in a letter to Green.[57] He had traveled the state of Arkansas in similar fashion in preparation for his Commonwealth College mural and no doubt envisioned a similar experience with in his new position with RA.

But even though he was poised to work for the agency extensively, other projects—or perhaps conflicts within the agency—seemed to get in the way.[58] He only worked with the RA for a six-week special appointment, from mid-July to late August 1936, producing images of struggling families and drought-stricken scenes based on his travels in the area designated as Region III (an area that included Illinois, Iowa, Indiana, Missouri, and Ohio). Despite its brevity this experience clearly moved him deeply. Almost immediately after his appointment ended, he applied for and received a Guggenheim Fellowship to further record the effects of the Dust Bowl. Citing his RA experience on the application, he argued that he needed more time fully to capture the serious ecological and social devastation he had witnessed. "Entire populations have been uprooted and impoverished, the land apparently destined to become a desert," he wrote. "I feel that, under the unstultifying terms of a Guggenheim fellowship, I could produce a series of drawings and paintings calculated to bring a clearer understanding of the difficulties and problems of an extremely distressed section of America."[59] Upon receiving the fellowship he traveled throughout the Midwest and West to such sites as eastern Colorado and the Texas Panhandle, producing images based on his observations. As with his RA appointment, only a small selection of drawings, watercolors, and paintings survive from the time of this fellowship.

If the Old Courthouse and Commonwealth College murals bring to life a vision of the Midwest as a site of agitation, these few surviving works from Jones's RA and Guggenheim experiences evoke a narrative of dislocation. In several of the sketches and watercolors, he draws on familiar motifs that imbue the region with a sense of melancholy and loss. In studies entitled *Midwestern Landscape* (1936) and *Windmill and Two Bulls* (1936), for example, he includes an abandoned windmill as an eloquent symbol of the social and ecological tragedy. Although windmill technology had been vital for Great Plains farmers in need of water, during the Dust Bowl the mechanism had come to stand for poor land management practices.[60] In Jones's vision, the windmill is transformed into a solemn, haunting artifact of a moribund era. It has become a modern-day ruin, representing a population that tried and failed to take root in the land. In other paintings he meditates instead on the disaster's psychological effects. In *Departure* (ca. 1937), for instance, a man walks purposefully away from his farmstead, which now lies partially covered by drifting soil. This man is now an exile, representing, along with other figures in Jones's Dust Bowl imagery, the more than two million people forced to leave their homes during the unfolding of that environmental tragedy.

Many Dust Bowl motifs also appear in documentary photography of the time.[61] And, like a documentary photographer, Jones saw his work as bringing attention to the enormous disaster. After completing his appointment with the RA in 1936, he published a small selection of his sketches as a pictorial essay, "In the 'Seventh Year' of Drouth," which appeared in the *St. Louis Post-Dispatch*.[62] The vignettes in this essay—of emaciated animals, a prairie fire, and farmers hauling water—were meant to operate as a kind of journalistic record. Jones himself also took photographs during his trip, many of which served as preparatory studies for his drawings. His Dust Bowl images seemed to be influenced by photography in other ways as well; many of them have a spontaneous quality reminiscent of snapshots or candid, unposed compositions.

In tone, though, these works share a haunting vision of the Midwest that also appears in many of the literary accounts from the period. Consider, for example, Meridel Le Seuer's description of the Midwest in a paper presented at the American Writers' Congress in 1935, a piece that Jones may have been familiar with through his friend Conroy at the *Anvil:* "The Prairie of the Middle West is very large. Nothing has ever been rooted there. Now it is blowing away because nothing has been rooted there to hold the soil into the earth. The rooted things have been torn up by the greed for lumber, coal, iron, railroads, and wheat. Man has not been rooted in it either."[63] Like Le Sueur, Jones constructed the region as a transient space made so by a pervasive insistence on economic exploitation. Although he was not as openly critical as Le Sueur, he used similar, familiar symbolism that made his views understood. In this way her works complement Jones's more explicitly agitating imagery, such as *Roustabouts*. Yet they are also qualitatively different, presenting not a vision of social upheaval but rather a bleak and pointed portrayal of one of the greatest problems of the Great Depression. They are works born out of a sense of documentary realism, that through their directness ultimately aspire to revolutionary critique.[64]

• • •

Together with his imagery of labor and social justice Jones's Dust Bowl–themed works construct an entirely different conception of regionalist art than that which dominates present-day art historical discourse. This imagery can be tied to Jones's own working-class background, yet like his other images, it is ultimately also shaped by his membership in the Communist Party. Taken as a whole, his 1930s works form a vision of the Midwest as a site under constant transition and bring to the forefront a proletarian sensibility. He also constructs in his imagery a Midwest that is adamantly contemporary. His workers in the Old Courthouse mural can be tied to the Nut Pickers' Strike; his dockworkers in *Roustabouts* could be found anywhere near the St. Louis Hooverville along the Mississippi.

In these ways Jones was explicitly countering the very notion of regionalism found in the work of Benton and Wood. Although both of these artists claimed to capture elements of contemporary society, their work was grounded in a nostalgic vision of the Midwest that downplayed serious social conflict. This is the case even for their more progressive works, such as Benton's well-known state capitol mural, *Social History of Missouri* (1935). Scholars have praised the mural for its consideration of the darker elements in Missouri history, including the role of slavery.[65] Yet nowhere among these scenes do there appear themes of a reordering of conventional society. As Botkin wrote of such representations, it is as if the artist took "a certain social background for granted and a certain social order as final."[66] By contrast, in Jones's works the disenfranchised not only appear but act as agents in charge of their own destiny.

When considered within the broader context of regionalism, Jones's work and vision seem to show some appropriate parallels with the writing of Le Sueur. "We have never, in the Middle West, had ease or an indigenous culture," claimed Le Sueur, in her American Writers' Congress essay. "We have been starved since our birth. . . . Revolution can spring up from the windy prairie as naturally as the wheat."[67] Like Le Sueur, Jones grounded his regionalism in this sensibility of transience, turning the Midwest into a space for dynamic activism. It was their awareness of the absence of native culture, or the Midwest's "lack of roots," that set the midwestern radical regionalists into sharp relief from their conservative colleagues.[68] While his colleagues in the visual arts attempted to create a comforting vision of the Midwest, Jones began with a blank slate. The Midwest had no deeply rooted culture; it was a template upon which history was made.

In art-historical discourse regional art has been the site of a particularly rich body of revisionist scholarship. Researchers seeking to deepen earlier simplistic interpretations of the art of Benton and Wood have drawn important connections between regionalist expression and a history of aesthetic modernism.[69] Yet while these efforts have served to enrich our understanding of these artists, they have only attended to one aspect of regionalist art history. Jones's career speaks to a counter-narrative that explicitly asserts itself in opposition to this better-known discourse. His career complicates our very conception of regionalist art, invigorating it with a vital political energy.

NOTES

1. Howard Devree, "In Galleries: Current Exhibitions and Other Events," *New York Times*, July 28, 1935. Some of the positive reviews include Clarence Weinstock, "Joe Jones," *Art Front*, July 1935, n.p.; Lewis Mumford, "The Art Galleries: In Capitulation," *New Yorker*, June 3, 1935, n.p.; and Edward Alden Jewell, "Taking Stock of Local Prospects," *New York Times*, June 2, 1935, X7.

2. Erika Doss, *Benton, Pollock, and the Politics of Modernism: From Regionalism to Abstract Expressionism* (Chicago: University of Chicago Press, 1991), 138 (quoted).

3. For a discussion of Jones's later career see Karal Ann Marling, "Joe Jones: Regionalist, Communist, Capitalist," *Journal of Decorative and Propaganda Arts* 4 (Spring 1987): 46–59; and Bryna Campbell, "Chronology," in *Joe Jones: Radical Painter of the American Scene*, ed. Andrew Walker (St. Louis: Saint Louis Art Museum, 2010), 179–203.

4. Benjamin A. Botkin, "Regionalism and Culture," in *The Writer in a Changing World*, ed. Henry Hart (Equinox Cooperative Press, 1937), 141, quoted in Michael Denning, *The Cultural Front* (London: Verso, 1997), 133.

5. For a discussion of Jones's youth and early career see Janeen Turk, "Joseph Jones: A Conservative Modern in St. Louis," in *Joe Jones*, 15–32.

6. *Landscape* is presently in the collection of the Mildred Lane Kemper Art Museum in St. Louis. For an analysis of this work see Bryna Campbell, "Joseph Jones, *Landscape*," Spotlight Essay, Mildred Lane Kemper Art Museum, February 2008, http://kemperartmuseum.wustl.edu/files/spotlight2.08.pdf (accessed June 23, 2010).

7. "In Joseph Jones' Show," *Art World*, November 1931, 1; see also Turk, "Joseph Jones."

8. These documents form the core of the John Green Papers, now at the State Historical Society of Missouri, St. Louis. (John Green was the father of Elizabeth Green.)

9. Guy Forshey, "From House Painting to Portrait Painting," *St. Louis Post-Dispatch Sunday Magazine*, June 14, 1931, 5.

10. The group was first known as the High Hats but adopted the permanent name New Hats before their first exhibition in December 1931. See "'High Hats,' New Modern Group Is Organized Here," *St. Louis Art World*, November 1931, 3; and "Forty Paintings in First Show of New Hats," *St. Louis Art World*, December 1931, 1.

11. Orrick Johns, *Time of Our Lives: The Story of My Father and Myself* (New York: Stackpole, 1937), 338.

12. "Provincetown Makes Artist a Communist," *St. Louis Post-Dispatch*, September 21, 1933. Just whom Jones met during this trip remains unknown, but Provincetown had a well-established leftist identity in the 1930s. See Melissa Wolfe, "Joe Jones: Worker-Artist," in *Joe Jones: Radical Painter*, 33–54.

13. "Joe Jones Tries to Knock Holes in Walls," *Art Digest*, February 15, 1933, 9.

14. Elizabeth Green, travel journal, May 15–June 2, 1933, Green Papers.

15. Clippings in the Green Papers show that some of the local patrons included City Art Museum director Charles Nagel, J. Lionberger Davis, and members of the Mallinckrodt family.

16. Elizabeth Green to Francis Henry Taylor, January 22, 1934, Green Papers.

17. "Joe Jones Stirs up A Row," *St. Louis Post-Dispatch*, January 21, 1934.

18. "Social Unrest Mural in Old Court-house," *St. Louis Post-Dispatch*, February 16, 1934.

19. For more on this interpretation see Wolfe, "Joe Jones: Worker-Artist."

20. "Social Unrest Mural in Old Court-house."

21. Andrew Hemingway, *Artists on the Left: American Artists and the Communist Movement, 1926–1956* (New Haven: Yale University Press, 2002), 35. For more on women's participation in the strike see Katharine T. Corbett, *In Her Place: A Guide to St. Louis Women's History* (St. Louis: Missouri Historical Society Press, 1999), 262–63.

22. "Old Courthouse Display of Soviet Art Torn Down," *St. Louis Post-Dispatch*, March 5, 1934.

23. Orrick Johns, "St. Louis Artists Win," *New Masses*, March 6, 1934, 28. For more on Conroy's role in the Nut Pickers' Strike, see Douglas Wixson, *Worker-Writer in America: Jack Conroy and the Tradition of Midwestern Literary Radicalism, 1898–1990* (Urbana: University of Illinois Press, 1994), 294.

24. Orrick Johns to Jack Conroy, March 5, 1934, Jack Conroy Papers, Newberry Library, Chicago.

25. Many of the details can be traced in the Green Papers. For a detailed summary of these events see Campbell, "Chronology."

26. Elizabeth Green to Harriette F. Ryan, February 22, 1935, Green Papers.

27. Wolfe, "Joe Jones: Worker-Artist."

28. Joe Jones, "Repression of Art in America," February 1936, reprinted in *Artists Against War and Fascism: Papers of the First American Artists' Congress,* ed. Matthew Baigell and Julia Willliams (New Brunswick, N.J.: Rutgers University Press, 1986), 75–77.

29. For details on his New York trip see Green, travel journal, Green Papers. For more on Jones's trip to Detroit see "Provincetown Makes Artist a Communist."

30. Jones, "Repression of Art in America," 75–77.

31. *Struggle for Negro Rights,* exhibition brochure (New York: ACA Gallery, 1935). For an extended discussion of this exhibition see Helen Langa, "Two Anti-Lynching Art Exhibitions: Politicized Viewpoints, Racial Perspectives, Gendered Constraints," *American Art* 13, no. 1 (1999): 11–39.

32. Jones's name appears in issues of the *Anvil* at this time. For a discussion of his termination see Walt Snow to Jack Conroy and William Wharton, n.d., Jack Conroy Papers.

33. Elizabeth Green, announcement, n.d., Green Papers.

34. Clippings and announcements tied to these events can be found in the Green Papers.

35. Individual works by Jones had already appeared in East Coast venues. For instance, *American Justice* (1933) had appeared in *Exhibition of American Painting Today* at the Worcester Art Museum in Worcester, Massachusetts in December 1934. See Campbell, "Chronology," for other examples.

36. The Downtown Gallery and Rehn Gallery both turned Jones down. For more on his travels to New York see the Green Papers.

37. Herman Baron, *ACA Gallery. 61 and 63, East 57th Street* (New York, 1945).

38. "Grant Wood in the East," *Art Digest,* May 1, 1935, 18; Elisabeth Luther Cary, "Two Artists' Drawings: Sidelights on Curry and Benton Revealed in their Exhibition at the Ferargil," *New York Times,* September 22, 1935, X10.

39. Mumford, "The Art Galleries: In Capitulation"; Edward Alden Jewell, "Ex-House Painter in Art Show Here," *New York Times,* May 22, 1935, 17

40. Stephen Alexander, "Art: Joe Jones," *New Masses,* May 28, 1935, 30.

41. Alexander, "Art: Joe Jones.," 30.

42. Alexander, "Art: Joe Jones."

43. Alexander, "Art: Joe Jones."

44. Doss, *Benton, Pollock, and the Politics of Modernism,* 92.

45. Hemingway, *Artists on the Left,* 38. For a discussion of the Bingham exhibition see Andrew Walker, "Joe Jones and the Dust Bowl: A Search for Social Significance," in *Joe Jones: Radical Painter,* 55–80.

46. For a history of Commonwealth College see William H. Cobb, *Radical Education in the Rural South: Commonwealth College, 1922–1940* (Detroit: Wayne State University Press, 2000).

47. For discussions of the commission and completion of these murals see "Significant Mural to Adorn Commons," *Commonwealth College Fortnightly,* August 15, 1935; Al Lehman, "Brilliant Murals by Joe Jones Decorate Labor College Walls," *Daily Worker,* August 31, 1935; and "Mural in Commons Nears Completion," *Commonwealth College Fortnightly,* September 1, 1935. A fragment of this mural was recently exhibited in the fall 2010 exhibition *Joe Jones: Radical Painter of the American Scene* at the Saint Louis Art Museum;

see the exbhition catalogue, *Joe Jones,* 153; see also http://ualr.edu/www/2012/06/08/grant-to-help-restore-jones-mural/ (accessed August 17, 2012), describing restoration efforts by the mural's host university, University of Arkansas, Little Rock.

48. Jones to Green, August 6, 1935, Green Papers.

49. Jones to Green, August 19, 1935, Green Papers. See also William Henry Cobb, "A Commonwealth College: A History," M.A. thesis (University of Arkansas, Fayetteville, 1963), 163–79.

50. Cobb, *Radical Education in the Rural South,* 146.

51. Cobb, *Radical Education in the Rural South,* 147–48.

52. Walter White, *Rope and Faggot: A Biography of Judge Lynch* (Salem, N.H.: Ayer, 1929; reprinted, 1992), 237.

53. For a discussion of the relationship between the Scottsboro trial and anti-lynching imagery in the period see Langa, "Two Anti-Lynching Art Exhibitions."

54. Reviews of this exhibition include "Joe Jones of Missouri: A 'Success Story,'" *Art Digest* January 15, 1936, 15; and "Joe Jones Celebrates Missouri's Wheatfields." *Art News,* January 25, 1936, 8.

55. Green's efforts as Jones's patron can be tracked through a series of exchanges she had with Edward B. Rowan, director of the Section of Painting and Sculpture, now in the Green Papers.

56. For a more detailed discussion see Walker, "Joe Jones and the Dust Bowl."

57. Jones to Green, September 12, 1935, Green Papers.

58. For an analysis of these events see Walker, "Joe Jones and the Dustbowl."

59. Joe Jones, "Fellowship Application Submitted to John Simon Guggenheim Memorial Foundation," October 15, 1936, in the Foundation's Archives, New York.

60. See Walker, "Joe Jones and the Dustbowl."

61. See Walker, "Joe Jones and the Dustbowl."

62. "In the 'Seventh Year' of Drouth," *St. Louis Post Dispatch Magazine,* September 6. 1936, 1.

63. Meridel Le Sueur, "Proletarian Literature in the Middle West," in *American Writers' Congress,* ed. Henry Hart (New York: International Press, 1935), 135.

64. Walker, "Joe Jones and the Dustbowl."

65. One of the richest analyses of *Social History of Missouri* can be found in Doss, *Benton, Pollock, and the Politics of Modernism,* chapter 2.

66. Benjamin A. Botkin, "Regionalism and Culture," 150, quoted in Denning, *The Cultural Front,* 133.

67. Le Sueur, "Proletarian Literature in the Middle West," 138.

68. Denning, *The Cultural Front,* 133 (quoted).

69. See, for example, Debra Bricker Balken, *After Many Springs: Regionalism, Modernism and the Midwest* (Des Moines: Des Moines Art Center, 2009); James M. Dennis, *Renegade Regionalists: The Modern Independence of Grant Wood, Thomas Hart Benton, and John Steuart Curry* (Madison: University of Wisconsin Press, 1998); and Doss, *Benton, Pollock, and the Politics of Modernism.*

PART II
THE GREAT PLAINS AND TEXAS

The Great Plains and Texas have had a volatile political history. Seen as bastions of conservatism today, the plains states and Texas have been surprisingly fertile ground for left-wing protest in the past. Beginning with abolitionist turmoil in Kansas and Nebraska in the 1850s, peaking again during the Populist revolt against eastern monopoly capitalism in the 1890s, and rising once more amid the environmental and economic devastation of the 1930s, leftist dissent has cropped up repeatedly in the vast austerity of prairies and plains stretching from the Dakotas to Texas.

The fiery dissent of John Brown, Carrie Nation, and William Jennings Bryan; Elizabeth Mary Lease's call to "raise less corn and more hell"; the lionization of Jeremiah "Sockless Jerry" Simpson; the emergence of Texas "Bible socialism" in the 1890s—these are but a few examples of mid- and late-nineteenth-century left-wing protest across this vast region. The massive popularity of Julius Wayland's socialist journal *Appeal to Reason*, published in Girard, Kansas, from 1897 until 1922, and the widespread appeal of agrarian socialism reflected in North Dakota's powerful Non Partisan League, founded in 1915; Oklahoma's Green Corn Rebellion in 1917; and the rise and fall of the Texas Socialist Party among Anglo and Mexican farmworkers in the decade before World War I—all are examples of radical dissent in the Great Plains and Texas in the early years of the twentieth century.[1]

This tradition emerged from both a sense of endless possibility in this vast space and a sudden awareness of its limits, as a last frontier. Commenting on Kansas's early radicalism, a recent critic has remarked that "it was as though the blank landscape prompted dreams of a blank-slate society, a place where institutions might be remade as the human mind saw fit."[2] Witnessing the emergence of regional consciousness on the plains in the 1890s, Frederick Jackson Turner detected a darker edge: "In the remoter West, the restless, rushing wave of settlement has broken with a shock against the arid plains, and all this push and energy is turning into channels of agitation. . . . The forces of reorganization are turbulent," he concluded, "and the nation seems like a witches' kettle."[3]

Mari Sandoz (1896–1966), Sanora Babb (1907–2005), Benjamin Botkin (1901–1975), and Angie Debo (1890–1988) were heirs of the plains tradition of radical agitation, the sense of boundless dreams betrayed. Native Texans J. Frank Dobie (1888–1964) and Américo Paredes (1915–1999) devoted most of their writing to the south Texas borderlands, giving their work a distinctive Anglo-Mexican orientation that stands apart from the four plains regionalists. The three women of the plains—Sandoz, Babb, and Debo—were all born on the arid edge of the region at the end of the homestead era, while New York–born, Harvard-educated Botkin came to the region in his early twenties and spent his most formative decades there. Grouped in Oklahoma and Nebraska (often within the orbit of occasionally progressive state universities) and profoundly shaped by the Dust Bowl disaster, these four Great Plains writers expressed a hard-won loyalty to their flawed and fragile region by bravely speaking out against social, economic, environmental, and racial injustice.

Three of the four plains regionalists lived and worked in Oklahoma. Unlike fellow left-leaning Oklahomans Ralph Ellison, Woody Guthrie, and Will Rogers, who left for greater fame elsewhere, Debo, Babb, and Botkin achieved much of their greatest work while resident in the state. Just as the University of Oklahoma served as a nurturing though increasingly difficult home base for Botkin and Babb, the University of Nebraska was a source of inspiration for Sandoz, with the famed folklorist Louise Pound, the populist historian John Hicks, and the influential regionalist editor Lowry Charles Wimberly on the faculty and the memory of Willa Cather's earlier presence still vivid.

In his masterfully written chapter on Mari Sandoz, Robert Dorman traces the author's career from the harsh beauty and "wilder side of life" experienced in her Sand Hills childhood and youth to the intellectual stimulation of Lincoln. He argues that whereas land dispossession was a central theme for Babb and Debo, forebodings about the rise of homegrown fascism preoccupied Sandoz during her most productive years, from the 1930s to the mid-1940s. With the possible exception of Carey

McWilliams in California, Sandoz foresaw the danger of totalitarianism more vividly than any other regionalist on the left. Depicting the death of liberal egalitarianism and the rise of jackboot demagoguery and brutal plutocracy on the plains, her three dystopian heartland novels offer few hopeful alternatives. Fleeting glimpses of a democratic "regionalist middle landscape" of well-ordered towns and fields and images of heroic Oglala Sioux and Cheyenne leaders like Crazy Horse and Dull Knife, whose biographies absorbed Sandoz's attention late in life—each provided faint streaks of hope for this tough-minded radical regionalist.

Sanora Babb had much in common with Mari Sandoz. Both grew up on hardscrabble homesteads on the region's western edge—Babb on the Central High Plains of Oklahoma and Kansas and Sandoz on the Nebraska Sand Hills. And both writers were haunted by the fragile beauty of the land and profoundly shaped by harsh, mercurial, frontier-driven fathers. The title of Douglas Wixson's wide-ranging chapter, "Radical by Nature," emphasizes how Babb's political convictions grew from love of the land and indignation over what capitalism had done to it. Witnessing the Dust Bowl's impact on the High Plains as well as in California's Central Valley, Babb brilliantly documented both ends of this bleak American exodus. She traveled extensively in the United States and Europe, engaged in a spectrum of leftwing and antifascist causes, and interacted with other radical regionalists including Meridel Le Sueur, McWilliams, and Carlos Bulosan. As Wixson convincingly argues, Babb wrote as compellingly about sense of place and uprootedness as any writer in the 1930s, and her final work, *Whose Names Are Unknown* (2004), a novel that had remained unpublished for more than sixty years, poignantly captures the voices of the dusted-out folk with a profound sympathy that rivals John Steinbeck's greatest work.

Jerrold Hirsch's chapter admirably covers the nearly two decades that the transplanted folklorist Benjamin Botkin spent in Oklahoma while becoming the nation's foremost advocate of radical regionalism and a one-person clearinghouse for nearly every strain of regionalism in the interwar decades. Only Howard W. Odum and his colleagues at the University of North Carolina and perhaps Lewis Mumford and his regional planning associates in New York equaled Botkin in their regionalist zeal during the Depression decade. To an even greater degree than his fellow western apostles Conroy, Le Sueur, and McWilliams, Botkin preached the gospel of an all-inclusive regionalism grounded in a dynamic theory of folklore, and the controversy this sparked at his university and elsewhere reveals a common predicament for regionalists on the left.

Although not a regional theorist like her colleague Botkin, Angie Debo was a fearless regional historian who also pushed the limits of the haltingly progressive university they both served. Shirley Leckie Reed's finely detailed chapter describes how Debo's unblinking vision of a state steeped in racial misdeeds threatened the academic establishment and sacrificed her career. Driven by critical affection for her region, she devoted herself to uncovering painful truths about the unjust land grab at the heart of Oklahoma's frontier. Understanding the frontier from the perspective of Native Americans, she saw America's "real imperialism" as its mistreatment of its indigenous peoples. And more than any other western regionalist, Debo was also a true cosmopolitan. Balancing deep loyalty to her immediate homeland with social justice commitments in Europe, Mexico, and Africa, she was both a devoted native daughter and a citizen of the world—a rooted cosmopolitan in the very best sense of the term.

Like Debo, Texans J. Frank Dobie and Américo Paredes also developed transnational visions of regionalism. In the final chapter of Part II, José Limón skillfully narrates how these two seemingly antithetical figures achieved this cosmopolitan perspective and became fellow regionalists on the left toward the end of their careers. Separated by a generation and by ethnic and ideological differences, both men were born near the Texas-Mexico border. Both were steeped in the rich folk culture of their native region—Dobie largely from an Anglo and Paredes from a Mexican point of view—and both pursued careers in folk studies at the University of Texas. Usually seen as a crusty, Anglocentric regionalist in the mold of his university colleague Walter Prescott Webb, Dobie bravely moved to the left during the late 1930s and early 1940s as war broke out in Europe and repressive corporate forces descended upon the Austin campus. Also shaped by the war, particularly by his military and Red Cross experiences in the Far East, Paredes returned to Texas in the late 1940s and developed a far more inclusive version of the ethnonationalistic program he had promoted as a young man before the war. Limón's intricate tale of two seemingly different regionalists' eventually meeting on the left is a fitting capstone to this portion of the book.

NOTES

1. For a classic analysis of agrarian socialism in the Great Plains and Texas, see James Green's *Grass-Roots Socialism: Radical Movements in the Southwest* (Baton Rouge: Louisiana State University Press, 1978).
2. Thomas Frank, *What's the Matter with Kansas? How Conservatives Won the Heart of America* (New York: Henry Holt, 2004), 31–32.
3. Frederick Jackson Turner, "The Problem of the West" (1896), in *The Frontier in American History* (New York: Holt, Rinehart & Winston, 1920), 194–95, 196.

Mari Sandoz. Courtesy of Archives & Special Collections, University of Nebraska–Lincoln Libraries.

CHAPTER FOUR

Blowout Grass

MARI SANDOZ, HISTORICAL PESSIMISM,

AND GREAT PLAINS REGIONALISM

Robert L. Dorman

R*edfieldia flexuosa*, also known as blowout grass, thrives—if such a word captures its precarious existence—in the blowouts or barren pits that the wind scours randomly from the slopes of the Nebraska Sand Hills. *Redfieldia* is often the first plant to appear in the crater, spreading its roots shallowly through the sand to hold it in place. "At this point," wrote the ecologist Frederic Clements, who developed his general theory of plant succession from observing Nebraska's grasslands, "the bluestems of the bunch-grass formation, which hitherto had been unable to enter, quickly take a foothold, the blow-out grasses disappear before them, and the change from blow-out to hillside is complete. The first to disappear, as it is the first to enter, is Redfieldia," which "yield and retire to begin their work anew in some other blow-out."[1]

The blowout grass of the Sand Hills may serve as something more than a metaphor for the regionalism of Mari Sandoz (1896–1966). The Sand Hills landscape was formative for her, its volatility and hard-won bounty, its disappointments and triumphs, its beauty and fragility. Here her political education began in earnest. She experienced her first real freedom and independence, witnessed the range of human depravity and virtue, and saw justice done, all in the Sand Hills. She learned the lesson of the blow-out grass: to struggle for redemption relentlessly, whether it is possible or not.

Consider Sandoz in 1934: she was thirty-eight years old, on the cusp of her major achievement as a writer, the publication of *Old Jules*. To afford to live alone in Lincoln, she starved herself on a diet of stale bread and restaurant-table crackers. Everything, all of her, was devoted to her art. Now it was April, and her still-tenuous career had reached an equilibrium of sorts. She had gotten an editorial job with the state historical society, paid from New Deal relief funds. Her office was on the ninth floor of the new state capitol tower, a building rife with symbolism for her, with its friezes of pioneers and bison and its dome-top statue, *The Sower*. Then one day that April, all day long, she looked down from her window at a dust storm blown up from the southern plains; not even the streetlights were visible. Afterward, in a letter to the folklorist B. A. Botkin, she commented on a new book by the botanist Paul Sears, *Deserts on the March*: "Of course deserts march both ways," she wrote. Somewhat later she would recall the storm for the historian Bernard DeVoto: there were "those of us who lived long in Nebraska wind and like it," she told him.[2] Two of her five books from the 1930s and 1940s end with the accession of a dictator, one with an assassination, and one with a nuclear blast. The pessimistic mode came to her naturally. Blowouts happen, after all.

• • •

Much of what Sandoz learned into her early maturity taught her to be a historical pessimist—except for her own life. Born in the year of agrarianism's defeat, when William Jennings Bryan lost the apocalyptic election of 1896, she grew up in a highly politicized household still feverish with the grievances of Populism. In Nebraska, Populism had an afterlife beyond 1900 because the frontier had not yet closed there. One of the scraps of unclaimed land that remained was the Sand Hills region, on the edge of which young "Marie's" family lived at their River Place on the Niobrara. Covering much of the northwestern one-quarter of the state, the Sand Hills looked decidedly unpromising as farmland. Their name was purely descriptive: they were sand dunes, some of them immense, that shifted in the High Plains wind unless anchored by grass. But where they sheltered watered dales and valleys, whether from springs, lakes, or along the Niobrara, the Sand Hills showed their richness. Sandoz's father, Jules, who planted extensive orchards and developed a plum adapted to the local environment, was one of those who saw the area's potential for agriculture. So did ranchers like Bartlett Richards, who in 1901 began to fence large areas of the Sand Hills and carve out a private empire. Then in 1904 and the years following, the "Kinkaiders" arrived to take advantage of the government's offer of 640 acres of the very same land under the terms of the Kinkaid Land Act. As a self-appointed homestead locater and a connoisseur of feuds, the irascible Jules Sandoz was in the thick of the ensuing conflict, which culminated in twenty years of bad blood and ended only after the intervention of federal inspectors and of President Theodore Roosevelt himself: "Gentlemen, the fences will come down," he announces triumphantly in *Old Jules*.[3] Richards and a partner went to prison in 1910.

Sandoz was a young teenager at the dawn of this new era of justice, "the discovery of a new America," she later called it.[4] It marked her developing political consciousness with what seemed to be a rare victory for social democracy on the plains, where otherwise the plenitude of discontent could not find an effective political outlet. Jules had served as a Populist committeeman and candidate in the mid-1890s, only to be defeated; thereafter he flirted with agrarian socialism to the extent of receiving positive notice in the newspaper *Appeal to Reason*, the movement's principal organ. Some of this the young Marie was aware of or would hear stories of later, when she was researching *Old Jules* in the 1920s. What she also witnessed as a child from some unobtrusive spot behind the kitchen stove was her father holding court and talking politics with neighbors and relatives, fellow immigrants, often speaking in German. She saw Jules welcome the Oglala Sioux who still visited as in the old days before Wounded Knee, bringing their children to play with Marie and her younger siblings. From this obscure but richly textured regional background it was no great leap to issues of fascist aggression and class struggle in the 1930s and minority rights in the postwar years.

In 1909 Jules filed a claim on 480 acres of Kinkaid land in the Sand Hills, and the family began building a new farm, with Marie playing an important part. We must take Sandoz at her word that such a frontier life was a kind of "paradise," as she later insisted to Bernard DeVoto, and not speculate on her capacity for self-deception. Yet her tragic sense must come from somewhere. What remains with every reader of *Old Jules* is that her father, for all his virtues as a community leader and defender of the little man, was also a pathologically short-tempered, habitual abuser of women and children. He was, as well, what some today would call a "gun nut"—the ultimate threat of masculine violence. The volatile temper that kept the big-money ranchers thinking twice could mean hell on earth for

Jules's family. Sandoz relates how in her infancy Jules beat her for crying, until she lay "blue and trembling"; she describes one incident in which her "balky" mother was scourged with wire, and another in which she herself was threatened at gunpoint.[5] The last time that she was beaten, Jules broke a bone in her hand with a club.

Thus the advent of the Sand Hills homestead must have come as a liberation, or so Sandoz's biographer suggests.[6] In 1910 Marie and one of her brothers were delegated to spend the late summer alone at the homestead in order to watch it; during the summers of 1912 and 1913 they stayed at the River Place while Jules and rest of the family worked the homestead. Such was Marie's first taste of independence; yet it, too, came with a price. The Sand Hills were beautiful and also brutal, especially the weather, which rolled in unmitigated out of the Dakotas. In this environment a false sense of security was an occupational hazard: rainy years encouraged dreams, plans, investments; then the drought came, or hail, or locusts. In that first summer of 1910, the idyll was interrupted by a massive, terrifying wildfire. The following spring Marie was permanently blinded in one eye while out herding stray cattle after a blizzard. In her world, no happiness goes unspoiled, every good fortune invites a bad turn, and progress is reversible. Small wonder that she developed a lifelong belief in the occult, in the perverse rule of chance and fate.

The year 1913 was the beginning of the end of Jules's petty patriarchal tyranny. While staying at the River Place, Marie secretly took the state teachers' examination—"she must get away," Sandoz asserts repeatedly in *Old Jules*. In 1914 she would begin a short, unhappy marriage but was at least apart from her father, if not yet separated from him. That process would require his death in 1928 and the decade or more that it took to write *Old Jules*. She moved to Lincoln in 1923, and the rest of her life would be lived in cities, except for an occasional retreat to the Sand Hills when her health or money gave out. Her existence in these years was not exactly that of the "gay divorcee," as her brother Jules recalled, because she was so poor.[7] She disciplined herself into the life of a freelance writer, for which farmwifely frugality well prepared her; under sheer force of will it approached a near-asceticism devoted to freedom from the rule of a man. She kept her married name, Macumber, for most of the 1920s, until changing it back to Sandoz, along with her own stamp of "Mari," for marketing reasons.

In all these ways, moving to Lincoln "marked a sort of hundredth meridian in the life" of Sandoz, to borrow a conceit that she later used in *Son of the Gamblin' Man* (1960). She attended classes at the university sporadically when she could afford them, becoming (like Willa Cather) a member of the Louise Pound admiration society. Pound, a pioneering folklorist (also Botkin's mentor and academic advisor), was not the only Nebraska faculty member to shape Sandoz's emerging regional consciousness. The classicist John Andrew Rice taught her Greek history, philosophy, and drama. Perhaps most important was her exposure to the historian John Hicks's overview of the Populist movement, framed in terms of Frederick Jackson Turner's frontier thesis, which provided her with a historical context in which to understand her father's and her own politics. Hicks's history of Populism raised local events in the Nebraska Panhandle and Sand Hills to national significance and lent them a moral majesty easily obscured by all the grasping and bitterness of the range wars. In his hands the Populists became part of what Sandoz would call the "great tradition of mid-western liberalism, the agricultural liberalism of the Bryans, the LaFollettes, the Manahans and the Norrisses," with their vision of a good society forged on the frontier and upholding republican producerism, democratic egalitarianism, and agrarian communitarianism. In *Old Jules* she was thus able to offer her father redemption as a hero in the battle between the plain folk and concentrated wealth. As she wrote, "He had never failed his community. . . . He brought them in as penniless homeseekers, many on passes, helped them to stay. . . . He it was who helped them open the range and put the cattlemen and their agents under indictments, into the penitentiary."[8]

As she endured the maelstrom of the 1930s, however, Sandoz could not sustain Hicks's confidence in the progressive march of American reform. She had survived too long on the wilder side of American life and lived there yet. Things looked different from the Sand Hills and other subregions of the national outback. Sandoz agreed with Turner that the frontier process recapitulated human social evolution. Like Frederic Clements in his locally inspired plant ecology, she believed that Nebraska history was a microcosm of the universal. But in *Old Jules* and her debut novel, *Slogum House* (1937), she challenged Turner's idea that the frontier gave universal history the peculiar twist toward greater freedom and democracy known as American exceptionalism. As she later put it, "Here we have the period from the dispossession of the so-called savage to transcontinental air service . . . all in the span of a living man's lifetime. . . . Here, within one lifetime, we have assembled the conflicts of the nationalities and races from all over the world."[9] The frontier myth might draw "penniless homeseekers" to Nebraska, but rather than escaping history through America's natural abundance, they fell into an armed struggle over land with wannabe gentry, whether Bartlett Richards in real life or Gulla Slogum in Sandoz's fictive retelling of the range wars.

This turn to novel-length fiction—never her strong suit as a writer—is puzzling at first glance, but there were deeper personal and ideological reasons behind it. In the claim locator Leo Platt, her protagonist in *Slogum House*, Sandoz could recreate her heroic father minus the betrayal of his appalling private brutality. Yet in reimagining her Sand Hills heritage, she also gave it a much darker spin with the character of Gulla, a farm woman who is less earth mother than succubus, bent on devouring all the men and women around her by destroying their republican virtue. The women, including some of her own daughters, are literally prostituted by Gulla, whereas the men are dispossessed or turned into tenants. These machinations of Gulla's are not posed as a historical anomaly, nor does Sandoz offer much comfort with historical distance. *Slogum House* covers much the same period as *Old Jules*. Gulla reigns from the late nineteenth century up to the present, her ever-expanding empire mapped in red pencil. Thus Nebraska mirrored the ever more frightening world of the 1930s. Sandoz told a correspondent that she envisioned Gulla as a "will-to-power individual" and claimed that the novel, which she began writing in 1933, was inspired by a reading of *Mein Kampf*.[10] That the present included the possibility of a homegrown American fascism was to be one of Sandoz's principal themes in coming years, only the message of *Slogum House* was worse: the potential had always been there.

Slogum House was actually the most hopeful of the trio of heartland fascism novels that Sandoz published in the decade after 1937. With the climactic scene of Leo Platt and his fellow farmers winning mortgage relief from the state legislature, she suggested that the great midwestern liberal tradition had life in it yet to renew American liberty, even as the Kinkaid Act had reopened the frontier that everyone had pronounced closed. But the years 1933 to 1937, when *Slogum House* was written and published, were the floodtide of the New Deal; thereafter its fortunes began to reverse.

Sandoz would hardly have predicted otherwise. The Kinkaiders in both *Old Jules* and *Slogum House* are shown going bust, moving on. Writ large, it was the cycle of dashed hopes that scarred Mari's youth. During the 1930s this pessimistic cycle became her philosophy of history.

The temptation is ascribe this worldview to a post-frontier perspective and to compare Sandoz to someone like Rose Wilder Lane, a fellow child of the frontier who never outgrew her fixation on a mythicized pioneer individualism, or to Turner himself, who floundered for decades trying to write a second act for American history after 1890. There is the swelling crescendo of freedom and opportunity up to 1890, as Americans take possession of the wilderness continent, and then the more regimented, more oppressive recessional that is all subsequent history. To be sure, Sandoz was never entirely free of the frontier myth, the "paradise" of her youth, despite her radical revision of it. But to her, post-frontier decline was merely a modern symptom of the pessimistic cycle that was part of the nature of things—fate governs all, disaster looms out of every good fortune, and every cause, in the long run, is a lost one. Her other readings of the 1930s reinforced this mindset. John Strachey's *The Coming Struggle for Power* (1932) referred to the Stoics' cyclical and catastrophist view of history and highlighted Nietzsche's doctrine of the "eternal return of all things." Writing of Nietzsche, Strachey might have been describing any adherent of the frontier myth, Sandoz included: "His discovery of the ineluctable conditions of destiny caused him the utmost agony, for he mistook the doom of his particular category of civilization for the doom of civilization itself." Sandoz also waded into the four volumes of Vilfredo Pareto's *The Mind and Society* (1916), which briefly became all the rage among some American intellectuals of the time (Sandoz's friend DeVoto promoted him in the pages of *Harper's*). Pareto, too, surveyed history and concluded: "A period of 'individualism' (when ties are weak) paves the way for a period of 'collectivism' (when ties are strong), and *vice versa*. . . . Now we are in a descending period of freedom and an ascending period of 'planning.'" It is said that Sandoz always reread Franz Kafka's absurdist exercise in bureaucratic futility, *The Castle*, before beginning her own writing projects, and one suspects that she was not merely looking for stylistic pointers.[11]

It can be difficult to make art—certainly popular fiction—out of such a pessimistic worldview. Sandoz's trio of novels, especially *Capital City*

(1939), were a case in point. That she allowed *Capital City* to be published at all signified the urgency of the times—it was less a novel than the notes for one. In it she completed the historical sequence begun with *Slogum House*, shifting the scene to the parasitic city of Franklin in the fictional plains state of Kanewa. That she fictionalized the setting (she was still living in Lincoln at the time) signified her own growing fear of violent repression, and in fact one of the novel's characters is a young woman writer persecuted for publishing a historical exposé of Franklin. The more hopeful conclusion to *Slogum*, with its brief reprieve for protesting farmers, has died out in the corrupt and class-riven world of *Capital City*, where plutocracy rules and the down-and-out are kept in their place by a fascist-style organization called the Gold Shirts. Although she could take her Marxism straight from writers like Strachey, and Pareto suggested an alternate model of oppression by elites, Sandoz needed no further schooling in class-consciousness beyond that which she had gotten in the Sand Hills. What Pareto did provide was an extended analysis of propaganda, rationalization, false consciousness, and the self-interest inherent in language, especially political rhetoric. In *The Tom-Walker* (1947) Sandoz simply called these the "guyascutus," a mythical beast or bogeyman used to distract the masses.[12] Examples abounded in 1930s America and abroad.

Sandoz rings down the cycle in *Capital City* with the election of a demagogue portending dictatorship, and she does the same at the end of *The Tom-Walker*, the third novel of the trio, after having recounted the whole cycle anew from the 1860s to the end of World War II. Her regional canvas is broader this time, tracing the action from Ohio out to Wyoming, and the booms and busts endured by the characters are all too familiar in Sandoz's works: town worthies gone bankrupt; marriages turned loveless; veterans dishonored; homesteaders dispossessed. The frontier myth haunts the narrative in the person of Milton, a Civil War amputee who becomes a legendary western vagabond known as Iron Leg, about whom yarns are invented. Iron Leg's descendants keep pushing westward, generation after generation until the 1920s, when they reach bounty lands in Wyoming and begin to coax a farm into being with the help of a New Deal irrigation project. But by the time that she wrote *Capital City* and *The Tom-Walker*, a radicalized Sandoz already believed that the "great tradition of mid-western liberalism . . . is dead." In *The Tom-Walker*, Iron Leg's daughter-in-law keeps a scrapbook of the tall tales told of him and, alongside it, a "scrapbook of midwestern liberals . . . like LaFollette and Norris."[13]

To reseed this ideological blowout, Sandoz in both *Capital City* and *Tom-Walker* strews glimpses of a regionalist social democracy in the West: "Here cheap and clean power and fruitful lands would be brought together in a new society centered around a farm-factory unit: labor free of the blight of the old factory community . . . ; agriculture free from the gamble of hot winds, drouth and floods. . . . An industrialized society . . . with the best in education and the arts, set up in a healthful, pleasant, semi-rural environment." Liberalism, she argued, must take the next step toward recognizing that "the earth is not a private chattel but a public trust, a trust held for posterity." Unfortunately, in the aftermath of World War II this vision was foreclosed—as actually occurred with the defeat of a proposed Missouri Valley Authority for regional development—by the ascendancy of Cold War reactionaries and the national security state. The "water's gone, cut off" from the Wyoming farm, Sandoz wrote, as timber interests, big cattlemen, and power companies seized control of national parks and forestlands: "The ditches of Seep Creek, they would be drying down, the fine lush greenness shrinking . . . the dust and sage moving in on the handsome place." She was not so blithe now about deserts marching both ways, as she had quipped to Botkin years before. Her mood turned darker still. The same forces shutting off water to small farmers presaged a "cartel world not so different from I. G. Farben's," a globalized corporate fascism.[14] The new American reich was inaugurated with an atomic warning-shot off the Atlantic coast. Every cycle of history must end with *ekpyrosis*—a conflagration—so the Stoics believed.

• • •

Before September 11, 2001, contemporary readers may have had trouble comprehending the bleak tone of Sandoz's novels of heartland fascism, but in the era of "homeland security" and "torture memos," her scenarios seem much less fantastic. In *The Tom-Walker*, Iron Leg's grandson Milton has a magic routine that he performs about the "Portable, Extradimensional Hole," and it is a measure of Sandoz's despair that Milton suggests that his family crawl into the Hole "safe from the A-bombs, the microscopic dusts and poisons, the dreadful power of the cosmic, and the schemes and plotting of all the evil men." Yet ultimately, Sandoz herself did not just hide from the fearsome, demoralizing politics of her time.[15]

Her own personal history belied the pessimistic cycle that she saw in regional and national history. In her frontiersman father's decline was her own liberation. She became freer the farther she moved from the frontier, going east to Lincoln and finally to New York City. An urban lifestyle, not rural, saved her from the time-consuming regimen of farmwife drudgery. And there in the city her relentless pursuit of a writing career defied the cycle yet again. For despite her fears of the exhaustion of liberalism, she held tightly to two articles of liberal faith throughout her life: the efficacy of the individual in history, and the force of moral publicity. The first article sent her in search of deliverer-heroes of the plain folk, modeled after the "usable father" that she salvaged from *Old Jules*. Leo Platt in *Slogum House* was one; Crazy Horse, in her 1942 biography, performed much the same role for the Oglala Sioux. The second article was embodied in her heartland fascism novels, which were a tribute to the depth of her belief in moral publicity. Writing these novels was political activism, her way of fighting back against reactionary forces locally and nationally. If the novels were deficient aesthetically, the point was less in the plot or the characterization but in how they dramatized and amplified the political message. The assumption underlying moral publicity is that the audience is rational and shares a common ideology—in this case, belief in equity, the rule of law, and democracy. Once enlightened, the people will pressure lawmakers to redress social wrongs. As a character in *The Tom-Walker* puts it, "Let the people know: they will do right, whatever it costs them, they will do right."[16]

Of course, Sandoz was tough-minded enough to cast doubt on this faith, with her demagogue figures and "guyascutus" theme, even as she was exercising it. Her revisionist woman historian in *Capital City* arouses furious denials from the locals and loses her position at the university, but at the same time Sandoz was alluding directly to the more gratifying outcome of her own real-life inspiration, Ida Tarbell. In the end, her fictional revisionist historian is rewarded with a movie deal at a major studio, and so too Sandoz vested her hopes in a greater national audience that might bring the weight of its opinion to bear on the self-interested and self-deluded powers-that-be back home—an irony of regionalist cultural radicalism that probably was not lost on her.

It would nevertheless be misleading to pose Sandoz as always the fearless, invulnerable defender of the little man. In Lincoln, she received her share of death threats following the publication of *Capital City*, which is one reason that she relocated to Denver in 1940, before moving permanently to New York by 1943. To sustain some flicker of optimism in the dire political environment of the late 1930s and early 1940s, when fascism was aggressively expanding worldwide and an invasion or subversion of the United States was not a farfetched notion—this was an exhausting task, mentally and spiritually. It is clear that Sandoz sought refuge and rejuvenation in the past during these years, as did other American artists and intellectuals. Her focus remained regionalist rather than nationalist. Borrowing the idea from a fellow Nebraskan, the poet John G. Neihardt, she conceived a historical epic of the Great Plains that would span the story of *Old Jules*, the plains tribes, the cattlemen, fur traders, and others who had shaped the region, a project that took her much of the rest of her life to complete. But most immediately, she turned to American Indian history, especially that of the Northern Cheyenne and the Oglala Sioux.

Much like the California writer Mary Austin, Sandoz believed that she shared a mystical bond with Native Americans, an affinity that gave her peculiar insight into their cultures. She had plentiful childhood memories of friendly visits to the family farm by Indians from Pine Ridge and other nearby reservations. But it appears that it was not until 1930, when she accompanied a journalist friend to Pine Ridge to do research, that she began seriously to think of American Indians in literary terms. By 1936 she was fully engaged in a work featuring the chiefs Dull Knife and Little Wolf, who had led the flight of the Northern Cheyenne from Indian Territory to Montana Territory in 1878-79. When this work was preempted by the publication of another writer's book on the same subject in 1940—which devastated Sandoz—she then shifted her attention to Crazy Horse. *Crazy Horse: The Strange Man of the Oglalas* (1942) is considered by some to be Sandoz's best work, and along with Angie Debo's *And Still the Waters Run* (1940), it marked a postcolonial sea change in the portrayal of American Indians by European American scholars.[17] For Sandoz, the Crazy Horse biography was almost therapeutic in providing her with the imaginative sanctuary of the Plains Indian world, while at the same time fulfilling her political need for a deliverer-hero. Yet what also drew her to the story must have been the way it synchronized so well with the pessimistic cycle that still dominated her thinking; after all, the story ends with Crazy Horse's assassination.

On balance, Sandoz's Native American histories would prove to be less a refuge from politics than a path toward more direct and engaging advocacy than her baleful novels ever were to be. Much as DeVoto spent his final years fighting the wholesale plundering of public lands in the West, so she took up the cause of the impoverished Northern Cheyenne during one of the bleakest periods in their relations with the Anglo world: the postwar "termination" era, during which the federal government proposed the dissolution of tribal government, landownership, indeed, tribal identity itself, as a fast track to complete assimilation.

In a letter to President Harry S. Truman in 1949, Sandoz admitted, "The calamities of the present compelled me to shift my interest from the old buffalo hunting days to the problems of the present."[18] At times she felt the Cheyennes' plight so keenly that she donated money and clothing directly to their reservation. More broadly, she used her growing fame to plead their cause in popular magazine articles as well as through radio and television appearances. She coordinated her individual efforts with organizations such as the Association on American Indian Affairs and also took up the cause of other tribes, including the Oglala Sioux. Yet if American Indian history, declining from a golden past, fit so readily into the pessimistic cycle, how was she able to avoid political demoralization and paralysis? Sandoz survived a bout with breast cancer in 1954, which in itself may have stirred her to greater political commitment. Fate might be defeated by sheer will; she had already proven this to herself. Survival—and a new chapter—were possible. But it is also clear that her work on the harrowing story of the flight of the Northern Cheyenne, during the years prior to her illness, helped to break Sandoz free of the pessimistic trope.

Cheyenne Autumn (1953) was perhaps Sandoz's most compelling book, well suited to her fictionalized method of history writing, which she used to convey the manifold horrors endured by the Cheyenne people in their attempt to return to their northern plains homeland. As she told a correspondent in 1950, "It's hell to be a minority." The captivity of Dull Knife and his followers at Fort Robinson, Nebraska, evokes the Nazi concentration camp. Their massacre "while trying to escape" was one of the darkest moments of the American West. But unlike Crazy Horse's assassination, which also occurred at Fort Robinson, the massacre did not mark the culmination of a downward cycle of tragedy. Instead, in *Cheyenne Autumn*, it comes to represent a sacrifice that delivers Chief Little Wolf's surviving band of Cheyenne refugees toward the hope of a Montana reservation, thanks to the national outrage that greeted news of the atrocity. Beyond "this hard Cheyenne autumn and its frozen winter," Sandoz wrote in a key passage, "must be a new springtime . . . a springtime in which the Cheyennes were once more a warm, a well-fed, a straight-standing people." Her depiction of the episode was a testimony to her abiding faith in the force of moral publicity. The deeper radicalism of the book was the challenge that it offered to the contemporary termination policy—which Sandoz referred to in letters as "extermination"—a challenge that grew in significance during the 1950s as Native peoples across the West resisted the federal assault on tribal communalism, rooting their defiance in an identity tied to reservation homelands. Sandoz's Northern Cheyenne fought to the death for theirs. She recognized the termination policy for what it was: the "unlanding of the Indians."[19]

• • •

In her volume *Love Song to the Plains* (1961) Sandoz reports that during the hard times of the 1930s, Sand Hills cattle ate the "grass roots out of the ground, until the hills . . . were bald and cupped into blowouts, the valleys stripped so there was nothing but weeds when the rains returned where the grass had once stood to the saddle skirts." Like the expropriation of Native American lands, this environmental destruction was the product of "the white man's incumbency on the Great Plains," the subject of her projected multivolume epic. In *The Beaver Men* (1964), the last book of the epic that she was able to finish before succumbing to cancer in 1966, Sandoz wrote that as the epic took shape, book after book, she "discovered that what the white man did to the Great Plains, good and bad, was largely a repetition of what man of any color did elsewhere, Europe, say, or Asia, from Stone Age to the present."[20] Just as someone lost in the Sand Hills might find direction with the knowledge that blowouts tend to happen on southeastward slopes, so Sandoz's historical pessimism revealed an order of sorts in the brutalities and catastrophes of "what the white man did to the Great Plains."

Once she had universalized that history, Sandoz had the perspective to find meaning in it, the "good and bad," just as she had in the story of her father. Beyond the autumn of the pessimistic cycle, human will and effort could bring about something better to ameliorate, to compensate. Despite his villainies, Jules achieved a measure of redemption as a "creative builder" who befriended the dispossessed and enhanced the barren

Sand Hills with orchards. Under "intelligent management" by local ranchers and government experts, the Sand Hills and Niobrara valley as a whole "came back," she wrote, "blossomed as none had ever seen them before" after the drought of the Depression years. A staunch agrarian, she was less a devotee of raw wilderness than of this kind of cultivated middle landscape of well-ordered towns and fields balanced with a wild fringe—a vision that had captivated regionalists in the West and elsewhere since the time of Thoreau. Here Sandoz could be at peace; in fact, she requested a solitary grave in the Sand Hills with a view of her father's orchards. For her, it was a vision not only of a past redeemed but also of a brighter future, which she emphasized in a late essay suggesting how the "small and pleasant farm-factory or ranch-factory community" of the Plains might become nuclear-powered.[21]

To create this regionalist middle landscape, however, required care, commitment, and rootedness. By raising historical consciousness through her own works, Sandoz strove to instill a strong sense of place and, like the blowout grass, to foster a more lasting attachment to the land. As early as 1927, when she published the lead story in the inaugural issue of the Lincoln-based *Prairie Schooner* literary magazine, she steadily encouraged the development of major regional cultural institutions, becoming an important booster of the University of Nebraska Press as well. Her own growing corpus and fame anchored the emergence of modern Great Plains literature, and aspiring writers, some of them American Indians trying to find their voices during a painful era of cultural suppression, sought her support and advice. Inviting a broader range of perspectives, such as her own, to see beyond the racial triumphalism of the frontier myth was essential not only to regional justice and community, but also to finding out the truths of plains history. "I hope to understand something of what modern man does to such a region," she once wrote, "and what it does to him."[22]

Perhaps the metaphor of blowout grass shapes this account of Sandoz's life too neatly. But she herself was not above using such devices in her writing. Kingsley M. Bray, who wrote the authoritative *Crazy Horse: A Lakota Life* (2006), is among the most recent of her critics to note that "Sandoz forced her materials to fit dramatic unities." This tendency suggests why she had such difficulty finishing her novelization of the frontier boyhood of the painter Robert Henri, *Son of the Gamblin' Man* (1960).

She labored on the book sporadically for nearly two decades, the same years in which she learned to write her way out of the pessimistic cycle. Henri's story required something more of her: to come to terms with her own rise to fame from backcountry obscurity and from under the shadow of a larger-than-life pioneer father, just as Henri had. The artistic Henri was "a stranger, an alien" to his worldly, volatile father, John Cozad, a land promoter like Jules. So long abused in her own childhood, so belittled and neglected, Sandoz imagined a closing scene of recognition and reconciliation between Henri and Cozad—with the son quietly painting his father's portrait—such as she had never experienced with Old Jules. Her yearning was apparent enough—unaccountably, Jules has a cameo in this very same scene of *Son of the Gamblin' Man*, through a quoted piece of correspondence with Cozad. It was as if she wished Jules to bear witness to Henri's (and her own) assertion of identity. Henri "wanted most of all," she wrote, "to live his life as himself," as someone who had surpassed the father and whose art could redeem him and his frontier world.[23]

The source of this self-affirmation, and of growth as an artist, was regionalism, in Sandoz's portrayal, though it was not quite clear whose growth she was describing. For dramatic effect, she granted it to young Henri as an epiphany, just as she gave to the mature artist a closure about their shared childhood on the plains that one doubts she ever felt entirely herself. Henri "had never really seen it or comprehended it until today," Sandoz wrote. "All the valley here, the people and all, were no longer just a sort of accidental accumulation," but were "all part of a pattern, a part of a community ... a body of people and ground and sky."[24]

NOTES

1. Roscoe Pound and Frederic E. Clements, *The Phytogeography of Nebraska*, 2nd ed. (Lincoln: Botanical Survey of Nebraska, 1900), 367–68. On blowouts and *Redfieldia flexuosa*, see Great Plains Flora Association, *Flora of the Great Plains* (Lawrence: University Press of Kansas, 1986), 1217; Charles Barron McIntosh, *The Nebraska Sand Hills: The Human Landscape* (Lincoln: University of Nebraska Press, 1996), 4; and Paul A. Johnsgard, *The Nature of Nebraska: Ecology and Biodiversity* (Lincoln: University of Nebraska Press, 2001), 78–79. The Sand Hills are also spelled "Sandhills" by many writers, including Sandoz.

2. Sandoz to B. A. Botkin, Lincoln, May 19, 1936, in *Letters of Mari Sandoz*, ed. Helen Winter Stauffer (Lincoln: University of Nebraska Press, 1992), 105; Sandoz to Bernard

DeVoto, Lincoln, December 12, 1936, in *Letters*, 113. Biographical information for this essay is taken from the standard work by Helen Winter Stauffer, *Mari Sandoz: Story Catcher of the Plains* (Lincoln: University of Nebraska Press, 1982).

3. Mari Sandoz, *Old Jules* (1935; reprinted, Lincoln: University of Nebraska Press, 1985), 247. On Richards's land scheme to create the Spade Ranch see McIntosh, *Nebraska Sand Hills*, 206–13.

4. Mari Sandoz, *Slogum House* (1937; reprinted, Lincoln: University of Nebraska Press, 1981), 219.

5. Sandoz to Bernard DeVoto, Lincoln, April 9, 1936, in *Letters*, 102; Sandoz, *Old Jules*, 215, 230; on Jules's abuse see also Dorothee E. Kocks, *Dream a Little: Land and Social Justice in Modern America* (Berkeley: University of California Press, 2000), 70. Jules Sandoz's land acquisitions are exhaustively detailed in C. Barron McIntosh, "One Man's Sequential Land Alienation on the Great Plains," *Geographical Review* 71, no. 4 (October 1981): 427–45.

6. Stauffer, *Sandoz*, 32–33.

7. Sandoz, *Old Jules*, 366; Carol Sandoz Pifer and Jules Sandoz, Jr., *Son of Old Jules: Memoirs of Jules Sandoz, Jr.* (Lincoln: University of Nebraska Press, 1989), 112.

8. Mari Sandoz, *Son of the Gamblin' Man* (1960; reprinted, Lincoln: University of Nebraska Press, 1976), 11; John R. Wunder, "Mari Sandoz: Historian of the Great Plains," in *Their Own Frontier: Women Intellectuals Re-Visioning the American West*, ed. Shirley A. Leckie and Nancy J. Parezo (Lincoln: University of Nebraska Press, 2008), 104–105; Sandoz to the Daughter of James Manahan, Lincoln, October 24, 1936, Mari Sandoz Collection, Box 4 Item 44, Archives & Special Collections, University of Nebraska-Lincoln Libraries; Sandoz, *Old Jules*, 326. See also John D. Hicks, *The Populist Revolt* (1931; reprinted, Lincoln: University of Nebraska Press, 1961), esp. 404–23.

9. Mari Sandoz, *Hostiles and Friendlies: Selected Short Writings of Mari Sandoz* (1959; reprinted, Lincoln: University of Nebraska Press, 1992), 164.

10. Sandoz to F. B. Griffith, Denver, January 7, 1941, in *Letters*, 181.

11. John Strachey, *The Coming Struggle for Power* (1932; reprinted, New York: Modern Library, 1935), 233; Vilfredo Pareto, *The Mind and Society: A Treatise on General Sociology*, vol. 2 (1935; reprinted, New York: Dover, 1963), 1860, 1912. On Pareto and American intellectuals see Lewis A. Coser, *Masters of Sociological Thought*, 2nd ed. (New York: Harcourt Brace Jovanovich, 1977), 422–23. Kocks is suggestive on the role of *The Castle* in her chapter on Sandoz in *Dream a Little*, 87. Other cyclical views of history in the interwar years are explored in Ernst Breisbach, *Historiography: Ancient, Medieval, and Modern*, 3rd ed. (Chicago: University of Chicago Press, 2007), 408–10.

12. Mari Sandoz, *The Tom-Walker* (1947; reprinted, Lincoln: University of Nebraska Press, 1984), 60.

13. Sandoz to the Daughter of James Manahan, Lincoln, October 24, 1936; Sandoz, *Tom-Walker*, 217.

14. Sandoz, *Tom-Walker*, 350–51, 318, 343, 346.

15. Sandoz, *Tom-Walker*, 351.

16. Sandoz, *Tom-Walker*, 351.

17. For an analysis of Sandoz as a postcolonial writer see Laura R. Villiger, *Mari Sandoz: A Study in Post-Colonial Discourse* (New York: Peter Lang, 1994).

18. Sandoz to Truman, New York, October 18, 1949, in *"I Do Not Apologize for the Length of This Letter": The Mari Sandoz Letters on Native American Rights, 1940–1965*, ed. Kimberli A. Lee (Lubbock: Texas Tech University Press, 2009), 84; the volume well documents Sandoz's postwar activism.

19. Sandoz to Margaret Marshall, New York, January 31, 1950, in *"I Do Not Apologize,"* 88; Mari Sandoz, *Cheyenne Autumn* (1953; reprinted, Lincoln: University of Nebraska Press, 2005), 258–59; Sandoz to F. H. Sinclair, New York, January 30, 1960, in *"I Do Not Apologize,"* 115. On reservations as homelands see Paul C. Rosier, "'They Are Ancestral Homelands': Race, Place, and Politics in Cold War Native America, 1945–1961," *Journal of American History* 92, no. 4 (March 2006): 1300–26.

20. Mari Sandoz, *Love Song to the Plains* (1961; reprinted, Lincoln: University of Nebraska Press, 1966), 265; Sandoz, *The Beaver Men* (1964; reprinted, Lincoln: University of Nebraska Press, 1978), xiv–xv.

21. Sandoz, *Sandhill Sundays and Other Recollections* (1970; reprinted, Lincoln: University of Nebraska Press, 1984), 19–20; Sandoz, *Hostiles and Friendlies*, 51; Sandoz, *Love Song*, 274–75. On Sandoz's gravesite and for an excellent contemporary account of the Sand Hills region see Stephen R. Jones, *The Last Prairie: A Sandhills Journal* (Lincoln: University of Nebraska Press, 2006), esp. 101–102.

22. On Sandoz's relationship with American Indian writers see *"I Do Not Apologize,"* 145–74; Sandoz, *Beaver Men*, xv.

23. Kingsley M. Bray, *Crazy Horse: A Lakota Life* (Norman: University of Oklahoma Press, 2006), xvi; Sandoz, *Son of the Gamblin' Man*, 317, 331.

24. Sandoz, *Son of the Gamblin' Man*, 220.

Sanora Babb. Courtesy of The Harry Ransom Center, The University of Texas at Austin.

CHAPTER FIVE

Radical by Nature

SANORA BABB AND ECOLOGICAL DISASTER

ON THE HIGH PLAINS, 1900-1940

Douglas Wixson

The promise of free land and self-sufficiency attracted Anglo settlers to the western High Plains at the end of the nineteenth century and the beginning of the twentieth. Enduring drought and economic failure, they clung tenaciously to their dryland farms. For some the dream of a new beginning as independent tillers of their own land became a nightmare of dispossession and a desperate quest for survival in the Depression era. Long periods of drought and failed crops forced them to uproot and seek work farther west, where they suffered further deprivation and humiliation as seasonal laborers in the agricultural fields of Arizona and California. Popularized in Woody Guthrie's songs and John Steinbeck's *The Grapes of Wrath*, the farmer-refugees, termed "Okies" by their hostile hosts, entered a long and difficult struggle to gain fair wages and decent working conditions against the grower-owners of large-scale enterprises, who had long profited from cheap labor, hiring Mexican and Filipino migrant workers. The plight of American families, camping in ditches, their children without schooling or adequate health care, following the harvests, threatened to become a national disgrace. In 1935 the U.S. government established the Resettlement Agency, later the Farm Security Administration (FSA), which set up temporary camps in California's three main agricultural valleys, providing shelter and health and sanitation facilities and organizing the refugees in self-governance councils.[1]

Working in the FSA government camps as an assistant to administrator Tom Collins was a young woman named Sanora Babb (1907-2005), a native "Okie" who had come to California by a very different route.[2] Raised on the windswept central High Plains, she had left home in 1929 for Los Angeles to pursue a career as a journalist, which would allow her the means to write short stories and eventually, she hoped, a novel. Drawing from her memories of the High Plains, she would ultimately produce some fifty short stories and three novels. She constructed a collective memory of place, a lived world that delineated the components of space and place in the yawning, limitless vastness of the High Plains and endowed them with meaning and cultural significance. Her writings dramatize the growth and development of an individual consciousness engaged in a communal and ecological life-world, both in her native High Plains and later among dispossessed plains folk in California. Her radical regionalist voice foregrounds and dignifies the ordinary and gives expression to timeless social injustices such as homelessness, poverty, discrimination, inequality, economic hardship, and repression of dissent. Widely published in radical and mainstream literary magazines of the 1930s and 1940s, she wrote *Whose Names Are Unknown* (1939), *The Lost Traveler* (1958), and *An Owl on Every Post* (1971), as well as two collections of short stories, *The Dark Earth and Other Stories* (1987) and *The Cry of the Tinamou* (1996), and a volume of poems, *Told in the Seed* (1998).

Babb's early years were spent among farmers and townspeople who, she realized, were shaped in distinctive ways by the harsh and isolating conditions of the High Plains. Her writings put a human face on the short-grass steppe west of the 100th meridian, giving voice to a people who typically left little written record of their own lives and received scant representation in histories. Deeply affected by the difficult conditions of her childhood and the natural beauty of her surroundings, she was determined to make these the subjects of her writing. Her challenge was to find the artistic means to give the unbounded, featureless physical space of the central High Plains artistic expression and to extract a cultural memory of its people from the spare circumstances of their lives.

The passionate vision of Alexandra Bergson, in Willa Cather's *O Pioneers!*, wresting wealth from the land in "the Divide" of southeastern Nebraska; the bitter struggle of Mari Sandoz with her tyrannical pioneer father in western Nebraska's Sandhills; the brooding figure of Beret Hansa in O. E. Rölvaag's *Giants of the Earth*; Angie Debo's studies of the social forces that shaped community life in early Oklahoma; and Babb's own stories of how a people afflicted by failure, dispossession, and disgrace reconstitute their lives—these Great Plains writers all locate a unique sociocultural landscape, distinct in its historical and geographical diversity, in which individual memory is linked to broader humanistic concerns, and the relations between people and nature are revealed as conflicted and precarious, yet ultimately sustaining.

THE HIGH PLAINS AS BIOREGION

The central High Plains, where Babb grew up, is a unique bioregion inscribing a fragile human environment delicately balanced between settled place and dispossession and the location of a wealth of diverse plant and animal life not immediately apparent to the unobservant eye. In his study of bioregionalism Michael Kowalewski points out that bioregional definitions of place "underscore the formative interrelationship of both human and nonhuman forms of life" and that "bioregional writers emphasize an awareness of 'place' as a living, interactive force in human identity. They attempt to counter the rootless and displaced character of contemporary American society by illuminating the complex ecology of local environments and how those environments affect the life of those who live within them."[3] Babb was keenly aware of the interdependence and interconnectedness of all nature and how individual species, including humans, adapt to a specific bioregion—in this case, the central High Plains—characterized by ecological associations, peculiarities of flora and fauna, and specifics of topography, climate, history, economics, and occupation. State lines are merely political and geographic demarcations; the bioregion of her experience and writings is a contiguous, nearly uniform ecological system embracing southeastern Colorado, southwestern Kansas, and western Oklahoma.

Particular circumstances affected the High Plains of Babb's youth: cycles of drought and violent weather that continue today; farming methods inappropriate to the arid conditions and soil composition; fluctuating agricultural market prices that impoverished families without sufficient means; physical isolation, loneliness, lack of schools, medical facilities, and cultural amenities. In the 1930s financial exigencies compelled many to stay put; dispossession exposed families to great peril, both financially and emotionally. The Great Depression, comments Michael Steiner, "abounded with disruptive events that evoked a keen desire for the stability of place in the lives of many people."[4] Dislocation sharpens the yearning for location, for the memories of the stability of place and region. Dispossessed of their homes, people clung through memory to what they had lost. Storytelling and an interest in regional differences and folklore were in part responses to the longing for one's own native home and place. Babb's writings in the 1930s reveal the sense of loss of place felt by uprooted Dust Bowl people who longed for the homes they left behind on High Plains farms and in small towns.

The dryland farmers west of the 100th meridian had long attended the school of risk, and their tests had been unsparing. As early as 1877 the explorer and geologist John Wesley Powell, in his *Report on the Lands of the Arid Region of the United States*, questioned the wisdom of opening the semiarid grasslands of the American West to farming. Submitting to the pressure for land, however, Congress had opened public domain of the Great Plains in a series of land laws, beginning with the Homestead Act in 1862. The special conditions of the semiarid lands west of the 100th meridian were such that the common unit of land, the 160-acre section, proved inadequate to support a family. Moreover, recognition that water was a limited commodity in the West brought about provisions (in the Desert Land Act of 1877) affecting water rights: "A monopoly of water," as Walter Prescott Webb observed, "was a monopoly of land." The early settlers, as Webb further noted, accustomed to the productive soils of the forestlands of Kentucky, Ohio, and Virginia, adapted with difficulty to the demands of this dry, wind-swept land.[5]

In the course of opening public lands west of the 100th meridian to settlement, agricultural scientists and promoters like Hardy W. Campbell devised special techniques for breaking and cultivating the grasslands of the West, employing new types of plows and tillage techniques such as letting the land stand fallow alternate years, and introducing hardy varieties of grasses and new planting methods.[6] The archeologist Cyrus Thomas, a member of Powell's expeditionary team, coined the maxim "The rain follows the plow."[7] But all too often the rain scorned the plow, while the wind seemed drawn to it. During the dry cycles, three or four years might intervene between rains. In the meantime farmers had no crops; and when the wind blew hard, the topsoil went with it. Some people suggested that the land be returned to grazing. After all, the deep roots of native grasses had held the soil for longer than recorded history. Before the arrival of first Spanish and American explorers the High Plains of eastern Colorado traditionally were buffalo hunting territory for the Comanches and the Arapahoes, not a place of permanent settlement. Superb horsemen, they were nomadic people who, as Webb notes, "had no settled village life."[8]

The early Anglo settlers took root like native grasses. They weathered the bad years and prospered when the rains returned. But dryland farming became increasingly dependent on distant markets and improvements in machinery. When the market went sour for too long, the banks could no longer carry the loans they had issued. With financial resources exhausted, many farmers had no alternative but to leave. Periodic dust storms were not alone the sole root problem; lacking adequate capital resources to provide irrigation and subject to the economic uncertainties of grain markets, the settlers were both dried out (no water) and left hung out to dry (by the market).

The periodic hard times affected the High Plains people in various ways. Those unable to weather periodic droughts and economic downturns were uprooted. But others stayed on, selling their machinery and stock but keeping their land. Those who remained were stubborn survivors. Many who left dreamed only of returning, so great was their attachment to the treeless, barren High Plains. From their dugout home in Baca County, Colorado, Sanora's mother said, the horizon looked like the edge of the Earth, where one might fall off. Unhappy about leaving her home in north central Oklahoma for an isolated dryland farm in southeastern Colorado, Jennie Babb had acquiesced to her husband's almost whimsical attempt at rural yeomanry. Her attachment was to her children; as long as they were provided for, she was reconciled to the lonely existence. Sensitive to the subtle beauty of the High Plains, Jennie made the best of it, knowing that her restless husband would eventually move the family to town (somewhere on the High Plains), where he could play baseball and, she hoped, return to baking.

A few farmers invested in deep water wells and dams, but most did not possess adequate capital and were dependent on rainfall. What nature did not provide freely, they extracted from the ground and from stream runoff. A few wealthy farmers, drawing on capital resources, invested in groundwater irrigation. But most farmers simply made preparations to last out the dry years. Irrigation set up economic divisions that made a subsistence economy ever more problematic. The "chicken and feather" farmers—chicken one year, feathers the next—were less able to compete in the new money economy. After World War II the independent family farm began to cede to large-scale capitalized operations and, with this, the heavy use of irrigation, supplied by the Ogallala aquifer and delivered by powerful deep-well turbine pumps. (Someday, however, even the great Ogallala aquifer will be taxed beyond its capacity; groundwater wells will face exhaustion, and the ecological credits will come due.)[9]

HIGH PLAINS CHILDHOOD AND YOUTH

Sanora Babb knew intimately the land, the weather, and the people among whom she grew up. Her parents were living in Red Rock, Oklahoma Territory, in 1907, when she was born, six months before statehood. Her father, Walter, had lived for many years in Oklahoma Territory, learning several Indian languages and organizing baseball teams of "Sooners" and Native Americans. In Lansing, Kansas, where his father ran a bakery, Walter met Anna Jeanette (Jennie) Parks, Sanora's mother. Jennie, raised in genteel circumstances in Kentucky and Kansas, was fifteen in 1905, when she married Walter, aged twenty-four. Beginning in 1870, four railroads—the Missouri, Kansas & Texas, the Chicago, Rock Island & Pacific, the St. Louis & San Francisco, and the Atchison, Topeka & Santa Fe—were instrumental in opening the Indian territories to Anglo settlement. In the spring of 1905 a Santa Fe train brought the newly wed Walter and Jennie across the Kansas line into Oklahoma Territory, to the Otoe reservation, where Otoes on horseback, members of Walter's baseball team, whooping and shouting like "wild Indians," welcomed the terrified bride.

Walter had grown up in the Unassigned Lands ceded by the Creek and Seminole Indians to the United States at the close of the Civil War. The territory was a wide-open frontier for gamblers, thieves, boomers, adventure-seekers, and land speculators when Alonzo, Walter's father, had made the 1889 land run. With Walter and Walter's sister (their mother had died several years before), Alonzo settled in the new town of Mulhall, Oklahoma, and practiced his baking trade there until he moved to Lansing circa 1902. Largely unsupervised, Walter learned to gamble by watching older men play faro and poker in Mulhall's taverns. The fever of development in the new territorial towns of pre-statehood Oklahoma encouraged gambling, alcohol, guns, and corruption among business promoters, railroad interests, and politicians. Historian Angie Debo describes these towns vividly in *Prairie City*: "The saloons drew more people than ever; the proportion of drunken men on the streets increased with the accelerated speed of town life.... Most of the players here were farm hands and other young men from the country. But the same saloon had a special room in the back, a secret hide-out, where most of the business leaders, infected with gambling fever by the chances of the Strip race and the excitement of town site promotion, played late at night for high stakes."[10]

Red Rock, where Walter moved after Mulhall, had its beginnings as a railroad station on Otoe land. Honoring a promise to Jennie to earn his living respectably, Walter opened a bakery, serving new settlers and the Otoes. Walter played baseball, organizing a team with Otoe players that competed with other towns in the territory. Later on, the Otoes invited Sanora to their summer and winter camps, where, given an Indian name, she lived for periods of time and participated in the ceremonies. Like her Great Plains contemporaries Meridel Le Sueur, Mari Sandoz, and Angie Debo, she developed a lifelong identification with Native American spiritual beliefs and attitudes toward nature and community, among them, a sense of the present as part of a continuum, and a connectedness with all creatures in nature.

Sanora's father, on the other hand, was restless and hungered for the challenges he found in matching wits in two-hand poker and faro.[11] Jennie tolerated patiently Walter's mercurial moods and dominating behavior, devoting herself to her daughters' well being while making do with often slender means. (A second daughter, Dorothy, was born in 1909 in Waynoka, Oklahoma.) The Babbs moved frequently, and Walter gambled with businessmen and travelers in hotels late into the night. Laws and mores were changing fast in the early years following statehood (which occurred in 1907). In the new towns informal codes of "respectability" were invoked against illicit activities. Community disapprobation imposed a heavy emotional burden on Jennie, who longed desperately to raise her two young daughters in more secure circumstances. Each time the family moved to another town, Jennie felt humiliation and a sense of defeat. She had made her choice to marry Walter, her mother reminded her; now she must remain with him. Her marriage vows had become a prison sentence.[12]

Walter took pride in matching his skill and mental acuity against the "suckers," as he called his gambling opponents, refusing to cheat unless the family's resources were running out. Partly from an impulse to try his luck at homesteading and partly to rejoin his widowed father, Walter moved the family in 1913 to Baca County in southeastern Colorado to raise broomcorn, one of the few cash crops that were adapted to the soil and harsh weather conditions. The Babbs and Alonzo, Sanora's grandfather, lived in a single-room dugout home; cramped, poorly ventilated, the dugout was an unhealthy setting for raising young children. Leaving Alonzo, who seemed to prefer his solitary life, the Babbs moved to a rented house on a small creek seven miles away. Ill-nourished, remote from formal schooling, and lacking contact with other children, Dorothy and Sanora created their own imaginative world. Their companions were the Babbs' draft horses, dogs, and the small, indigenous creatures—prairie dogs, mink, jackrabbits, fox squirrels, burrowing owls, rattlesnakes, and a wide diversity of bird species—in which the High Plains abounds. From closely observed impressions of her immediate surroundings—the land, nature, and people—Sanora gathered the material that later furnished much of her writing.

She knew very early in life that she wanted to write. The conditions for success were formidable for a young woman who had known only a hardscrabble existence on the High Plains and a nomadic life as a gambler's daughter. Like the Russian novelist Maxim Gorky, whose literary work she read with great interest, she turned personal hardship into compassion for the outcast, the marginalized, and the voiceless poor, all subjects of her writing.

She turned for inspiration again and again to her High Plains childhood despite the difficulties and frequent insecurity she had endured; her attachment to both the beauty and the hardships associated with place and landscape fueled her imagination. The plight of the Dust Bowl farmers, dispossessed and forced to leave their homes, was an extension of this attachment. It was the destiny of the dryland farmers, for whom weather, economy, drought, aridity, and inappropriate farming methods brought failure ultimately to their dreams of yeoman independence, that became the subject of her three novels, reportage, and numerous short stories.

In her third novel, *An Owl on Every Post* (1970), she recalls this landscape and the deep impression it made upon her as a youth:

> There was nothing in sight on the open prairie. The high clear air shimmered with moonlight. The silence deepened into a sound of itself, a palpable atmosphere through which we walked to what destination I did not know. In this unpeopled place what destination could there be? An intensely felt but not understood part of me was being stretched in every direction to the circular horizon and upward to that immense field of stars. I was aware of my hunger then, a hunger that stirred me to living life, a knowledge that I was more than myself, that self of the hours of day and night, that the unknown answer lay all about me, that everything spoke to me and yet I could not understand.[13]

In 1919, the family moved to Forgan, in Oklahoma's Panhandle, where Sanora graduated valedictorian of her high school class and worked as a printer's devil for the newspaper. At graduation she was not permitted to deliver the valedictory address; such was the penalty imposed upon a gambler's daughter. In 1924, shortly after her graduation, the Babbs moved to Garden City, Kansas. Sanora attended the University of Kansas but, lacking financial means, left after her first year to work as a reporter for the *Garden City Herald*—an experience that pushed her toward a career in writing and journalism. The situation at home grew steadily worse. Walter rented a room in the Windsor Hotel, where he gambled with salesmen who stopped over in Garden City. When he "cleaned out" a salesman's stake, Walter would give back some of the earnings. On the other hand, when his earnings were low, he marked his cards. Jennie, who had long endured the humiliation and insecurity of a gambler's wife, found work as a grocery-store clerk. As his fortunes declined, Walter became increasingly frustrated and domineering. Following several angry confrontations with her father, Sanora decided to leave home. Dorothy was away at college in Emporia. Prominent businessmen, including some who had gambled with Walter, decided it was time Walter left town. Jailed several times for short periods, Walter found a gambler's life too "hot" in Garden City. Divorced from Jennie, he began a life of restless moves, a "suitcase" gambler playing casinos and bars across the West. (This tumultuous period in her life became the inspiration for Babb's novel *The Lost Traveler*.)

In 1929 Sanora left for Los Angeles to pursue a journalism career and try her hand at writing short stories for the "little magazines" that were springing up everywhere even as the country experienced its worst economic crisis. She applied for work at several newspapers but soon discovered that women journalists were the first to be fired and the last to be hired. Unable to afford her rent, she joined other homeless job seekers sleeping in Lafayette Park. By the spring of 1930 she had found work in the Warner Brothers building in Hollywood, and soon thereafter she was writing scripts for KFWB, the Warner Brothers radio station.

The work was not demanding; she set about writing sketches and short stories that drew upon her journalistic and storytelling abilities. She submitted these to literary magazines that sought fresh, vigorous writing about contemporary reality. The hard times of the Depression era elicited literary and documentary expression in urban centers like Los Angeles as well as in rural areas and small towns in the hinterlands of the nation. Little magazines such as *The Midland*, edited by John T. Frederick, and *The Anvil*, edited by Jack Conroy, and some mainstream book publishers (Covici-Friede, for example) welcomed young writers like Babb who drew from their own knowledge and experience to tell the stories of those who do not write.[14] Literary expression was on the left movement's agenda until the Popular Front called for more urgent priorities in the struggle against fascism in the late 1930s. Babb's leftist friends were William Saroyan, John Fante, Carlos Bulosan, Meridel Le Sueur, John Sanford, Tillie Olsen, Nelson Algren, and Carey McWilliams—all young, aspiring writers at the time. They talked about writing, traded tips on where to publish, and shared their dreams. No one had any money, she recalled; yet they had stories to tell in the early years of the Depression and editors who encouraged them, certain that some would succeed, as, indeed, some did.

The 1930s witnessed the proliferation of little magazines responding to the renewed focus on regional difference and the value of local knowledge in a collaborative effort of editors, printers, and writers, who saw their work as a shared enterprise, a cause, really, that called for generosity and a spirit of camaraderie. Despite their short run, little magazines of the 1930s such as *The Anvil, Pagany, Partisan Review*, and *Contempo* served an important role in introducing little-known writers to mainstream publishers. And despite the continued domination of the national publishing industry by New York firms and intellectuals, a number of literary magazines promoted regionalist interests, among them *Southwest Review, Prairie Schooner, Southern Review, New Mexico Quarterly*, and *The Kansas Magazine, Black & White, The Clipper*—to name some of those in which Babb published many of her short stories and poems.

Frederick's *Midland* (January 1915–May/June 1933) deserves citing as an outstanding example of a region-focused little magazine. Established in Iowa City in 1915, while Frederick was on the faculty of the university there, the magazine in its editorial philosophy urged that "serious writers should remain in their native regions where they might develop their art unfettered by the standardizing and commercializing influences of New York."[15] Babb's short story "The Old One" appeared in one of the last issues (March/April 1933). Set on a western prairie, the story, one of her earliest, tells of a young girl hired for domestic farm work coming to awareness of eros and death, themes that Babb would continue to explore in short stories and novels.[16]

DUST BOWL DEPRESSION: THE MAKING OF A RADICAL

In 1934 Babb returned to western Kansas to visit her mother. One afternoon she looked to the northwest to see what appeared like huge wave, black and ominous, obscuring the sun. The dust storm settled on the town, sifting through windowsills and darkening the sky. Farmers strung ropes to guide their way to their barns. People wrapped wet towels around their faces and hung oil-soaked paper in the windows. Many fell sick with "dust pneumonia," and stray cattle suffocated. Droughts and dust storms on the High Plains were familiar to Babb, who had known them in her youth. But the intensity and duration of the 1934 storm were greater than anything she had ever experienced—a cataclysm or, at the very least, the end of the precarious existence that dryland farmers had known for two generations.

Droughts have brought down civilizations: a protracted period of drought between A.D. 800 and 1000, a period known as the Classic Maya Collapse, brought death to millions of Mayans. The Maya failed to adjust their behavior and culture to the changing climatic conditions; internal political and social failures ultimately brought ruin. Radical environmental change has collapsed other once-great societies in later times. The Aral Sea in the former USSR, once a fertile fishing ground and source of life-giving water, is today a dry salt bed, an ecological tragedy perhaps unparalleled in human history. Periodic droughts plagued the High Plains of the American West, where Babb had grown up. From the days of early settlement (around 1855) onward, successive droughts and periodic enormous swarms of locusts had led to crop failure and exodus; each time the dryland people survived and returned to farming. In the early 1930s a failed economy and four dry years drove the people away in the largest mass exodus ever known in American life.

In flivvers loaded with pots, blankets, boxes of clothes, and threadbare spare tires they fled the drought-stricken Great Plains of the "dirty 'thirties." Some 600,000 dispossessed farmers and their families scattered like migrating birds, most heading west, seeking work in New Mexico mines, Arizona cotton fields, California's harvests. They were a valiant, hardy people, proud of their pioneer ancestors, who had lived in sod houses and dugouts and survived hard times, creating a tenuous existence on the land in pursuit of rural independence and autonomy. The homesteaders had met hard times, but things were different now. Low crop prices and years of drought had left the farmers destitute and dispossessed. There were no social programs, no farm subsidies, no price controls, and no alternate sources of water. Over a half-million people left their homes in the plains states in search of jobs farther west. In California they experienced the deep humiliation of a proud, independent people confronted with police control points and unfriendly townspeople. Despite a hostile reception they clung to the expectation that California was a land of new beginnings. They held to their purpose: rural independence and self-reliance. Although few had read or heard of them, Thomas Jefferson's views on agrarian independence and Ralph Waldo Emerson's on self-reliance represented values shared among the settlers on the Great Plains.[17]

Babb left her job as script writer at KFWB in 1936 to travel on a theater tour to the Soviet Union with a small group headed by Herbert Kline, the editor of *New Theatre*, a Los Angeles publication that had printed her article on the local Federal Theatre Project.[18] Active in progressive causes, including the Spanish Aid Committee and the Anti-Fascist League, she joined the Hollywood branch of the Communist Party USA (CPUSA) after returning from Europe—not for ideological reasons, she said, but because the party, with its unemployed demonstrations and strike activities, had shown success in representing the rights of dispossessed workers left to fend for themselves. Restless with the discipline and doctrinal views the party called for, she eventually left it in the 1950s, convinced that it had lost the progressive aims that had first attracted her.

In the long run, Communism offered no romantic attraction or ready-made declaration of faith for Babb. She had known the protocommunism of the Otoe Indians, who shared their commonly owned land and provided for one another through collective structures of governance. The Communism she knew in the 1930s was part of a larger progressive movement in response to the Depression and the threat of fascism. The literary cell of the party in Hollywood that she was associated with had not yet become the Cold War spook demonized by McCarthy inquisitions and laced with factionalism and betrayals. In the 1930s CPUSA was a legitimate political party that placed candidates in elections and fostered labor reforms, however incommensurate its aims and methods were with American cultural traditions and democratic practices. The list of those joining the party in the 1930s, or lending their support to its programs, reads like a who's who of American intellectuals and artists. The Nazi–Soviet Nonagression Pact of 1939 split the left; the Stalinists in CPUSA justified the pact, arguing that it delayed the Nazis' inevitable invasion of the USSR, giving the Soviets time to prepare.

Stalin's crimes disgraced the very Marxist-Leninist principles that Soviet society purportedly embraced. No thinking person could condone his record of terror against his own people after Khrushchev exposed it at the 1958 Communist Party Congress of the Soviet Union. For American leftists the Soviet Union had been the workers' republic and an ally against fascism in Europe. Yet its leaders betrayed its people; the Soviet Communist Party no longer represented the worker's cause. Not for the same reason, obviously, workers' rights in the United States lost ground in the postwar period. Legislation, like the Taft-Hartley Act (1947), severely undercut union activity. Babb's engagement with CPUSA had been a matter of the heart more than of reason, of contingency rather than of principle. Her relation to the party had always been on her own terms; her purpose was not "art as a weapon" for any political aim, but rather writing that gave voice to the marginalized, those who do not write. When that no longer seemed possible within the party, she severed her connection.[19]

To trace Babb's radical roots one would have to look earlier, to political traditions in western Oklahoma that were still very alive when she was growing up there. These traditions grew out of what has been termed a "culture of political revolt."[20] This culture of protest produced the Farmers' Alliance, the Populist movement, and Oklahoma's Socialist Party. Sanora's grandfather Alonzo was a Socialist when the Socialist Party was a strong political presence in the territories and early statehood; the spirit of its ideals and intent of its reform positions influenced in part the writing of Oklahoma's constitution when it was drafted in 1907.[21] Alonzo subscribed to *The Appeal to Reason,* the socialist publication appearing from J. A. Wayland's press in Girard, Kansas. An influential voice for progressive reforms, *The Appeal* was a persuasive force in supporting Eugene Debs's socialist presidential candidacy in 1912, at which time its circulation approached one million. "*The Appeal* was published by and for people," notes Elliott Shore, "who objected to the course being charted by American society. It was an angry paper, a partisan paper that spoke for the cares and hopes and for the frustrations and dreams of people who were united in their desire to change what they saw into a curious mixture of what could be and what they believed once was."[22]

Alonzo was drawn to *The Appeal's* indigenous variety of socialism that found resonance among local Socialist Party groups in western Oklahoma. It was Babb's grandfather Alonzo, then, to whom we should look for her political grounding, not in any formal way but as the spark that ignited her natural inclination to side with the outsider: minorities, the poor, the oppressed. Her writings, together with her editorial roles with *The Clipper* (August 1940–November1941) and *The California Quarterly* (fall 1951–spring 1953), reflect her lifelong concern for social justice and humanitarian activism.

FARM SECURITY ADMINISTRATION: TOM COLLINS

After returning from England in 1938 Babb went to work for the Farm Security Administration as an assistant to a camp manager, Tom Collins. Founded in 1934 as the Resettlement Agency, the FSA was established to aid dispossessed Anglo farmers, not the migrant workers, mainly Mexican and Filipino, who had done the harvesting in the years before the diaspora of Dust Bowl migrants flooded California's Central Valley in the "dirty 'thirties." Working as a team, Collins and Babb followed the harvests, from the Imperial Valley in the south through California's San Joaquin and Sacramento valleys to the Oregon border, setting up tent camps and providing rudimentary amenities. Babb's job was to encourage the farmer-refugees camping in ditches and cars to find shelter in the tent camps provided by the FSA, and to organize them through self-governing committees. Collins called it "Democracy Functioning." The idea was to implant among the refugees the same rudimentary democratic practices of organization and self-governance that their frontier parents had known in settling new towns and protesting the power of banks and railroad interests. These practices were a resounding success, in contrast to the exploitive, inhumane conditions of the growers' company camps. Spartan in their construction, the FSA camps in California's principal agricultural valleys provided clean, safe, orderly living conditions. At night after work Babb wrote detailed sketches of the people she met and made notes of the day's work.[23]

During one of John Steinbeck's visits to the camps to gather material for his novel on the Dust Bowl migrants, Collins invited Babb to join them at a café in a nearby town and talk about the camps, the refugees' plight, and the Associated Farmers, the powerful political lobby of farm owners. Two years earlier Steinbeck's novel *In Dubious Battle* (1936) had appeared, based upon the 1934 strikes in the lettuce and pea fields near Brawley in California's Imperial Valley. Soon after the novel's publication, the *San Francisco News* hired Steinbeck to write a series of reports on the refugees, later published in pamphlet form as *Their Blood Was Strong*. Steinbeck visited the Arvin Sanitary Camp in August 1936, where he met Collins, then a Resettlement Agency administrator. Steinbeck's subject was, of course, the plight of the "Okies," a name that bespoke the resentment that small town Californians felt toward the refugees. For his source material Steinbeck relied heavily on the FSA field notes provided by Collins and the experiences of FSA workers such as Babb. Collins was eager to help Steinbeck; his novel would help publicize the plight of the "Okies" and perhaps induce Congress to grant support for the camps. In return Steinbeck promised to help Collins get his own memoir into print.[24]

Tom Collins was a gentle, compassionate, dignified man, an ex-schoolteacher who had worked in South America and the Philippines. Reticent about his past, according to Steinbeck's biographer, Jackson J.

Benson, he had left two wives and families. Lean, wiry, tireless, Collins was an able and dedicated administrator. Steinbeck was impressed with Collins's method of organizing the camps. The refugees were told to set their own rules and police their own affairs. They were a proud, independent, literate people in the main, except, as Babb recalled, for certain backwoods Arkansawyers, who remained clannish and suspicious of other dispossessed farmers. "Tom Collins," she said, "a truly humanitarian person, was setting up camps: tents, outhouses, a tent-office, registering hundreds, thousands of families. [It was] One of the most moving experiences of my life. What courageous, enduring people. Little food, if any, 40 cents an hour field work. We worked like beavers. Many were ill, hungry, desperate, but dignified. They were farmers (not the regular migratory workers) from the dust-ruined farms in the Midwest."[25]

Collins and Babb met frequently to exchange their views on what they had experienced and on ways of improving the conditions in the camps. Collins asked her to share her field notes with Steinbeck, as he had done with his own. The success of the theater version of *Of Mice and Men* (1937) had vaulted Steinbeck into literary prominence. The spirit of little magazine contributors had deeply influenced Babb: to view writing as a common enterprise, to share ideas and to criticize one another's work were her apprenticeship in writing. She had gone to "school" on the steps of the Los Angeles Public Library, where she had spent afternoons with John Fante, Carlos Bulosan, and other young writers discussing their work, trading tips, and enjoying one another's success in placing a story. Now she felt the urgency of making known the plight of the "Okies." It was in this spirit that she lent her field notes to Collins, who passed them to Steinbeck.

Babb was composing her own sketches of the Dust Bowl refugees while in the camps. She reframed her impressions and sketches of people and incidents encountered in the course of her work into a novel manuscript, her story of the Dust Bowl refugees.[26] Her approach was immediate, personal, and affective. The immediacy of her writing derived from her intimate childhood memories among the dryland farmers on the High Plains and her work in the refugee camps. She had seen a crude inscription, "Whose Names Are Unknown," scrawled on a decrepit shack in a grower's improvised settlement for migrant workers, and she used it as the title of her novel. The title embodied the bitter fact that to the corporate owners, the field workers were nameless peons, expendable labor "units." Her sketches give the refugees their names and retell their personal experiences.

Steinbeck's Joads, in *The Grapes of Wrath* (1939), function on several levels: the symbolic, drawn from biblical sources and marine science; folklore (and folk speech); and literary realism. The novel embraces a powerful social message in addition to functioning as a vehicle for Steinbeck's philosophical views, the best known being his notion of organic group behavior. Babb's Depression-era writings, on the other hand, reflect traditions of literary radicalism nurtured in Socialist publications like Wayland's *Appeal*, magazines of the left such as *The Masses* and *The Liberator*, and the host of little radical regional magazines of the 1930s like *The Midland*, *The Anvil*, *Hinterland*, *Pagany*, *Windsor Quarterly*, *The Magazine*, *The Clipper*, and others, to which she contributed. Her literary radicalism is a form of critical realism in which the characters and events problematize contemporary social and political realities, based upon her own reportorial observation and personal experience.

The refugees, she perceived, were not hapless, uninformed "Okies" who came late to political consciousness. Their aim was to reestablish themselves as independent farmers or set up small businesses—as many subsequently did. Radical initiatives fell on deaf ears; in their minds they shared little in common with the industrial workers of the Midwest. Yet when conditions became unbearable, they organized strikes and permitted visits from journalists, photographers, and Hollywood liberals, who, expressing solidarity, brought them food and clothing, and toys for their children. The refugees remained aloof and distant from outsiders, as people do when they feel patronized. By contrast they accepted Babb warmly; after all, these were her people: she had walked the roads with them, lived among them, organized the women into committees to provide education and medical help—and on occasion organized their strikes for better working conditions.

Local schools did not accept the children of the refugees, and sometimes hospitals would refuse to treat them. Collins and Babb served as midwives numerous times, when women bore their children in tents on newspapers spread on the ground. She met some families repeatedly at different camps as the harvesting moved. Later she particularly recalled the King family. After work they played the traditional music their parents had brought to Arkansas from eastern Kentucky. In the evening the men sat about, "hunkered down" in the absence of chairs, discussing their plans and their prospects. On weekend nights Collins organized dances accompanied by camp musicians. Most of the refugees came as families.

Bachelors tended to live in one section of the camps, cooking on their stoves placed outside the tents. The women baked on crude outdoor stoves and did their laundry in tubs or in streams. Another family she remembered, the Beckenwirths, had lived for a time in company-owned shacks. They were moved out when the harvest ended, camping in their car until finding work again.

Powerless against the large growers, the displaced Dust Bowl farmers were nonetheless reluctant to organize in collective forms of protest; they viewed themselves as independent farmers, not as industrial workers. As the terms of work and living conditions grew worse, the refugees' anger and frustration reached a breaking point. Strikes sprang up spontaneously in the fields; leaders emerged from among the refugee-farmers. Babb met with strike leaders who planned their next protest action and counseled others how to handle "thugs" sent by the growers to intimidate them.

During one strike she was arrested and jailed for a night, along with Dorothy Healey, a Communist organizer, who had been jailed for a longer period during the 1934 lettuce strike. Babb's attempts to organize a strike near Modesto failed. Children were employed there without pay to harvest walnuts in order to supplement their parents' meager income. She was unable to gain support from the CIO, which shied away from farm workers, who, because of their itinerant occupation, were considered poor candidates for union membership. Strike organizers suffered great risks from the police and from thugs hired by the farm owners. The Associated Farmers, an organization of large growers, were in league with local politicians and the sheriff.

At a lunch counter one day two thugs sat down on either side of Babb. "You'd better get out of town fast," they said, "or they'll find your body floating in a canal." When she told Collins of this, he advised her to leave immediately and to relocate at another FSA camp. With her few possessions she moved to the Weed Patch Camp near Bakersfield and continued her work.[27]

CONCLUSION: WHOSE NAMES ARE UNKNOWN

In the summer of 1939 Babb sent several chapters of the manuscript of "Whose Names Are Unknown" as a blind submission to Bennett Cerf, the legendary director-editor at Random House. Cerf paid Sanora's airfare to

New York, put her up at a hotel, and told her to finish the novel. Steinbeck's *The Grapes of Wrath* had appeared from Viking Press the previous April. By summer it had become a huge market success, fulfilling Collins's hope that Steinbeck's book would serve to publicize the refugees' plight. Cerf called Babb in and told her to put the manuscript of her own refugee novel in a drawer until a later time. It was a brilliant piece of writing, he told her; and a number of other editors, including Maxwell Perkins, concurred. Market conditions dictated Random House's decision and subsequently the decision of other publishers who read the manuscript. The present market, Cerf said, would not welcome two novels on a similar subject. Kyle Crichton, a Random House editor, who had written satiric pieces for *New Masses*, took the manuscript to other publishers, who responded similarly. Babb was advised to wait; with time, the subject would gain interest through its "historical perspective." She had worked in the FSA camps several months too long, and that had made all the difference. Had she brought a completed manuscript to Random House a few months earlier, *Whose Names Are Unknown* rather than *The Grapes of Wrath* might be required reading in high schools across the United States today.

The simple fact was that the sensational success of Steinbeck's novel overshadowed Babb's ill-fated manuscript and dashed her hope that her writing would finally win the recognition that a string of editors had predicted she deserved. Deeply discouraged, she returned to the settings and people she had known early in her life on the High Plains. Twice (1950, 1960) her short stories were included in Martha Foley's *Best American Short Stories*. In 1958 her novel *The Lost Traveler* appeared after a long struggle to come to terms with her insecure childhood and her charming, domineering father. *An Owl on Every Post*, a closely observed, environmentally sensitive novel-memoir of the Baca County dryland farm where her family had struggled to survive, appeared in 1971. Both novels reflect her long apprenticeship in the discipline of writing, nurtured in the little magazines circuits of the 1930s and 1940s. Postwar America witnessed profound changes in literary publishing, in response to readers' altered tastes, and Cold War anxieties led editors and publishers to steer clear of working-class subjects and radical themes.

World War II created jobs in wartime industries for the Dust Bowl refugees; many enlisted or were drafted. People looked forward to better times economically. There was little interest now in accounts of Depression-era subjects and social concerns affecting the unemployed and deepening class divisions. A chilly reception from publishers greeted literary radicals such as Nelson Algren, Jack Conroy, Meridel LeSueur, Tillie Olsen, John Sanford, and Sanora Babb. Some screenwriters, filmmakers, and writers on the left wrote under pseudonyms or moved abroad to escape intimidation. Babb's own history of activism with progressive causes brought her under FBI scrutiny. When agents visited her home she acted to protect her husband, cinematographer James Wong Howe, whose career might have been threatened by his association with her. Companions for many years, they were finally permitted to marry in 1949, after California overturned its miscegenation law. Born in China but living in the United States from the age of five, Howe held permanent citizen status, yet under California's Exclusion Law he was not permitted full American citizenship; the law was finally rescinded in the early 1950s. Fearing that their association, together with his noncitizen status, would make it difficult for Howe to obtain film work, Sanora lived in Mexico City in the early 1950s, during the worst of what Ceplair and Englund have called the "Hollywood inquisition."[28] Even being merely associated with a participant in the progressive movement was enough to place someone's artistic career in jeopardy.

Near the end of her long life, persuaded by her friends, Babb finally consented to let her long-silenced manuscript of the Dust Bowl refugees, "Whose Names Are Unknown," be published. *Whose Names Are Unknown* (2004) is centered on the everyday lives of the refugees; reportorial in its unembellished recounting of hardship and life-affirming resourcefulness, it represents one of the choicest fruits of American literary radicalism, rooted in traditions of critical realism, literary naturalism, protest literature, and reportage.[29]

For Steinbeck and Babb, only literary techniques could adequately embrace and give meaning to the refugees' unfolding tragic diaspora. So great was the subject in its scope and so overpowering in its emotional impact on the sensitive observer that a merely naturalistic or journalistic treatment would have proved inadequate. If the refugees did not recognize themselves in the figures of the Joads, they did so in the characters' plight; the powerful sweep of Steinbeck's novel was eloquent witness to the tragic calamity they had experienced.

The characters in *Whose Names Are Unknown* represent people whom, under different circumstances, we might have known as neighbors and, in a different time, with whom we might have shared a similar destiny.

The power of her novel lies in its creative restructuring of reportage and personal experience into literature. Babb hewed close to testimonial witnessing in novelizing her personal observations, focusing on day-by-day existence, recording the adversities, stoic endurance, and humor of her characters' beleaguered existence. The freshness and vigorous, rawboned quality of the narrative reflect the material conditions attending the composition of the novel.

The epic of displacement that Steinbeck created in *The Grapes of Wrath* swept across the nation, causing storms of protest and swells of praise, finally achieving an unassailable iconic status, as eponym of the Great Depression.[30] With no less compelling vividness and emotional impact, Babb's Dust Bowl novel reflects the conditions of its production in the FSA camps, written at night amid the fatigue and dust and sorrows of the displaced people. She knew the poor and the working class intimately from early childhood through adulthood, both as writer and radical activist, for she too had overcome great hardship.

To study Sanora Babb's life and work is to gain an understanding of the High Plains, its people, and how they shaped their environment and in turn how it shaped them. It is also a story of forced migration, and what happens to a dispossessed people's sense of place. It is a story about landscape, belief, and commitment, as well as a vision of connectedness—the continuity of all things, human and nonhuman. She wrote of difficult choices made under trying, frequently ambiguous circumstances. Balancing open-eyed, unsentimental observation with a sense of mystery and wonder, she believed in the capacity of the individual consciousness, rejecting the authority of ideology or political creed, to develop empathetic understanding and tolerance of difference. The real revolution, she said, must occur in the human heart, not on the streets. Like her gambler-father, but for entirely different reasons, she believed in taking chances in life and trusting in instinct—an instinct formed by a broad diversity of experience and a deep compassion for all living things.

NOTES

1. Sources include James N. Gregory, *American Exodus* (New York: Oxford University Press, 1989); Walter J. Stein, *California and the Dust Bowl Migration* (Westport. Conn.:

Greenwood Press, 1973); Paul Bonnifield, *The Dust Bowl: Men, Dirt, and Depression* (Albuquerque: University of New Mexico Press, 1979). Babb's own Dust Bowl account is told in Douglas Wixson, *On the Dirty Plate Trail: Remembering the Dust Bowl Refugee Camps* (Austin: University of Texas Press, 2007).

2. Sources for this chapter and details about Babb's life and work include my own extensive interviews and correspondence, from 1983 through 2003, with Babb as well as with her friends and colleagues. My thanks to Michael Steiner and to my wife, Suzanne Chamier Wixson, for their helpful advice and careful editing.

3. Michael Kowalewski, "Bioregional Perspectives in American Literature," in *Regionalism Reconsidered: New Approaches to the Field*, ed. David Jordan (New York: Garland, 1994), 33, 31.

4. Michael Steiner, "Regionalism in the Great Depression," *Geographical Review* 73 (October 1983): 446.

5. Walter Prescott Webb, *The Great Plains* (New York: Grosset & Dunlap, 1931), 415. Also see Webb's polemical essay "The American West: Perpetual Mirage," *Harper's* 214 (May 1957): 25–31.

6. Mary Wilma M. Hargreaves, *Dry Farming in the Northern Great Plains* (Cambridge: Harvard University Press, 1957), 21, 84–88; Webb, *The Great Plains*, 369.

7. First appearing in Charles Dana Wilber's *The Great Valleys and Prairies of Nebraska and the Northwest* (1881), these four simple words achieved near proverbial status in the drylands during the time when dryland cultivation techniques like the Campbell system were actively promoted by private entrepreneurs (ca. 1890s–1920). For an overview of settlement on the drylands see Wallace Stegner, *Beyond the 100th Meridian* (New York: Penguin, 1992); Henry Nash Smith, *Virgin Land: The American West in Symbol and Myth* (New York: Vintage, 1957); W. Eugene Hollon, *The Great American Desert* (New York: Oxford University Press, 1966).

8. Webb, *The Great Plains*, 59.

9. See, generally, John Opie, *Ogallala: Water for a Dry Land* (Lincoln: University of Nebraska Press, 1993).

10. Angie Debo, *Prairie City: The Story of an American Community* (Tulsa: Council Oak, 1985), 94.

11. See Douglas Wixson, "Romancing the Desiring Machine: Edna Ferber's *Cimarron* and Sanora Babb's *The Lost Traveler*," *MidAmerica* 14 (2008): 92–105.

12. First published in 1958, Babb's novel *The Lost Traveler* (now reprinted, with introduction by Douglas Wixson, Albuquerque: University of New Mexico Press, 1995) recalls her early years, clashing wills with a headstrong, dominating father. The novel merits close comparison with Mari Sandoz's narrative portrait of her own father in *Old Jules* (1935).

13. Sanora Babb, *An Owl on Every Post* (1970; reprinted, Albuquerque: University of New Mexico Press, 1994), 117.

14. For a detailed study of radical writers and the little magazine circuits of the 1930s see Douglas Wixson, *Worker-Writer in America: Jack Conroy and the Tradition of Midwestern Literary Radicalism* (Urbana: University of Illinois Press, 1994).

15. Milton M. Reigelman, *"The Midland": A Venture in Literary Regionalism* (Iowa City: University of Iowa Press, 1975), 45.

16. She published short stories in a number of radical little magazines in the 1930s, among them "Dry Summer" in Conroy's *Anvil* (September–October 1934), a highly

esteemed publication that drew the attention of establishment publishers looking for new talent.

17. On this tragic episode in the destiny of the dryland farmers, see Wixson, *On the Dirty Plate Trail*, based in part upon Babb's field notes and reports from the period (1938–39) during which she worked for the Farm Security Administration in California's three principal agricultural valleys.

18. Sanora Babb, "The Los Angeles WPA Theatre Project," *New Theatre* 111, no. 6 (1936): 22–23.

19. This subject, including Babb's involvement, is treated in considerable detail in Wixson, *Worker-Writer in America*.

20. Elliott Shore, *Talkin' Socialism: J. A. Wayland and the Role of the Press in American Radicalism, 1890–1912* (Lawrence: University Press of Kansas, 1988), 5.

21. Useful sources for the People's Party and the Socialist Party in Oklahoma include Worth Robert Miller, *Oklahoma Populism* (Norman: University of Oklahoma Press, 1987); John Thompson, *Closing the Frontier: Radical Response in Oklahoma, 1819–1923* (Norman: University of Oklahoma Press, 1986); Davis D. Joyce, ed., *"An Oklahoma I Had Never Seen Before": Alternative Views of Oklahoma History* (Norman: University of Oklahoma Press, 1994); Danney Goble, *Progressive Oklahoma: The Making of New Kind of State* (Norman: University of Oklahoma Press, 1980); Oscar Ameringer, *If You Don't Weaken: The Autobiography of Oscar Ameringer*, introduction by James R. Green (Norman: University of Oklahoma Press, 1983).

22. Shore, *Talkin' Socialism*, 8.

23. See Wixson. *On the Dirty Plate Trail*. A general source on the FSA is Sidney Baldwin, *Poverty and Politics: The Rise and Decline of the Farm Security Administration* (Chapel Hill: University of North Carolina Press, 1968).

24. See Jackson J. Benson, *The True Adventures of John Steinbeck, Writer: A Biography* (New York: Viking, 1984), 361–62, 378.

25. Sanora Babb, Hollywood, to Douglas Wixson, November 11–12, 1996, in author's possession.

26. See Wixson, *On the Dirty Plate Trail*, chapters 2–5.

27. Babb shared these memories with me many times during the twenty years I knew her.

28. Larry Ceplair and Steven Englund, *The Inquisition in Hollywood: Politics in the Film Community, 1930–60*. Urbana: University of Illinois Press, 2003.

29. *Whose Names Are Unknown* (Norman: University of Oklahoma Press, 2004).

30. On the issue of reception, see Rick Wartzman's *Obscene in the Extreme: The Burning and Banning of John Steinbeck's "The Grapes of Wrath"* (New York: PublicAffairs, 2008).

B. A. Botkin. Courtesy of American Folklore Society and Archives & Special Collections, University of Nebraska–Lincoln Libraries.

CHAPTER SIX

Theorizing Regionalism and Folklore from the Left

B. A. BOTKIN, THE OKLAHOMA YEARS, 1921–1939

Jerrold Hirsch

R egionalism "has received a black eye from its association with lost causes," declared B. A. Botkin (1901–75) at a meeting of the leftist American Writers' Congress in June 1937. He had come to the conference not just to criticize conservative regionalists but, more importantly, to lay out the case for proletarian regionalism before an audience many of whose members thought the term an oxymoron. For almost a decade, Botkin had not only been defending regionalism from detractors who associated it with conservatism, but had also been developing a radical approach to regionalism and folklore. That hardly anyone, other than a few scholars, remembers Botkin as a leftist theorist of folklore *and* regionalism is a central and startling fact. And yet that is exactly what he was during the period between 1929 and 1939.[1]

Botkin was one of the few interwar regionalists familiar both with the urban world of recently emergent racial and ethnic minorities and with the older world of rural America. The former knowledge was part of his inheritance as the child of poor Lithuanian Jewish immigrants who had settled in Boston, where Botkin was born in 1901 and later, with the help of scholarships, attended Harvard University from 1916 to 1920. The latter knowledge he acquired during his years as an English professor at the University of Oklahoma and from his graduate studies with ballad scholar Louise Pound at the University of Nebraska.[2] Botkin differed from many regionalists who primarily viewed literary, social, and economic issues entirely through the lens of their own regions and their particular approaches to regionalism. Lewis Mumford, the brilliant self-taught student of American life, who was based in the Northeast, influenced Botkin's cosmopolitan and national view of regionalism, as did southern sociologist Howard Odum, who thought that regional planning could alleviate poverty in the South and the rest of the nation. Unlike many technocrats, Mumford and Odum maintained that regions had a cultural dimension and that regional planning needed to acknowledge and embrace the aesthetic and emotional aspects of regionalism. Like Mumford, Botkin was not antiurban, as many then (and now) imagine all regionalists to be.[3]

To achieve his goals, Botkin taught standard courses in the university's English department as well as specialized courses on regionalism and on contemporary American writing. He eventually also taught folklore in the university's anthropology department. This placed him in a different position from virtually all academic folklorists, who were based in either English or anthropology departments, with the former concentrating on European folksong and the latter on the culture of Native American groups. From early on in his career, Botkin's courses in both departments focused on contemporary American folk and lore as both literature and culture. His goal was to help students understand the place of folklore in American life, to study and appreciate it as part of both a regional and a national culture. This made him almost unique among academic folklorists of his era. Nor did he stop with English and anthropology. He also studied geography, sociology, and history.

Nor was he content to teach only students. He sought to be a public intellectual by writing book reviews for the local newspaper about both contemporary modernist and regional writers, by encouraging regional writers, by supporting folk festivals, and by participating in workshops for elementary and high school teachers. He gladly seized on every opportunity that a far midwestern university's mission of public service and promotion of "culture" offered him. These were opportunities largely missing in the nation's great northeastern universities, although as Botkin would discover, at a public university he would have to contend with state politics. He was interested not only in the "Great Tradition," what Matthew Arnold had thought of as the best of Western high culture, but also in the tradition of the provincial, the nearby, the folk, and the relation between the two traditions.[4]

Botkin's 1929 manifesto, "The Folk in Literature: An Introduction to the New Regionalism," was a bold initial step in a journey in which cultural politics and theory were deeply intertwined. His ideas are still important, not only as part of the history of regionalism and folklore studies but also as a legacy for those who want to explore the relevance of regionalism today. Yet even with the revival of talk about "critical regionalism," of a new-new regionalism, in the present age of globalization, Botkin remains an unclaimed ancestor. Those who today reject regionalism as inherently a static view of society do so for largely the same reasons that critics of regionalism did in the 1930s, but they show no awareness of that fact. Nor are they aware of Botkin's leftist formulations of theory about folklore and regionalism, nor of his criticisms of conservative, reactionary regionalism. He is not a resource for them, when he should be someone they could build on or wrestle with to their benefit.[5]

While recent reassessments of proletarian writing in the 1930s have been welcome, they have rarely mentioned Botkin and for the most part have given only cursory, if any, attention to radical regionalist writers and theorists. Nevertheless they have moved us beyond the clichés that served during the Cold War as final judgments and as a means for the New Critics to establish a canon that had a place for high modernists but not for proletarian or regionalist writers. The reassessments have demonstrated that proletarian literature was not monolithic. Not all proletarian writers adhered to formulaic plots about the great strike leading to revolution or about the young man discovering his true identity when he realizes he is part of the working class and embraces radical politics. Reassessments have also established that many proletarian writers were nevertheless influenced by the high modernists of their era. As Marcus Klein has maintained, "proletarian literature was a literary rebellion within a literary revolution, to which it was loyal." Barbara Foley has spelled out the point in greater detail: "In short, much Depression-era literary radicalism was intimately involved with the project of 'mak[ing] it new.' The conflation of 'modernism' with the high modernism of Eliot, Joyce, and Pound . . . can be argued only at the risk of fundamentally distorting the intentions and perspectives of those who were actually engaged in literary production during the proletarian period. The literary proletarians were part of modernism." Botkin deserves a place in post–Cold War studies on proletarian writing, but one will barely find him mentioned there.[6]

But what happens if we put Botkin back into the story? We are forced to rethink clichés that still obscure much about 1930s radical writing and regionalism and about Botkin himself, who argued that regional writing could be part of proletarian literature. We will have to allow for the existence and achievements of a leftist regionalist and folklore theorist. The very title of Botkin's 1929 manifesto links folk, literature, and regionalism and promises a new theoretical turn. He opens with a fighting declaration and a rejection of commonly accepted ways of constructing modernity: "The arbitrary division between folk-lore and literature has had the unfortunate effect of obscuring the relationship between the two." He insists that this so-called division is a "difference in degree" and not "in kind or content." The "real antithesis," he claims, lies "between oral, or unwritten, and written tradition, a given piece of lore being just as much literature before it is written down as it remains lore after it is written." By calling the division arbitrary, he indicates that he wants to clear the ground for new thinking and that he knows what he is up against from those who held the earlier theories he had studied, learned from, modified, and on key points rejected. With the word "arbitrary," he is claiming that this division has no validity, that whatever value and theoretical content it once had has become hardened convention without justification or justice to America's diverse folk, lore, and regions.[7]

The seeds of ideas that Botkin would develop as he became more politically involved are planted in this manifesto. His position that lore and literature were one before "the invention of writing and printing, the stratification of society, and the growth of modern individualism, sophistication and 'private property,'" echoes a central theme in the work of folklorists, at least from the time of the romantics, if not earlier. Note, however, that he makes "private property" part of the list of the sources that have alienated human beings from the wellsprings of communal fellowship and creativity. And despite a large consensus among his predecessors and contemporaries in folklore studies that lore could not be created under modern conditions, he was interested in showing that folk creativity could flourish in the present. Like many folklorists, he saw folklore as modern society's "other," but he did not see modernity as folklore's nemesis. Orthodox folklorists looked for that other in remnants of the past that resided and survived yet among the rural folk. Botkin, however, saw "folklore in the making," as he later called it, which was a byproduct of modernity. It was emerging within the new spaces and the conflicts that a bureaucratic, urbanizing, and industrializing society created in the present and would create in the future.[8]

Like one strand of romantics, who M. H. Abrams analyzed in his classic study of romanticism, Botkin saw "the fall [modernity] as a fortunate self-division, because it was the necessary first step upon the educational journey by which thinking and striving man works his way back toward his long integrity, along a road which looks like a reversion, but is in fact a progression." Unlike a larger number of romantic thinkers and artists and among the many folklorists deeply influenced by romanticism, he did not stop with ruing, as Abrams puts it, "man's departure from the ignorance and self-unity into the multiple self-divisions and conflicts attendant upon the emergence of self-consciousness." His manifesto had a place for not only the self consciousness of intellectuals like himself, but also for ordinary folk, who, he maintained, were not always the spontaneous, natural, un-self-conscious bearers of traditions, as so much folklore scholarship deeply influenced by romanticism had assumed as foundational.[9]

Roughly forty years before folklorists began to give the issue some attention, Botkin theorized about the relationship between high culture, modern forms of popular culture, and unwritten tradition. He claimed not only that there is downward transmission, but that there is also movement from the bottom up. In his view, they "play back and forth." Unlike most folklorists and many regionalists who wanted to find a pure, untouched and isolated folk and to avoid dealing with what they thought of as contamination caused by the interaction of the folk and lore with modernity and with high and popular culture, Botkin asked scholars to analyze this interaction and encouraged regionalist writers to facilitate it by forging "culture literature which, brooding over folk materials and motifs, rehandles and recreates them." In the modern United States, he maintained, writers could aid in bringing folk regional traditions into the public space of democratic middle-class culture.[10]

But from the beginning he was interested in *difference* as well as unity. There are, he argued in his manifesto, "not one folk but many folk-groups— as many as there are regional cultures or racial and occupational groups within a region." His emphasis on diversity within a region separated him from many, but not all, of his fellow regionalists. Leftist regionalists like Botkin paid attention to diversity and class conflict within a region. The very title *Folk-Say: A Regional Miscellany* (an annual compilation he published 1929–32), with its emphasis on the present as well as the past, with its use of a new term for folklore, or at least a supplement to it, further separated him from many folklorists. Botkin was already taking a position where he observed the regionalist movements from within and without. Although he considered himself a southwestern regionalist, he sketched in his manifesto regionalist developments in every part of the nation. Nor did he ignore the New Negro Renaissance.[11]

His interest in a regionalism and folklore of the present did not mean a rejection of the past—far from it. He made a deliberate link between the English Romantic movement and the new regionalism. But history, for him, was not a search for still-surviving traditions that were dying out and therefore needed to be studied before it was too late. Instead, having a sense of history and tradition meant "realizing that only in the light of the past can one understand one's environment." He maintained that Americans of his era had "a genuine need of taking root, of finding solidarity and unity in identifying oneself and the community, a need growing out of the world unrest and conflict during and since the [World] War." He argued for a regionalism "seeking to unite the streams of written and unwritten tradition, of academic and folk culture," explaining that "by setting the scholar and the artist at work upon oral tradition it is creating a general myth and fable, and by setting the myth-making instinct at work upon actual characters it is creating an American epic and saga." Note how he wants academic and ordinary people, scholars and artists, to work together and not to put up No Trespassing signs—to treat boundaries as fluid and to not view crossing them as transgressions.[12]

From this early manifesto onward Botkin did not see a region as existing outside history, something Robert Dainotto has recently claimed that all regionalists do. If Dainotto had gained a deeper sense of the history of regionalist thought, he would recognize that Botkin and other leftist regionalists of the 1930s did not "naturalize a process of historical formation . . . to negate the historical forces, struggles, and tensions, that made a culture what it is." Nor did Botkin see regionalism as inherently a vision of "idyllic regions and perfect communities." In fact he allowed for conflict, declaring, for example, that "ours is an age of taking root and of the resulting conflict and compromise, within a locality, of varied racial stocks and varying orders of civilization." And although Dainotto thinks that coupling Marxism and regionalism is "an untenable project," Botkin's work increasingly showed the influence of Marx on his thinking.[13]

Botkin's immersion in Oklahoma culture and the regionalist movement began with his study of the American play-party—a form of adult social recreation that combined song and movement, and that by rarely using musical instruments and not engaging in sustained partnered dancing avoided fundamentalist religious objections. University of Nebraska folklorist Louise Pound directed Botkin's dissertation on the play-party. His field work in this area led him to reconsider the issue of the meaning of folk and lore and to reformulate the issues of creativity at the heart of ballad studies. He developed a fresh understanding of the connection between place and folk, the individual and the group, the region in its relationships to other regions, the provincial and the cosmopolitan, the local and the universal. Drawing also on modern social science as an aid, he reformulated answers to these issues in terms that focused on folklore *and* regionalism and that were both academic and activist.

By the middle of the Depression decade he had begun revising and further intertwining a folklore and regionalist theory in ways that took into account his deepening knowledge of social science and ballad theory and spoke to regional, national, and international issues of the day. In all of this his desire to promote a literary and cultural revival remained central. And while he compared the regionalist revival of his day to the poets of the English Romantic revival, unlike them he looked as much or more to the present and the future than to the past.

• • •

Shortly after his arrival in Oklahoma, in 1921, Botkin mentioned being taken with the "picturesqueness of the local scene, character, speech, custom, and the possibilities of Oklahoma as literary material." He quickly determined that he favored the "local homespun school" of writers over "the harlequin school of sophisticated lyrists." He encouraged Oklahoma writers to consider "Oklahoma backgrounds and materials." As a poet, he wanted to help in "restoring the oral popular tradition to poetry." He participated in the poetry and ballad revival centered at the University of Oklahoma campus. The iconoclastic critic H. L. Mencken wrote glowingly about the literary revival in Oklahoma, and he and Botkin worked on showcasing a collection of Oklahoma poets in Mencken's famous literary magazine *American Mercury*.[14]

Seemingly the pieces for a regional literary revival in Oklahoma and the Southwest were falling into place in the 1920s. William Bennett Bizzell became the university's president in 1925 and encouraged regionalist activities there. Botkin became president of the Oklahoma State Folklore Society in 1924 and of the Oklahoma Authors' League in 1927. Regarding the latter, he could not resist writing his in-laws: "and that's not too bad for a Jew, is it?" The arrival of Joseph Brandt in 1928 to direct the newly established University of Oklahoma Press soon led to the publication of Botkin's *Folk-Say: A Regional Anthology* (1929). Brandt and Botkin became fast friends. But as Botkin, Brandt, and others would later discover, Bizzell could support their activities only as long as they did not speak to and become part of present-day controversies.[15]

Beginning with his early studies of the play-party, an offshoot of the ballad tradition, Botkin made it clear that he was interested in "hybrid, eclectic" folklore forms and the role of conflict as well as consensus in the creation of lore and regional culture. What excited him about the play-party was the importance of these materials as a source for historical study and a stimulus to creative regional writing: "Interest in folk-lore has always been attended by exploitation in literature. So it was in the Romantic Movement, and so it has been in the new movement in poetry in this country—a movement concurrent with the revival of American folk-song and the birth of the blues." Botkin self-consciously tried to promote a literary revival. He examined the present as much as the past. The regional and nationalist implications of his project stressed heterogeneity, not homogeneity. The national treasure, the cultural and literary foundation of the customs and ways that could bind a diverse American people together, would not consist exclusively of an accumulation of items from some distant past, long, very long, before modernity, a time that did not exist in the United States. Beginning with his *Folk-Say* anthologies, Botkin made himself and other writers aware of the way cultural expression flowed back and forth between lore, popular culture, and high culture.[16]

Botkin's regionalist work is about new beginnings, not origins. Beginnings give us a fascination with difference, with sudden moments of change. The search for origins gives us warrants, ratifications for honoring that which is old, or claims to be old. The conservative nationalistic implications of the latter have been well explored by folklorist Roger Abrahams. It is possible to see just how radical Botkin's approach is by contrasting it with what Abrahams describes as an all-pervasive conservative nationalist tradition from at least the time of the Romantics. Abrahams connects folklorists' concern with the mystery and power of the very old, dislocated remnants of the past with a nostalgic sense of loss, which they sought to overcome by fetishizing the remnants of the past. Botkin saw instead a mystery and power in the folklore of the present, which he thought could help create a better, more egalitarian future.[17]

As Abrahams notes, there are "manifest ironies" in sentimentalizing ways of life that are disappearing. If Botkin sentimentalized anything, however, it was the emergence of new classes, of a proletariat, and, even more, of the lore of those making the transition from an older agrarian to a newer industrial way of life, and of oppressed groups' struggling to be recognized as equal citizens by their fellow Americans. He was not concerned with sentimentalizing a past that was gone but with studying and celebrating the lore of ordinary people created in the struggles of the present. He saw not "ruins in the landscape" but people in transition creating a new, often industrial lore of the present and future. For him, the shore behind the horizon was not some distant past but the future.[18]

• • •

It was no coincidence, then, that both Botkin's article on the Oklahoma play-party and the first volume of the annual *Folk-Say* appeared in the same year, 1929. Each called for a revival of regional literature tied to Botkin's broadening concept of folklore. The first *Folk-Say* and the three that followed until publication ceased in 1932 comprised Botkin's response to his own call for a new regional literature. Looking back at mid-decade, he judged it only a limited success. Most of the material for the first volume came from Oklahoma; only about one-third of the book was devoted to literary material that, according to Botkin, "did not even pretend to great literary merit." He concluded, "Although I tried to emphasize the contemporary aspects of folklore by including 'lore in the making' and by demonstrating the interplay between folk and popular influences, the emphasis seemed to fall on the primitive and the past. *Folk-Say* was still in the stage of collection and comment, rather than of interpretation, and still in the 'sentimental and anachronistic' stage." He was, however, too harsh in his self-assessment. His manifesto, which opened the first volume, provided a theory and overview of the movement. It contributed to his growing contacts with regionalists throughout the nation.[19]

Botkin took responses to the first volume of *Folk-Say* seriously, and none more so than that of Carey McWilliams in his chapbook *The New Regionalism in American Literature* (1930). McWilliams placed Botkin at the center of the movement: "It is seldom that a contemporary movement is fortified by a complete exegesis. But 'the New Regionalism' has found an able spokesman in B. A. Botkin who, in his introduction to *Folk-Say: A Regional Miscellany*, outlines the philosophy of the movement with commendable precision." Given the onset of the Great Depression, McWilliams was impatient with regionalists in general and some of the content of *Folk-Say* in particular: "In times so strenuous as ours, it is rather annoying to discover intelligent men devoting their talents to such tasks as listing the animals and plants in Oklahoma folk-cures and noting, with infantile delight, the eroticisms in the folk speech of taxi-drivers." He failed to notice that while examining home remedies constituted a study of a dying tradition, recognizing the folk speech in the language of users of modern technology was just the opposite.[20]

For McWilliams, Botkin's manifesto and the regionalist movement were fundamentally flawed. He found Botkin's efforts to distinguish the New Regionalism from the older, local-color movement unconvincing. Botkin, McWilliams claimed, was asking the "modern mind" to "will to be naïve"—which was impossible, for writers were a product of their time and were not savages or even semi-savages, or part of the folk. He found in the New Regionalism "the modern tendency . . . to escape from the tumultuous present into the glamorous present." Regionalism, he argued, was hopelessly provincial: "The futility of reconciling, let alone incorporating, a yearly batch of cast-off and internecine traditions, which have no relevancy to problems other than the particular problems that brought them into being, has bred a reactionary mood. Regionalism voices this feeling in its effort to check the influx of foreign influences." The focus on the unique qualities of a region invites endless unmoving "rhapsody."[21]

Botkin so respected McWilliams's critique that he made the book assigned reading in his classes and wrote for himself pages of response to it. Later the two men came to see each other as friends and allies working together in a regionalist movement of art and reform.[22] It was not so much that Botkin changed his mind as that McWilliams helped him clarify and develop his thinking: "At least the movement is here; there is something concrete, something to go on. We have discussion, we have criticism. Maybe out of the folk of the past and the present, out of the tradition of the past and present, we shall forge a folk and a tradition for the future." He acknowledged that much of folklore was anachronistic, "but out of it," he wrote, "must come the symbolism and imagery, the new mythology of the future." This he thought would replace what McWilliams had referred to as "the galvanized determination" of writers to rhapsodize over their region's novelty. "Moreover," Botkin noted, McWilliams seemed unaware that "there is the folklore of the present—in our industrial life, in our cities."[23]

Botkin thought the 1930 volume of *Folk-Say* might have answered "some of [McWilliams's] questions." Regarding the will to be naive, Botkin pointed out he had anticipated McWilliams's question when he himself had asked, in the introduction to *Folk-Say* (1930), "to what extent can the individual artist lose his self-consciousness in order to merge his individuality with that of the group?" Botkin stated that "I did not mean to imply that literature should be folklore, but I did mean that folklore is literature." He then took a step that he had not yet spelled out in print: "Unwritten or folk literature is just as self-conscious and artistic as culture literature." Here he broke with the Romantic tradition's emphasis on the unconscious, the spontaneous, the natural. McWilliams, however, although he rejected the Romantic tradition, had also imbibed many of its basic assumptions: "[McWilliams] still thinks of folk-lore or folk-lit [sic] as a group creation, its material belongs to the group and it is inherited by the group." Botkin found that as with so many Romantic theories of folklore, McWilliams did not allow for the existence of a creative individual in the folk group or in the process of creating folk-lore. "The suspension of disbelief that legend requires," he indicated in a note, "is not restricted to the semi-savage artist: it is also found in the civilized poet. For the poet then to put himself in the place of the folk-artist requires no violent effort but simply a willing suspension of disbelief."[24]

In the same introductory essay (*Folk-Say*, 1930) Botkin also responded to all "who called for a redefinition of the 'whole question of what is folklore?'" He made it clear that he wanted to reopen discussion and was willing to include in this forum views he disagreed with as well as those with which he agreed. Some contributors thought that "we are in danger of losing the folk in America" because of mass education and that "folklore is inseparable from 'noble illiteracy.'" Botkin also opened the subject to a consideration of the relationship between folklore and popular media. Aware that he was using "folk" and "lore" in ways that stretched their traditional meaning, he opined that "perhaps they alone have themselves to blame, who in the past insisted too narrowly on the letter of the meaning." He continued to play with the idea that "if the terms no longer conform to the facts, why not change the terms or drop them altogether?" But as always, "the actual conditions and problems facing the artist in America" remained a central concern. He reiterated his commitment to embracing and celebrating American diversity: "And whether we have not yet developed a folk or whether we are fast losing it, is it not more important to recognize that we have in America a variety of folk groups, representing different racial, regional, and even industrial cultures; that this very variety, while it may stand in the way of the synthesis beloved by the scholar, constitutes the strength and richness of American lore?"[25]

The last two volumes of *Folk-Say* emphasized short stories that drew upon the materials of contemporary lore and life. When a public outcry in Oklahoma was raised against *Folk-Say IV: The Land Is Ours* (1932), for its increased attention to class, gender, racial conflict, and aspects of human sexuality, officials at the university bowed to the pressure. President Bizzell ordered the volume withdrawn from sales because "it violated the canons of good taste." The combination of charges of radicalism and prurient writing were particularly explosive and made the book seem especially subversive to some Oklahomans. Botkin himself was outraged at the outrage of various officials who had been offended by the book. Those who thought the book "dangerous," he pointed out, noted "that it calls attention to the fact that some of our farm laborers are communists." Individuals unwilling to acknowledge "that among the poor whites of the South religion is mixed up with sex," he said, had labeled the book "sacrilegious."[26] He lamented how genteel Oklahomans did not want *Folk-Say* to disturb their comfortable denial that sex and religion were often interrelated forces in human thought and behavior. Those who regarded folklore as quaint and cute had found *Folk-Say IV* a rude awakening. The volume is an explicit reminder that Botkin's radical folk regionalism was part of the literary and social currents that made sex and class major touchstones in writing of the interwar era. Those who wanted to keep folklore in a nice, safe compartment would find no support from him: he saw lore as intertwined with every fundamental aspect of life.

Folk-Say had provided a forum that in defying the realities of the literary marketplace had hoped to contribute to the growth of the regionalist movement. It existed outside the New York commercial publishing industry and outside the tastes that regionalists believed the industry was catering to and imposing on the nation. Literary historian Douglas Wixson maintains in his biography of Jack Conroy that *Folk-Say* provided one of the reasons in the early 1930s that "there was hope that the experience of migratory workers, the dispossessed, the assembly line stiffs, mill workers, and farmhands might serve to reintegrate culture into everyday life." Wixson also argues that because of such efforts as *Folk-Say*, Conroy's *Rebel Poet* and *Anvil* magazines featuring radical writers, John T. Frederick's more conservative magazine *Midland*, the fiction and anthropology of Zora Neale Hurston, and the popular scholarship of Constance Rourke, a fresh vernacular sense of American culture, rooted in folklore, folk music, and humor, emerged before the arrival of the Popular Front. Putting it more succinctly and poignantly, Conroy wrote to Botkin: "And, of course, the suspension of *Folk-Say* was a major tragedy for literature. Isn't there any hope of reviving it?"[27]

Although Botkin saw no way of continuing *Folk-Say* in the immediate future, he tried to influence the direction of the regionalist movement in other ways. For one thing, he worked to give the movement a critical history that he hoped would shape its future. In his essay "We Talk about Regionalism—North, East, South, and South" (1933) he sought to provide the movement with a typology of its differences and his critical assessments of the strengths and weaknesses of various approaches, for as he declared in the first sentence, "Regionalism is an inclusive term for a variety of movements to relate the artist to his region." He identified four types of regionalists: the "localist," identified with the Northwest, who was empiric in approach; "the naturist," found primarily in the Southwest, who contemplated the environment and the indigenous culture as a path to the mystical and cosmic; the "traditionalist," largely in the South, who stressed viewing the past as a source of symbols and values that could guide life in the region; and the "culturist," living mostly in the metropolitan and cosmopolitan Northeast, "who like Lewis Mumford, is the social cosmopolitan regionalist, combining and transcending other approaches, interested in shaping life as well as literature to the needs of interrelated regions," with their emerging urban hubs.[28] Botkin held that "the future of regionalism" would depend on the culturists' ability to build a synthesis that both drew on and transcended the other three regionalist approaches. It is clear that he identified most strongly with Mumford's approach. For Botkin, Mumford seemed to state "the newness of the 'new regionalism'" when he argued that "all that is legitimate in folklore, historical curiosity, and regional pride will thrive best when they are taken, not as escapes from contemporary fact, but as contributions to living culture."[29]

In this essay Botkin also sounded a radical political note more clearly than ever before. He conceded that "it is important to draw the line between originality and decadence," as some northwestern regionalists had argued; but he did not stop there: "it is also important to distinguish between literature that reveals a decadent society and literature that glosses it over." Not surprisingly, he draws on Emerson in moving the discourse farther left: like Whitman, Emerson had looked to the democracy of the future as an ideal unfolding in the present. Echoing Emerson's radical individualism and cultural nationalism, Botkin asserts that "a regionalist may thus feel himself at the end of a tradition as well as the beginning of one." A thoroughgoing radicalism, he continued, can involve what Emerson called "an original relation to the universe ... a poetry and philosophy of insight and not of tradition." Then comes a transition to the Great Depression and 1930s politics: "this radicalism includes those who, refusing to accept a heritage that leaves the individual in economic and cultural bondage, asks not only, 'Where did we come from?' but also 'Where do we go from here?'—who are interested not only in submerged culture but also in submerged society; who, posing the past of their regional childhood and ancient mythologies against the present of America's 'pessimism of defeat' and 'exasperation of progress' seek a way out."[30]

Two years later, in 1935, Botkin reassessed his experiences as a regionalist editor who had sought to address the issues of how regionalist writers might survive and publish in the midst of the Great Depression. After the demise of *Folk-Say*, he wrote, he had created and edited *Space* (1934–35), a little magazine devoted entirely to publishing experimental writing. It sounded both modernist and regionalist themes in its very title. As he liked to point out, *Space* was an answer to *Time* magazine. The journal was also modernist in its critique of modernity. *Space* was an extension, not a repudiation of Botkin's folklore interests, which were compatible with modernist literary experiment.

Looking back at his experience editing *Folk-Say* and *Space,* Botkin concluded that whatever the merits of the two series, they had failed to fulfill the larger goals he had envisioned and that their failure was a reflection of the larger society that he alone could not solve. The *Folk-Say* experiment in combining folk literature with literature about the folk had not found a wide audience and thus had not solved the problem of writers' relation to society, nor had it reinvigorated the culture of the larger society by reintroducing it to the diversity and richness of its regional folk traditions.[31]

Not only his experience with the demise of *Folk-Say* but also the continuing Depression led Botkin to become more pessimistic about the future of writing in his adopted state. "Oklahoma," he explained ruefully, "was settled on the run ... Oklahomans have been, are, and in my darker moments, I fear always will be on the make." He judged his attempt both to nurture an Oklahoman tradition and to import the best of outside culture to Oklahoma as having proven somewhat futile. The state, he complained, had "no standards except success" and had "more or less sold out to the Babbitts." In his view there was a clear tie between culture and economics, for "the centralization and standardization of literature is but a phase of the centralized economic structure of American business." The "fundamental issue confronting the writer everywhere today," he concluded, is "Can the artist ignore politics and economics?" He saw a universal question emerging from his provincial Oklahoma experience: "Does the real development of regionalism lead from *Folk-Say* through *Space* to the whole problem of the contemporary economic system?"[32]

By the mid-1930s Botkin was becoming better known among leftist writers. The radical Minnesota regionalist Meridel Le Sueur asked if she could reprint in her journal *Midwest* Botkin's "Regionalism: Cult or Culture?"—which had just appeared in the *English Journal*. He corresponded with *New Masses* editor Joseph Freeman, and in 1937 sent him a copy of *Folk-Say IV: The Land Is Ours,* "which is my contribution to proletarian anthologies ... I want you to have it because *Folk-Say* is nowhere mentioned in *Proletarian Literature in the United States.*" (He refers here to the landmark anthology, edited by Granville Hicks and others, that had appeared in 1935.) Malcolm Cowley, a *New Republic* editor, and author of the classic *Exiles Return*, corresponded about Botkin's poetry and his ideas regarding regionalism. "Your piece on regionalism," Cowley wrote, "interested me a great deal. I think you are on the right track." Cowley told Botkin about his plans for holding a writers' conference in New York; he wanted regionalism on the agenda: "I wanted to have somebody show that it wasn't necessarily connected with reactionary political opinions."[33]

In the summer of 1937 Botkin gave just such a paper, titled "Regionalism and Culture," before the American Writers' Congress. It marked the end of a transition for him. It was an embracing of Popular Front cultural politics, but as always in his distinctive manner. It should come as no surprise that Meridel Le Sueur was interested in Botkin's work. Both of them focused on the class-conflict dimensions of industrialization of predominantly agriculture regions and in the relationship between the exploitation of the poor and of the natural environment. Le Sueur had given a powerful and perceptive talk, "Proletarian Literature and the Middle West," at the 1935 Writers' Congress but had found the reaction disappointing; she recalled fierce attacks on regionalism by Communist Party members in response to her address. It seems that Botkin's more theoretical and social science–oriented approach to regionalism was not much more successful in 1937, with an audience of predominantly urban leftists.[34]

Regionalism, Botkin told participants at the congress, was relevant to writers on the left despite the reactionary positions some regionalists took. It was relevant as fact and as theory. He had become impatient with a southwestern regionalism that set itself in opposition to the machine age. Regarding the Southern Agrarians, he rejected the false dualism between contemplation and action, their glorification of "a private world and a static one, individualistic and aristocratic," which defines "culture as the aim of life" and identifies "culture with private or individual well-being and sensibility." At the same time, those interested in class analysis, Botkin maintained, had to recognize that "regional acceptances and resistances must be reckoned with in initiating the class struggle on any broad scale." In his view regional and proletarian writers represented complementary, not antagonistic, approaches, one focusing on the rural and the agrarian folk in transition, the other on the urban and industrial masses: "In short, there is a common ground for regional, class, and other forms of collective consciousness."[35]

The most significant regional writing, he argued, focused on "occupational and industrial trends, especially as these deal with the transition from agriculture to industry." As an inheritor of the modernist tradition, regional writing "does not simply provide source material—it can create new forms ... by drawing upon place, work, and folk for motifs, images, symbols, slogans, and idioms." Like other modernists, Botkin thought that questions about form, symbols, and idiom were crucial; however, the answers were not to be discovered by the writer-seer's unique esoteric insights but rather "by seeking a way out of the chaos of individualism by a revaluation of folk and group symbols and patterns."[36]

His defense of regionalism as literature, social science, and politics did not carry the day at the Writers' Congress. Literary historian Douglas Wixson sees the rejection of the legitimacy of a radical regionalism as a turning point in 1930s writing: "In the beginning, the possibilities seemed very fresh that a new strain of literature might evolve, deriving from orality, certain types of speech acts, folk tradition, and ordinary experience, reflecting the heterogeneity of American common life." Proletarian regionalists felt rejected by the leftist literary movement they were committed to, by fellow leftists who could only see regionalism as reactionary. They also thought that the number of leftist journals that would publish their work was shrinking. The irony, according to Wixson, was that "the United States government"—through its Federal Writers' Project (FWP) and the work of Botkin as its folklore editor—"filled a vacuum created when the left largely abandoned its sponsorship of worker-writing."[37]

News of Botkin's talk eventually reached the university in Norman, and the consequences were painful for him. President Bizzell sent him a *Saturday Review of Literature* reporter's account of the Writers' Congress paper. Bizzell underscored key passages, asked for a copy of "Regionalism and Culture," and awaited an explanation. In his written reply, Botkin denied that he advocated class struggle. He stressed instead that his scholarly analysis demonstrated that in America's various regions economic issues became more important as cultural isolation broke down. All that Botkin maintained in this letter to Bizzell about the controversial paper was true, but it was also disingenuous in the way Botkin stressed the scholarly and tried to erase the politically radical from his analysis of regionalism, when in fact it had been his purpose to use research and theory to support his leftist positions.[38]

Nothing immediately developed from this exchange. Bizzell did not interfere with the leave of absence Botkin had already received to use a Rosenwald Foundation fellowship to study southern culture at the Library of Congress. Two more leaves were granted after he became National Folklore Editor of the FWP in 1938. Nevertheless, a file had been created. It would not be long before the FBI also started a Botkin file.[39]

Botkin thought his scholarly, informed theorizing could contribute to the causes he cared about; he believed that scholarship and political advocacy could go hand in hand. Indeed, he believed that they enriched each other, although this was not the argument he thought he could make to his university's president. In Oklahoma and in the Southwest he had tried to organize chapters of the League of American Writers but found that few in Norman or Santa Fe were interested. He had already transgressed disciplinary boundaries in his efforts to rethink folklore and regionalism, academic and public boundaries in his commitment to the regionalist movement, and scholarly and creative boundaries in publishing challenging fiction at a university press, and he saw no reason not to cross the boundaries between scholarship and engagement in using whatever conceptual tools the left offered him as a scholar, a public intellectual, and a visionary.[40]

Some of Botkin's friends who were politically to the right questioned what they saw as his move leftward. Brandt, who considered himself a liberal, thought Botkin had decided that "the only way to stop fascism was to become a Communist." To writer Haniel Long's news that "John Gould [Fletcher] insists you are becoming an incendiary communist," Botkin responded both humorously and seriously: "when I returned from New York in June, I was ready to lick the world, but always there is a hole somewhere to curl up in. . . . if you and John think me an incendiary communist my incendiarism must consist of ringing false alarms." On the other hand, he wrote, "I am trying to figure things out and arrive at some consistent interpretation, if only a materialistic one." There was a lot at stake: "Anyway, there's something burning in me, and if it doesn't burn me up and out it may keep a steady (if not a hard gem-like) flame glowing in me."[41]

Later he wrote to Edward Burgum, editor of *Science and Society: A Marxian Quarterly*, about possibly publishing a conference paper, "Folklore and Culture," with Burgum rather than in the *English Journal*. In this request Botkin was both humble and assertive: "I have attempted not a Marxist interpretation so much as a transition to the Marxist interpretation

I hope to someday write." Burgum replied that he "was attracted to what the paper implies about the relationship between folk and proletarian literature," and much discussion ensued before the *English Journal* suddenly went ahead and published its copy of the paper. It was perhaps a missed moment in the history of 1930s radical regionalist literature, for although the audience for *Science and Society* was small, the quarterly had an influential following among left-wing writers that the *English Journal* did not.[42]

• • •

In January 1938 Botkin wrote to Louise Pound that he had been offered the position of National Folklore Editor for the Federal Writers' Project. He was eager to take the job and another year's leave of absence from his university position. Everyone, he wrote, seemed to be encouraging him to do it, and he was eager to follow their advice: "Since the suspension of *Folk-Say* I have always speculated on the possibility of reviving the series. Now with the facilities of the Federal Writers' Project to draw upon, there doesn't seem to be any limit to the possibilities." He took the position in the spring.[43]

Although the Living Lore units Botkin created within the FWP focused primarily on urban-industrial lore, he drew on everything he had learned in Oklahoma in advising the writers who participated. He was, however, overly optimistic about the future of the FWP. The program was greatly curtailed in the summer of 1939. Botkin then became the head of the Library of Congress Unit of the Writers' Program, as the FWP was rechristened. There too he tried to make the projects he had already undertaken into a permanent government institution, and failed. When he submitted a request for a third leave of absence from the university in Oklahoma, Bizzell cautioned him against it on practical grounds and noted he was still a controversial figure with the university's Board of Regents. Botkin had been named in a report published by the House Committee on Un-American activities as a member of the American League for Peace and Democracy, which the committee had labeled a Communist Front Organization. The university Board of Regents turned down his request for further leave and he was encouraged to resign, which he did.

In the spring of 1938 Botkin wrote to Joseph Brandt that "personally I think the regionalism movement is almost played out, and this might be a good time to take stock."[44] Botkin and his activities in Oklahoma had become a hub of regionalism, so he was in a good position to assess the movement. He had brought diverse writers into conversation with each other, and they in turn influenced his thinking by giving him a broad perspective on the nation's diverse regions. He not only contributed to the movement his own theoretical perspective on regionalism, but he understood and critiqued the theories of other regionalists. He also knew that many Americans, including many of those who attended left-wing writers' conferences, dismissed folklore as "dead or phony stuff."[45] It is not clear that he won that battle in the 1930s, or indeed that it has been won today. Botkin never completed the history of regionalism that he proposed writing, which might have helped in winning that battle. It is up to us to return him to the conversation about theorizing regionalism, then and now.

NOTES

1. B. A. Botkin, "Regionalism and Culture," in *The Writer in a Changing World*, ed. Henry Hart (New York: Equinox Cooperative Press, 1937), 140; for an overview of Botkin's life and work see Jerrold Hirsch, "Folklore in the Making, B. A. Botkin," *Journal of American Folklore* 100 (1987): 3–38; and *America's Folklorist: B. A. Botkin and American Culture*, ed. Lawrence Rodgers and Jerrold Hirsch (Norman: University of Oklahoma Press, 2010).

2. Botkin and Pound's relationship is discussed in Robert Cochran, *Louise Pound: Scholar, Athlete, Feminist* (Lincoln: University of Nebraska Press, 2009).

3. Botkin, "We Talk about Regionalism—North, East, South, and West," *Frontier* 13 (1933): 286–96.

4. Botkin to [?] Barber, September 15; to Louise Pound, October 11, 1932, Benjamin A. Botkin Papers, Benjamin Botkin Collection of Applied Folklore, University of Nebraska, Lincoln, box 56; Laurence Vesey, *The Emergence of the American University* (Chicago: University of Chicago Press, 1968), 100–113.

5. Botkin, "The Folk in Literature: The New Regionalism," in *Folk-Say: A Regional Miscellany*, ed. B. A. Botkin (Norman: Oklahoma Folklore Society; printed by the University of Oklahoma Press, 1929), 9–20; Mary Hufford, "Interrupting the Monologue: Folklore, Ethnography, and Critical Regionalism," *Journal of Appalachian Studies* 8 (2002): 62–76.

6. Marcus Klein, "The Roots of Radicals: Experience in the Thirties," in *Proletarian Writers of the Thirties*, ed. David Madden (Carbondale: Southern Illinois University Press, 1968), 137; Barbara Foley, *Radical Representations :Politics and Form in U.S. Proletarian Fiction, 1929-1941* (Durham, N.C.: Duke University Press, 1992), 62. Botkin figures much more in Robert Dorman's excellent *Revolt from the Provinces: The Regionalist Movement in America, 1920–1945* (Chapel Hill: University of North Carolina Press, 1993), but Dorman does not fully explore the issue of folklore and regionalism.

7. Botkin, "The Folk in Literature," 9.

8. Botkin, "The Folk in Literature," 9; Botkin, "The Folkness of the Folk," *English Journal* 26 (1937): 469.

9. M. H. Abrams, *Natural Supernaturalism: Tradition and Revolution in Romantic Literature* (New York: W. W. Norton, 1971), 217.

10. Botkin, "The Folk in Literature," 10.

11. Botkin, "The Folk in Liteature," 10, 18–20.

12. Botkin, "The Folk in Literature," 14.

13. Roberto M. Dainotto, *Place in Literature: Region, Cultures, Communities* (Ithaca: Cornell University Press, 2000), 2, 30, 27; Botkin, "The Folk in Literature," 10. In general the renewed interest in regionalism has focused more on local-color writers than the interwar regionalists. In *American Literary Regionalism in a Global Age* (Baton Rouge: Louisiana State University Press, 2007) Philip Joseph argues for the point of his title but treats Mary Austin as the sole example of interwar regionalism, in a very short chapter. Even as smart a book as Carrie Tirado Bramen's *Uses of Variety: Modern Americanism and the Quest for National Distinctiveness* (Cambridge: Harvard University Press, 2002) refers to local-color writers as regionalists but totally ignores interwar regionalists.

14. Botkin, "*Folk-Say* and *Space*: Their Genesis and Their Exodus," *Southwest Review* 20 (1935): 323, 324; Botkin, "The 'Oklahoma Manner' in Poetry," *University of Oklahoma Magazine* 14 (1925): 22; H. L. Mencken, "Oklahoma Poets," *American Mercury* 8 (May 1926): 14–17; Lawrence Rodgers, "'In the Beginning Lore and Literature Were One': B. A. Botkin's Literary Legacy," in Rodgers and Hirsch, *America's Folklorist*, 21–34.

15. Botkin to his in-laws, April 24, 1927, Botkin papers box 36. On the university's tolerance of regionalist activities see Richard Lowitt, "Regionalism at the University of Oklahoma," *Chronicles of Oklahoma* 17 (1995): 150–71.

16. Botkin," The Play-Party in Oklahoma," in *Follow de Drinkin' Gou'd*, Publications of the Texas Folk-Lore Society, No. VII, ed. J. Frank Dobie (Austin: The Texas Folklore Society, 1929), 9.

17. Roger D. Abrahams, "Phantoms of Romantic Nationalism in Folkloristics," *Journal of American Folklore* 106 (1993): 3.

18. Abrahams, "Phantoms of Romantic Nationalism," 4, 12, 16.

19. Botkin, "*Folk-Say* and *Space*," 325.

20. Carey McWilliams, *The New Regionalism in American Literature* (Seattle: University of Washington Book Store 1930), 15, 23; Botkin, "On Reading *The New Regionalism* in American Literature," January 5, 1931, Botkin papers, box 234.

21. McWilliams, *The New Regionalism*, 21, 23, 31, 34.

22. See, e.g., Botkin to McWilliams, July 12, 1932, Botkin papers, box 56.

23. Botkin, "On Reading *The New Regionalism*," 1.

24. Botkin, "On Reading *The New Regionalism*," 1, 2–3.

25. Botkin, "Introduction," in *Folk-Say: A Regional Miscellany*, 15–18.

26. Botkin to Haniel Long, November 17, 1932, marked not sent, Botkin papers, unidentified box. Richard Lowitt, "Regionalism at the University of Oklahoma,"164–65.

27. Douglas Wixson, *Worker-Writer in America: Jack Conroy and the Tradition of Midwestern Literary Radicalism* (Urbana: University of Illinois Press, 1994),418, 421; Conroy to Botkin, September 23, 1937, Botkin papers, box 59.

28. Botkin, "We Talk about Regionalism," 286.

29. Botkin to Harry Moore, April 23, 1936, Botkin papers, box 56; Botkin, "We Talk about Regionalism," 286–90, 293–95.

30. Botkin, "We Talk about Regionalism," 289.

31. Botkin, "*Folk-Say* and *Space*," 333.
32. Botkin, "*Folk-Say* and *Space*," 333, 335.
33. Telegram, Meridel Le Sueur to Botkin, September 12, 1936; Botkin to Freeman, July 19, 1937, Botkin papers, box 59; Cowley to Botkin, May29, 1936, box 58. See also *Proletarian Literature in the United States: An Anthology*, edited by Granville Hicks, Joseph North, Paul Peters, Isidor Schneider and Alan Calmer, with a critical introduction by Joseph Freeman (New York: International, 1935).
34. Meridel Le Sueur, "Proletarian Literature and the Middle West," in *American Writers' Congress*, ed. Henry Hart (New York: International, 1935), 135–38.
35. Botkin, "Regionalism and Culture," 147–52.
36. Botkin "Regionalism and Culture," 156–57; Jerrold Hirsch, "T. S. Eliot, B. A. Botkin, and the Politics of Cultural Representation: Folklore, Ethnicity, and Pluralism." in *Race and the Modern Artist*, ed. Jacob Jarab et al. (New York: Oxford University Press, 2003), 16–41.
37. Wixson, *Worker-Writer in America*, 418, 421.
38. Botkin to Bizzell, June 21, 1936, Botkin papers, box 59.
39. Lowitt, "Regionalism at the University of Oklahoma," 165–68; The Botkin file is in Bizzell/University Press Folders, Western History Collections, University of Oklahoma, Norman; to see these files requires securing permission from the archive. See also Susan G. Davis, "Ben Botkin's FBI File," *Journal of American Folklore* 122 (2010): 3–30.
40. Botkin to Ray [?], July 7; Ray to Botkin, July 12, 1937; "Report on the Second American Writers' Conference . . . ," draft for the executive committee of the Southwest Writers' Conference, Botkin papers, box 59.
41. Fletcher and Gould as quoted in Lowitt, "Regionalism at the University of Oklahoma"; Haniel Long to Botkin, November 26; Botkin to Haniel Long, December 22, 1937, Botkin papers, box 59. The "hard, gem-like flame" is an allusion to a famous passage from Walter Pater's *Renaissance* (1883), on the mind's engagement with beauty and creativity.
42. Botkin to Edwin Burgum, December 1937, Botkin papers, box 59.
43. Botkin to Louise Pound, January 13, 1938, Botkin papers, box 59. For an analysis of Botkin's role on the FWP see Jerrold Hirsch, *Portrait of America: A Cultural History of the Federal Writers' Project* (Chapel Hill: University of North Carolina Press, 2009).
44. Botkin to Joseph Brandt, March 1, 1938, Botkin papers, box 59.
45. Botkin, "WPA and Folklore Research: 'Bread and Song,'" *Southern Folklore Quarterly* 3 (1939): 14.

CHAPTER SEVEN

Discover the Truth and Publish It

ANGIE ELBERTHA DEBO AND THE ROOTS

OF AMERICA'S "REAL IMPERIALISM"

Shirley A. Leckie Reed

Angie Elbertha Debo (1890–1988) centered her study of history on Oklahoma and its peoples, especially its American Indians and their collision with the non-Indians among them. As a regional writer she viewed U.S. Indian policy as America's "real imperialism" and was convinced by the 1940s that until her fellow citizens understood the tragic history of their interaction with Native peoples, their ability to relate wisely to the new nations that would emerge from colonialism would have no sound foundation. From her beginning as a proud daughter of struggling sodbusters of the southern frontier of the Great Plains to her emergence as a courageous critic and voice of protest in the 1930s and 1940s, she embodied many of the best qualities of progressive regionalism and became, by the end of her long and productive life, one of America's most cosmopolitan yet regionally rooted historians. Debo may have lived most of her life in the small and vanishing town of Marshall, Oklahoma, yet she was, despite the Oklahoma cadences of her speech, one of America's most far-thinking intellectuals, who wrote regional history as United States history writ large and lived her last decades as a true citizen of the globe.

As with all children in all families and cultures, Angie's view of the world began with an origin myth—in this instance, the myth of indomitably enduring ancestors. It was a good myth to build a life on, because it contained a kernel of solid and inspiring truth; still, like all myths, it was partial, for it evaded other truths and was heavily idealized. In November 1899, when the Debo family arrived in Marshall, then in Oklahoma

Angie Debo. Courtesy of the Angie Debo Collection, Oklahoma State University.

Territory, nine-year-old Angie and her eight-year-old brother, Edwin, listened to their parents' accounts of family history as the children helped them farm and in the evenings assisted them in repairing and expanding their one-room shack. Their father, Edward, explained that the Debo family, originally from France, had arrived in the United States from Prussia, where it had relocated during the Napoleonic wars. After those wars, the Debos had felt increasingly unwelcome in Prussia, and a later generation moved to the United States in 1854, becoming engaged in farming in the Midwest and in Wyoming Territory—unfortunately, with little success.[1]

Lina Cooper Debo's story began with her father, Alfred Cooper, and his trek to California in 1859. Returning home thinner and poorer, he moved his family to northeastern Iowa and, finding no prosperity here, took them in 1879 to Rooks County in western Kansas. There Lina, as the second of seven children and the oldest daughter, helped erect their sod house. Her family soon encountered drought and insects that "seemed to drop out of the Kansas sky." To help with the family's finances, Lina left school at fourteen and by "working out" (that is, out in the community, not at home) assisted mothers of newborns with their housework for fifty cents a day. In 1883, during a "starving time," Alfred Cooper moved his family to Beattie, Kansas. There Lina later met and married the "cyclone [corn] shucker" in the community, Edward Debo. She gave birth to Angie in 1890 and to Edwin the next year. When the Debos, tenant farmers, managed to earn enough to buy railroad land and then sell it at a profit in 1898, they moved to Oklahoma. For both parents, pride in the pioneering perseverance among their forebears represented their primary bequest to their own children, growing up in Oklahoma.[2]

Edward and Lina also shared with Angie and Edwin their deep love for the land. Debo's most vivid recollection of her father involved the day that she had watched him transplant trees from the near creek in back of their house into the front yard. As he rocked the roots gently into place, he seemed to be tucking them into bed.[3] Angie also remembered the day several months after the first planting of winter wheat, when she and her mother took their wagon to see the ripening fields. That day, when "the sky was blue the way Oklahoma skies can be," Lina showed rare emotion. "When I look out on the country like this, the tears come to my eyes," she confided to her daughter. "I don't know why." Angie understood, for the surrounding beauty and fertility moved her in the same way.[4] This attachment to the land that her parents instilled within her inspired her, in 1947—when she had moved beyond seeing only cause for celebration in the opening of new land—to lament the loss of Oklahoma's topsoil. As the last area opened to non-Indian settlement, Oklahoma represented a process at work: "To establish a family on the land, to build a new society—this was the American ideal." "Unfortunately," she added, "slashing the timber, destroying the grass, mining the soil—this was noble, too; this was a part of the process as well."[5]

By 1913 Edward Debo had sold his farm and opened and closed an unsuccessful hardware store in downtown Marshall. The family that bought the Debo farm, however, located oil on the property. Angie recalled that her father never expressed regret over selling the land. Instead, whenever he passed the site, he remembered their family's good times in their old homestead, thereby teaching Angie what the old timers meant when they spoke of the "spirit of Oklahoma."[6] Angie's mother added her voice to this lesson by instructing her daughter to meet life's inevitable hardships with equanimity and courage. One demonstrated concern for suffering, but one never dramatized tragedy or willingly played the victim's role.[7] True Oklahomans, both parents agreed, met bad luck with outward humor and grace, for frustrations and setbacks were best encountered with cheerful stoicism. In years to come, Angie would encounter many frustrations and setbacks; but, in the spirit of Oklahoma, she would for the most part sublimate these disappointments by finding refuge in creative work.

Those setbacks began early, for while Angie loved Oklahoma, she also loved school. When she finished ninth grade, in 1906, further high school classes in Marshall were nonexistent. After spending four years teaching in Logan and Garfield counties' one-room schoolhouses, she entered the newly built high school in 1910 and graduated among the first alumni, in 1913.[8] With her high school diploma, she resumed teaching for another two years, before entering the University of Oklahoma.

There she encountered Edward Everett Dale, the tall, slim, "unprofessorial figure," so different from other teachers, when he strode into the classroom with his "cowboy walk, his soft voice, and his alert far-seeing eyes."[9] His Harvard thesis adviser, Frederick Jackson Turner, had introduced him to "a new heaven and earth in the field of American History," and Dale wanted to inspire the same enthusiasm in his own students, the offspring of pioneering families.[10] Oklahoma, Dale taught them, had provided the setting for the last act of an amazing drama. The Five Civilized Tribes—Creek, Choctaw, Chickasaw, Cherokee, and Seminole—the state's original pioneers, had entered the eastern portion of Oklahoma, then known as Indian Territory, in waves of settlement during the first half of the nineteenth century. They brought with them their diplomatic skills, honed from earlier dealings with European powers and their later, although tragically unsuccessful, resistance to removal from their traditional lands. In their new homeland, they continued their struggles with an encircling EuroAmerican population. When Oklahoma became a state, although Indians numbered only 6 percent of the population, they supplied, Dale estimated, 20 percent to 25 percent of its most notable leaders.[11]

Their neighbors were traders, military men, cattlemen, and farming families, sweeping westward in successive waves across the newly opened Indian territories and seeking opportunities unavailable in older, settled regions, who created a boom in population for the future state of Oklahoma. Dale claimed that as each of these waves "revert[ed] to primitive conditions," the region's society rebuilt itself anew: owing less each time to European influences, Oklahoma became the most American of all areas. Dale was building here on his mentor's ideas, as expressed in Turner's "Significance of the Frontier in American History," an address to the American Historical Association at the Columbian Exposition in Chicago in 1893.[12]

When non-Indian settlers joined the Native peoples in Indian Territory, they created a unique state that encapsulated the entire history of the larger United States.[13] Having "grown up on the prairies" of Oklahoma Territory, Dale told his students, he had "observed its change from the frontier of the hunter to that of the cowboy, the pioneer settler, and the prosperous farmer, and had witnessed the coming of towns and cities and all the complex organizations of commercial and industrial life."[14] Thus history was not only about the elite; it was what he and other common folk had lived through. Most amazing of all, this former cowboy, with few financial resources, had earned a bachelor's from the University of Oklahoma, and then had earned his master's from Harvard University. For Debo, Dale seemed a kindred soul who had overcome barriers she now faced. Following in his footsteps, she decided, she would become a history professor someday.[15]

As she ended her freshman year in college, Angie was elated at the possibilities before her and wrote to Lina, confiding ambition to make her mother's life easier once her own dreams became fully realized. Earlier, Lina had "been chained down on that old farm and nothing could be done to make that nightmare tolerable." But, Angie vowed that, once armed with degrees, she would give her mother a life of ease and pleasure that included "a diamond ring [for] every finger and thumb," constant movie going, and frequent travels abroad.[16]

After graduating from college, Angie taught in western Oklahoma's public schools and served as principal in one, as she saved to enter the University of Chicago. The 1920 Republican victory and the United States' failure to ratify the Treaty of Versailles with its League of Nations meant that her country had reverted to its earlier stance of isolationism, as before World War I. She wanted to understand why these events had occurred. With that ambition, she entered the University of Chicago in fall 1923 and enrolled in the curriculum for international relations.[17] Faced with a dearth of male students in the aftermath of the war, graduate schools welcomed women more readily than before, and female students now constituted about 40 percent of those working toward advanced degrees.[18]

At Chicago, majoring in history and minoring in political science, Debo wrote her master's thesis under James Fred Rippy, an expert on the United States and Latin America and on the role of the Americas in world history. She quickly discovered that isolationism did not originate in 1793 with George Washington's Proclamation of Neutrality following the outbreak of war between France and England, as was then commonly believed. Even before the thirteen colonies had declared their independence, isolationism had been a firmly established principl among American leaders.[19]

In the earlier decades of the twentieth century a master's degree opened the door to teaching in higher education at most colleges and universities, whereas a doctorate remained the credential for researchers at prestige-seeking institutions that offered graduate programs. As June 1924 approached, Debo searched for a faculty appointment at a college or university. Unfortunately, twenty-nine of the thirty institutions that contacted Chicago entirely ruled out employing a woman, and the sole exception would do so only if a qualified man were unavailable. Although Debo knew that women faced prejudice, she had grown up when opportunities in college teaching had been relatively plentiful for her sex. At the turn of the century, openings for women in higher education had outpaced those in medicine and law, largely because of the earlier expansion of women's colleges and teacher training schools.[20]

Beneath the surface, however, trends were working against women in higher education. Although the growth of female institutions of higher learning had given women 36 percent of the positions at colleges and universities in the 1880s, that ratio had declined to 20 percent between 1890 and 1910 as many exclusively female institutions, seeking more renown, began hiring male teachers. The modern university of Debo's time, including elite women's colleges, increasingly stressed graduate training through seminars and the scholarly productivity of a faculty that would expand fields of knowledge rather than simply present its most current findings to students.[21] Women, whose ultimate destiny was seen as marriage and motherhood, were viewed as less capable of conducting the sustained research that would enhance the reputation of a university or college department.

When Debo returned to Marshall, she contacted teacher training colleges, which led her to two with openings.[22] She selected West Texas State Teachers College (founded 1910), in the town of Canyon. Enrollment totaled about 2,000 students, the offspring of pioneering ranchers, much like those Debo had encountered while attending the University of Oklahoma.[23] She hoped to instill in them the same appreciation for their families' historic role in the non-Indian settlement of the West that Dale had inspired in his students. When she arrived at the Canyon campus, however, the chair of the department, Lester Fields Sheffy, assigned her as assistant professor to the Demonstration School attached to the college, a unit devoted to teaching education majors how to approach various subjects. Debo stayed there from 1924 through the 1929–30 school year, with no promotion or change, as other professors were hired, spent time in the Demonstration School, and then were promoted to associate professor in the department of history.[24] Eager to advance, she took a leave of absence in 1930 to obtain her doctorate at the University of Oklahoma. She studied again under Edward Everett Dale, who having earned his Harvard Ph.D. under Turner in 1922, now headed the history department. When Debo received a research fellowship, she extended her leave to two years.

Dale proved "knowledgeable, patient, and generous with compliments," and Debo was spellbound by his humorous tales, which often recounted the chicanery and corruption that non-Indian settlers had perpetrated to defraud Indians. As she examined Dale's books and articles, however, she noticed that he left out "anything that wasn't pleasant."[25] During the winter of 1930–31 she critiqued her professor in a seminar paper, "Edward Everett Dale: Historian of Progress." Such action, unusual for a graduate student, suggests her growing ambivalence regarding Dale's views on writing history. She now questioned his approach to Euro-American settlement of the West, even though her gratitude toward him never wavered. Once a student "sleeping on the prairie," she noted, he had become a world-famous scholar. Small wonder, then, that "imperialism, if he thinks of it at all, is the march of civilization across the waste places of the earth."[26] Debo was beginning to form her own scholarly identity apart from Dale.

When she lacked a dissertation topic, Dale sent her to the Phillips Collection, which Frank Phillips, an Oklahoma oilman, had donated to the university library. Within its extensive collection of primary sources on American Indians and western history, she discovered volumes containing the Acts and Resolutions of the General Council of the Choctaw Nation for various years and began researching the Choctaws' history as a separate republic in Indian Territory.[27] When she realized that her inquiries would require further archival research in Washington, D.C., Dale was able to help with letters of introduction to prominent colleagues there. He had participated in the Survey of Indian Affairs of 1926, led by Lewis Meriam, which had led to an authoritative report, *The Problem of Indian Administration*, in 1928 (soon widely known as the Meriam Report).[28] The report had uncovered extensive and pervasive poverty among Indians, which it attributed to deplorable health conditions and inadequate educational opportunities in their communities.[29] Primarily, however, the report blamed an overreliance on assimilationist policies that had emphasized Indian ownership of private property as a panacea for recovery following the destruction of tribal economies. (Dale, as a member of Meriam's team, certainly knew that Native peoples nationwide and those in Oklahoma had suffered grave losses under these assimilationist policies.) Well received, the report had already led to reforms in the federal Indian Bureau. It was in this new climate that Debo arrived in Washington with Dale's introductions in hand. She easily gained access to government documents located in the basement of the old Department of the Interior building.[30]

Debo also investigated the Choctaw files in the Office of the Superintendent of the Five Civilized Tribes, in Muskogee, Oklahoma. Here she met Grant Foreman, a lawyer who had served from 1899 to 1903 on the Commission to the Five Civilized Tribes, better known as the Dawes Commission. Foreman, having embarked on a new career as a historian, was awaiting publication of *Indian Removal: The Emigration of the Five*

Civilized Tribes of Indians, scheduled to appear as the second volume in the Civilization of the American Indian series inaugurated in 1932 by the University of Oklahoma Press, with strong support from the University's president, William Bennett Bizzell. The press had opened in 1928, and its first director, Joseph A. Brandt, a former Rhodes Scholar and one-time city editor of the *Tulsa Tribune*, had initiated the series with *Wa'Kon-tah: The Osage and the White Man's Road* (1932), by the Osage writer John Joseph Mathews. In Brandt's vision, the series would highlight the achievements of America's Indigenous peoples and their contributions to the state and nation.[31] In addition, the communalism of American Indians attracted intellectuals of the 1920s, who were dissatisfied with American individualism and materialism. Especially notable was John Collier, a former social worker from California who would become, by 1933, President Franklin Delano Roosevelt's commissioner of Indian affairs.[32] Other similar critics of American culture who welcomed serious investigations into Indian cultures included the southwestern archaeologist Edgar Lee Hewitt, the writer Mary Austin, and the patroness of writers, artists, anthropologists, and archaeologists, Mabel Dodge Luhan.

Debo soon found her topic compelling. She felt the Choctaws' sorrow when they were forced in 1830 to sign the Treaty of Dancing Rabbit Creek, giving up their southeastern homeland in the recently formed (1817) state of Mississippi. Only assurances that they would maintain "jurisdiction and government of all the persons and property that may be within their limits west" forever and that "no Territory or State" would ever be allowed "to pass laws for the government of the Choctaw Nation of Red People and their descendants" had persuaded them to exchange their home for land in Indian Territory.[33] With these guarantees the Choctaws moved westward. Initially they prospered in their new homeland by blending tribal traditions with borrowings from the non-Indian world. By combining elements of English common law and what Debo termed "savage custom," they created a legal system in which, for example, in property and marriage, women held the same rights as their husbands.[34]

During the Civil War the Choctaws, along with the Chickasaws, a closely related tribe forced to join them in Indian Territory, had supported the Confederacy. Afterward the federal government retaliated by appropriating their western lands as reservations for the Plains Indians farther west. The Choctaws also struggled with vestiges of slavery during

Reconstruction. By adopting their former slaves and awarding them limited citizenship rights, they overcame some of their racial turmoil.[35] Their greatest threat came, in Debo's view, from outsiders who brought railroads, mining companies, and growing numbers of non-Indians into Choctaw country. By 1890 the new groups, comprising 75 percent of the population and increasing in numbers, clamored for an end to tribal government and the breakup of communally owned Indian lands.[36] The Dawes Commission assisted them by painting a grim picture of conditions within the Choctaw republic. In annual reports, from 1893 on, the Dawes Commission depicted Choctaw government as dominated by a mixed-blood elite that exploited full-bloods, cared little for non-Indians within their midst, and ruled through violence and corruption.

Debo admitted that the elite at times resorted to corruption and bribery that spawned political violence. High crime rates, brought on partly by unruly outsiders, also plagued the community,[37] but overall, she noted, the Choctaw republic had increased public health and education for its own people, areas that lagged seriously among contemporary Indian tribes and nations according to the Meriam Report. Finally, whereas the Dawes Commission had portrayed tribal ownership of land as the way leaders exploited full-bloods, Debo found that all Choctaws valued communal ownership.

Faced with the Curtis Act of 1898, which brought the Five Tribes under the provisions of the Dawes Severalty Act and swept away their laws and courts, all residents of Indian Territory now came under federal jurisdiction. Despite resistance among conservative full-bloods, the majority of Choctaws and most of the Chickasaws as well ratified the Atoka Agreement of 1897, which gave them individual allotments of up to 320 acres. In 1902 a supplementary agreement created a citizenship court and established procedures for selling mineral lands, with the proceeds going only to those who registered their allotments.[38] Choctaw representatives, as well as delegates from the other four of the Five Tribes and progressive non-Indian reformers such as William H. Murray and Charles N. Haskell, then met at the Sequoyah Convention in 1905 and petitioned Congress (unsuccessfully) for permission to form a separate Indian state. Two years later Indian Territory and Oklahoma Territory merged into the new state of Oklahoma.[39] Debo, who viewed the now disbanded Choctaw republic as an entity that its people had supported and that had enjoyed its share of successes, saw that beyond the new requirements of allotment and termination lay a deeper loss. Almost beyond calculation was the spiritual cost of giving up a deeply traditional way of life.[40]

By fall 1932 the Great Depression had ravaged the economy, and professors in Texas colleges and universities were being laid off. When Debo returned to West Texas State Teachers' College, she learned that Ima Barlow, the woman who had replaced her during her leave of absence to earn her doctorate, would now replace her at the end of the school year—even though Debo was the first woman faculty member to earn a Ph.D. President Andrew Jackson Hill found her a part-time position as director of the college's newly established Panhandle Plains Historical Museum, but Sheffy, chair of the history department—who never earned his doctorate, but headed the museum's oversight committee—excluded her from the museum's events. Had she attended, she would have met individuals such as Warren K. Morehead, former member of the federal Board of Indian Commissioners, who might have helped her find new employment.[41]

As Debo worked in the museum the following year, the University of Oklahoma Press published her dissertation as *The Rise and Fall of the Choctaw Republic* (1934). A year later the book would receive the Dunning Prize from the American Historical Association. Despite her achievement—the prize gave a strong boost to the careers of men who received it during the 1930s and early 1940s—Debo met only rejection as she applied for academic jobs everywhere.[42] She became so depressed that at one point her adherence to the "spirit of Oklahoma"—stoic cheerfulness or at least equanimity in the face of hardship—gave way. She and several women friends were traveling by car, and while they stopped to change a tire, Debo stood in the road. Alarmed, her companions summoned her away from oncoming traffic, but in a "flat voice" she responded, "Oh, it doesn't matter"—meaning that "it didn't matter to her at that moment if she [lived or] died."[43]

In the end, Debo's resilience convinced her that she should return to her parents' home in Marshall, Oklahoma. After much self-examination she recognized that "each one of us has our life and that's all we have. If we waste that, we waste everything."[44] The saving grace was that "if we are committed to use that life in the best way that our special talents will permit us to use it . . . we will be divinely guided into the kind of use that we were intended for."[45] For Debo, the best way to use her special talents was as a writer of history. At home in Marshall she now began work on the history of the Five Tribes as they struggled with the end of their autonomy and the loss of their communal lands after their merger into the State of Oklahoma in 1907.

Supported with a grant of $800 from the Social Science Research Council, Debo again discovered that the Dawes Commission came down on the side of non-Indians, publicizing Indian Territory's crime rate and the lack of schools for non-Indian children. It also portrayed the leaders of the protectorates as oligarchs who exploited full-bloods by monopolizing common property.[46] She contested that statement and the commission's assertion that only the elite among the Five Tribes had resisted allotment, while the large majority of Indians had supported it. Her evidence indicated that the reverse was true. Among some full-bloods, opposition to the breaking up of communally owned lands into allotments was so fierce that they refused to accept their newly allotted acreage, which left them pauperized.[47] Then, following the liquidation of tribal holdings and governments early in the twentieth century, a "criminal conspiracy," as Debo termed it, would rob members of the Five Tribes of much of their remaining land and its resources as the new state of Oklahoma took form and identity.[48] Although she had encountered instances of white duplicity in her earlier work on the Choctaws, nothing had prepared her for the enormity of these new discoveries.

Debo had uncovered a process that historians of the westward movement had largely neglected. The subject was important, for "the reaction of this process upon the ideals and standards of successive frontier communities is a factor in the formation of the American character that should no longer be disregarded by students of social institutions."[49] Building on the work of Frederick Jackson Turner, she now moved beyond him and his student, her mentor, Edward Everett Dale. More clearly than either, she saw the material and spiritual cost that the Five Tribes had sustained from unbridled economic development.[50] Even more important, she saw the history she had uncovered as a case study that showed the ugly underside of the settlement process that Turner and his disciples had so unequivocally celebrated. Although Oklahomans prided themselves on their mixed cultural heritage, the actual story of the Five Tribes, especially that of the full-bloods, remained an unacknowledged tragedy. Baffled by the new land system that often gave families both a homestead and noncontiguous lands farther away, and confused by the constantly changing legal and bureaucratic systems, they had been easy prey for white and mixed-blood exploiters.

Taking into account the internal divisions within the Five Tribes, which were based on differences between full-bloods and mixed-bloods plus varying degrees of assimilation into white society, and on unsettled relationships with the black citizens among them, Debo delineated the responses of these diversified peoples to new conditions and demands. Through the testimony of non-Indians and some acculturated or assimilated Indians on one side and traditional Indians on the other, she described the collision between opposing worldviews. The result was a more sophisticated study than her history of the Choctaws and one more chilling in its findings.

The downturn began in 1908, when Oklahoma's congressional delegation won federal legislation removing restrictions from land belonging to members of the Five Tribes who were freedmen and freedwomen or mixed-bloods of less than one-half Indian ancestry. When the current holders of allotted lands died, restrictions on the sale of Indian lands would be almost gone, and for those too young to have received allotments, any remaining restrictions against them as heirs of allottees could be withdrawn under probate court approval and oversight.[51] This opened the way for the "grafters," the term for those who exploited the ambiguities within these complex legal changes. Earlier they had capitalized on Indians' naiveté by leasing their land for ninety-nine years at low prices and subletting at higher rents to farmers or mining or oil drilling companies.[52] Now they wrested holdings from "consenting" adults whom they had confused or intimidated. Sometimes when oil was discovered on Indian land, the grafters kidnapped the owners and held them captive, forcing them to sign over their possessions. Sometimes the grafters simply murdered them.

The grafters discovered that attaining guardianship of orphaned or homeless minors was another way of gaining access to Indian land and its resources. After siphoning off royalties from mineral deposits or productive oil wells, many grafters left their young charges penniless. But why stop with children when adults who also owned resources, especially oil, could be declared incompetent and brought under "protection"? Then, by levying fees against their holdings for such arduous "services" as depositing or cashing checks, Oklahoma's grafters could appropriate much of their victims' remaining possessions.[53]

As Debo untied dusty old packets in the basements of various archives, she discovered that the ranks of the grafters had included well-known officials, including Governor Charles N. Haskell and Senator Robert L. Owen. Back in her rented room in Washington, D.C. and in other places, she realized that the names appearing in the society pages of the local Oklahoma newspapers were often those of the wives and relatives of prominent legislators, lawyers, judges, business people, and developers whose actions she was uncovering. As she explained in later oral history interviews, had she known what she would find, she would not have started her investigation, very likely because she feared the prominence of these people and their ability to retaliate. Once into her subject, however, she felt compelled "to go on with it."[54]

More than dedication to her current writing project was at work this time, however. As Robert L. Dorman has observed, Debo was uncovering "on one level, a depression-era parable of the systematic exploitation of the powerless by the powerful, of the 'common man' by 'economic royalists.'"[55] Given her background and her own situation, the dispossession of the Five Tribes was a compelling plunge into living history. Imbued with the "spirit of Oklahoma," she could express her anger over the fate of the Five Tribes in a way that she could never have expressed anger over her own situation, due, at least in part, to gender injustice. She saw in the Indian world, moreover, qualities that attracted her as an individual. Unlike many Oklahomans, whose values extolled growth and development, most full-bloods of the Five Tribes retained an attachment to tradition and place, priorities that Debo upheld for herself her entire life.

Throughout the summer of 1936, as she sat at her typewriter, the intense heat, combined with days upon days without rain, deepened her foreboding as her narrative progressed. The drought-stricken land turned "desolate under blazing sun and fiery wind. Trees died in great numbers along the creeks," she recalled years later, "their limbs standing out gaunt above the tortured vegetation." As the thermometer rose to 113, 114, and 115 degrees, the aged, sick, and frail died in increasing numbers.[56] She worked diligently at her desk, sweat trickling down her back, until early evening, when she read her typed pages to Lina. Often her mother, shaking her head, warned her, "nobody will ever publish that." Debo believed, however, that Brandt, determined to establish the University of Oklahoma Press as the leading producer of Indian history, would publish her work.[57]

By mid-March 1937, after her first glowing review from an anonymous reader for the univesity press (actually D'Arcy McNickle), Debo impatiently awaited her second reader's report.[58] A year earlier, Oklahoma had passed the Oklahoma Indian Welfare Act. A modified version of the federal Indian Reorganization Act of 1934, which (under the aegis of Commissioner of Indian Affairs John Collier) sought reinvigoration of tribal culture and the restoration of tribal lands, the Oklahoma act allowed groups of Indians numbering ten or more to form cooperatives and apply for loans to purchase land from a $2 million fund. Many members of the Five Tribes, especially the elite mixed-bloods, favored assimilationist policies and opposed both the Indian Reorganization Act and the Oklahoma version. Businessmen and politicians who objected to removing Indian land and subterranean resources from state tax rolls joined them.[59] Given this controversy, Debo wanted her work published quickly. Although she included "no propaganda" for Commissioner Collier or his Indian Reorganization Act, she wrote to Brandt in 1937 that as her prospective publication was "the only scientific study that has ever been made of the question about which such a bitter fight has raged for the past four years ... it would please me to think that sincere people on both sides could have some facts available as a basis for their arguments." If the "despoilers of the Indians" were to triumph again, it should not occur because of "lack of knowledge."[60] Shortly after, Debo received a glowing review from the press's second reader and relaxed. Publication was set for October 1, 1937.

That spring, impoverished and entirely dependent on her parents for food and housing, Debo wrote to Dale, asking him to consider her for one of two vacancies in his department at the university in Norman. She could not have replaced the Latin American scholar, but she might have filled in, at least temporarily, for Morris Wardell. After receiving his Ph.D. from the University of Chicago, Wardell was leaving the classroom to become assistant to President William Bizzell. The University of Oklahoma Press would soon publish his dissertation as *The Political History of the Cherokees, 1838–1907* (1938), so he and Debo shared subject matter. Debo suggested that Dale consider bringing her into the department as a temporary instructor, and "the future would take care of itself." Admittedly, she had "one disqualification," or "defect." She was a woman, few of whom, she noted, "were employed on history faculties." Perhaps her "productive scholarship" and record as a teacher could offset this weakness.[61] After assuring her of her fine qualifications, Dale devoted most of his letter to explaining why he had to hire a Latin American historian. He never referred to the possibility that Debo might replace Wardell, even on a part-time basis, and he gave her no encouragement that he would ever consider her for any teaching position in his department.[62]

While respectful and courtly toward women, Dale had displayed, in a Harvard seminar paper written in 1913, a bias that probably still colored his feelings about women as potential colleagues. In "Woman's Influence on the French Revolution" he had asserted that women had influenced the revolution mainly because the male revolutionaries were, at times, "imbued with a fatal feminism, a strange sentimentality that causes them to act more like excited, hysterical women than like sober law-givers to whom has been entrusted the task of creating a new form of government for France." These men, when their histories were examined, were found to "waste time on trifles, they talk endlessly, and they show in many ways incapacity for business, sentimentalism, a failure to 'make the head rule the heart,' and other characteristics which we in America usually regard as peculiarly feminine. Thus," he concluded, "not only did the women of France have a large share in the Revolution but there was also apparently a strain of 'femininity' or at least a lack of masculinity in the men of the period."[63]

If this misogyny remained a part of Dale's thinking, it explained, in part, why he had brought Wardell, a former high-school teacher, into his department even before Wardell had earned his terminal degree, and had given Debo's request for part-time employment no consideration. Dale likewise had carefully mentored Wardell's advance toward tenure and promotion. Despite Debo's prestigious award from the American Historical Association and her production of another manuscript on a very complex subject, involving the fate of the Five Tribes, and disregarding her reputation as an "excellent" teacher in the classroom, Dale would never do for her what he had done for his male friend.[64]

By spring 1937 Debo felt anxious that her forthcoming work on the termination of the Five Tribes in Oklahoma might bring retaliation against the University of Oklahoma Press. After all, she had identified prominent individuals in the state as exploiters of Indians.[65] At her urging, Brandt submitted her manuscript to President William Bizzell, who in turn ordered his assistant—none other than Wardell—to evaluate the manuscript. Wardell issued a negative report questioning Debo's impartiality and concluding that publication of this work would generate criticism, libel suits, and retaliation against the press and the university.[66] Debo soon received her canceled contract in the mail.[67]

Debo assumed that Dale had written this negative appraisal, or perhaps their recent correspondence had planted that idea. More likely, she recalled that although Dale as a teacher had told his classes of the treachery whites had practiced against Indians, he had left such incidents out of his publications. In the end, her manuscript was not published until Princeton University Press, having wooed Brandt away from Oklahoma, published the book late in 1940 as *And Still the Waters Run*. Then, although the academic reviews were excellent, the work received little coverage in the popular press.[68] With the eruption of World War II in Europe, public attention turned to foreign affairs. In this context the voices of intellectuals, who had seen in American Indian cultures qualities valuable to the nation as a whole, received less attention. Still, despite the frustrations and disappointments of bringing *And Still the Waters Run* into publication, Debo had received another grant from the Social Science Research Council and was completing a history of the Creek Nation. Again, she uncovered a chronicle of white deceit, and once more, she told her story from the Indian perspective.

Her research revealed another story of broken treaties and betrayed trust. When southern whites seized Native lands in the Southeast, the Creeks were "dragged from their ancient homes and flung down upon a raw western frontier to conquer it or die."[69] In Indian Territory, nonetheless, the Creeks reconstructed their lives and their republic, retaining the Euro-American ways that they found serviceable while steadfastly maintaining their ancient traditions. They also struggled to work out their relations with neighboring western tribes. Despite the pain of adjustment and lingering divisions over removal, the Creeks had prospered until the American Civil War intervened. That conflict heightened dissension among them, pitting Creek against Creek as some supported the Confederacy and others, who became fugitives, joined the Union cause.[70]

After the war, like all the Five Tribes, the Creeks faced continuing dissension. They also confronted "the encircling menace of a new frontier"—in the continuing encroachment of newcomers upon their land. Despite fierce attachment to their old ways, the Creeks were forced to capitulate to federal demands. Yet even as the majority accepted the Curtis Act in 1898, which shattered their tribal lands into "deeds and land titles," some, under Chitto (Snake) Harjo, resisted until their leaders were brought to trial in 1901.[71]

Among the Creeks, Pleasant Porter impressed Debo the most, mainly for his leadership after the passage of the Curtis Act. As he counseled his people to move beyond their lost hopes and into the future, he understood the continuing importance of the Creek heritage to Oklahoma and the nation. Fittingly Debo ended her work with his moving statement to the Creek Council in 1900: "The vitality of our race still persists. We have not lived for naught. We are the original discoverers of this continent, and the conquerors of it from the animal kingdom, and on it first taught the arts of peace and war, and first planted the institutions of virtue, truth and liberty." Those achievements, Porter maintained, showed European Americans that "it was possible for men to exist and subsist here." His people had bequeathed to them "our thought forces—the best blood of our ancestors having intermingled with [that of] their best statesmen and leading citizens. We have made ourselves," he closed emphatically, "an indestructible element in their national history."[72]

When the University of Oklahoma Press, short of funding due to the Great Depression, finally scheduled an early 1941 publication date for *The Road to Disappearance*, Debo was employed in Oklahoma City as head of the Oklahoma Writers' Project for the Works Progress Administration. Her employment there had come as she faced the severest poverty yet, for she had held only one other position since leaving Texas and that had entailed serving in February 1937 as an interviewer for the Indian-Pioneer Papers under the Works Progress Administration in Oklahoma. To travel to her interview at the state capitol she had been compelled to borrow the fifty-cent train fare and, armed with sandwiches from home, had stayed at the local YWCA (Young Women's Christian Association) overnight. Her WPA duties included overseeing the production of a state history. Although she welcomed the relief from penury, she soon found that working for a bureaucracy and supervising often inept writers was difficult. A year later she resigned.[73]

In late 1941, when *Oklahoma: A Guide to the Sooner State* arrived in print, she was appalled.[74] She and her colleague at the WPA office, John M.

Oskison, were listed as coeditors of the volume, but the chapter on the history of Oklahoma was not hers. Whereas her opening sentence had begun, "Although Oklahoma is young as a state, and the region came early within the scope of the white man's imperial ambitions," the substitute chapter made no reference to imperialism. Debo resented being censored; worse yet, the chapter contained numerous errors, leaving her deeply embarrassed that her name as first editor was on the volume's cover.[75]

That same year—1941—John Collier, still commissioner of Indian Affairs, asked Debo to critique a speech he was giving. Afterward, Debo sent him a draft of "Indian Policy as a Problem in Colonial Administration," which she hoped to publish. In it, she argued that although Great Britain and later the United States had recognized the sovereignty of Native peoples and dealt with them as nations, both powers had sought to add Native land to their holdings. Her topic was not about colonial administration, Collier responded, but rather imperialism. Doing justice to that subject meant examining Indian-white relations "in the context of national development." That, he advised her, required writing a book, not an article.[76]

With other projects already under way, she could not begin such an ambitious study in the foreseeable future. In 1943 she published *Tulsa: From Creek Town to Oil Capital*, and, a year later, *Prairie City: The Story of an American Community*, the story of a composite town.[77] If Frederick Jackson Turner's 1893 "Significance of the Frontier in American History" had presented individualism, democracy, and pragmatism as traits arising from the frontier experience and pivotal to the formation of American character, Debo's study of a pioneer settlement was, in part, a eulogy for an earlier sense of community that technology and political divisions had largely erased from the population.

At the same time, she demonstrated the ways in which the larger world, with its cycles of boom and bust and war and peace, increasingly shaped and reshaped the lives and fortunes of citizens in a Great Plains hamlet. Ending her work, as young people were leaving home to participate in World War II as soldiers or defense workers, Debo predicted that Prairie City would endure but in a different form. "Why not," she asked, never knowing that, in a sense, she was predicting the rise of the Internet age, "a new village of farmers, citizens of the world through schools and radio and space-consuming transportation, grouped together in friendly sociability, building directly upon the soil?"[78] Although *Prairie City* had disappointing sales in 1944, it gave Marshall, Oklahoma, its chief inspiration, a measure of immortality. By the 1980s, the work had become required reading for Oklahoma's schoolchildren.

During World War II, Debo, like many women above age thirty-five in the United States, found new employment opportunities—but not in higher education. In addition to teaching high school history in Marshall, she served as lay minister for the local Methodist Church. Her parishioners recalled later that she often concluded an interment with the words, "With this loved soil of Oklahoma, which you tilled for so many years, I bury you."[79] When peace was again in sight, she wrote to Savoie Lottinville, Brandt's replacement as director of the University of Oklahoma Press, asking if he would consider a study of America's "real imperialism," its treatment of its Native peoples. If her country could not overcome its past mistakes in this era, she explained, "we may as well admit that the colonial problems that will be left from this present war are beyond our solving." Lottinville, seeing little market for such a book, suggested another topic: perhaps Debo might write a history of the Indians of North America, something the press had long wanted to add to its listings. Debo responded that she might one day be willing to tackle a more modest endeavor, a history of the Indians of the United States.[80]

A quarter-century later, in 1970, Debo's *History of the Indians of the United States* appeared in print and became her best-selling book. In the intervening years she had served as curator of maps at Oklahoma A&M University (presently Oklahoma State University, Stillwater) during the school year and had continued researching, writing, and editing books and articles in the summers, before retiring in 1955 at the then-obligatory age of sixty-five.

In retirement she had visited Russia, a goal she had nurtured since, as a fifteen-year-old, she had read in January 1905 an account in the *Kingfisher* [Oklahoma] *Free Press* of Czarist troops firing on petitioning workers at the Winter Palace in St. Petersburg. Other travels took her throughout Europe, Mexico, and much of Africa, as she became a citizen of the world in her attitudes towards the value of increasing living standards, educational opportunities, and safety for all people, and most especially for women in Africa.[81] In 1976, when she was eighty-six, she published *Geronimo, The Man, His Time, and His Place*, which won three national prizes, including the esteemed Wrangler Award. Constantly she bought stamps "like wallpaper" to keep her ever-widening circle of activists informed and in contact with representatives and senators on behalf of American Indians and the Indians, Aleuts, and Eskimos of Alaska.[82]

In 1978 Debo's health gave way, and until her death in 1988 she was blind in one eye, almost deaf, and suffering the agony of osteoporosis. Still, she engaged in oral history interviews from 1981 through 1985 with a team comprised of the American historian Glenna Matthews; Gloria Valencia-Weber, a friend from the American Civil Liberties Union who has since become a professor of American Indian Law; and Aletha Rogers, a skilled interview technician. These interviews became the basis for the hour-long PBS documentary *Indians, Outlaws and Angie Debo* (1988). In 1985 Debo went to her "hanging" (her term), at which her portrait, painted by Charles Banks Wilson, was formally unveiled in the capitol rotunda in Oklahoma City. It resides there today alongside those of the Cherokee scholar Sequoyah, the American Indian athlete Jim Thorpe, the humorist Will Rogers, former governor of Oklahoma and U.S. senator Robert Kerr, former Speaker of the U.S. House of Representatives Carl Albert, and, most recently, in 2012, historian John Hope Franklin. The American Historical Association honored her with its Lifetime Achievement Award shortly before her death on February 21, 1988.

Debo never saw the PBS award-winning film about her life, but she knew during her last decade that she had changed Oklahoma history, western history, and American Indian history. "Sometimes," she observed in a letter in 1979 to Edward Shaw, Savoie Lottinville's successor at the University of Oklahoma Press, "I play with a half-formed conviction that Savoie invented the word 'ethno-history' and that I invented [that] kind of writing."[83]

Major historians have agreed. In response to *Indians, Outlaws and Angie Debo* Richard White characterized her as having "invented the 'new' Indian history long before there was a name for it."[84] Terry Wilson (Potawatomie) in an American Historical Association pamphlet, *Teaching American Indian History*, published the results of a survey he had conducted among scholars in the field: "Only a single book published before 1945 was mentioned more than once and that was Debo's *And Still the Waters Run*." It was also the sixth most often cited, and some scholars commented that it had significantly changed the field.[85]

Angie Debo is buried today outside of Marshall, Oklahoma, where her grave stone reads simply: "Historian, discover the truth and publish it."

But although her remains are close to home, her life taken as a whole was an odyssey in which she traveled far from the mental landscapes of her childhood. As she noted in June 1985, "[T]here's no spot on the globe that is as far away from my knowledge and understanding as the Indian Territory was when I was growing up in the Territory of Oklahoma."[86]

Placing herself on the other side of Turner's frontier and viewing the story of westward expansion from the perspective of Native Americans undergoing dispossession, she saw a different reality behind the idealized version of the history she had inherited from her extended family and her beloved mentor, Edward Everett Dale. As a regionalist historian, she viewed US Indian policy as America's "real imperialism," and she was certain by the 1940s that, until her compatriots understood the history of their often tragic interaction with Native peoples, their relationship to the new emerging nations of formerly colonized peoples would be forever compromised. By moving beyond her own origin myth, Angie Elbertha Debo bravely challenged the widespread myth of national innocence. She insisted that her compatriots honor their commitments, not only for the sake of Native peoples in the United States but because they owe at least that much to their better selves as they constantly discover anew that they cannot escape the immense and historically-based problems of a postcolonial world.

NOTES

1. Angie Debo, "The Debo Family" and "History of the Debos in America," ed. John Tilden, 1972, Angie Debo Papers (ADP), Manuscript Collections, Edmon Low Library, Oklahoma State University, Stillwater, box 7, folder 66.

2. "For Bruce and Gitte," December 16, 1984, typescript copy of handwritten draft of family history, in possession of Hugh and Ramona O'Neill, Marshall, Oklahoma, copy in author's personal collection; "Lina Debo" (obituary), *The Marshall News*, June 17, 1954.

3. Typescript of interviews conducted with Debo (ADTI), by Glenna Matthews, Gloria Valencia Weber, and Aletha Rogers, November 11, 1984, 1, ADP.

4. ADTI, July 25, 1984, 14.

5. Angie Debo, *Oklahoma: Foot-loose and Fancy-free* (Norman: University of Oklahoma Press, 1987), 75. She was indebted to the work of environmentalists of the era; Edward H. Faulkner's *Plowman's Folly* (1943) and Paul Sears's *Deserts on the March* (1935) and *This Is Our World* (1937) were all published by the University of Oklahoma Press during that era.

6. Sara Doyle to Debo, March 28, 1958, ADP, box 1, folder 42.

7. Angie Debo, "Bender and Goldberry," typescript story of the Bender and Goldberry feud that resulted in a murder, ADP, box 7, folder 9; "For the Grandchildren of Zebedee and Ida Halsted," typescript family history, box 7, folder 64.

8. *Marshall Tribune*, September 1910; Lola Clark Pearson, a clubwoman, spearheaded the move to build the Marshall high school. See Linda W. Reese, "'Dear Oklahoma Lady': Women Journalists Speak Out," *Chronicles of Oklahoma* 58 (Fall 1989): 286.

9. Angie Debo, "Edward Everett Dale: The Teacher," in *Frontier Historian: The Life and Work of Edward Everett Dale*, ed. Arrell Gibson (Norman: University of Oklahoma Press, 1975), 28-29.

10. Edward Everett Dale, "Turner—The Man and Teacher," *University of Kansas City Review*, Autumn 1951, 25.

11. Edward Everett Dale, "The Spirit of Soonerland," *Chronicles of Oklahoma* 1 (June 1923): 167-69.

12. Dale, "Spirit of Soonerland," 175-78. For a complete analysis of Frederick Jackson Turner's Frontier Thesis, his sources of inspiration, his delivery of that thesis at Chicago, and its relation to his later work, see Allan G. Bogue, *Frederick Jackson Turner: Strange Roads Going Down* (Norman: University of Oklahoma Press, 1998).

13. Edward Everett Dale, course outlines, Edward Everett Dale Collection (EEDC), Western History Collection, University of Oklahoma, Norman, box 181, folder 1; box 176, folder 10.

14. Dale, "Turner—The Man and Teacher," 25.

15. ADTI, November 20, 1981, 2-3.

16. Angie Debo to "Dear Mamma" (Lina Debo), May 15, 1916, ADP.

17. ADTI, November 20, 1981, 4; August 15, 1983, 2.

18. William H. Chafe, *The Paradox of Change: American Women in the 20th Century* (New York: Oxford University Press, 1991), 99.

19. Fred James Rippy and Angie Debo, "The Historical Background of the American Policy of Isolation," *Smith College Studies in History* 9 (April-July, 1924), 71, 125, 131. Rippy wrote no part of her published thesis.

20. Nancy Cott, *The Grounding of Modern Feminism* (New Haven: Yale University Press, 1987), 218; ADTI, November 20, 1981, 9-10.

21. Nancy Woloch, *Women and the American Experience*, 5th ed. (Boston: McGraw-Hill, 2005), 285-86; Patricia A. Graham, "Expansion and Exclusion: A History of Women in Higher Education," *Signs* 3 (Summer 1978): 759-73.

22. ADTI, December 12, 1981, 2.

23. *Randall County News* (Canyon, Texas), February 26, 1925.

24. *West Texas State Teachers College* [Canyon, Texas] *Quarterly Bulletin*, nos. 39-69, 1925-33.

25. ADTI, June 8, 1985, 17.

26. Seminar paper, University of Oklahoma, 1930-31, ADP, box 7, folder 2.

27. ADTI, December 16, 1981, 6-7. Frank Phillips set up the Phillips Collection, which under Professor Edward Everett Dale became the basis of the present-day Western History Collection at the University of Oklahoma, Norman. Dale received annual funds from Phillips to add primary sources. Debo's bibliography in her revised and published work, *The Rise and Fall of the Choctaw Republic* (Norman: University of Oklahoma Press,1934) cites

the *Acts and Resolutions of the General Council of the Choctaw Nation,* giving full information on their publication into volumes year by year. The first volume includes proceedings from 1852 to 1857 and was printed in Fort Smith, Arkansas. Scholars interested in these acts and resolutions can still locate them in the Western History Collection and they are available at other colleges and universities with degree programs in American Indian Studies.

28. This was the first extensive survey of conditions among American Indians since Henry Schoolcraft had published his multivolume work in the 1850s. See now *The Problem of Indian Administration,* with a new introduction by Frank C. Miller (New York: Johnson Reprint, 1971). Meriam had been a statistician with the Institute for Government Research in Washington, D.C., and it was the institute, supported by the Rockefeller Foundation, that produced the original edition of *The Problem of Indian Administration* in 1928. For information on the Meriam Commission see Donald Parman, *Indians and the American West in the Twentieth Century* (Bloomington: Indiana University Press, 1994), 84–86.

29. *The Problem of Indian Administration,* 21–51, 189–429. See Paul Prucha, *The Great Father: The United States Government and the American Indians,* 2 vols. (Lincoln: University of Nebraska Press, 1984), 2: 808–10.

30. For information on the reform movements that began in the 1920s see Randolph C. Downes, "A Crusade for Indian Reform, 1922–1934," *Mississippi Valley Historical Review* 32 (1945–46): 337–45. See also Prucha, *The Great Father,* 2: 927–31; Dale to Debo, July 2, 1931, EEDC; ADTI, December 12, 1981, 8.

31. Morris L. Wardell, "William Bennett Bizzell: Bibliophile and Builder," *Chronicles of Oklahoma* 30 (Autumn 1952): 256–61; Arrell M. Gibson, "A History of the University of Oklahoma Press," *Journal of the West* 7 (October 1988): 553–61; Steven Crum: "Bizzell and Brandt: Pioneers in Indian Studies," *Chronicles of Oklahoma* 66 (summer 1988): 178–91.

32. See John Collier, *Indians of the Americas* (n.p.: Mentor, 1954). See also Lawrence C. Kelly, *The Assault on Assimilation: John Collier and the Origins of Indian Policy Reform* (n.p.: Olympic Marketing, 1983).

33. Angie Debo, "History of the Choctaw Nation from the End of the Civil War to the Close of the Tribal Period," Ph.D. dissertation, University of Oklahoma, 1933.

34. Debo, "History of the Choctaw Nation," 10–23.

35. Angie Debo, *The Rise and Fall of the Choctaw Republic* (Norman: University of Oklahoma Press, 1934), 101–109, 249. Chapters 4 through 12 of that work were taken entirely from her dissertation.

36. Debo, *Rise and Fall of the Choctaw Republic,* 221–44.

37. *Rise and Fall of the Choctaw Republic,* 143–93. See Devon Abbott Mihesuah, *Choctaw Crime and Punishment, 1884–1907* (Norman: University of Oklahoma Press, 2009), for her more thorough and illuminating research into the question of how much the crime and violence among the Choctaws was due to outsiders and how much arose from the Choctaws themselves. She finds that whereas earlier in the republic's history much of the violence was due to outsiders, as time progressed more of the violence came from increasing factionalism among the Choctaws themselves and had to do with politics, such as progressives (assimilationists) versus conservatives (traditionalists).

38. Debo, *Rise and Fall of the Choctaw Republic,* 259–71, 277–83.

39. Debo, *Rise and Fall of the Choctaw Republic,* 277–90.

40. Debo, *Rise and Fall of the Choctaw Republic,* 110.

41. Connie Cronley to Shirley Leckie, December 28, 1998, author's personal collection. During Debo's later years Cronley was one of her best friends.

42. Francis B. Simpkins, Richard Leopold, and Oscar Handlin were among the early recipients of the Dunning Prize.

43. Connie Cronley to Shirley Leckie, October 8, 1996, author's private collection.

44. Art Cox, "Town Turns Out to Honor Its Own Living Legend," *Enid Morning News*, February 2, 1986, newspaper clipping, ADP box 1, folder 5.

45. ADTI, November 20, 1981, 16; August 17, 1983, 6.

46. Angie Debo, *And Still the Waters Run* (Princeton: Princeton University Press, 1940), 25.

47. Debo, *And Still the Waters Run*, x, 1.

48. Debo, *And Still the Waters Run*, 197, 312.

49. Debo, *And Still the Waters Run*, ix–x.

50. On Turner's indifference to Indians see Richard Hofstadter's comments in *The Progressive Historians: Turner, Beard, and Parrington* (New York: Knopf, 1969), 104–105.

51. Debo, *And Still the Waters Run*, 176–81.

52. Debo, *And Still the Waters Run*, 92–125.

53. Debo, *And Still the Waters Run*, 181–317.

54. ADTI, December 12, 1981, 8.

55. Robert L. Dorman, *Revolt of the Provinces: The Regionalist Movement in America, 1920–1945* (Chapel Hill: University of North Carolina Press, 1993), 172.

56. Angie Debo, *Prairie City: The Story of An American Community* (New York: Knopf, 1944), 218.

57. ADTI, June 8, 1985, 5.

58. D'Arcy McNickle, reader's report on "As Long as the Waters Run" (original title of Debo's manuscript), included in a letter from Brandt to Debo, September 15, 1936, Joseph A. Brandt Collection (JABC), Western History Collection, University of Oklahoma, Norman.

59. Graham D. Taylor, *The New Deal and American Indian Tribalism: The Indian Reorganization Act, 1934–45* (Lincoln: University of Nebraska Press, 1980), 35–36; Peter W. Wright, "John Collier and the Oklahoma Indian Welfare Act of 1936," *Chronicles of Oklahoma* 50 (Autumn 1972): 347–71.

60. Debo to Brandt, March 10, 1937, JABC.

61. Debo to E. E. Dale, June 19, 1937, EEDC.

62. E. E. Dale to Debo, June 23, 1937, EEDC.

63. E. E. Dale, "Woman's Influence on the French Revolution," unpublished paper from the Frederick Jackson Turner's seminar "History of the West," fall 1913– spring 1914, EEDC.

64. E. E. Dale to M. L. Wardell, June 11, 1930, EEDC. See also Richard Lowitt, "Regionalism at the University of Oklahoma," *Chronicles of Oklahoma* 73 (Summer 1995): 170, n. 19.

65. Debo to Brandt, July 16, 1937, Angie Debo Collection, Western History Collection (ADCWHC), University of Oklahoma, Norman.

66. ADTI, December 12, 1981, 10; [Morris Wardell,] review titled "Miss Debo, As Long as the Waters Run," University of Oklahoma, Office of the President, W.B. Bizzell Correspondence (WBBC), box 124, Western History Collection, University of Oklahoma, Norman. Although unsigned, an accompanying letter from William Bizzell to Joseph A.

Brandt, dated July 20, 1937, indicates that the enclosed review is Wardell's and that given that review, the University of Oklahoma Press should not publish this work.

67. Bizzell to Brandt, July 20, 1937, WBBC; ADTI, December 12, 1981, 10–11; Brandt to Debo, July 26, 1937, JABC.

68. ADT, December 11, 1981, 10; June 8, 1985, 14. The better-known publications reviewing the work were *Christian Century*, November 20, 1940, 1451; *The Nation*, January 4, 1941, 26; and Stanley Vestal, "Despoiling the Indians," *New York Herald Tribune*, January 5, 1941, 3.

69. Angie Debo, *The Road to Disappearance: A History of the Creek Indians* (Norman: University of Oklahoma Press, 1941), vii.

70. Debo, *Road to Disappearance*, viii, 142–75, 376.

71. Debo, *Road to Disappearance*, 360–76.

72. Debo, *Road to Disappearance*, 377.

73. Angie Debo diaries, ADP, box5, folder 3, March 11, 1940; Mary Ann Slater, "The Oklahoma Writers' Project: 1935–1942," M.A, thesis, Oklahoma State University, 1985, 109–12; Debo to Dale, January 17, 1941, EEDC; ADTI, May 4, 1983, 5–6.

74. Norman: University of Oklahoma Press, 1941.

75. Debo used this deleted chapter as her historical chapter, which starts on page 15 in *Oklahoma Foot-loose and Fancy-free* (Norman: University of Oklahoma Press, 1947); Debo to Dale, January 11, 1942, EEDC.

76. John Collier to Debo, December 8, 1941, ADCWHC.

77. *Tulsa: from Creek Town to Oil Capital* (Norman: University of Oklahoma Press, 1943); *Prairie City*.

78. Debo, *Prairie City*, 245.

79. Employers preferred women over thirty-five years of age because they were less likely to have children under school age at home; they were the first hired to replace men in offices, secondary schools, and factories. See *A Statistical Portrait of Women in the United States*, Current Population Reports, Special Studies, Series P-23, #58, U.S. Department of Commerce, Bureau of the Census (Washington, D.C.: Government Printing Office, 1976), 31, cited in Carl Degler, *At Odds: Women and the Family in America from the Revolution to the Present* (New York: Oxford University Press, 1980), 511, n.1, On Debo's time as a minister see ADP box 1, folder 18: The Methodist Church, Local Preacher's License for Miss Angie Debo, November 21, 1944; H. R. Doak, Ted Merrell, Raymond Bryson, and Bert Burlew to "Dear friends," September 26, 1946. See also Gloria Valencia-Weber, "Eulogy, Angie Debo, 1890–1988," ADP box 1, folder 3.

80. Debo to Savoie Lottinville, September 27, 1944; Lottinville to Debo, September 30, 1944; Debo to Lottinville, October 3, 1944, Savoie Lottinville Collection, Western History Collection, University of Oklahoma, Norman.

81. In her will Debo bequeathed money from her estate to educate the children of Betty Nakede Mubiru of Uganda. Once their schooling was taken care of, the remainder of her estate (ongoing royalties, primarily) was to be given to the Global Ministries of the United Methodist Church, to be used for the education of African women. She specified that funds should go first to Zaire; if that country failed as a nation, the monies from her estate were to go to women in Africa or wherever the Global Ministries determined it was most needed for women in the Third World.

82. Many American Indian activists saw Debo as a scholar-warrior, a term that came originally from Rayna Green. See Shirley A. Leckie, *Angie Debo, Pioneering Historian*. Oklahoma Western Biographies 18 (Norman: University of Oklahoma Press, 2000), esp. 151–73.

83. Debo to Edward A. Shaw, 2 September 1979, JABC.

84. Richard White, Review of *Indians, Outlaws and Angie Debo*, in *Journal of American History* 76 (December 1989): 1010.

85. Terry Wilson, *Teaching American Indian History*, is part of the American Historical Association's series Diversity within America, edited by Nell Irvin Painter and Antonio Rio-Bustamante (Washington, D.C.: American Historical Association, 1993); see pages 16–17.

86. ADTI, 11 November 1984, 1.

CHAPTER EIGHT

Texas, the Transnational, and Regionalism

J. FRANK DOBIE AND AMÉRICO PAREDES

José E. Limón

According to the editor of this volume, Michael Steiner, the turn to regionalism in the 1930s and into the early 1940s was motivated by the "search for... the indigenous or the primal basic America, a desire for a stable community, and a reverence for the past—especially the memories that could bring a sense of order and certainty to a tumultuous present."[1] Such regionalisms could be adopted in the name of either a right-wing or a leftist politics but were directed against the same adversary: a centralized, urbanized capitalist modernity.[2] By these measures, the two best-known Texas literary intellectual regionalists, J. Frank Dobie (1888–1964) and Américo Paredes (1915–99), were ultimately regionalists on the left, or so I generally argue here.

Other theorists of regionalism caution that regionalism "is not an unproblematic move," because "as a political and literary discourse" it is "underpinned by assumptions that warrant interrogation... like race, gender, class and sexuality... and must be theorized not in isolation but in relation to other elements central to the construction of subjectivity and of literature."[3] More specifically, Malini Johar Schueller has stressed the centrality of race and "the urgent need for local knowledge dealing with how subalterns," such as racial minorities but also racial dominants, "are historically, nationally and regionally constructed."[4] My own argument likewise speaks of such complications and contradictions as those emerge in Dobie's and Paredes's relationship to their shared native ground of Texas

J. Frank Dobie. Courtesy of Dolph Briscoe Center for American History, The University of Texas at Austin.

and ultimately to each other, principally but not exclusively as mediated by race.

Dobie's parents came to Texas in the 1870s as ranchers in upper south Texas. Born in 1888, Dobie would grow up knowing the workaday world of the cowboy even as his mother assured that he was also well read in the

Américo Paredes. Courtesy of The Harry Ransom Center, The University of Texas at Austin.

English literary classics. He was sent to a nearby small town for his high school education, a rarity in those times, and from there to a college education at Southwestern University in Georgetown, just north of Austin.[5] His family members were neighbors to the famous, sprawling King Ranch established on land previously owned by Mexicans who traced their ancestry to the Spanish explorations and settlement of the area dating back to the eighteenth century.⁶ This settlement occupied the southern portion of the territory straddling the Rio Grande on both banks but extended up to the Nueces River and even beyond it. After the founding of the Republic of Mexico in 1821, Mexican settlers added to the population. Dobie's family came to acquire their land when it was passed over to the United States after the U.S.–Mexican War of 1846–48. How this land passed over to new owners like Dobie's parents remains a hotly contested topic even today. As David Montejano relates, "Taxes, mortgage debts, legal battles, the effects of the erratic cattle and sheep market, outright coercion and fraud, as well as the cash offer of land speculators, all combined once more to reduce the number of Mexican landowners."⁷ Dobie himself records still other unconventional land transactions in his first book on his native regional culture, *A Vaquero of the Brush Country* (1929). One of his informants saw "many little ranches in the lower country deserted by their Mexican inhabitants; he saw too the remains of various Mexicans hanging from trees."⁸

Américo Paredes was born into such a family of eighteenth-century Spanish-Mexican origin and grew up in relatively safe seclusion from racial distress and violence in the predominantly Mexican American city of Brownsville, Texas. But racist violence did affect Mexican communities in almost every other part of south Texas, and the young Paredes was quite aware of it. Indeed, he was born in the very same year, 1915, that some Mexican Americans, the *sediciosos*, launched an armed, left-wing insurrectionist revolt against Anglo domination throughout south Texas. This insurrection had nineteenth-century antecedents, including the south Texas rebellion of the journalist-guerilla Catarino Garza, eventually suppressed by U.S. Army units led by the well-known anthropologist, military officer, and western explorer John Gregory Bourke, in 1892.⁹ Indeed, whereas Dobie mentions anti-Mexican violence in his first book, Paredes opens his own first book with a dedication to his father, "who rode a raid or two with Catarino Garza."¹⁰

Although both men became Texas regionalists, Paredes would dedicate himself largely to the southern part of the state, while Dobie's claims would be less specific and yet still regional. But both men experienced earlier, less than regionalistic phases, in their personal, intellectual, and political lives, and each added a transnational dimension occasioned by the two world wars.

After graduating from Southwestern University in 1910 with a major in English, Dobie tried his hand at newspaper work, but also at college teaching as an English instructor, primarily at the University of Texas at Austin. The university at Austin required an advanced degree if he aspired to rise to a professorship, and in 1914 he earned an M.A. in English from Columbia University. He returned to Austin in 1914, just as the "guns of August" went off in Europe; the United States would enter the bloody fray in 1917. An adventurous young man with stories of the wars in Texas in his head, Dobie enlisted but did not see combat, arriving in France late in October 1918 on the eve of the armistice. Once in Europe, however, Dobie, whose life had assumed a largely regional dimension up to that point—he had disliked New York during his studies at Columbia—fell in love with France and chose to remain in the army through May of 1919, in order to visit famous cultural sites and to take classes at the Sorbonne. Once back in Austin, he became profoundly dissatisfied with the life of a professor of composition and canonical literature, a career that threatened his ranch-formed sense of self. His depression became so serious that in 1920 he left the university to return to ranching, managing an uncle's ranch back in the Nueces River area.

Since his undergraduate days, Dobie had been interested in the vernacular culture of Texas and the Southwest, and during this brief stint as a rancher with a literary sensibility he discovered the riches of Mexican folklore from the Mexican cowboys (*vaqueros*) who worked on the ranch. He immediately sensed that he had found his life's calling. Not only did this folklore flow from his home region, but he became convinced that such folk material belonged in the curriculum of university literary departments. In this he was supported by the example of John Lomax (1867–1948), a fellow Texan who had been a student at the university in Austin in the 1890s, had earned a Ph.D. at Harvard, and pursued a long career collecting Texan and other regional folklore. Dobie could never be persuaded to acquire a doctorate himself, a problem that would have impeded his academic progress under conventional circumstances. Dobie was not conventional.

He gave up ranching to return to the university in Austin in 1921, to launch his new program of research and teaching in Texas regional folk culture. Although he never lost his interest in Mexican folklore (more will be said on this below), he never developed fluency in Spanish, and that obstacle seemed to be the principal factor encouraging him to focus on the Anglophone culture of Texas cowboys and others of his own ancestry. He also turned to a more generalized region that might be described as "southwestern Texas," for he had little to say about the cotton fields and later the oil industry of eastern Texas, even as the oil industry would become his principal adversary after World War II. Beginning with his very first work, *A Vaquero of the Brush Country: The Life and Times of John D. Young* (1929), based on the reminiscences of a working Anglo cowboy, Dobie wrote and published a series of books of collected and archival Anglo-Texan and southwestern vernacular culture, which he typically rewrote in a more literary style. Appearing from the 1930s into the postwar period, these eight enormously popular books were consonant with the great flowering of regionalism during that time.[11] As a result of his highly popular class English 342, "Life and Literature of the Southwest," at the university in Austin, along with numerous speaking engagements across the country, Dobie soon came to be called "Mr. Texas," the foremost exponent of Texas regionalism.

Américo Paredes likewise had his time in a kind of wilderness before fully affirming his native ground. His would spend the first thirty years of his life largely in his hometown of Brownsville. With a high school and junior college education, he developed a multifaceted initial professional identity and lifestyle that one historian of south Texas has characterized as "bohemian."[12] While keeping day jobs in journalism and aircraft maintenance at a local airfield, Paredes pursued his real vocations: literature, music, and the life of a single and very attractive young man. But even within the modernist, self-inspired "portrait of the artist as a young man" in his poetry and fiction from that period, he did begin a first, if contradictory, exploration of a regional identity keyed to the sociocultural life of the Lower Border. In some of this early work, such as his short story "The Hammon and the Beans" (1936) and the poem "The Mexico-Texan" (1939), he articulates a critical perspective on the Anglo domination of Mexican Americans in left-of-center, ethnonationalist terms. But other, later writings, including the short stories "Macaria's Daughter" (1943), "A Cold Night" (1940), and "Revenge" (1949), take a more generalized Marxist perspective in the sense that labor and class are the primary categories of his critique, with race always hovering in the background. Each of these stories speaks of the degrading effects of urban, proletarian life for Mexican Americans, always in implicit contrast to country life and the old ranching society, which clearly begin to emerge in his work as the true basis for Mexican American regional identity in Texas. This ruralized regionalism, set in contrast with the city, is displayed in another later short story, "Rebeca" (1950), even though it too is overlaid with a class analysis.[13]

This theme of the dangers of leaving the rural, regional, but also working-class life is carried over into his major work of this period and possibly his entire career, the long novel *George Washington Gómez*.[14] Set in deep south Texas, the novel opens in the year 1915, at the moment of Guálinto's birth; the scene includes the baby's mother, Maria, and his grandmother and sisters, as well as his father, Gumersindo, and his uncle, Feliciano, Maria's brother. The family debates a formal proper name for the new child, finally deciding on George Washington Gómez, because his parents, at least, believe that the name of a great American leader is very appropriate for a son who, they hope, will be a "leader of his people." But the grandmother, who speaks only Spanish, cannot pronounce "Washington," saying it as "Guálinto," which makes a very Mexican-sounding nickname.

This naming debate foreshadows what will become the central issue in Guálinto/George's development. The novel also foregrounds the violent revolt, also in 1915, of the *sediciosos* against Anglo-American authority in the Valley, an insurrection bloodily intertwined with the Mexican Revolution, then in progress. Many Mexican nationals had crossed over into nearby Texas to escape Porfirio Díaz's oppression and the violence of the Revolution. Guálinto's father, Gumersindo Gómez, is one such refugee. By contrast, Guálinto's maternal uncle, Feliciano García, traces his origins not to recent immigration but to the older Spanish-Mexican ranching culture of the Valley; he participates in the 1915 insurrection. Feliciano survives the revolt, but the Texas Rangers kill Guálinto's noncombatant father, Gumersindo. These two themes—loss of his father, and the emergence of Anglo-American dominance of the area after 1915—assume pivotal roles in the formation of Guálinto's character.

After Gumersindo's death, Feliciano moves the family to nearby Jonesville (a fictional name for Brownsville) for their safety and stability. In the city Guálinto's developing identity emerges as a necessarily antagonistic argument in his consciousness between his Mexican cultural origins, his knowledge of his region's history (principally gained from his uncle), and the now competing cultural force of Anglo-American dominance that is rapidly becoming institutionalized in the Valley, especially in the educational system.

The novel takes several twists and turns and adds many more characters as Guálinto matures in Jonesville. At his high school graduation, he listens to a commencement address by K. Hank Harvey, a professor at a place called the University, who is described as an expert on Texas history and culture, including that of its Mexican residents. Harvey gives a racially condescending speech, extolling the virtues of Anglo-Texas to a predominantly Mexican American audience, who listen politely as most of them do not understand his English. With thinly veiled sarcasm, the narrator says: "Harvey's fame grew too big even for vast Texas, and soon he was a national and then an international figure" who "filled a very urgent need; men like him were badly in demand in Texas."[15] Art imitates life. Paredes revealed elsewhere that he modeled Harvey after Dobie, who did come to Brownsville in the 1930s to give a speech that the young Paredes heard. "Dobie was constantly in the news at that time," he recalled. "His books were being touted for the truth of their representations of Texas folklife."[16]

Although Harvey's speech embitters Guálinto even more toward Anglo-Texas, the bitterness will not last, as the novel takes a decisive turn. Guálinto will eventually become a seemingly fully assimilated American subject, especially after attending the University of Texas in Austin (where Dobie taught), becoming a lawyer, marrying an Anglo-American woman, and securing employment in Washington, D.C., as a covert federal agent gathering intelligence on seditious activity among Mexican Americans. He also begins to use his Anglo-based formal name, George—and develops a classic ethnic self-hatred, which he freely voices in one of his infrequent returns to the Lower Border, dismissing old friends now involved in political organizing as "a bunch of clowns playing at politics. And they're trying to organize yokels who don't know anything but getting drunk and yelling and fighting. . . . Mexicans will always be Mexicans."[17] The novel ends with a bitter parting, especially between Guálinto and his uncle, as Guálinto/George leaves the Lower Border for what appears to be the last time. His uncle remains behind as a kind of living repository of the rural, working-class regional existence that Paredes seems to value, as once again, class mobility, urbanization, and the movement from periphery to center threaten to destroy a vital regional folk culture.

Regarding the pre–World War II period when he wrote the novel and similar shorter fiction, Paredes recalled, "I was a fiery, loud radical." He goes even further: "my own politics were really quite radical. I've often thought that if there had been a Communist Party cell in south Texas at the time, I would have joined it."[18] At the time, he also wrote a fiery poem attacking Franklin D. Roosevelt's famous enunciation in address to Congress, in 1941, of the Four Freedoms: freedom of speech and of worship, and freedom from want and from fear. The speaker in the poem argues that "this 'Four Freedoms' nation / can offer us nothing." Only a regional, ethnonationalist identity based on "Language, Culture, Blood" can suffice.[19]

Ramon Saldívar has praised Paredes's critical posture, arguing that it must be seen in relation to what he calls the "historical documents of Mexican American modernity" that emerged among other Mexican American activists from that era, such as George I. Sánchez, a professor at the University of Texas at Austin, and the San Antonio native Emma Tenayuca, with her husband, Homer Brooks, members of the Texas Communist Party, also beginning in the 1930s.[20] Within their distinctive ideological points of view Sánchez and Tenayuca were also full activists beyond their writing: he (a Democratic liberal) with the League of Latin American Citizens and as an expert resource and witness in school desegregation legal challenges, she (a Communist) in organizing and participating in often violent labor strikes in poverty-ridden San Antonio. Saldívar presents an extraordinary assessment of the ultimate significance of Paredes's poems within that highly charged context. Such "Mexican American intellectuals," he writes, "deployed the liberal rhetoric of American national unity to justify its reformation but not to imagine the framework of a new *mexicano* consciousness. In stark historical contrast, Paredes, as a young native intellectual seeking to invent a site of decolonized consciousness, offered a difference ... [that] prefigures an era of renewed cultural integrity in the imaginary ground between two worlds in borderlands of culture."[21]

Nevertheless Saldivar may have overstated the importance of Paredes's poem in relation to Tenayuca, Brooks, and Sánchez. The collapse of such disparate voices into one single vision of modernity is by itself debatable especially when, as Communists, Tenayuca and Brooks would have had the ultimate aim of creating a breakthrough into revolution, not "reformation"—the latter objective a well-known, but only initial, Popular Front tactic. Yet to attribute the fomenting of "mexicano consciousness" only to Paredes clearly suggests that Tenayuca, Brooks, and Sánchez had no interest in such an issue, which also seems too dismissive. Tenayuca was clearly interested in the "national question," and Sánchez had strong affirmative interests in what Paredes's poem calls "language," "culture," and "blood" in education. However, they articulated these views with nuance and care in comparison to the young poet's proclamation of primordially rooted sentiments, uttered in nationalist idioms that could easily have been on the lips of then active European but also American fascists, some in Texas, and also directed against President Roosevelt. Such is the character of primordial nationalisms.

But two other, more critical issues, are at stake here. Both Tenayuca and Sánchez were active in the public arena of consciousness: that is, they published their work and spoke of it in many public forums. The young Paredes likewise spoke his poetic views, but to whom? Other than perhaps among his circle of young poets in Brownsville, this poetry was never published in its time.[22] Tenayuca, Brroks, and Sánchez were also public activists in politics, labor strikes, and legal proceedings at some risk to their lives in Texas. Paredes has no such record of participatory politics. Although he did say that he would have joined "a Communist Party cell in south Texas" if one had been available, it does seem that this self-described "angry young man" whose politics "were really quite radical" was neither angry nor radical enough to travel up the road to work with Tenayuca's cell in nearby San Antonio, at the height of the Pecan Shellers' Strike in 1938–39 or, better yet, to organize a cell in rural south Texas to serve its oppressed Mexican agricultural labor force.[23]

Alternatively, and especially as a native Spanish-speaker of more Spanish than mestizo ancestry, Paredes might have joined his age-mate, fellow poet, and later cultural nemesis Octavio Paz, in fighting and writing for the Republican leftist cause in the Spanish Civil War (1936–39). Instead, this self-perceived exponent of a radically new "mexicano consciousness" chose instead to articulate that consciousness through largely private poetry, fiction, and musical activities in the politically benign world that was Brownsville, Texas. His early, inexperienced poetry also vented leftish anger at an American president who, like today's Barack Obama, was trying to resolve a substantial economic mess inherited from prior administrations while fending off attacks from the entrenched right and also from a dissatisfied far left.

By late 1944 Paredes had left Brownsville and his unpublished fictions and poetry to enter military service during World War II. The war was drawing to a close, and he wound up in Occupied Japan after August 1945. With some experience as a journalist in the lower Rio Grande valley, he served out his tour working for the U.S. Army's newspaper, *Stars and Stripes,* covering and filing stories on small and large events happening in postwar Japan. One might think that a young soldier with his strong regional attachments would immediately return home, once released from duty, to the Lower Border, but after his discharge in 1946 Paredes worked for the Red Cross in Asia in humanitarian aid efforts and also spent several years in Korea and China. During this period he also worked as a journalist, filing stories on Asian culture and politics for newspapers in Mexico even as he continued to write fiction principally set in Asia and largely featuring American characters, principally military. Little of this work, however, focuses on the Lower Border as a region, as if Paredes, now in a transnational existence beyond that of his youthful experience with nearby Mexico, was taking a respite from his native soil.

He returned to the United States in 1950 to Dobie's University of Texas at Austin to resume a college career. But by 1951 it was no longer Dobie's school and public platform. Much had happened since the young Paredes had last seen Dobie at that speech in Brownsville, changes principally occasioned by Dobie's surprising leftward political turn. Perhaps consistent with his condescending and sometimes racist attitudes toward Mexicans, and also toward African Americans, Dobie's general politics in the 1930s were decisively right-wing and conservative, especially when it came to dealing with national conditions, and he had construed his opposition to Roosevelt and New Deal policies in regionalist terms. For Dobie, Texas was the last depository of personal freedom symbolized by the open range of the nineteenth century, and he thus called for opposition to an expanding, activist federal government. "I have no use for Roosevelt and no use for his plans," he had said.[24]

But things began to change by the late 1930s and early 1940s, as a much greater threat to Dobie's vision of Texas clearly emerged in September 1939. For him this threat revolved around the seemingly unlikely conjunction of Great Britain, oil, and the University of Texas at Austin, all in relation to an increasingly conservative right-wing and white Texas political and business establishment (which persists to the present day). In keeping with his love for the English literary classics, he was an ardent supporter of England in the Battle of Britain, against Nazi air attacks, even as he grieved for France. On June 26, 1940, he wrote to his friend Tom Lea: "The fate of England and France... hangs like a pall over us." Before December 7, 1941, the Texas oil establishment, in league with isolationists, had opposed Roosevelt's attempt to help Great Britain while maintaining U.S. neutrality, and some had openly sympathized with what they saw as an industrially and militarily dynamic and Aryan Nazi Germany. The oil establishment abhorred Roosevelt and the federal government's increasing regulation of big business and also disdained Eleanor Roosevelt's call for "equal rights for African Americans" as well as the president's "support for an anti-lynching bill."[25]

Disturbed by such corporate blindness, Dobie threw in his lot with Roosevelt and began to advocate for racial integration, particularly of the university at Austin. This latter issue became even more of a focal point of resistance when Texas big business, operating through the university's politically appointed Board of Regents, openly tried to suppress or fire professors who were, in their eyes, engaged in "subversive activities," including the use, in their classes, of books such as John Dos Passos's *U.S.A.* trilogy. Dobie was also attacked for advocating the teaching of Russian at the university. Eventually the regents fired university president Homer Rainey, on November 1, 1944, when he defended academic freedom and openly opposed them. The campus erupted in protest, and students boycotted classes. According to Davis:

> More than any other factor, these attacks on academic freedom caused Dobie to reassess his deeply held, almost instinctive political beliefs. He realized that the greatest threat to individual freedom was no longer the government—it was right-wing business interests. With this insight, fifty-three year old Dobie became a political liberal. He wrote to a friend, "Here in the University we have a fight for academic freedom on, against a board made up almost entirely of millionaires and corporation lawyers, Roosevelt-haters, and new-style fascists. I am expected to take the lead on the side of the liberals, and I am expecting to be called on the carpet for taking part in politics."[26]

Thereafter Dobie did indeed take a liberal-left perspective on most issues, at considerable distance from his former conservative, anti-Roosevelt views of the early 1930s, views that he associated with his sense of Texas as a region. It cost him dearly in popularity as "Mr. Texas" within some conservative circles, and his new views strained his friendship with intellectual figures such as the famous regional folklorist John Lomax, an archconservative, who accused him of "stirring up class feeling." "You're disgracing yourself," Lomax wrote to Dobie, " and you're disgracing Texas. You'll ruin your reputation writing trash like this."[27] Yet as I have suggested elsewhere, we must also wonder if Dobie's new stance might have been conditioned by his never quite forgotten involvement with Mexican Americans. His feelings toward them, though conflicted, even early on included admiration for their traditional place-related culture, in contrast to American capitalist modernity, an appreciation most evident in his *Tongues of the Monte* (1935).[28]

In 1943 Cambridge University invited Dobie to spend a year there teaching American history and culture. As an ardent Anglophile, Dobie readily accepted, seeing the appointment also as a way to help the British cause in the war, with so many English faculty having enlisted in the war effort. Dobie loved the experience so much that he extended his leave of absence for another year, on an unpaid basis; he was making a good living from the sales of his very popular books and other investments. In 1947 he applied for further extension of this unpaid leave so that he could finish another book project. The request was approved at every administrative level but was ultimately denied by the president's office. The new university president at Austin was T. S. Painter, an archsegregationist who also had invited the FBI to investigate subversive activities on campus. Dobie had publically referred to him as "a flunky of the Laval pattern." Dobie was told to report for teaching duties in the fall of 1947; he refused and was fired. The firing only intensified his liberalism and his popularity with ordinary Texans and people across the world, as he continued to write about his beloved Texas in books such as *The Voice of the Coyote* (1949). For good political measure, he did not support Harry Truman in the 1948 presidential election but revealed his decidedly left regionalism by backing the third-party, leftist candidacy of Henry Wallace.

Dobie continued to fight from the left through the 1950s and early 1960s, bravely opposing the House Un-American Activities Committee's anti-Communist crusade and supporting the 1954 Supreme Court decision in *Brown vs. Board of Education of Topeka*. His opposition to HUAC drew the personal ire of J. Edgar Hoover, who sent FBI agents to investigate Dobie for "subversion." In his final few years, Dobie led a counterattack on an ultraconservative group called Texans for America who demanded, among other right-wing initiatives, that school textbooks at all levels delete references to authors disloyal to America, notably "Albert Einstein, William Faulkner, Ernest Hemingway, Willa Cather, Langston Hughes, Carl Sandburg, and several others"—including J. Frank Dobie.[29]

In the afternoon of September 18, 1964, Dobie died at his home in Austin near the university. That morning, he had received the first advance copy of his latest book, *Cow People*, which featured a variety of Texas and southwestern characters.[30] Although in his lifetime he had expressed some doubts about Texas, in the end he returned to it with critical affection. "It was a handsome book," his biographer, Steven L. Davis, tells us, "and the portraits he assembled contained some of the strongest, most disciplined writing he had ever achieved. He no longer romanticized the old-timers; instead he saw them for what they were—fellow humans who were tough and admirable in some ways, limited in others."[31] So it might be said of Dobie, as a Texas regionalist, that in the end he surpassed his initial limitations.

When Dobie died, Américo Paredes was living in Austin, indeed by then serving as an associate professor of English at the university in Dobie's old department, a new career begun when he had returned from Asia in the fall of 1950 and enrolled at the university. A man of uncommon academic talent and discipline, Paredes had completed his B.A. in the summer of 1951, in the record time of one year, and then decided to fulfill a life-long dream to become a professor of English. He stayed on at the university for an M.A. (1953) and a Ph.D. (1956). He then took a position at a small west Texas college, but for only one year. In an extraordinary move, the English department at the university in Austin invited him to join their faculty in the fall of 1957. In 1958 his doctoral dissertation was published, and by 1960 he was awarded tenure.

Paredes specialized in the professionalizing field of folklore studies, focusing on the folklore of what he soon called Greater Mexico but with a decided emphasis on south Texas. His scholarly work was devoted to recovering popular folk balladry, notably the *corrido* but other forms of folk culture as well, such as legend and proverb. He was also interested in present-day folk culture, analyzing food and joke forms not as residuals but as active elements of contemporary regional identity. He interpreted these and other folk expressions as widely distributed elements of a democratic culture—a poetics of everyday life—originating with the Mexican people of south Texas and speaking against racist domination. His principal and best-known writing is *"With His Pistol in His Hand": A Border Ballad and Its Hero* (1958). The book issued from his dissertation, which for the first time recorded and analyzed a folk genre, the corrido or ballad, that was created by the Mexican American community for the specific purpose of naming and celebrating their resistance to Anglo-American domination.[32]

In its focus on folk and popular culture understood as a critique of domination, Paredes's critical work may be compared to that of the Birmingham (England) Marxist cultural studies project launched at about the same time that he began his own.[33] Although Paredes in his youth had identified at least in spirit with the Communist Party in the 1930s, by the 1950s and 1960s Marxism in the Birmingham sense was not explicitly evident in his work. What can be seen in his later work is what Renato Rosaldo has described as an imbedded perspective that clearly relates culture to domination.[34] In contrast to Dobie's regionalist leftist activity, Paredes's contribution remained confined largely to his writing and to academic interests throughout his life; that is, he eschewed any public and active political participation. This reticence regarding political causes seems characteristic of the man, for in choosing to remain for six years in Asia, he effectively removed himself from joining what can now be recognized as a watershed, politically active generation of Mexican American World War II veterans, among whom his journalistic skills would have been of great service.[35]

Occupied with professional and family obligations during his graduate student and early teaching days at the University of Texas at Austin, Paredes at first did little in the postwar public sphere. This reserved stance changed remarkably with the onset of the Chicano student movement beginning in 1967, whose high point on the Austin campus was the establishment of the Center for Mexican-American Studies in 1970. As someone who was present and active every step of the way, I can testify that Paredes, by then an established full professor, was deeply involved with the movement, attending meetings, advocating to the administration, helping to draft position papers, traveling to coordinate with similar efforts throughout the Southwest, and later serving as the first director of the new center. For the most part, however, he served his cause of critical and leftist south Texas regionalism through his academic writings.

This chapter has traced the careers of two Texas regionalists over the first half of the twentieth century, with some emphasis on the 1930s, when both first articulated their respective regionalisms in writing. At that moment, Paredes seemed to flirt with a literary and musical modernist identity, but one must also recognize his initial development of a regionalist perspective. His early regionalism had a decidedly ethnic and leftist cast seen most evidently in his desire for a Communist Party affiliation but also in his literary critique of Anglo-inspired Mexican American class mobility and urbanized assimilation, always against the backdrop of a rural, self-sustaining traditional Mexican American society centered in the Lower Border region of south Texas. After an intervening and transnational postwar career in Asia, his later years were largely spent returning to his earlier regionalism, but now as an accomplished scholar, a career he had actually begun before his war service, with his first scholarly publication, in 1942, in which his enduring interest in the balladry of resistance is already evident.[36]

The university at Austin was also the site for Dobie's articulation of his regionalism, based on a more diffused Texas geography than that of Paredes. Unlike Paredes, Dobie originally placed his regionalism decidedly on the political right, but later his transnational affiliations with England and Europe played a role in shifting his allegiances toward the left. It was under this transnational influence that he developed what his most recent biographer correctly calls "a liberated mind," a shift in identity that led him, momentarily at least, to question his fundamental regional allegiance to Texas. Toward the end of his life he said: "I wonder why and how I used to think that I could not live happily anywhere but in Texas and wanted no intellectual pabulum but Texas. . . . Intensity can make a fool of a man."[37] Yet though he began to long for a world beyond the regional, he also said, "I'll always have roots in Texas"—and it must be recalled that his last book was, indeed, *Cow People*.[38] But as his career developed and toward the end, he brought this love for Texas into a more universal and global framework, asserting, for example, in 1960 that "unless the regional has elements of the universal it is country-minded and is, therefore, damned . . . I ask of the regional that it enlarge, not diminish me."[39]

In closing, it is fitting to recall the moment when these two careers overlapped personally. Back in the 1930s Paredes had written a scathing, satirical portrait of Dobie in the fictional character of K. Hank Harvey. But Dobie never saw that writing, because the manuscript of Paredes's novel *George Washington Gómez* was not retrieved from his archives and published until 1990. Paredes had also mildly criticized Dobie's views toward Mexicans in "*With His Pistol in His Hand*" in the 1950s, and in other writings—and these Dobie did see. Yet Dobie admired and promoted the book when it appeared.[40] In an exquisite irony given Dobie's ranching origins, "Dobie's reading of Paredes also influenced his view of the King Ranch," writes Davis. "Dobie now understood that the King Ranch and the Texas Rangers who worked on its behalf were accused of illegally dispossessing Mexicano land grant families."[41] The King Ranch is often credited with inventing cattle ranching itself, a falsehood Dobie exposed. "Millions of Spanish-Mexican cattle had been raised in south Texas," he observed, "before King owned an acre or a cow."[42]

During Paredes's early career Dobie and his wife were still living close to the university campus in Austin, even after Dobie was dismissed in 1947. Of their overlapping time there, Paredes had this to say in the 1990s: "I was pretty harsh on Dobie in the novel because I didn't know him when I was writing the novel. Later, when I came to the University of Texas, I finally did meet him. I found him to be a very lovable old ... fraud. I was invited to his house several times, and I think we even visited him at his Paisano Ranch. But as I said, he was a lovable old fraud [laughter] as far as Mexican materials were concerned. . . . When I did get to know him, we would talk about a number of things, but never about Mexicans."[43]

There is no record that Paredes ever returned the courtesy by inviting the Dobies to his home, but he did pay Dobie the respect of singing a corrido about him at the Texas Folklore Society meetings after Dobie's death, a corrido composed by Longino Guerrero of Austin, Texas. Whatever Dobie's early failings when it came to Mexicans, one must still wish that he and Paredes had become able to talk frankly about Mexicans and Anglos and Texas, and also that Paredes could have viewed Dobie in other than largely racial terms. There is no record that Paredes was ever able to see and perhaps appreciate Dobie's stalwart politics in defense of racial equality and academic freedom, which were legendary on the Austin campus and in liberal circles in Texas during Paredes's early academic career. Uttered late in his life, Paredes's use of the phrase "old fraud" seems uncharacteristically unkind and contributes to what Davis has correctly identified as a marked tendency of younger Mexican American scholars to see Dobie solely "as a perpetrator of racist histories."[45] That these two regionalists on the left could not make common cause to articulate a bilingual, bicultural progressive Texas in the face of capitalist and racist domination remains sadly true today for the two peoples who have inherited their regional legacies. For the most part, in Texas we remain neither friends nor strangers.

NOTES

1. Michael C. Steiner, "Regionalism in the Great Depression," *Geographical Review* 73 (October 1983): 432.

2. Steiner, "Regionalism in the Great Depression," 430.

3. Herb Wylie, Christian Riegel, Karen Overbye, and Don Perkins, "Introduction: Regionalism Revisited," in *A Sense of Place: Re-evaluating Regionalism in Canadian and American Writing* (Edmonton: University of Alberta Press, 1997), xii.

4. Malini Johar Schueller, *Locating Race: Global Sites of Post-colonial Citizenship* (Albany: State University of New York Press, 2009), 3.

5. Here and throughout, my biographical commentary on Dobie is informed by Steven L. Davis, *J. Frank Dobie: A Liberated Mind* (Austin: University of Texas Press, 2009). See also Lon Tinkle, *An American Original: The Life of J. Frank Dobie* (Boston: Little, Brown, 1978).

6. Don Graham, *Kings of Texas: The 150-Year Saga of an American Ranching Empire* (New York: Wiley, 2003).

7. David Montejano, *Anglos and Mexicans in the Making of Texas, 1836–1986* (Austin: University of Texas Press, 1987), 113.

8. J. Frank Dobie, *A Vaquero of the Brush Country: The Life and Times of John D. Young* (Austin: University of Texas Press, 1929), 62.

9. On the 1915 revolts see Benjamin Johnson, *Revolution in Texas: How a Forgotten Rebellion and Its Bloody Suppression Turned Mexicans into Americans* (New Haven: Yale University Press, 2005). On Catarino Garza see Elliot Young, *Catarino Garza's Revolution on the Texas-Mexico Border* (Durham: Duke University Press, 2004).

10. Américo Paredes, *"With His Pistol in His Hand": A Border Ballad and Its Hero* (Austin: University of Texas Press, 1958).

11. Steiner, "Regionalism in the Great Depression," 430.

12. Emilio Zamora, as quoted in Manuel F. Medrano, *Américo Paredes in His Own Words: An Authorized Biography* (Denton: University of North Texas Press, 2010), 32.

13. Américo Paredes, *The Hammon and the Beans and Other Stories* (Houston: Arte Publico, 1994).

14. Américo Paredes, *George Washington Gómez: A Mexico-Texan Novel* (Houston: Arte Publico, 1990).

15. Paredes, *George Washington Gómez*, 271–72.

16. Ramón Saldívar, *The Borderlands of Culture: Américo Paredes and the Transnational Imaginary* (Durham: Duke University Press, 2006), 117–18.
17. Paredes, *George Washington Gómez*, 300.
18. Saldívar, *Borderlands of Culture*, 120, 91.
19. Paredes, "The Four Freedoms," in *Between Two Worlds* (Houston: Arte Público, 1991), 58. Quoted in Saldívar, *Borderlands of Culture*, 215–16.
20. Saldívar, *Borderlands of Culture*, 240.
21. Saldívar, *Borderlands of Culture*, 241.
22. Saldívar, *Borderlands of Culture*, 93.
23. Saldívar, *Borderlands of Culture*, 91.
24. Davis, *J. Frank Dobie*, 99.
25. Davis, *J. Frank Dobie*, 143 (to Tom Lea), 144 (oil companies' opposition to the Roosevelts).
26. Davis, *J. Frank Dobie*, 152–53.
27. Davis, *J. Frank Dobie*, 157.
28. José E. Limón, *Dancing with the Devil: Society and Cultural Poetics in Mexican-American South Texas* (Madison: University of Wisconsin Press, 1994). J. Frank Dobie, *Tongues of the Monte* (Boston: Little, Brown, 1935).
29. Davis, *J. Frank Dobie*, 228.
30. J. Frank Dobie, *Cow People* (Boston: Little, Brown, 1964).
31. Davis, *J. Frank Dobie*, 233.
32. Paredes, *"With His Pistol in His Hand."*
33. Simon During, "Introduction," in *The Cultural Studies Reader*, ed. Simon During (New York: Routledge, 1993), 1–25.
34. Angie Chabram-Dernersesian, ed., *The Chicana/o Cultural Studies Forum: Critical and Ethnographic Perspectives* (New York: New York University Press, 2007), 116.
35. Maggie Rivas-Rodríguez and Emilio Zamora, *Beyond the Latino World War II Hero: The Social and Political Legacy of a Generation* (Austin: University of Texas Press, 2009).
36. Américo Paredes, "The Mexico-Texan Corrido," *Southwest Review* 27 (1942): 470–81. See my exchange with Ramón Saldívar on the issue of Asia in relation to Paredes's later career: José E. Limón, "Border Literary Histories, Globalization and Critical Regionalism," *American Literary History* 20 (2008): 160–82; Ramón Saldívar, "Asian Américo: Paredes in Asia and the Borderlands: A Response to José E. Limón," *American Literary History* 21 (2009): 584–94; José E. Limón, "Imagining the Imaginary: A Reply to Ramón Saldívar," *American Literary History* 21 (2009): 595–603.
37. Davis, *J. Frank Dobie*, 186.
38. Davis, *J. Frank Dobie*, 171.
39. J. Frank Dobie, "Out of Regionalism: A Larger View," *Saturday Review*. 60 (May 21, 1960), 17. Also see Dobie, "The Writer and His Region," *Southwest Review* 35 (Spring 1950): 81–87.
40. Davis, *J. Frank Dobie*, 210–11.
41. Davis, *J. Frank Dobie*, 214.
42. Davis, *J. Frank Dobie*, 214. The King Ranch as the beginning point of cattle ranching is most vividly articulated in the George Stevens film *Giant* (1956), based on Edna

Ferber's novel of the same name, which was in turn based on the King Ranch and partially written on the ranch itself.

43. Saldívar, *Borderlands of Culture*, 117, 119.

44. The corrido and a brief discussion may be found in F. E. Abernethy, "Longino Guerrero's Corrido on J. Frank Dobie," in *Corners of Texas*, ed. Francis Edward Abernethy (Denton: University of North Texas Press, 1993), 197–200.

45. Davis, *J. Frank Dobie*, 236. I do take exception to Davis's blanket indictment of all Mexican American scholars. I believe that my own earlier assessment of Dobie is more evenhanded. See my *Dancing with the Devil*, chapter 2, "J. Frank Dobie."

PART III

THE NORTHERN WEST

Although the Northern West lacks strong identity as a unified cultural region, the stretch of land that includes Montana, Idaho, Washington, and Oregon has a long tradition of fiery class and labor protest. Remindful of historical patterns on the neighboring Great Plains, the leftist labor politics of this northern tier reached a flash point between 1890 and 1920, and the radical regionalism that followed in the 1930s had a stronger literary, environmental, and racial slant than its predecessor.

The Northern West's turbulent labor history, fairly well known, is noted for flamboyant leaders such as William "Big Bill" Haywood, Frank Little, John Reed, Louise Bryant, and Anna Louise Strong, as well as the election of socialist mayors and state senators in every state of the region in the early twentieth century. A highly independent, anarchic streak of environmental and social protest continues today.[1] Birthplace of some of the nation's most militant labor unions—including the Western Federation of Miners (1892) and Industrial Workers of the World (1904)—and site of a string of virulent labor battles and protests—including the Coeur d'Alene and Butte labor wars beginning in the 1890s, the Spokane Free Speech Fight (1906), the Everett Massacre (1916), the Centralia Massacre (1919), and the Seattle General Strike (1919)—the Northern West and the West Coast have seen working-class protest more violent and vivid than in the rest of the nation.

Labor radicalism across the Northern West has been widely recognized, but the more self-conscious cultural regionalism that followed in the 1930s is a less familiar story. Compared to other western regions, the Northern West has evolved a diffuse cultural identity that has bred fewer conspicuous groups of regional writers, artists, and social critics. A significant cluster of regionalist painters, including Mark Tobey, Maurice Graves, and Guy Anderson, emerged in Washington in the 1930s. Oregon-based novelist H. L. Davis published appeals for a tough-minded northwestern regionalism and achieved this goal in his Pulitzer Prize–winning novel *Honey in the Horn* (1935), and the irascible Idaho writer and social critic Vardis Fisher advocated a retrograde form of regionalism during the 1930s and beyond. The most influential Northern West regionalist of the era, however, was Harold Guy Merriam, a devoted English professor at the University of Montana who, much like Benjamin Botkin at the University of Oklahoma, edited a nationally recognized literary magazine, in this case *The Frontier* (1927–39), sponsored regional writers' conferences, taught generations of Montana-based writers, and laid the groundwork for the writing renaissance that would come to the region in later decades.

The Northern West's left-wing regionalists tended to be maverick intellectuals, without supporting networks like those that emerged in the Midwest or in California and to a limited extent in the Great Plains and Texas. Crusading Montana journalist and historian Joseph Kinsey Howard (1906–51), mixed-race Montana writer and intellectual D'Arcy McNickle (1904–77), and Washington State proletarian novelist Robert Cantwell (1908–78) were independent-minded critics who identified with the marginalized and the oppressed. Their radical visions of racial, economic, and environmental injustice in their native grounds have universal implications.

Tim Lehman's lucidly written chapter presents Joe Howard as a fearless critic of predatory capitalism and outspoken advocate for the dispossessed. In many ways the consummate radical regionalist, this provocative Great Falls journalist and historian used his finely tuned sense of place, sympathy for the underdog, and unblinking awareness of the dark corners of history to create an inclusive, forward-facing vision of what his region might become. Among many other things, Lehman illuminates the background and significance of Howard's two path-breaking books: *Montana: High, Wide, and Handsome* (1943) and *Strange Empire: Louis Riel and the Métis People* (1952). At the publication of his first book—one that would become arguably the most popular ever written about Montana—Howard endured slander and death threats because of his unflinching depiction of the systematic looting of the state by distant corporate powers. In his second book Howard ennobled the scorned Métis people of the U.S.-Canadian borderlands, whose mixed-race heritage pushed them beyond the pale of both white and Indian culture. To even a greater degree than Mari Sandoz, Howard saw Indian societies as a "model for interdependent communities," and with the Métis he "championed the cause of a society that he saw as a repudiation of the exploitive individualism that ravaged the region." With his vision of cultural pluralism across national boundaries, Lehman concludes, "Howard the regionalist had become a globalist, the historian of the transnational frontier."

Howard's fellow Montanan D'Arcy McNickle, whose maternal grandfather had fought with Louis Riel in the Métis Rebellion of 1885, was a direct descendant of the people Howard wrote so eloquently about. Like Howard, McNickle became an acclaimed writer with a complex vision of race, region, and politics. William Bevis's impressionistic chapter traces the growth of this distinctive tribal-regional stance that transcended right, left, and liberal ideologies. Following McNickle's intellectual odyssey, from his mixed race upbringing to his cosmopolitan education and lifestyle in the 1920s to his work in the Bureau of Indian Affairs in the 1930s and beyond, this chapter explores the local and global implications of McNickle's thought. Through a close reading of *Wind from an Enemy Sky* (1978), Bevis explains how McNickle ultimately rejected the "Bad Medicine" offered by liberal capitalists and radical Marxists alike and opted for the deeper radicalism of a tribal perspective.

Farther west, in the Depression-ravaged lumber town of Aberdeen, Washington, young writer Robert Cantwell drew upon local memories of IWW labor radicalism and his harsh work experience in a plywood factory to complete *The Land of Plenty* (1934), among the most highly praised proletarian novels of the 1930s. In T. V. Reed's insightful chapter we see how Cantwell achieved this sophisticated work of literary leftism to become, along with Jack Conroy and John Steinbeck, the archetypal proletarian regional novelist. Reed's careful and nuanced reading of *The Land of Plenty* reveals how Cantwell created a politically charged, regionally rooted novel that endures as a sophisticated and compelling work of art. Along with the work of Howard and McNickle, Cantwell's dark-edged narrative, deeply sensitive to issues of class, race, and gender, stands as a powerful contribution to radical western regionalism.

NOTES

1. See, e.g., Jeffrey A. Johnson, *"They Are All Red Out Here": Socialist Politics in the Pacific Northwest, 1895-1925* (Norman: University of Oklahoma Press, 2008); and Carlos Schwantes, *Radical Heritage: Labor, Socialism, and Reform in Washington and British Columbia, 1885-1917* (Seattle: University of Washington Press, 1979).

Joseph Kinsey Howard. Courtesy of Montana Historical Society Research Center, Archives (PAC 90-46 f4).

CHAPTER NINE

Wrong Side Up

JOSEPH KINSEY HOWARD AND THE WISDOM

OF THE DISPOSSESSED

Timothy Lehman

Regionalism ... means fullest recognition and utilization of the resources of one's area and their integration into the national and world scene; and of course it welcomes new brains and new blood for the regional effort. Provincialism means sitting around on one's fat rump and yelping that everything is rosy as it is and we mustn't be disturbed and asked to think. Montana isn't regional enough and it's too damned provincial and always has been.

—Joseph Kinsey Howard, 1946

Joe Howard, Montana's muckraking journalist and most provocative historian, always trusted a pithy story to get to the heart of the matter. One of these stories began with a North Dakota farmer who suddenly noticed a "solemn Sioux Indian" watching him plow his fields. The farmer observed with amused condescension while "the old Indian knelt, thrust his fingers into the plow furrow, measured its depth, fingered the sod and the buried grass." Slowly standing, the Indian solemnly pronounced, "Wrong side up."[1] Although this story had originally been told to reveal the "ignorance of the poor Indian," Howard liked to explain that the real joke was on the patronizing farmer, who would realize the value of the grassland only years later, after the devastating drought of the 1930s caused dust storms throughout eastern Montana and the Great Plains. Howard's story turns over more than grass; like a biblical parable it inverts the notion of who is foolish and who is wise, just as it shows that possessors of land must learn from the dispossessed.

The story also reveals Howard's finely tuned sense of place, of a region given shape by biology and history. His northern plains were an abused grassland peopled with ecologically wise but tragically outnumbered societies: Indians and cowboys. In a letter to a friend, he wrote, "All through the country the Indians fought their last battle to keep their land and their meat. A decade or two later the cattlemen, on the same ground, fought against the homesteaders to keep their land and their meat, wrested from the Indians. Both the Indians and the cattlemen were right, and the homesteaders were wrong, but numerous."[2] Indians and cowboys alike, Howard believed, possessed the land without destroying it; both groups embodied an implicit ecological sensibility of how human society should develop in harmony with nature. In his view, protecting the land required greater respect for the folkways of those who knew it best. His ecological vision came from an appreciation of the cultural wisdom of the dispossessed. The powerless were better guides for society than the powerful. Ultimately "wrong side up" applied as much to society as it did to soil.

Joseph Kinsey Howard's personal background prepared him to view history from the underside. Born in Iowa in 1906, he was five years old when his family moved to Alberta, and thirteen when they returned from Canada to settle in Great Falls, Montana. In Alberta his father worked as a mine manager, and young Joe, influenced by his mother, came to sympathize with the mine workers. As a boy on the prairies of western Canada, he learned with other boys to play war—not the impersonal, mechanical war then raging in Europe but the adventurous, glamorous war of an earlier time when the Métis, descendants of French fur traders and Indian women, fought for independence against the overwhelming power of the Canadian Mounted Police. This childhood play taught him the Métis story, which would become the basis for his magisterial history *Strange Empire: Louis Riel and the Métis People* (1952). Although it was decades before he conceptualized this child's play in terms of Canadian manifest destiny, even as a child he realized that he was the only boy eager to take the side of the Métis, "to adopt the role of the traitor," to become a member of "the side that couldn't ever win, made up of people who—shamefully, somehow—weren't even white."[3]

Joe Howard's father left the family while they were still living in Canada. When they moved to Great Falls in 1919, Joe, an only child, and his mother had to fend for themselves. Struggling to make her way as a single mother, Josephine Howard found a small apartment that they would share as their primary home for the rest of their lives. The experience of living "two against the world" strengthened the bond between mother and son even as it put them both more than ever "on the side of the underdog," according to friends.[4] From his mother, Joe acquired at an early age compassion, idealism, and a love of learning. He frequented the town's lone bookstore and discussed books and ideas with her. Although he flirted with socialism when he was young, his was a heroic more than a scientific socialism. He never lost the idea that individuals could make a difference. Committed to the ideal of self-improvement, he kept a notebook of quotations reflecting his sympathy for the oppressed and his commitment to making a difference in the world. Containing selections from literature, poetry, and philosophy, the notebook reflected a commitment to lofty ideals and heroic struggle, sometimes socialist and often romantic.

After high school Howard found a job as a reporter in Great Falls and in three years was promoted to copy desk editor, a job he held until 1944. Acquaintances described him as hard-working, brilliant, charismatic, attractive, and enthusiastic. While working full-time, he helped to organize the newspaper guild, an activity that cemented his life-long appreciation for unions. For him, unions meant decent working conditions and a "worker's right to a good life in a good town." He subscribed to the labor theory of value but, at least in a public speech, associated it not with Marx but with Lincoln. Even though he believed militant strikes were sometimes necessary if workers were to obtain their rights in a capitalistic democracy, he was never quite comfortable with socialist orthodoxy. His leftist tendencies made him "convinced as ever of the inevitability of the revolution," but he was in no hurry for it, he wrote to a friend, because his nonconformist ways would make him "one of the first ones shot."[5] He was attracted to a socialist solidarity with the working class, but he was too pragmatic and too much of an individual to fit neatly into any category or movement. At bottom, he was the champion of the underdog more than a believer in a system, Marxian or otherwise. In the late 1930s Howard brought this perspective to the national scene with articles for periodicals such as *Harper's Magazine, The Saturday Evening Post, The Progressive,* and *The Nation.* These attracted the attention of editors at Yale University Press, who invited him to write a book-length history of Montana. In five years of working evenings and weekends, he produced *Montana: High, Wide, and Handsome* (1943)—the book that would introduce him to the wider literary world and change the way people thought about Montana.

Blending colorful characters, rugged landscapes, and unpredictable weather, all held together by a strong theme of exploitation, *Montana: High, Wide, and Handsome* became the most popular book ever written about Montana. Howard's theme from the beginning was the colonial exploitation of the region. He portrayed the state's history as "an object lesson in domestic imperialism." Quoting Baker Brownell, who later would become Howard's colleague in a regional cultural effort known as the Montana Study, he wrote that Montana's history had been warped by eastern financial interests who exploited the region "as a hinterland, draining wealth and youth . . . without corresponding return."[6] In his notes for the book he stated his position that "Montana has been looted," that "resource exploitation" formed the core of the region's history. Yet he also promised to tell this story not as "propaganda" but with "color and romance," anecdotes of "cowboy and homestead life, epic fires and blizzards, gun fights, rustler roundups, Indian raids, underground copper battles and the 'war of the copper kings.'"[7]

Both within the region and throughout the nation, response to the book was always strong but never neutral. Some bookstores in Montana apparently refused to carry it, and one reporter noted that finding Howard's book was almost as delicate a procedure as buying moonshine from a bootlegger.[8] The Anaconda Copper Mining Company, a frequent target of the book, discouraged people from being friends with Howard, a situation that led him to feel as if he were on the company's blacklist. Nevertheless the book gained immediate popularity and catapulted him into a new career as a writer. *Montana: High, Wide, and Handsome* went through eight printings in three years and has never been out of print. Reviewers across the country praised its grit, integrity, and readability. A *New York Times* reviewer called it a "brave, clear-sighted book" with an "anger that steadily flashes" from its pages, from "a man bitter about the betrayal of a place he loves." Another called it "one of the best books about an American state ever written." Part of the book's appeal came from Howard's journalistic habits of probing for revealing vignettes, outlandish characters, and moments of meaning among commonplace people and events. One Seattle reviewer wrote privately to Howard, "your mention of those unknown people is not provincial. It's just what the goddamned stuffed-shirt historians of this country need thrown in their faces at every opportunity."[9] Years before social historians promised to rewrite history from the bottom up, Howard told a story peopled not with the powerful, the celebrities, and the aristocrats, but with the powerless, the anonymous, and the commonplace. To his critics, it must have looked like history with the wrong side up.

Even if they were not sure about Howard's politics, many readers were drawn to his strong descriptions of the High Plains grassland environment. "The best Montana stories," he wrote, "deal with the erratic and unpredictable character of Montana weather."[10] He colored his descriptions of the northern plains not only with delightfully eccentric human heroes but also with a wildly variable Nature: chinooks that come too late to warm freezing cattle, winds that always blow, rain that refuses to fall, winter storms that freeze a body stiff, and summer heat that wilts a wheat field.

As Montana readers recognized, blizzards, chinooks, and sweltering heat were central to living in the region. As Montanans knew from lived experience, the natural environment played a crucial role in the development of the state. Early in the book Howard devoted an entire chapter to grass, and he repeatedly referred to the love of grass as one of the defining characteristics of a true westerner. For him, grassland was the Edenic paradise, Nature in pure balance, the canvas on which all subsequent history was painted. In Montana's past, the prairie grasses were abundant because of "Nature's meticulous planning," by which he meant the symbiotic relationship between grass and bison: "This was Nature's controlled grazing: vast herds of ponderous, hungry bison ranging across millions of unfenced acres, eating their fill—but moving on. The springy sod which had formed through centuries of growth and death of this grass cushioned pleasantly the great weight on their hooves; and the wind—for there had always been wind—blew the flowering heads of the bluestem against their bellies."[11]

All subsequent invasions of this Eden were judged, in Howard's dramatic scheme, by how well the newcomers harmonized their activities with the demands of the grassland regime. Plains Indians understood this, he maintained, and "lived in honorable alliance" with Nature. They knew uses for all varieties of native plants and "husbanded their game resources cautiously even in times of plenty."[12] Later, cattlemen occupied the range and, under fierce competitive pressure, overstocked and overgrazed the range. Nature, in the form of the unforgivingly frigid winter of 1885–86, answered back with a chastening message that cattlemen took to heart. If ranchers had learned by their mistakes to live with Nature, pioneer farmers and their plows represented a new and thoroughly unnatural actor in the historical drama. The cattleman had "been here long enough to learn" and "genuinely loves the grass which the plow is destroying," but the farmer did not even understand the delicately balanced system he was ruining.[13] Again Nature, this time in the form of wind, drought, and blowing dust, administered the appropriate punishment to those who would destroy Eden.

Howard borrowed themes for this grassland morality tale from other regional writers of his day. Stuart Chase, in *Rich Land, Poor Land* (1936), had also written a chapter on grass and told similar stories that emphasized the need for conservation. Walter Prescott Webb, in his classic *The Great Plains* (1931), had narrated an environmentally determined history of the region, in which the lack of rainfall and the scarcity of trees were key constraints on plains development. Howard was influenced by these writers, but his dramatic rendition gave nature a more active role than either of those authors had suggested. For Webb, the aridity of the Great Plains presented a barrier to frontier settlement, but a barrier that could be overcome with sufficient American ingenuity. Chase shared Howard's concern with grass, but his emphasis was on the politics of planning and conservation. Whether consciously or not, all three authors reflected the reigning ecological paradigm of a balanced, climax grassland ecosystem as taught by Nebraska botanist Frederick Clements, whose classic study of prairie grassland was the ultimate example of the "balance of nature" approach that dominated ecological thinking during much of the twentieth century. As these and other authors argued, agriculture inevitably meant the destruction of nature's equilibrium. But it was Howard, more than the rest, who presented Nature not only as a stage, and as the scenic backdrop for action, but as an actor in the drama who would pronounce judgment on the ecologically arrogant and instruct the ecologically wise in prudence and humility. No wonder that Howard usually capitalized "Nature."[14]

When Howard turned to western history as a source for his protests against abuse of the land, he relied on a nonconformist whose life was a great story in itself and whose work was often misunderstood or ignored: John Wesley Powell. The one-armed Civil War veteran and explorer of the Colorado River had published in 1878 his *Report on the Lands of the Arid Region*, a discarded blueprint for ecologically sensitive development in the American West. Howard first wrote about Powell during the 1930s, in a piece for *The Survey Graphic* entitled "Prophet without Honor." He saw Powell as "a scientist with an amazing prophetic vision": his ideas were ignored, "and the plains people perished." Powell had proposed that homesteading in the West should proceed only after land had been classified into three broad ecological categories: pasture, irrigation, and forest. Each type of land required a different pattern of settlement—large spreads for grazing land, small parcels for labor-intensive irrigated farms, and shared management of forested lands. The arid conditions of the West, Powell believed, meant that the individually owned farm settlements of the East could not be reproduced there; rather, all types of land use required group cooperation and shared control of precious water resources. Powell's proposals for land classification and settlement in the West, according to Howard, amounted to a "draft constitution for a new society in the western United States, a co-operative, free society composed of individuals who realized their responsibility to each other and acknowledged their debt to the soil." This new society was the sort that might have been developed by the Indians, because it "incorporated as much as it could of the best features of their society, their intimate colleagueship with Nature."[15]

Howard recognized in Powell's ideas the core concept that both Indians and cattlemen used land according to its natural purpose, that sensitivity to the land placed natural limits on what it could sustain. But his own environmentalism came not so much from a love of pure nature, as Powell's had, as from an appreciation of the dispossessed cultures that had inhabited the land. One friend described Howard as "bored to death" on a pack trip in the wilderness and called him "the antithesis of an outdoor person."[16] Howard did own a cabin along the Teton River not far from his Great Falls apartment, but his affection for the cabin came not because it brought him closer to nature, rather because it reminded him of the

Métis who had once frequented the area. He was drawn to Powell's ideas not for some sentimental attachment to an idealized nature, but because he saw Powell as another underdog in need of a champion. Land use wisdom, as Howard saw it, came from dispossessed societies and disinherited prophets.

Although he had hard words for anyone who abused the land, Howard saved his sternest invective for the city of Butte, which he termed "the black heart of Montana." In his view the Anaconda Copper Mining Company had found the "richest hill on earth" and carted away its millions of dollars' worth of minerals to far-off urban centers. He maintained that of "all the 'colonial' cities of the American West," Butte formed the "outstanding example of exploitation by that peculiarly American imperialist capitalism which has outstripped the resources of its own frontier in half a century." The Company, as Montanans generally called it, had "plundered" the public's resources for millions while treating the lives of miners with indifference. He claimed that during the boom years the mines had lost one miner per day and that there were so many injuries that the drugstores advertised sales on crutches. The Company controlled the police, the courts, the state government, and the newspapers. It "thrust its finger into every man's pie to make brutally manifest its absolute economic domination of the state, its power of life and death over the common man." Contrary to the image of the western frontier as an example of individualist democracy, Butte had become the picture of "monopolist concentration of the means of production." Men came west and found not opportunity but endless toil, market vulnerability, and injury or death, all the while with real wealth accumulating not in Montana but in corporate headquarters on the East or West Coast. "The ideals of laissez-faire capitalism," he claimed, "have been committing suicide in Butte."[17]

Howard's suggested alternative to predatory capitalism was New Deal-style, grassroots, regionally based, cooperative land use planning. He championed three distinct projects that had Montana origins and had in fact gained support from the federal government during the 1930s: unified county planning that coordinated federal subsidies with local needs, first tried in Teton County, near his home in Great Falls; a cooperative grazing district, pioneered in Montana's Powder River country and incorporated into the 1934 Taylor Grazing Act; and the Milk River farm resettlement program, which purchased marginal dryland farms (with the grass turned "wrong side up") and resettled farmers on federally supported irrigated farms. What the projects had in common was a cooperative focus and an attention to using land according to its natural limitations—ideas Howard had absorbed from Powell. If the rule on the northern plains was "cooperate or perish," this logically meant some sort of land use planning. It had to be, Howard maintained, "grass-roots planning, the only kind that can ever succeed." Even if New Deal land use plans represented a fulfillment of Powell's vision for the West, still "the planners had to be Montanans, with dust on their pants."[18]

Unfortunately for Howard and for regional development in Montana, these plans received much less attention than the historical chapters in his book that set the stage for them. As his editor foresaw before publication, "It would happen of course that the chapter on planning which you have been building up to all through the book is inevitably one of the least interesting ones. That always seems to be true—that constructive legislation, etc., is not as good reading as scandals and disaster."[19] The truth was that Howard was better as a muckraker than a reformer.

Regardless of what readers thought of his political reforms, *Montana: High, Wide, and Handsome* altered the way people thought about the region. Some historians picked up the theme of Montana as an especially beautiful land that had been despoiled by predatory capitalists; K. Ross Toole, perhaps the state's most popular historian of the mid-twentieth century, wrote a best-selling history of the state as an "uncommon land" whose resources and people had been exploited by the forces of distant corporate greed. Other historians challenged this view, arguing that Howard had overdramatized the state's history, exaggerated the extent of Anaconda's control over the press and the courts, and unfairly stereotyped homesteaders as poor, ignorant farmers. Howard's interpretation, they suggested, adhered too closely to a cattlemen's view of Montana history and degraded homesteaders by characterizing them as "honyockers," a term that perhaps had originated as a racial slur and carried connotations of ignorance and failure. Yet even critics of his interpretation admitted that his way of understanding the state—as a beautiful land cruelly exploited by outsiders for corporate profit—helped to explain how a state with a strong conservative streak could also have significant environmental and anti-corporate sympathies. Even historians who rejected his views as excessively moralistic and melodramatic concluded that the book had "probably affected people's thinking about Montana more than any other work."[20]

Publication of *Montana: High, Wide, and Handsome* also enlarged permanently the horizons for Howard's career. His literary agent had thought that the book would do well to sell enough copies to repay the $500 author's advance from the press, but robust sales very quickly made Howard more than five times that amount.[21] The royalties never made him rich, but they did provide him with enough of a financial cushion to quit his regular job as a newspaper editor in 1944 and pursue his writing career. The book also brought him a wider circle of literary friends, including the western historian and popular essayist Bernard DeVoto—who had likewise, and famously, described the West as a "plundered province" that had been "looted, betrayed, and sold out." For DeVoto, as for Howard, over the long haul the "dispossessed have the last laugh on their conquerors." Recognizing a kindred spirit, DeVoto described Howard as one of a "small handful of first-rate writers" from the West, and the two western writers, one in Cambridge, Massachusetts and the other in Great Falls, Montana, immediately became friends.[22] They shared a common interpretation of the West and a commitment to writing history for a popular audience. In 1947 Howard spent time with DeVoto and others at the prestigious Breadloaf Writers' Conference in Vermont. His book proved to be part of a renaissance of interest in John Wesley Powell, helping to create the explorer's legacy not as an ignored prophet but as a visionary advocate of irrigation-based agrarian democracy in the West. A decade after Howard's book appeared, DeVoto's friend Wallace Stegner published the first full-length treatment of Powell's life and work, citing Howard as one of a trio of scholars who had "discovered" Powell.[23]

Using the increased visibility he gained from the wide readership of *Montana: High, Wide, and Handsome*, Howard focused from 1944 to 1946 on solving the region's problems that the book had identified. Like other writers of the western plains, including Walter Prescott Webb, Angie Debo, Bernard DeVoto, J. Frank Dobie, and Mari Sandoz, he adopted a regionalism that was not tied to a mythical past with a vanishing frontier, although his view contained sadness for what had been lost. Instead, like many of these other regionalists, he faced the future more than the past. As Robert Dorman has written of these regionalists, they "came to share in this hope that regionalism could provide a map not just for cultural reconstruction but for social, economic, and political reform as well."[24] Howard's interest in political reform led him to support federal plans for a regional upper Missouri River development authority modeled on the Tennessee Valley Authority. Because he worried that distant corporations siphoned away both wealth and people from the region, he argued that a Missouri Valley Authority could provide cheap energy that would support local industry, job creation, and economic development. He wrote articles and testified in Congress as a self-described "lone innocent out of the West" that the northern plains suffered from rural depopulation caused by the flight of manufacturing and the mechanization of agriculture. The population left behind was growing smaller, older, and poorer as a result, and their communities had little to offer in the way of economic vitality or cultural life. "Unless these trends are arrested," he warned, "unless we are able to establish a more diversified economic base for Montana, we are going to become a state of vast agricultural plantations and a couple of extractive industries living on declining natural resources, metals, and timber."[25]

A federally funded, regionally based Missouri Valley Authority could not only provide flood control, irrigation, and navigation on the river, but its system of dams could generate hydroelectric power that would attract industry. As Howard envisioned it, this was exactly the sort of program Powell might have approved. Opponents thought the proposal would violate states' rights, involved too much federal control, and perhaps smacked of socialism. In the end the Missouri Valley Authority never made it out of congressional committee. When Congress did authorize a series of dams on the Missouri River under the Pick-Sloan Plan, engineering concerns rather than Howard's version of regional community building dominated the process.

If Howard's efforts at a political version of regionalism were thwarted, he was more successful with his cultural efforts. In 1944 Ernest Melby, chancellor of the Montana University System, established (with funding from the Rockefeller Foundation) the Montana Study, an ambitious organization aimed at improving the cultural and intellectual life of small towns in the region. Based on the idealistic regionalist philosophy of Baker Brownell, of Northwestern University, the Montana Study set out to cultivate local art, literature, and history as means of reviving interest and drawing people to the countryside. Brownell wrote to Chancellor Melby that he was "very interested in work of this sort and have long felt and written that the hope of our civilization in America is in regional development and culture." Twentieth-century mass society represented for him the triumph of industrial concentration and standardization, epitomized in large, faceless cities and homogenous, sterile cultures. Brownell, whose work Howard had quoted in *Montana: High, Wide, and Handsome*, was known in academic circles for his commitment to stabilizing rural communities, finding ways of making rural living both economically viable and culturally appealing so that rural populations would balance the strong magnetism of urban life. "The entire concentrative movement of population into the great urban regions," Brownell had written, "has reached a point of over-balance."[26]

Making small towns both interesting and viable was not merely a technical matter but also required a focus on the intellectual life, the arts and humanities, of the local culture. The way to do this, Brownell believed, was to form study groups that would work as "the modern version of the town meeting."[27] Representing the entire community, and pursuing no partisan or ideological objective, the Montana Study researchers would inventory available cultural resources, discuss local history, analyze community problems, and create means for increasing the intellectual vitality of small towns. Nothing less than the future of American democracy was at stake, Brownell contended, for without revitalization in the countryside, "the democratic community and functional family will continue to decline in American life."[28]

The best person to implement this vision in Montana, Brownell and Melby agreed, was Joe Howard. Fresh from reading *Montana: High, Wide, and Handsome*, Brownell wrote to Howard, "The book is about the finest thing that I have seen in the kind of job it undertakes. I like immensely its emphasis and anger, the color and hard-rock facts with which it is filled. Whether or not we in the United States can move towards the kind of regionalism which you support seems to me the most critical question that this country now faces."[29] When the Montana Study hired Howard for its field staff, he responded to Brownell that this was a chance "to renew my faith in the possible improvement of conditions in a state I love very much."[30] From 1944 through 1946 Howard traveled the state, listening to the people in small towns, lecturing to university and public audiences, and writing. He stressed a "new and more liberal concept of education" that would emerge from the fruitful collaboration of campus and community. "Making the communities more interesting," he stressed, "can help to check the drain" of young people away from the small towns. Advocating a blend of adult education and public humanities, he urged the entire state "to become one vast university in which all of you are teachers or research students."[31]

Although it had some successes, the Montana Study was never able to accomplish this ambitious agenda. It sponsored many study projects in small towns and fostered local history pageants and community theater productions, but it could never shake internal administrative obstacles and external political opposition. Its work became caught up between feuding campuses in the Montana University System and was perhaps a victim of poor administration. Externally, Howard functioned as a lightning rod for criticism that the Montana Study had socialist leanings or was even a Communist front organization. A former representative of the Montana Power Company, a firm that he had frequently criticized for corporate abuse, complained that "Howard has long been our trouble maker in Montana." His writings were "not only radical but Communistic," so much so that "Howard carried a card of membership in the Communist Party." Republican Governor Sam Ford warned Brownell that "our people do not want socialism in any form," claiming that Howard's visible left-leaning approach hindered the popularity of the Montana Study. Brownell and Melby defended Howard's right of free speech, and some participants from small towns spoke in favor of the work of the Montana Study, but Howard's participation always proved contentious. As one observer of the Montana Study concluded, even though Howard possessed an intimate knowledge of the state and was widely respected, "in Montana's top political and financial circles Howard was about as popular as a rattlesnake." When he resigned from his position, Howard noted ruefully, "Damned if I didn't become a dangerous so-and-so, just by writing a book!" At the same time, he noted that he relished the chance to "talk it over with somebody" when he received critical news. Clearly he felt some intellectual nourishment from the conversations he had with friends during these years. Not having had the opportunity to attend college, he noted that working with professors such as Brownell had enriched his intellectual life immeasurably. A few months later he confided to Brownell that his two years with the Montana Study "have been the happiest of my life, without any question."[32]

Perhaps the most significant result of Howard's involvement with the Montana Study, and certainly the most enduring legacy, was his collection of Montana writing, published as *Montana Margins* (1946). He saw clearly that one characteristic of regional exploitation was that the culture of a region, like its economy or politics, became dependent upon outsiders. To prevent Montana from becoming a literary as well as an economic colony, he collected an anthology of writings by Montanans for Montanans, a sort of literary declaration of independence. Rather than expecting small town Montana to appreciate and perhaps imitate highbrow literature from elsewhere, he began with "the conviction that the resources of the Montana scene were culturally rich." He wanted citizens of the region not only to consume art and literature but to participate in its creation. "The fully functioning community will provide even the experience of beauty for its citizens," he wrote. "Space and freedom, sun and clean air, the cold majesty of the mountains and the loneliness of the plains, the gayety of a country dance, the easy friendliness of the people" were the "margins around the sometimes fretful business of earning a living."[33]

Montana Margins helped to build the image of the state as a vital source of regional culture and to make Howard a spokesperson for that culture. Reviewers praised the book as "one of the best of the many regional anthologies recently published" and an "authentic piece of Americana."[34] The book went through four printings and was widely used in Montana's schools. What respect accrued to the state's literary heritage, both in and out of the region, also called attention to the book's editor, who was by the late 1940s a figure on the national literary scene. In 1947 he not only participated with other notable writers in the Breadloaf Writers' Workshop, he also received a prestigious Guggenheim Fellowship to allow him time to pursue his next book project, which would become *Strange Empire*. In 1950 and 1951 he also directed a summer institute, the Northern Rocky Mountain Roundup of Regional Arts, as a "focal point for the gradually developing cultural movements of our state and region." He hoped the institute would nourish the "cultural enrichment of life in the Northwest" and sustain the "stimulation, expert counsel and leadership training needed by anyone interested in intellectual or artistic achievement, professional or novice."[35] Although his work was cut short by his early death in 1951, Howard successfully laid important groundwork for later efforts. The summer institute was a precursor of the University of Montana Writing

Program, which by the 1960s helped make Missoula a magnet for the region's writers, and by the 1970s the Montana Committee for the Humanities (later Humanities Montana) and the Montana Arts Council carried on the Montana Study's goal of enriching the cultural life of small towns. Had Howard lived to see these developments, he would have recognized them as at least a partial fulfillment of his efforts to build a vibrant regional culture that invited the participation of all.

Beginning in 1947 and enabled by his Guggenheim Fellowship, he turned his attention to the story that had haunted him since his childhood, the history of the Métis people and their valiant attempts to obtain independence, led by Louis Riel. Howard was naturally drawn to this story for several reasons. He admired native societies for the way they lived in harmony with the natural world—indeed, he may have romanticized them in this regard. He also saw in native societies a model of interdependent communities. In other words, he championed in the Métis the cause of a society that he saw as a repudiation of the exploitive individualism that ravaged the region. Most of all, the Métis represented the ultimate underdog, a society pushed so far to the margins that it was neither white nor Indian but existed in an intermediate and unrecognized space, literally invisible to most observers. The fact that the Métis developed their own identity, strong enough not only to survive but to foment armed rebellion aimed at political recognition, made this the ultimate example of an adversarial culture that resisted the homogenizing "progress" of mainstream America. If regionalism meant space for the survival of the dispossessed, for those who could not and did not want to assimilate into the forced sterility of the dominant culture, then this book was Howard's regionalism triumphant.

Writing *Strange Empire* thus had personal dimensions for Howard, and he tried to write as empathetically as possible about the Métis. He told his agent, "I have to write this book—and I'll write it whether anybody prints it or not." Not only had he known about the Métis since his Canadian childhood, during his newspaper years he had reported on Hill 57, a Métis settlement near Great Falls, where Métis residents "haul their water in barrels to ramshackle huts" and "the children die of malnutrition and dysentery while flies crawl over their faces." He mixed outrage with sympathy, even writing a few short stories from Indian and Métis points of view that were praised for their cultural sensitivity. He loved his cabin outside Great Falls, where he wrote most of *Strange Empire*, because it was in the same canyon where the Métis had found refuge in 1885. In a mystical as well as a practical way, he identified with Métis history, so much so that he originally attempted to write the book as a novel. Many months and 60,000 words later, he concluded, "I'm not a novelist." Even so, the book is a personal recollection, even using character sketches and interior monologues to create an intimate portrait of leading characters such as Louis Riel and the Lakota leader Sitting Bull.[36]

Descendants of French fur traders and Plains Indian women, the Métis lived across cultural and national borders and became the "cultural and economic intermediaries in the 'civilizing' of a continent." Forced out of Canada, they lived in uneasy exile in the United States, where they were denied legal recognition or land rights, often harassed, and sometimes rounded up and forced back into Canada. Exploited and discriminated against on both sides of the 49th parallel, an artificial boundary that was "the conceit of congressmen, not of ecologists," the Métis found a home and fair treatment on neither side. Notably, however, Howard did not frame the story merely as a personal or a local event; the Métis uprising was part of the "drama born of incessant struggle between men of irreconcilable races, faiths, and political principles, and between these men and Nature."[37] This larger war for the West took place in both Canada and the United States, linking the two nations in a common destiny that was, in his view, anything but manifest. Howard the regionalist had become a globalist, the historian of the transnational frontier. By placing the Métis story at what he called "the heart of the continent," he suggested that a Métis victory might have resulted in an independent republic that would have provided a refuge for Native peoples on both sides of the arbitrary international boundary. However hopeful, even unrealistic, this vision might have been, it shows Howard at his childhood and lifelong best: transcending racial and national boundaries, championing the lost cause, and locating his struggle in the context of a larger and universal struggle for human dignity.

On August 25, 1951, while revising the manuscript for *Strange Empire*, Howard died of a heart attack at his beloved cabin. His friend A. B. Guthrie, a fellow author, remarked, "We have lost our conscience." Bernard DeVoto, who had spent the previous three weeks with Guthrie, prepared the manuscript for publication and wrote an introduction that praised the book for its "sympathy for the dispossessed," its contributions to American Indian history, and its "very fine art."[38] Reviewers praised the book and heaped posthumous praise on its author for writing an important piece of Indian history that displayed "deep sympathy" for "lost causes" and "dreamers of better worlds to come." It was "the last impassioned plea of a writer to whom injustice was always a challenge, the last pen stroke of one who loved the West and pictured it with honesty and courage and sweep." In his native Great Falls, his old newspaper wrote, "Howard's devotion to the underdog is nowhere more evident than through this book."[39] He had died, his friend DeVoto wrote, not with "a sense of triumph" but with "scars." Howard's death at the age of 45, just as he was reaching the peak of his writing powers, was the final injustice in the story of the crusading journalist who spent his life trying to get things turned right side up.

NOTES

Epigraph: Joe Howard to Agnes Regan, February 22, 1946, Montana Study Collection, box 2, folder 1, Merrill G. Burlingame Special Collections, Montana State University, Bozeman (MSC-MSU).

1. Joseph Kinsey Howard, *Montana: High, Wide, and Handsome* (New Haven: Yale University Press, 1943; reprinted, Lincoln: University of Nebraska Press, 1983), 14.
2. Howard to Helen [King], n.d., Joseph Kinsey Howard Papers, Manuscript Collection 27, box 2, folder 6, Montana State Historical Society Archives (MSHSA), Helena, Montana.
3. Joseph Kinsey Howard, *Strange Empire* (New York: Morrow, 1952; reprinted, Minneapolis: University of Minnesota Press, 1994), 13.
4. Jyl Hoyt, "Montana Writer Joseph Kinsey Howard: Crusader for the Worker, Land, Indian, and Community," M.A. thesis, University of Montana, 1988.
5. Howard to Dr. Sid [Willis], January 9, 1938, Howard papers, Manuscript Collection 220, box 1, folder 2, MSHSA; Hoyt, "Montana Writer," 35–38.
6. Howard, *Montana*, 3, 7.
7. Notebook, Howard papers, Manuscript Collection 27, MSHSA; quoted in Hoyt, "Montana Writer," 70.
8. Jay Edgerton, *Minneapolis Star*, October 4–9, 1951, quoted in Hoyt, "Montana Writer," 74.
9. Quoted in Hoyt, "Montana Writer," 71, 72, 75.
10. Howard, *Montana*, 148.
11. Howard, *Montana*, 10.
12. Howard, *Montana*, 20, 23.
13. Howard, *Montana*, 13.

14. Stuart Chase, *Rich Land, Poor Land* (New York: Whittlesey House, 1936); Walter Prescott Webb, *The Great Plains* (New York: Grosset & Dunlap, 1931); for a description of Clements's ecological thinking see Donald Worster, *Nature's Economy: A History of Ecological Ideas*, 2d ed. (Cambridge: Cambridge University Press, 1994), chapter 11.

15. Joseph Kinsey Howard, "Prophet without Honor," *The Survey Graphic*, p. 4, Howard papers, Manuscript Collection 27, box 6, folder 8, MSHSA.

16. Mildred Walker Schemm, quoted in Hoyt, "Montana Writer," 14.

17. Howard, *Montana*, 85, 56, 90; see also Hoyt, "Montana Writer," 43–52.

18. Howard, *Montana*, 275, 287.

19. Roberta Yerkes [Editorial Department, Yale University Press] to Howard, June 9, 1943, Howard papers, Manuscript Collection 27, box 18, folder 6, MSHSA.

20. K. Ross Toole, *Montana: An Uncommon Land* (Norman: University of Oklahoma Press, 1959); Michael P. Malone, "The Close of the Copper Century," *Montana: The Magazine of Western History*, Spring 1985, 69–72; Michael P. Malone, Richard B. Roeder, and William L. Lang, *Montana: A History of Two Centuries*, rev. ed. (Seattle: University of Washington Press, 1991), 375.

21. [Bernice] Baumgarten to Howard, Howard papers, Manuscript Collection 27, box 18, folder 6, MSHSA; Hoyt, "Montana Writer," 77.

22. DeVoto's best essays have been collected and published as *The Western Paradox: A Conservation Reader*, edited by Douglas Brinkley and Patricia Nelson Limerick (New Haven: Yale University Press, 2000); material cited here appears on 3, 21, 42.

23. Wallace Stegner, *Beyond the Hundredth Meridian: John Wesley Powell and the Second Opening of the West* (Boston: Houghton Mifflin, 1954; reprinted, Lincoln: University of Nebraska Press, 1982), 350.

24. Robert L. Dorman, *Revolt of the Provinces: The Regionalist Movement in America, 1920–1945* (Chapel Hill: University of North Carolina Press, 1993), 52.

25. Statement of Joseph Kinsey Howard, Montana, on "Missouri—Valley of Opportunity," before Subcommittee of the U.S. Senate Irrigation and Reclamation Committee, September 22, 1945, Howard papers, Manuscript Collection 27, box 2, folder 3, MSHSA.

26. Brownell to Melby, January 17, 1944, MSC-MSU box 1, folder 2. See also Baker Brownell and Frank Lloyd Wright, "A Balanced Society," in *Architecture and Modern Life* (New York: Harper, 1937), 2 (quoted,"concentrative movement").

27. Brownell and Wright, "A Balanced Society," 22; Hoyt, "Montana Writer," 95.

28. Quoted in Carla Homstad, "Small Town Eden: The Montana Study," M.A. thesis, University of Montana, 1987.

29. Brownell to Howard, January 30, 1944, MSC-MSU box 1, folder 1.

30. Hoyt, "Montana Writer," 94.

31. Howard's address to the American Association of University Women, Great Falls, October 27, 1944, quoted in Hoyt, "Montana Writer," 100.

32. Richard Waverly Poston, *Small Town Renaissance: A Story of the Montana Study* (New York: Harper & Row, 1950), 29; Howard to Baker and Adelaide [Brownell], September 30, 1946, MSC-MSU box 2, folder 5; Howard to Brownell, MSC-MSU box 1, folder 6.

33. "Introduction," in *Montana Margins: A State Anthology*, edited by Joseph Kinsey Howard (New Haven: Yale University Press, 1946), viii–ix.

34. John T. Frederick, *Chicago Sun Book Week*, November 17, 1946; *New York Sun*, November 13, 1946; quoted in Hoyt, "Montana Writer," 120.
35. Howard, quoted in Homstad, "Small Town Eden," 70.
36. Hoyt, "Montana Writer," 130, 134, 139–40, 147; Nicholas C. P. Vrooman, "Introduction to the Reprint Edition," *Strange Empire* (Saint Paul: Minnesota Society Historical Press, 1994), xxviii–xxxi.
37. Howard, *Strange Empire*, 40, 25.
38. DeVoto, "Joseph Kinsey Howard," *Strange Empire*, 3, 9, 10.
39. Hoyt, "Montana Writer," 158–59.

D'Arcy McNickle. Courtesy of The Newberry Library, Chicago (Ayer MMS, McNickle, box 34, folder 290).

CHAPTER TEN

Bad Medicine

D'ARCY MCNICKLE LOCATES LIBERALISM AND

THE LEFT FROM A TRIBAL PERSPECTIVE

William W. Bevis

Since the 1980s, D'Arcy McNickle (1904–77) has increasingly become recognized as a pioneer in the field of Native American fiction and praised as a spokesman and organizer for American Indian rights. Yet from 1922, when he left the Flathead Reservation for good and entered the University of Montana, until 1977, he published only two adult novels and a handful of short stories. His second adult novel, *Wind from an Enemy Sky*, extensively rewritten in his last years (1974–76), was published in 1978, after his death.[1]

Within ten years after his death, McNickle's work was attracting intense attention among scholars of Native American and western literature. In 1990 John Purdy's *Word Ways*, on McNickle, and my *Ten Tough Trips*, on Montana writers, appeared, followed quickly by Birgit Hans's edition of McNickle's short fiction and Dorothy Parker's excellent biography in 1992. Several more books followed, including Purdy's anthology of essays, *The Legacy of D'Arcy McNickle*, in 1996. In that same year I published an article, "Region, Power, Place," focusing on McNickle's remarkable and prescient critique of liberal capitalism in the person of Adam Pell, the Rockefeller-like sympathizer and advocate for Indian causes in *Wind from an Enemy Sky*, who tries to return a lost medicine bundle to the Salish and dramatically fails.[2]

I would like now to revisit and extend that work by first considering McNickle himself, as revealed in the tribalism in his novels and the politics in his life. From that standpoint I look closely at McNickle's radical critique of the fictional Adam Pell and liberal capitalism. This background informs a discussion of McNickle's tribalism in relation to regionalism and localism in the age of ecology. I argue that in 1976 McNickle, with his ever keen analysis of cultural values, envisioned the core of liberal capitalism in a way that predicted, or at least imagined, the economic crisis of the early twenty-first century (the "Great Recession" of 2008), and illuminates our present understanding of regionalism and the left.

TRIBALISM IN HIS NOVELS AND POLITICS IN HIS LIFE

McNickle's vision of Adam Pell's liberal capitalism is inseparable from his understanding of tribalism in opposition to individualism. His work in the federal Bureau of Indian Affairs with John Collier in the 1930s and 1940s, as well as his lifelong respect for tribalism and community, led McNickle repeatedly to interpret tribal self-determination as a dissent from individualism and unbridled free enterprise. He knew both worlds; he had a White life, and an Indian pen. The road to Adam Pell's disastrous return of the Feather Boy medicine bundle, in *Wind from an Enemy Sky*, begins with tribalism as a culture very different from our own.

American whites keep leaving home. *Moby Dick, Portrait of a Lady, Huckleberry Finn, Sister Carrie, The Great Gatsby*—a considerable number of American "classics" tell of leaving home to find one's fate farther and farther away. The story we tell our children is of Huck Finn lighting out for the territories. In *Letters from an American Farmer* (1782), Crèvecoeur defined Americans as a people who leave the old to take the new: "He is an American, who, leaving behind all his ancient prejudices and manners, takes new ones from the mode of life he has embraced, the new government he obeys, and the new rank he holds."[3] The home we leave, to Crèvecoeur, is not only a place; it is a past, an "ancien régime," a set of values and parents, a way of government and life before the revolution.

Such "leaving" plots embody quite clearly the basic premise of success in our mobile society. The *individual* advances, sometimes at all cost, with little or no regard for family, society, past, or place. The individual is the ultimate reality; hence individual consciousness is the medium of knowledge, and "freedom," our primary value, is a matter of distance between one's self and the smoke from another's chimney. Movement, isolation, change: these are the ingredients of the American Adam. *His* is the story we tell and always in our ears is Huck Finn's strange derision: "I been there before."

In marked contrast, most Native American novels are not about going out, diverging, expanding, but about zooming in, converging, contracting. The hero comes home. "Contracting" has negative overtones to most Anglo-Americans, "expanding" a positive ring. These are the cultural habits we are considering. In Native American novels, coming home, staying put, contracting, even what we might call "regressing" to a place, a past where one has been before, is not only the primary story, it is a primary mode of knowledge and a primary good.

For instance, in *The Surrounded* (1936), McNickle's protagonist, Archilde, comes home from Portland, Oregon, where he "can always get a job now any time" playing the fiddle in a "show house," to the Salish and Kootenai (Flathead) reservation. He has made it in the white world and has come "to see my mother ... in a few days I'm going again." However, family ties, cultural ties, and growing ties to a decidedly "reservation" girl are spun like webs to bind him down. He does not leave and finally is crushed by the white man's law. It seems to be a "tar baby" plot: Archilde takes one lick and then another at his own backward people, and suddenly he is stuck. At first, being assimilated into a white world, he had expected to remain mobile, thinking of "wherever he might be in times to come. Yes, wherever he might be." McNickle's repetition underscores the plot: whites would leave, Indians come home.[4] Although whites would usually find in such a homing-as-failure plot either personal disaster or moral martyrdom, McNickle applauds Archilde's return to Indian roots. The novel offers profound respect for the past, for family and tradition, and asks us to admire Archilde's involvement on the reservation even as it leads to personal doom.

The plot of *The Surrounded* is typical. In McNickle's other novel centered upon contemporary Indians, *Wind from an Enemy Sky*, a young boy on the Salish Kootenai reservation is abducted by whites to a mission school (as had happened to McNickle himself) and four years later returns, an outsider, to his very traditional grandfather and tribe. The plot hangs on the tribe's attempt to recover from white authorities a lost Feather Boy medicine bundle. In the course of the book, the young boy and the reader gain increasing respect for this futile effort to "bring back our medicine, our power."[5] Just as Archilde had recovered his traditional mother, so young Antoine is initiated by his conservative grandfather into the tribe.

These novels and others of the Native American Renaissance—beginning in 1968 with M. Scott Momaday's *House Made of Dawn* and including James Welch's *Winter in the Blood* (1974) and *The Death of Jim Loney* (1979) and Leslie Marmon Silko's *Ceremony* (1977)—present tribal past as a gravity field stronger than individual will. Tribalism is respected even though it is inseparable from a kind of failure. The novels also suggest that "identity," for a Native American, is not a matter of finding one's self, but of finding a self that is transpersonal. To be separated from that transpersonal time and space is to lose identity. These six novels—the four named here, and McNickle's *Surrounded* and *Wind*—not only depict Indian individuals coming home while white individuals leave, but they also suggest—variously and subtly and by degrees—a tribal rather than an individual definition of "being." The tribal "being" includes a society (which is laws and customs, not just company), a past, and a place. The tribal society assumes that the individual is completed only in relation to others, that man is a political animal, and the group that must complete the individual's "being" is organized in some meaningful way.

The tribal past is a profoundly conservative authority; "progress" and "a fresh start" are not *native* to America. The past, too, is a part of tribal culture and identity. "Today talks in yesterday's voice, the old people said. The white man must hear yesterday's voice," McNickle stressed.[6] The connotations of "regression" are cultural; going back to a previous condition is not necessarily a romantic "escape." Indeed, Native Americans said and still say that the white attempt to "get away from the past" is an escapist fantasy that will not succeed. Ecologists, as we shall see, agree.

A striking aspect of tribalism in these novels by Native American authors is the centrality of place. In all six novels named above, the protagonist ends *where* he began. Place is not scenery or landscape: all six of these novels (and those of Louise Erdrich) are from inland western reservations not drastically displaced from their original territories or ecosystems. Place is not only an aspect of these works; the author's relation to a specific place may have made them possible.

In their scholarly work *Indians and Other Americans* (1959) McNickle and Harold Fey identified the concept of individual and transferable title to the land as the "prime source of misunderstanding" between whites and Indians. McNickle thought that Indians understood land payment as a gift and perhaps as a rental fee for land use, but he believed that probably, even late in the nineteenth century, western Indians could not conceive of private land ownership. (The Cherokees, in the East, by 1881 had learned and dissented: "the land itself is not a chattel.") McNickle and Fey eloquently state the difference between the white transmutation of land to money, and the Native American view: "Even today, when Indian tribes may go into court and sue the United States for inadequate compensation or no compensation for lands taken from them, they still are dealing in alien concepts. One cannot grow a tree on a pile of money, or cause water to gush from it; one can only spend it, and then one is homeless."[7]

In all of the six novels considered here, the protagonist seeks an identity that he can find *only* in his society, past, and place; unlike whites, he cannot find meaningful "being" alone. Individuality is not even the *scene* of success or failure; it is nothing. These novels constitute a profound and articulate continuing critique of modern European culture, combined with a persistent refusal to let go of tribal identity, a refusal to regard the past as inferior, a refusal—no matter how futile—of even the *wish* to assimilate.

McNickle was perfectly positioned to be the father of Native American novel plots that move between both worlds. His home life was a maze of ancestry. His father, William McNickle, was an Irish farmer who had fled the potato famine of the mid-nineteenth century to homestead in South Dakota, and then moved to an allotment on the Salish Kootenai reservation. His mother was an enrolled member of the Salish tribe, although she was not Salish but Métis (French and Cree), taken in by the Salish. McNickle's maternal grandfather, Isador Parenteau, had fought with Louis Riel in the Métis uprising in 1885. So from the earliest age, McNickle lived in an Irish/Cree/French household surrounded by the Salish.

He was born in St. Ignatius, Montana in 1904, only twenty years after the Riel rebellion was crushed and the last buffalo in the state was killed. In a letter written in 1974, McNickle recalled his childhood: "As 'breeds' we could not turn for reassurance to an Indian tradition, and certainly not to the white community." He played with Salish children and probably spoke Salish, French, and English as a child.[8] Against his and his mother's wishes, he was sent at age twelve to the Jesuit School in Oregon, where any respect for his "breed" life was supposed to be eradicated.

In 1921 McNickle entered the University of Montana at age seventeen. He loved literature, English, Greek, and Latin and was drawn to, and befriended by, H. G. Merriam, one of his professors, a man who would spend a long lifetime in Missoula (he lived until 1978) promoting Montana and western regional writing. At exactly that moment McNickle's education in radicalism, resistance, and activism began. A Rhodes Scholar from Wyoming, Merriam had come to the university in Missoula in 1917, and in 1919 he had started there the second creative writing program in the country (after Harvard). In 1921 he urged his students not to imitate mainstream American writers like Henry James but to write about their own lives in their own voices—advice that Richard Hugo at the University of Montana would, nearly a half-century later, pass on to the Irish/Blackfeet student James Welch. When Merriam found that New York was not interested in his students' "regional" work, he started *The Frontier* literary magazine (founded 1920), where his students *could* publish. Young McNickle walked into the middle of this excitement. He joined Merriam's magazine staff, which included emerging western regionalist writers such as A. B. (Bud) Guthrie and Dorothy Johnson.[9]

After leaving the University of Montana, McNickle (with Merriam's help) attended Oxford University. By the end of the 1920s, having lived in Oxford, Paris, Philadelphia, and New York, he had begun the drafts of his two novels set entirely in the Mission Valley on the Salish reservation, novels haunted by a traditional native life walking like a ghost through a world becoming white. That is how he must have felt about his own life: he had sold his allotment on the reservation to go to Oxford.

He joined the Bureau of Indian Affairs in 1935 under the progressive New Deal director John Collier, and his life as a self-trained anthropologist began. Seen from a distance, his life had wide pendulum swings, not just daily oscillations between the two cultures. He was a Native "breed" as a child in a remote Montana valley; then from 1921 to 1935 he was an aesthete, car salesman, editors' assistant, writer, and man-about-town in some of the world's most cosmopolitan cities. From 1935 to about 1945 he was a liberal Bureau of Indian Affairs activist and part of Collier's crusade, optimistic about improving the climate for self-determination on the reservations. *The Surrounded* had come out in 1936, and *Wind from an Enemy Sky* was a manuscript in his bottom drawer.

From 1945 to roughly 1960 McNickle was faced with a right-wing revolt: Congress was swept by the termination (or "de-reservation") movement. In 1944 McNickle was a co-founder of the National Congress of American Indians. Collier quit the BIA in 1945, and McNickle resigned in 1954. By the 1960s he had become an influential figure in private funding for Native American projects, and he was encouraged by the young activists emerging in the new decade. In 1962 Oxford University Press published McNickle's *Indian Tribes of the United States*, and in 1966 he received an honorary doctorate from the University of Colorado. By 1974, when he began the final version of *Wind from an Enemy Sky*, the climate had been altered again: on the one hand, he had become the founding director of the Newberry Library Center for the History of the American Indian and a respected elder in Indian affairs; on the other hand, he found himself giving politic advice to the young radicals of the American Indian Movement (AIM), who were battling the FBI at Wounded Knee. He was sympathetic to their cause, but disturbed by their means.

With his understanding of tribalism in profound tension with individualism and private ownership, McNickle made a career of being the go-between, the messenger, the translator. Yet in the rewrite of *Wind from an Enemy Sky* at the end of his life, he apparently gave up: when Bull, shot Adam Pell and Agent Rafferty, "the world fell apart." All is lost in translation, as Louis Owens and James Ruppert have observed.[10] Let us see how thorough this breakdown was, and how radical was McNickle's understanding of Pell. Nothing in his background has quite prepared us for this scene.

ADAM PELL AND MCNICKLE'S CRITIQUE OF LIBERAL CAPITALISM

Wind from an Enemy Sky is the most political of McNickle's works, and the Indians portrayed there are the most traditional. Although the Indians are already on a reservation assigned with a government agent, the climax of the book has the feel of "first contact," to the readers as well as to the characters. Adam Pell reveals his extraordinary point of view toward the loss of the Indians' medicine bundle, Feather Boy, in a private meeting with the white elite, an hour before he faces the tribe. The Indians have asked for Feather Boy to be returned, Agent Rafferty has notified Adam Pell, and Pell has searched the basement of his museum in Albany. Unfortunately, "the unending battle museums wage against rats, moths, organic decay, and an assortment of molds, mites, and enterprising worms had caught up with the medicine bundle."[11]

When Pell finally comes to the Salish reservation, supposedly to return Feather Boy, he has instead brought to the Indians everything that liberalism can offer. To the local doctor, the doctor's wife, and the agent, Pell shows his hand—that is, what the victorious first world has to offer the overrun, studied, collected, and impoverished third. Pell opens the mysterious wooden chest he has brought on the train. He hopes to restore to these Indians "something of the world they knew" by giving them "a Peruvian piece, probably pre-Inca, possibly a thousand years old." A "gold statuette." "Gold" is used three times in a half-page of narrative, the irony compounded by Pell's unconscious comparison of himself to conquistadors: "It is one of the relatively few larger pieces that the Spanish invaders failed to discover and melt down for bullion."[12]

Pell seems oblivious to the fact that he has "discovered" the statue himself (he found it at Christie's in London), and is using it for exchange. At least the Spanish were liquefying material assets; Pell is melting down a culture, and thereby unwittingly defining his own, a liberal's cultural imperialism. The figure's value is established in the mind of the individual connoisseur-collector, as he explains to his astonished audience: "'It grows on you, just study it.' Adam's voice was a disembodied sound hanging in the air." "Disembodied": McNickle knows exactly what he is doing. Liberalism is inseparable from abstraction ("a piece . . . study . . . disembodied . . . in the air") and individualism ("grows on *you*"). As Pell continues, it becomes clear that liberalism is also inseparable from capitalism: "I have to add that I prize this little piece above all the rare, even priceless, objects in my collection. And in that sense I suppose it might be comparable to the priceless thing they lost."[13]

There it is: valuation by an individual consumer's "demand" sets price, things are comparable in relation to that abstraction, and, paradoxically, the greatest value, "priceless," means, as we all know, "very expensive," for in our culture everything has its price. The "artifact," Feather Boy, was the tribe's identity and power; yet for Pell, with the very best of Enlightenment intentions, their assets as well as his own are liquid: values are commodified, while place is annihilated by structuralism. "I intend to tell them about the Indians of the Andes," Pell says to the stunned agent, Rafferty; "I hope they will understand the brotherhood." Columbus has landed again. All Indians—East Indians, West Indians—are one in relation to trade. Rafferty, no less white but a good deal more knowledgeable about tribes, says Pell is trying to "restore a lost world by a simple substitution of symbols."[14]

Clearly the ground of McNickle's opposing of cultures extends far beyond conquest, or primitivism, or a narrowly Marxist "capitalism," or tribalism as a kind of communalism. Pell thinks of things in relation to other things and how they are comparable. All thought is by analogy, as the white philosopher Alfred North Whitehead claimed. The natives, according to Native author McNickle, think of things as unique in relation to other unique things. Things are incomparable and therefore cannot be exchanged: their tribe, their bundle, their land. Pell has mobility, individual achievement, and freedom; the Indians have location, identity, and fate.

Finally, the most traditional of Indians, Bull, murders the best of liberal reformers, Pell. Thunderbird is not replaced by abstraction; Pell and Bull do not understand each other. The novel rejects not just imperialism, or capitalism, but the Enlightenment—liberal modernity—in a way that whites still can hardly imagine. Pell and Bull cannot represent each other's points of view; the gap cannot be crossed by good intentions, and the Indians have to speak in their own way. "No people," McNickle wrote to Matthew Lowman, "should have to depend on another and possibly hostile party to give its account to the world."[15] The end of *Wind from an Enemy Sky* is not about a failure of negotiations; it is about a culture that believes in the negotiable, trying to destroy through modernization a culture that does not.

"Assimilation" is not a big enough word for what we do here in mainstream America, in this strange amalgam of eighteenth-century liberty, twentieth-century industrial capitalism, and radically modern freedom. Let us call it "liquidity." When the head of General Motors says that if American workers price themselves out of the market, GM will move its operations elsewhere, one has to ask: what is an international manufacturing firm? It seems to be a moneymaking system remarkably divorced from family, tribe, nation, and place. It apparently serves nothing but profit. Now listen to that message not morally, as a pontification against greed, but anthropologically, as a description of an entire group of people willing to be divorced from their history, family, place. It is the liquidity, not the greed, that seems fascinating.

The basis of liberal capitalism is liquidity. Things become "commodities" in reference to their potential value on the exchange. The medium of exchange is money; the more money units (or equivalent commodity units) that can be put into circulation, the better. The natural tendency of capitalism is to liquefy assets, and liquidity—abstracting things to equivalent units that can be exchanged—lies at the core of capitalism as a culture. We have traveled far in that direction from our early phases of manufacturing, to credit capitalism and leveraged buyouts, and now to credit default swaps. Abstracting things to equivalent units that can be exchanged is exactly what Wall Street was doing by 2005: subprime mortgages were transformed into junk bonds that could be traded, and then hedged insurance could be bet against them, and a new pile of money based on phony equity could be put into motion. The cleverness was in how to liquefy mortgages, so that a new source of false collateral could be traded.

By unfreezing assets, liquidity puts enormous markets into motion. Furthermore, this industrial-economic liquidity arose within the European democracies during the exfoliation of other kinds of liquidity: the ideals of liberty, liberal humanism, and progressive notions of the modern. "Capitalist democracy" seems to many people a natural yoking and usually implies more: a "modern industrial capitalist democracy" wed to "progress," as if economic liquidity were necessarily linked to political freedom, social mobility, and individualism.

"The left" is often used to refer to socialism in opposition to capitalism, but in America it may be more useful to think of the big picture: "the left" accepts the mainstream narratives of modernism since the European Renaissance and attempts to apply liberty, equality, and fraternity to the new society of the Industrial Revolution, which means spreading the wealth—*spreading the freedoms of the new liquidity*—to the new lower classes, not just to the new middle class. Issues concerning wages, even ownership of means of production, are tweakings of the new system, compared to tribal objections. Contemporary observers from many points of view—Peter Drucker, John Lukacs, Christopher Lasch, Edward Said—feel the need to understand capitalist industrialism as a culture, modernity as an economics, and both as a politics; that is, to describe what seems to be a "first world" culture, above or beyond or permeating various national and local traditions, and vigorously exported. And vigorously resisted, by much of the rest of the world, including Native Americans.

What Bull and the Salish are rejecting in *Wind from an Enemy Sky* is a culture of individualism, freedom, mobility, change. This culture surrounds and nurtures contemporary liberalism and capitalism. Liquidity suggests, in economics, unfreezing as many assets as possible; in our social life, it suggests mobility, moving away from family, kin, background, and therefore it suggests individualism; in our culture, liquidity suggests the liberal substitution of principle and abstraction for specific belief, and is related to proceduralism: the way eighteenth-century rationality has become rule by bureaucracy and law. Such abstraction is related to cherished political ideals, especially freedom in the form of license, the right to do anything one wishes (free of background, race, kinship, place) unless it restricts another's freedom.

Outside of America and Europe, however, native skepticism does not look strange, extreme, or marginal. To the Muslim world, whether industrial development must come with the other freedoms of "progress" is a clear and pressing question. Our media tells mainly of horror stories: the Taliban, stoning, suicide bombings. But many moderates in the Arab world and in Muslim Malaysia and Indonesia are painfully aware of our first-world derision at anything less than the whole package—all freedoms, a liquidity of values. People, they think, need not only to *have* something; they need to *be* something. That "being" is in a social, historical, and often geographical context: we need to be someone beyond our name, to be of a people, a tradition, a place, even if, in America, it is sometimes a background we choose. For all its virtues and achievements, industrial capitalism does not deal with these issues: perhaps the real "bottom line" is not money—it is identity.

The postmodernists have perceived our liquidity and, like Pell, have taken it to its logical extremes. As Marshal Berman has argued, "To be modern is to find ourselves in an environment that promises us adventure, power, joy, growth, transformation of ourselves and the world—and at the same time, that threatens to destroy everything we have, everything we know, everything we are. . . . To be modern is to be part of a universe in which, as Marx said, 'all that is solid melts into air.'"[16] Berman, the ecstatic postmodern, is quoting from a remarkable passage in *The Communist*

Manifesto, in which Karl Marx describes, almost from a tribal point of view, what I am calling the liquidity of the modern age:

> Constant revolutionizing of production, uninterrupted disturbance of all social relations, everlasting uncertainty and agitation, distinguish the bourgeois epoch from all earlier times. All fixed, fast frozen relationships, with their train of venerable ideas and opinions are swept away, all new formed ones become obsolete before they can ossify. All that is solid melts into air, all that is holy is profaned, and men at last are forced to face with sober senses the real conditions of their lives and their relations with their fellow man.[17]

At the end of *Wind from an Enemy Sky* McNickle's understanding of what we call the left is bleak indeed. The left, in the person of Adam Pell, is the inheritor of Renaissance humanism, trade, the rise of the middle class. The left accepts the mainstream narratives of modern progress and attempts to spread the wealth of capitalist liquidity to the working class. All this, says McNickle, simply has nothing to do with Native American tribalism. Through Pell, McNickle has linked emblems of the liberal, the progressive, the capitalist, and the left to convey a single culture that I am calling liquidity, and that we all call freedom. Using a tribal perspective, McNickle has situated the left at the center of modern culture, instead of repeating its monologues of dissent. Pell's white audience (doctor, wife, agent) recoils in shock, for unlike McNickle they cannot bear to see that Pell's act is indeed the logical extension of, and therefore the exposing of, their own point of view: all cultures, for their own good, must become modern. The liberal *system* of liquidity is visible through Pell's honesty and good will, and it will fail the Indians. They do not want *a* "priceless statue." They want *their* medicine bundle. The Indians, however, know it is the end. "The world fell apart."

What brought McNickle to such a radical (from "root") analysis of liberal capitalism? He had made severe comments on greed and moneymaking throughout his life. Selling cars was "a daily betrayal of my birthright in opposition." "Everything I was called on to do, was a violation of instinct and desire."[18] The crash of 1929, of course, shook everyone's trust in capitalism. America's leaders, said McNickle, were "blundering opportunists, welshers, babbling panderers, senile optimists, contemptible bluffers,"[19] but these sentiments do not distinguish him from the conventional leftist-bohemian opinions of his times.

In his manuscripts and stories written between 1926 and 1936 we find a keen and realistic, even cynical mind open to change. In the first draft of *The Surrounded*, Archilde is happily assimilated into white society; in the final novel (1936) he stays on the reservation and is doomed. In "Snowfall," a seed story for *Wind from an Enemy Sky*, the white Indian agent realizes that if Henry Jim dies, farming will fail on the reservation and the "increased expenditure on farm equipment" for the reservation will not ensue.[20] That is, the agent's job is to keep one eye on the Indians and the other on the GNP. In the early drafts of the novel Feather Boy is returned intact and brings good fortune to the tribe. That manuscript was put away. In "Hard Riding" the cowboy capitalism of the Indian agent is clear: "Cattle ... that was the idea. Beef Cattle. Blooded stock. Good bulls. Fall round-ups. The shipment East. The cash profits."[21]

In his early work and letters McNickle is not naive, and he always has a sense of fairness as well as an ability to "follow the money." Many of the white agents like Rafferty are presented as good men doing their best. And old Montana white men—as in "Six Beautiful in Paris"—are honest, blunt, and respected, as are the French-Indian Métis.[22] However, in the 1960s and 1970s, leading up to his final rewrite of *Wind from an Enemy Sky*, we can see McNickle coming to the edge of his liberalism and looking into the abyss. He was surrounded by change: Momaday's *House Made of Dawn* (1968) was the most significant Indian novel since McNickle's own *The Surrounded*, published thirty years earlier. Dee Brown's popular "Indian history of the American West," *Bury My Heart at Wounded Knee*, appeared in 1970. The new Indian radicals of AIM took Alcatraz in 1969 and occupied the BIA office in Washington, D.C. in 1972, landmark events followed in 1973 by the modern-day standoff between the Sioux and the FBI at Wounded Knee. Then in 1973–74, as McNickle was beginning his final revisions of *Wind from an Enemy Sky* and AIM was seizing headlines, President Nixon resigned, and the Arab oil embargo and the stock market crash of 1974 shook us all in one of the worst downturns of modern history. The Dow Jones Industrial Average lost 45 percent of its value.

My father, who grew up in impoverished West Tennessee during the Depression, was only six years younger than McNickle and, like McNickle, left one world and worked his way up into another—he became a partner in Price Waterhouse, an accounting firm on Wall Street. In 1974, as McNickle was beginning his revisions, I asked my father about the stock crisis. His answer was almost as shocking as McNickle's presentation of Pell: "I sometimes think," he said, "that there should be a law against selling a stock within three years of buying it. The market should be a place to invest in competing firms, not a place for speculation."

Given my father's thoughts, I find it easier to believe that McNickle, in the same years, 1974–76, could have come to a radical reassessment of capitalism, to a sense of crisis, and to an instinctive "liquidity" theory that saw the basis of capitalism and liberalism in what Rafferty in the novel called "substitution" and Baudrillard, in postmodernist essays, would soon call "simulation." As Rafferty says, perhaps the misunderstandings between the two cultures come not just from language, but from "the map of the mind we follow."[23]

The crash of 2008 was the logical extreme of liquidity, what my father and McNickle most feared. By that year, more than 50 percent of the trading on Wall Street was conducted through computerized buying and selling programs that process millions of shares, in fractions of seconds, on fractions of pennies, making billions of dollars. These transactions have nothing to do with the company issuing the stock, or with its product or quality, or even with its future beyond the next three minutes, much less three years. Like Adam Pell and other good liberal capitalists, the mortgage brokers in this millennial scenario—creating investment money by turning worthless (unsecured) mortgage loans into bonds—had transformed a moth-eaten medicine bundle into a priceless gold statue. "All that is solid melts into air." If someone would buy the unsecured bonds simply because they could sell them to someone else, then no value is inherent, there is no collateral—and all value is set only by demand on the exchange. Then they took out insurance against the bonds' failure (a "credit default swap"). Pell's substitution of an Inca gold statue for a Salish medicine bundle presumed that the medicine bundle's value was only its value on the exchange. But the exchange value had no value to the Salish. The medicine bundle was invaluable in every sense—both without market value and yet priceless, inherently uninsurable as its loss was beyond recompense. Not all thought is by analogy.

In the 1970s, as he was rewriting *Wind from an Enemy Sky*, McNickle made a number of revisions to his earlier nonfiction work, all more radical. In 1975, in his new conclusion to *They Came Here First*, he wrote:

"Indian society lived under a sentence of death from the first landings of an alien race.... the nature of the relationship was always that of executioner and victim, poised in suspense."[24] But perhaps the clearest glimpse of McNickle's transcending of liberalism, in his last years, came in a paper he gave at a conference in Canada in 1974, "The Surfacing of Native Leadership." He had written a laudatory obituary in *The Nation* for his friend and mentor John Collier, in 1968. Now, six years later at the conference, McNickle suggested publicly, for the first time, the limits of Collier's liberalism. According to McNickle's biographer, Dorothy Parker, he first presented Collier as "a man of his time, whose thinking was shaped by the progressive reformers of the twentieth century."[25] Then McNickle continued: "Collier's mission as a man of reason was to create the opportunity for the Indians to develop and use modern political devices ... and as a man of his class and generation he saw no reason why he should not speak for the Indian people, no reason why they should not be satisfied to have him speak." McNickle now saw Collier, this direct descendant of the liberal revolutions of the eighteenth century ("a man of reason") arriving, like Pell, at the final impasse. Collier believed that his culture was a gift to Indians, but "he could not," McNickle went on to say, "substitute his will and his vision for Indian will and vision."[26] Note "substitute." McNickle might have written the scene of Pell's well-intentioned fiasco the next day. By a "simple substitution of symbols" (as Agent Rafferty puts it), the best of liberal reformers is offering the Indians a modernism, based on liquidity, that will destroy them.

TRIBALISM, REGIONALISM, AND THE NEW LOCALISM IN THE AGE OF ECOLOGY

The South is a region; the West is a region; Boston is a region, but only after the power moved to New York. Brittany is a region; Paris is not. A region is a margin, existing in relation to a center of power. Paradoxically, the controlling center pretends neutrality; the center is a no-place speaking a non-dialect; its unique "point of view" disappears into an "authority" so general it becomes invisible.

The unique but invisible point of view of our center is liberal capitalism. There may be, then, a kind of merit to the center's claim to neutrality. What kind of "region" is the center? In America, the center is the neutral space that denies place in favor of commodity. The center has liquified all its assets, put it all into circulation, so that it does indeed live nowhere, or at least its "where" is interchangeable with any other "where" and can be traded up. All regional literature, then, that affirms the importance of its regionality by privileging the point of view of located inhabitants subverts consumer capitalism by refusing to make a commodity of place.

One might object that "place" here is irrelevant; that, yes, subcultures are always threatened by the mainstream culture; but those are class and power problems, and geography is not the issue. However, our particular Euro-American capitalist arrogance—that all can be liquefied in order to be manipulated to our convenience—is itself the belief of a certain people at a certain time and place. The new ships and navigation of the European Renaissance, the available fossil fuels for the Industrial Revolution, the cheap energy resources plus today's new technologies have given us the illusion of being free of time and place: the sun will never set on our liberal democratic empires. That illusion is itself environmentally conditioned. That is, our arrogance itself has been a part of our relation to earth, water, air; the attitudes even of the center, its own belief that it is a not-region free to pursue any bargain it chooses, is shaped by the "place" of European history in time and space, the location of its imagination. Hence the brilliance and shock of Buckminster Fuller's vision of "this spaceship earth," announcing that we all—even the rich and privileged—do live *somewhere* (on a tiny earth, spinning through a void), and we can see the edge of our territory, our limits, our fragility.

Regional writing stands outside of both the capitalist project and its related postmodern project. Regionalists believe in voice, self, place. They speak with the old authority of limited, located personal experience. However, regionalists have often done so in resistance to the present and the future. As Michael Steiner has observed, to many regionalists of the 1930s and 1940s, regions were places where "primal cultures could flourish as stable correctives to a dangerously top-heavy machine civilization."[27] Note "primal," and "corrective." Or as Howard Odum said, regions were "tabernacles for the folk cultures of the world to maintain a quality culture in a quantity world."[28] Note "maintain," as in a museum. The movement had more than a little nostalgia and at times was Luddite—smashing the new machines.

Since the 1930s, however, the rise of ecology has redefined "region," which is no longer a quaint (out of power) place but a complex and specific fabric of interdependent organisms. This is a progressive, biological understanding of "place," not a nostalgic one. Not surprisingly, many of the essays in this present volume are rereading the old regionalists in the light of this progressive understanding of place, and finding them not so reactionary after all.

It is a great paradox that the two major intellectual innovations of our time, ecology and postmodernism, are utterly opposed. Ecology seems to return to the Enlightenment, reestablishing meaning with empirical authority, and speaking in the voice of reason. Postmodernists, on the other hand, argue for the end of authority, for non-meaning and not-voice. Yet both movements are radically reformist. Ecology mounts the first empirical critique of the idea of progress, turning the language of the priests of science against their own creed. Postmodernists attack similar antagonists. They deconstruct that progressive culture from within, while ecology, unembarrassed by new logos formation, constructs an alternative from without.

Ecologists and regionalists flirt with the destruction of liberalism by foregrounding place as an alternative to liquidity; postmodernists flirt with the destruction of liberalism by entering liquidity and taking it to its absurd extreme. The center, however, does have a face, is itself a region in biospheric history that may have had its day. New forms of regionalism may well lie in the future, not in the past. The contemporary movement toward the "local" is quite different from the old "regionalism" and offers versions of the place-centered tribalism that McNickle understood so well.

Let us follow McNickle's lead and turn back to tribalism for perspective. Think a minute about native, tribal societies in relation to liquidity on the one hand, and to ecological localism on the other. When an Amazon Indian said, "We will keep this land which is our blood,"[29] he was not speaking of acreage, he was speaking of a particular place that could not be exchanged. In the 1990s the Borneo natives along the upper Baram River, some of the last intact hunter-gatherer tribes in the world before the logging took their land, had an exhaustive ecological knowledge of their complex rainforest. Asked to draw a map of their territory on the ground, they traced rivers and ridges, then poked dots here and there and named them: "Ula Jek", etc. These were not villages or camps, but especially productive fruiting trees and clumps of sago palm, their basic sources of dietary starch. They could tell you when they had last visited each dot, what they had harvested, and what was left—for themselves, and for the wild pigs, their delicacy.[30] The Borneo natives were not "regionalists," if that term suggests "out of power" in relation to a center, or backward-looking. They were localists: they, like the Native American tribes, had learned to live within a unique place.

McNickle knew, and felt, the force of a tribal dependence not on *a* place, but on *the* place where they lived. When the ecosystem is destroyed, the traditional tribal life is gone. "When the Buffalo went away," said the Crow Chief Plenty-Coups, "the hearts of my people fell to the ground, and they could not lift them up again."[31]

In college in the 1950s, "regional" literature (Sarah Orne Jewett, Edith Wharton's *Ethan Frome*, Mary Austin), even if delightful, seemed limited, quaint, "local color," because it was out of the mainstream of liberal progress. If the gap between liberalism (from *liber*, "free") and McNickle's native tribalism is the gap between freedom and fate (limits to freedom), then the new regionalists, the localists and ecologists, while coming from a different direction than the tribal societies, are also pointing to limits, accommodation to local realities, a growing acknowledgment of shared fate on our spaceship earth. This is a noble endeavor, curtailing immediate success (domination) for long-term gain. But some tribes, in one place a long time, have done that. McNickle was sure that Pell's liberal liquidity was fundamentally flawed: not everything is possible.

If sustainability is woven into the definition of progress, everything changes. Sustainability is the key to the difference between the regional (in its historical use) and the local. The regionalist movement was sometimes backward-looking, nostalgic, resisting progress. The local movement is forward-looking, progressive, tied to new science, staking claims on the future. The concept of sustainability demands attention to the future, for a long time.

In 1974, the same year that McNickle began his final revisions of *Wind from an Enemy Sky* and began to question the basis of American liberal optimism, one of the nationwide bestsellers in the United States was E. F. Schumacher's *Small Is Beautiful*, a convenient marker for the beginning of the localist movement. Ecological thought was the foundation of this movement, and one could argue that localism is simply regionalism in the age of ecology. Ecological science offered a new natural realism rather than using nature as a retreat from reality, and under its umbrella other important strains of thought have emerged in recent decades, all of which lend credence to the popular slogan "Think globally, act locally." Research in bioregions and in ecological limitations has led to new economic theory, especially in Paul Hawken's *Ecology of Commerce* (1993) and Michael Pugh's *Natural Capital* (1995).

Historians like Donald Worster (*Nature's Economy*, 1994) and writers and critics like Gary Snyder (who was bioregional before bioregional was cool) began to weave new ecological thought into their work. Richard White's revisionist history of the American West, *It's Your Misfortune and None of My Own* (1991), stressed how often kinship and community, not Daniel Boone's retreat from civilization, were the basis of western settlement. The new communitarians in politics, including Missoula mayor Dan Kemmis (*Community and the Politics of Place*, 1990), were providing alternatives to "free individual" values; cities were looking again at neighborhoods versus highways. Most of the "alternative" economics books of the 1990s were in fact not against capitalism itself; rather, they were questioning unlimited liquidity. Money could be made, these books said, by firms responsive to limits, to the new need for energy efficiency, sustainability, and quality. Commodities could be improved and produced more sustainably. This was not a regressive movement; this would be the new progress.

The food reformers and "locavores" have been crucial. In thinking by analogy, like Pell offering a replacement for a unique heirloom, one priceless object can be substituted for another: Tyson's chickens "farmed" in vast, largely automated enterprises are analogous to barnyard chickens, but in their billions they can be viewed as chickens "liquified," that is, chickens transformed into chicken-like units easier to exchange, junk bond chickens. The "modern" way—Cargill, Monsanto, Tyson, sugar beets, corn syrup, monoculture—produces cheap food, yes, but denatured or simulated food that has become a national health hazard. Journalist Michael Pollan has mounted a fierce attack on the meat industry (*The Omnivore's Dilemma*, 2006), and Eric Schlosser's *Fast Food Nation* (2002) and Robert Kenner's documentary film *Food, Inc.* (2008) indignantly expose what large corporate agriculture is doing to us: ever cheaper ingredients for ever increasing profits, and the nightmare of genetic control and patent ownership of seeds, empire building. Right now, in Iowa and Nebraska, families and local cooperatives of what once were called yeoman farmers—Thomas

Jefferson's ideal of freedom and responsibility—are constrained to work on agribusiness plantations like Monsanto's under terms approaching economic slavery. If this statement seems too strong, look it up.[32]

It is important to distinguish the recent locavore movement from the "drop out" aspect of the hippies' "back to the land" movement in the 1960s. The locavores are building on ecological and biological critiques of our recent progress, including skeptical analysis of "better living through chemistry." They document how large-scale monoculture has necessitated pesticides, fungicides, and fertilizers previously unknown; how additives and preservatives for distant shipment and longer shelf life have downsides; how oil prices affect transportation economy; and what carbon footprints are left by the factory farm food that we eat. The details are not our business here: but note that these questions are not nostalgic, but practical. Our Missoula newspaper today has a picture of two men at the local "truck garden" farm. The tall, skinny guy is a local organic farmer, Josh Slotnik. He has a graduate degree in agriculture from Cornell. The big guy is a large-scale organic farmer from Big Sandy: U.S. Senator Jon Tester. They are conferring about a new agriculture bill in Congress. Both men see themselves as our future, not our past. They are not "local color."

I am offering (playfully) a local criticism, deliberately invoking my newspaper, my senator, my mayor, my father—the elders of my tribe—in a piece on our local elder, McNickle, and his elder, Merriam. My speech, located in a local culture, is an alternative to the liberal aspiration to detachment, to an omniscient voice. In that local vein, I am pleased to report that the Salish Kootenai College on the reservation, under tribal leader and college president Joe McDonald, dedicated The D'Arcy McNickle Library in 1987, ending a long estrangement from the "breed" who had sold his allotment and left, and who came home only in his imagination, over and over.

"Liquidity" is linked to liberalism, and of course "liberal" (like all "lib-" words) is related to our most sacred word, "free." But freedom has limits and a context. An individualist conception of freedom is already a tyranny: that is, what if the free individual does not want to be alone? The free individual is not simply a state of nature, but a problematic construct, as the tribal tradition has suggested. Plato and Aristotle believed that man is by nature a political animal, meaning that a human is an animal who lives in a polis, a city-state, no more complicated a statement than saying that wild horses live in hierarchical herds. "Wild" does not mean "free." Ecology preaches the interdependencies of wild nature.

"Freedom to choose" begs the question of what choices are possible. If we live in a polis, we need meaningful "political" choices from which to choose. It is very naive, and very American, to think that freedom is just the continuous, ideal state of a lone individual. Willie Nelson knows better: "Cowboys are special, with their own brand of misery, from being alone too long." Or as Janis Joplin sang, "Freedom's just another word for nothin' left to lose." It is time for our notion of freedom and liberty to grow up. Colonial expansion is over; the frontier is closed. The unbridled individual pursuit of a "greed" that is liquidity, transforming everything including people's homes into a commodity to be micro-leveraged up to a house of cards that crashes on everyone except those who have already moved millions to the Bahamas, is disastrous in the long run. Our Native American literature has consistently chosen identity over the liquid assets of freedom as the center conceives it, and new ecological thought gives form and urgency to the rethinking of place. Our biosphere is nonnegotiable. Much of the contemporary regionalism of the West contains a profound critique of our own Enlightenment values—mobility, individuality, exchange, freedom. So, rather than representing a region that is marginal to a neutral center, this literature defines the limits of the center, makes of the center a region increasingly marginal to reality, and joins much of the third world in predicting an end to the center's imperialism of liquidity, and, for better or worse, a return to the fate of place.

Both D'Arcy McNickle and my father recognized that all that is solid does *not* melt into air; not without changing the air. Every species lives within ecological, biological, and species limits. Unbridled freedom is not natural. Adam Pell's infinite freedom of choice—everything is negotiable, can be traded up—versus the Indians' choosing of their past, their society, their sacred place, should make us all think again. As McNickle so wisely observed: "One cannot grow a tree on a pile of money, or cause water to gush from it. One can only spend it, and then one is homeless."[33]

NOTES

1. D'Arcy McNickle, *The Surrounded* (1936; reprinted, Albuquerque: University of New Mexico Press, 1964); *Wind from an Enemy Sky* (1977; reprinted, Albuquerque: University of New Mexico Press, 1988); *The Hawk Is Hungry and Other Stories*, ed. Birgit Hans

(Tucson: University of Arizona Press, 1992). A book for young adults, *Runner in the Sun: A Story of Indian Maize,* appeared in 1954.

2. John Lloyd Purdy, *Word Ways: The Novels of D'Arcy McNickle* (Tucson: University Arizon Press, 1990); William W. Bevis, *Ten Tough Trips: Montana Writers and the West* (Seattle: University of Washington Press, 1990); Birgit Hans, ed., in McNickle, *The Hawk is Hungry and Other Stories;* Dorothy R. Parker, *Singing an Indian Song: A Biography of D'Arcy McNickle* (Lincoln: University of Nebraska Press, 1992); John Lloyd Purdy, ed., *The Legacy of D'Arcy McNickle: Writer, Historian, Activist* (Norman: University of Oklahoma Press, 1996); William W. Bevis, "Region, Power, Place" in Michael Kowalewski, ed., *Reading in the West: New Essays on the Literature of the American West* (Cambridge: Cambridge University Press, 1996), 21–43. I thank John Purdy for his generous replies to questions about McNickle's politics and economics. We are both surprised at McNickle's apparent lack of involvement with Joseph K. Howard and especially with James Welch.

3. As cited in Bevis, *Ten Tough Trips,* 94.
4. McNickle, *The Surrounded,* 2, 7, 5.
5. McNickle, *Wind from an Enemy Sky,* 18.
6. McNickle, *Wind from an Enemy Sky,* 28.
7. Harold Fey and D'Arcy McNickle, *Indians and Other Americans* (New York: Harper, 1959), 26–28.
8. Letter quoted in James Ruppert, *D'Arcy McNickle* (Boise: Boise State University Press, 1988), 6.
9. Guthrie and Johnson, by the late 1940s, had become well known writers of novels and short stories.
10. "No meadowlarks sang, and the world fell apart." A death song and the last words in the book. Louis Owens in *Other Destinies* (Norman: University of Oklahoma Press, 1992) and James Ruppert in Purdy's *Legacy of Darcy McNickle* have explored the complexities of "translations" between cultures.
11. McNickle, *Wind from an Enemy Sky,* 210.
12. McNickle, *Wind from an Enemy Sky,* 232–36.
13. McNickle, *Wind from an Enemy Sky,* 232–36.
14. McNickle, *Wind from an Enemy Sky,* 249.
15. Quoted in Parker, *Singing an Indian Song,* 241.
16. Marshal Berman, *All That Is Solid Melts into Air* (New York: Simon & Schuster, 1982), 15.
17. Karl Marx as cited in Berman, *All That Is Solid Melts into Air,* 21.
18. Quoted in Parker, *Singing an Indian Song,* 32.
19. Parker, *Singing an Indian Song,* 33.
20. McNickle, "Snowfall," in *The Hawk Is Hungry and Other Stories,* 41.
21. McNickle, "Hard Riding," in *The Hawk Is Hungry and Other Stories,* 4–5.
22. McNickle, "Six Beautiful in Paris," in *The Hawk Is Hungry and Other Stories,* 161.
23. McNickle, *Wind from an Enemy Sky,* 125.
24. McNickle, *They Came Here First: The Epic of the American Indian* (New York: Lillincott, 1949; reprinted, New York: Octagon, 1974), 283. My thanks to James Ruppert for the comparison in his *D'Arcy McNickle,* 36.
25. Dorothy Parker, paraphrasing McNickle in Purdy, *Legacy,* 26.

26. Parker, in Purdy, *Legacy*, 26–27.

27. Michael Steiner, "Regionalism in the Great Depression," *Geographical Review* 73 (October 1983): 433.

28. Howard Odum, *The American Blend*, as cited by Steiner, "Regionalism," 433.

29. U.S. National Public Radio, "All Things Considered," October 14, 1991.

30. William W. Bevis, *Borneo Log: The Struggle for Sarawak's Forests* (Seattle: University of Washington Press, 1995), 156.

31. Frank Linderman, *Plenty-Coup, Chief of the Crows* (1932; reprinted, Lincoln: University of Nebraska Press, 1962), 308.

32. Michael Pollan, *The Ominvore's Dilemma: A Natural History of Four Meals* (New York: Penguin, 2006); Eric Schlosser, *Fast Food Nation* (New York: Harper, 2005). A quick glance through Internet listings soon reveals a wide spectrum of opinion regarding Monsanto and other agribusiness companies. See, e.g., Monsanto's own website, www.monsanto.com (whose heading in Google reads "Monsanto—A Sustainable Agriculture Company"), and the countervailing site from Organic Consumers Association, www.organicconsumers.org/monsanto/index.cfm (suhead "Millions against Monsanto"), both accessed August 13, 2012. Wikipedia's article on Monsanto as of the same access date presented a lengthy description of the company's history, policies, products, legal battles, and public controversies.

33. Fey and McNickle, *Indians and Other Americans*, 28.

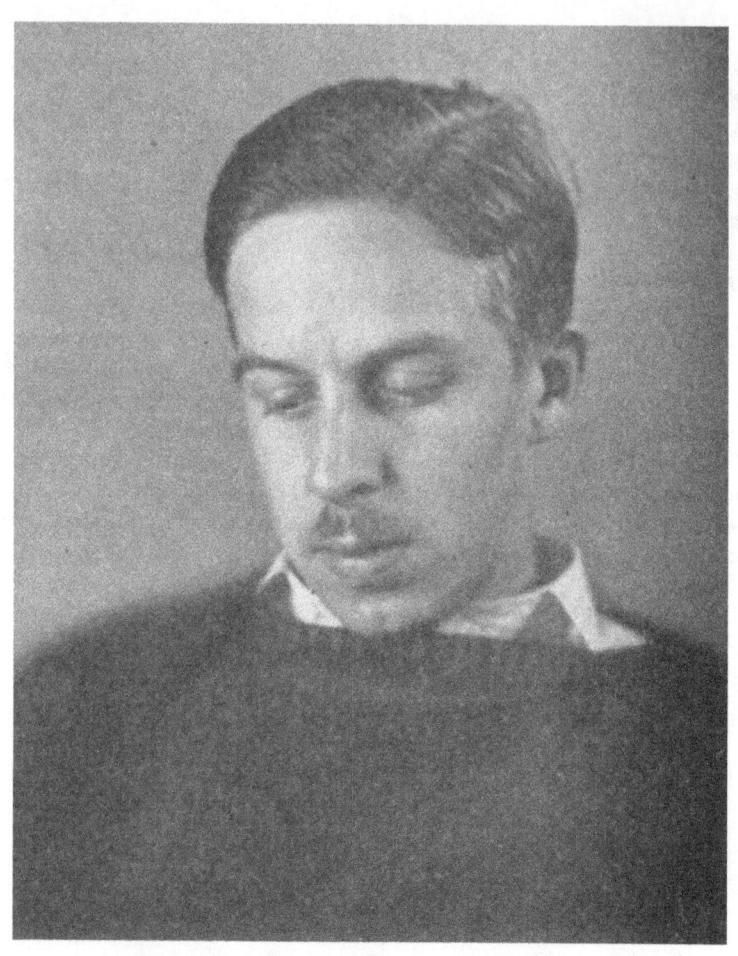
Robert Cantwell. Courtesy of T. V. Reed.

CHAPTER ELEVEN

Robert Cantwell and Northwest Left Literary Labors

T. V. Reed

Any history of literary leftism in the U.S. Northwest would certainly place Robert Cantwell (1908–78) at the center.[1] Born and raised in the lumber towns of western Washington, Cantwell went on to become the best-selling and best-reviewed figure in the "proletarian" literary movement of the 1930s. His novel *The Land of Plenty* (1934) is on virtually every historian's list of the most important fictional works about working-class life in the Depression era. He was in some respects a solitary figure who never had about him anything like the circle of midwestern writers who gathered around his friend and contemporary Jack Conroy.[2] Nevertheless, Cantwell can be fully understood only in the context of tensions and synergies between his Pacific Northwest homeland and national political and literary trends centered in New York City, where he lived from the 1930s until his death.

As regional manifestations of radical literary movements slowly have been brought to light, the Pacific Northwest has remained largely unexplored. The region has a rich, complicated history of radicalism, particularly labor radicalism, a history reflected, and reflected upon, in northwestern literatures of various types. Because of its relative isolation from such major centers of left and left-literary activity as New York and Chicago, the Northwest developed its own strand of literary radicalism, confined primarily to labor newspapers and radical magazines. Both the Populist Party and the Socialist Party had strongholds in the region. A significant bloc of northwestern voters supported the Democratic-Populist ticket in 1896 and voted for Eugene Debs and the Socialist Party in 1912.[3] After World War I the Communist Party had a very active presence in the state's labor movement. By 1936 the Communist movement in the state was such that the U.S. Postmaster joked, "There are forty-seven states and the Soviet of Washington."[4]

The most important radical influence was undoubtedly the Industrial Workers of the World (IWW), who were particularly active regionally in the lumber industry and in migrant agriculture up through World War I and who continued to influence the region's culture long after their heyday.[5] The Wobblies, as its members were known, have long been recognized for their radical individualism even amidst political collectivism, and their own rich culture of song, poetry, and the graphic arts must be seen as an element of the cultural legacy of the region's left.[6] Though perhaps best known for their parodic anticapitalist singing as exemplified in *The Little Red Songbook* (first published in 1909, now in its 38th edition) and for the career of the infamous Joe Hill (1879–1915), the Wobblies were responsible for an abundance of cultural production of all kinds, as were other unions. Poet, journalist, and activist Anna Louise Strong, for example, wrote poetry about the great general strike in Seattle of 1919, and virtually all of the union and left magazines of the period in the region had literary sections with poetry, short stories, and occasionally even excerpts from novels in progress. John Reed, famous as the author of the most widely read account of the Russian Revolution, *Ten Days That Shook the World* (1919), was born in Portland, Oregon, and brought his Northwest-bred sympathy for the Wobblies with him to the East, where he became involved in IWW-led textile worker strikes in Lawrence, Massachusetts (1912) and Paterson, New Jersey (1913). During the latter, Reed spearheaded one of the most spectacular radical cultural events of the twentieth century, the Paterson Strike Pageant. Held in Madison Square Garden, the event included more than 1,000 workers reenacting scenes from their strike. With sets designed by artist John Sloan and with Reed directing, the spectacular "play" is unique in U.S. cultural history.[7]

Whereas Strong and Reed became Communist internationalists and were among the handful of Americans granted a resting place in the Kremlin, Cantwell, though he too spent most of his fiction-writing years away from the region, focused the vast majority of his writing on the Northwest. Close study of his life and work makes it increasingly clear that his literary leftism had local roots. And though no fully developed left-literary coterie emerged in the region, one of the places Cantwell lived in Washington turns out to have been unusually productive of radical writing. Surprisingly that place was not the state's major city, Seattle, but the small coastal lumber town of Aberdeen.

No fewer than three proletarian novelists emerged from this town of 20,000 during the 1930s. In addition to Cantwell, Aberdeen housed Louis Colman, a friend of Cantwell's who likewise worked in a plywood mill and was author of *Lumber* (1931); and Clara Weatherwax, descendent of one of the city's founders and author of *Marching! Marching!* (1934).[8] Though neither of these novels achieves anything near the literary quality or political force of Cantwell's work, each reinforces a general sense of a broadly northwestern literary leftist perspective. *Lumber*, which Colman drafted while on strike from the mill where he worked, offers a realist chronicle of IWW organizing in the Northwest and the vicious mob resistance it often met from the local business communities. Weatherwax's *Marching! Marching!* is a more experimental novel (attempting to achieve a collective voice) that, while clumsy in execution, is rich in representing the range of ethnicities in the region as connected to various industries (for example, Filipinos in the canning industry and Scandinavians in timber), as well as presenting debates (with regional inflections) between IWW and Communist Party USA organizers. *Marching! Marching!* won a prize for best new writing about the working class sponsored by CPUSA's literary magazine *The New Masses*, an award based no doubt in part on the way the novel closely reflects then current party policy.

Cantwell himself offered an astute analysis of why three radical novelists might emerge from this relatively small town. In an article in the *New Republic* in 1936 he suggested that class stratification was more visible in timber country than in the big cities.

> There are twenty-four big mills around [Aberdeen], capable of producing about a billion feet of timber a year; there is a large Finnish population there, a big Filipino colony, a considerable number of half-breeds from the Chehalis, Quinalt and Taholah tribes, [and] a large proportion of Southerners who drifted to the Northwest.... It is almost entirely a working-class community. The major stores are chain stores, and most of the mill officials are hired representatives of Eastern capitalists; the absorbent layer of shopkeepers, small owners and professional people that in other places acts as a cushion to

break the clash of class antagonisms—or prevents their being recognized for what they are—is numerically and culturally unimportant. Consequently, class lines are firmly drawn, and the classes can hardly be said to be in that "state of flux, with a persistent interchange of elements" which Marx once observed to be a condition of American society in general. The history of the town is a record of violent labor disputes. The Wobblies were strong there during the War; the Ku Klux Klan got control of the city administration in 1925; the trade-union movement, intermittently powerful, had no continuity, so that organizational gains made during strikes were dissipated in the periods of relative inactivity between them.[9]

Cantwell further notes that the local immigrant Finns, Poles, and other ethnic minorities from the south side of town did not generally fraternize with the "Americans." And class divisions were written into the very geography of the city. The middle- and upper-middle-class children from houses on "the hill" above the city seldom moved in the same circles as children from the lower class homes on "the flats." The district where the mill workers lived was comprised of acres of closely packed wooden dwellings crowded between the bluff and the waterfront and was marked by a high incidence of tuberculosis. This was the context in which Cantwell spent his late adolescence and early adulthood. But to understand his regionally inflected literary leftism, we need to trace this history back a bit farther.[10]

BECOMING A DISCIPLE OF HENRY JAMES AND KARL MARX

At the turn of the twentieth century, the southwestern quadrant of Washington state was timber country, a region with dozens of logging camps in its hills, dotted with mill towns lining the railway lines and rivers that carried lumber to cities and the sea. Cantwell entered the world in one of these small mill towns, Little Falls, on January 8, 1908. Descendants of one of the first families to settle in Washington, the Cantwells remained in the region throughout Robert's childhood and adolescence. But the stability and class status these facts might seem to imply were undermined by the turbulent cycles of economic boom and bust that rocked all but the largest lumber companies, and these cycles, often combined with violent labor wars, wreaked havoc in and around the Cantwell family.[11]

Cantwell's literary imagination was clearly stirred by the presence of the IWW during his childhood. Wobblies were active throughout the region in the years of his youth, as indicated by the Wobbly-led Spokane Free Speech Fight of 1909, the Everett Massacre of 1916, and numerous other well-publicized events, including, most spectacularly, the first city-wide strike in U.S. history, the Seattle General Strike of 1919.[12] Prior to his move to Aberdeen, Cantwell spent his early teens near the town of Centralia, site of another deadly pitched battle between IWW members and the American Legion, a series of events known as the Centralia Massacre that he later memorialized in a short story, "Hills around Centralia" (1935).[13] The story concerns a young boy who encounters fleeing Wobblies in the woods near his home. Whether or not the young Robert actually experienced such an event, his literary re-creation makes clear that he experienced it imaginatively. He was fourteen at the time of the massacre, and despite much conservative propaganda in the local papers against workers, he was quite aware of their deplorable conditions and is likely to have been sympathetic to the colorful, bottom-dog revolutionists of the IWW.

After a series of good and not so good jobs in a number of towns, Cantwell's father found work in 1922 as a supervisor with Gray's Harbor Iron and Metal Works, a shop in Aberdeen that repaired and designed engines for the cargo ships that carried Washington lumber to ports around the world. Robert was to spend the next nine years there. After finishing high school (at Weatherwax High, named for Clara's great-grandfather) at age sixteen, Cantwell entered the University of Washington. But by the end of his first year in college his father had become seriously ill with tuberculosis, and it became clear that he would no longer be able to afford college educations for any of his four children. Robert and his elder brother, Jim, left college and found work at a plywood factory near Aberdeen. When their father died one year later, their mother took up work as a cook in a bakery-delicatessen on the waterfront but made far too little to support a family.

In *Laugh and Lie Down*, Cantwell's largely autobiographical first novel, the narrator describes the death of the father of the two brothers (both working in a mill) who are the novel's protagonists: "The last years of his life were spent in a vain almost an hysterical attempt to make some financial provision for the future of his family, as he had planned more pleasant careers for his children than additional lifetimes of drudgery."[14] When the father, an engineer who moved from town to town aiding in the design and construction of mills, falls victim to the "tubercular winds" that blow across the harbor, his sons are forced into just the kind of drudgery he had hoped to spare them.

This is precisely how Robert was forced into a working life he had not chosen. But while learning the pleasures and hardships of blue-collar work, he was also forming the literary ambitions that would eventually lead him out of the factory and away from the Northwest. As adolescents he and his friend Calvin Fixx had dreamed of "escaping to New York" to make names for themselves as writers, and shortly after Cantwell began work at the mill, Fixx did manage to "escape" to Greenwich Village. Through correspondence with Fixx and by continuing the writing he had begun in high school and college, Cantwell kept alive a self-image apart from his role as a veneer clipper-operator at Harbor Plywood. While working in the mill from 1925 to 1929 he managed to complete a half-dozen short stories, a play, and portions of a novel.

The tastes of the two young would-be writers ran clearly toward the modernists, with whom they shared an interest in things French. Cantwell read Gertrude Stein and James Joyce, sending Fixx a fairly detailed analysis of the latter's *Ulysses*, and claimed Henry James to be his literary and critical master (having deeply studied James's famous critical prefaces). He was able to live a kind of low-rent version of the "jazz age" from a distance. With Fixx acting de facto as his literary agent, he managed to publish a couple of short stories that led to a contract for his first novel. Finally, with that novel's publication in 1931, Cantwell permanently joined Fixx in New York City.

New York in the early years of the Depression was the center of intense debate concerning the political meanings and uses of literature. Cantwell had chosen to settle there during the most unsettling of times. He had come to pursue a literary vocation just as many of America's foremost writers and critics were calling the traditional life of letters into question. Edmund Wilson, among the most respected critics in the nation and literary editor of the prestigious then liberal journal *New Republic*, voiced the views of many writers when he noted that the economic crisis had made the disinterested pursuit of beauty seem utterly irresponsible.

Not long after the stock market crash, Wilson had temporarily abandoned literature and gone out among the people to gain a sense of the national mood. The reports he sent back to the *New Republic* in 1930 and 1931 portrayed a profoundly confused populace and spoke portentously of the shattering of traditional American beliefs. Wilson concluded that "Karl Marx's predictions are in process of coming true" and that capitalism, victimized by its own internal contradictions, had totally collapsed, ushering in an era of intensified class conflict.[15]

Wilson was far from alone in these observations and opinions, but rather reflected a general drift of the intelligentsia toward the Marxist left. Marxist ideas became common currency among intellectuals in the early 1930s, and nowhere was this influence greater than among critics of literature and writers of fiction. Cantwell's transformation from an F. Scott Fitzgeraldesque modernist (both Fitzgerald and Hemingway praised his work highly) into the most admired of "proletarian" writers came about through the coalescence of several forces: the political-economic collapse, reflections back on his own experiences as a mill laborer, and immersion in this rapidly radicalizing literary culture in New York. He met and was befriended by virtually all of the key writers (among them Hemingway, Dos Passos, Erskine Caldwell, and James T. Farrell), critics (including Wilson, Kenneth Burke, and Newton Arvin), and editors (Malcolm Cowley, T. S. Matthews, and later Henry Luce) of the Depression era. Through these contacts he secured a variety of always tenuous, never well-paid jobs as book reviewer and critical essayist, while continuing to work on his fiction.

By the mid-1930s, as he was completing his second novel, Cantwell was among the most respected young literary critics in the city. In October 1933 he took the opportunity provided by a *New Republic* review of recent fiction about workers to elaborate on his strong support for the proletarian literary movement. Calling the literature dealing with the conditions of workers the "most vital" of "all contemporary literary movements," he insisted that "no one who is interested in literature rather than in politics could disregard" proletarian fiction.[16] For him, these views were not just theoretical; it is evident that his critical perspectives on working-class literature were developing in dialogue with his practice as a novelist. His first years as a critic, 1932–34, were also the years in which he labored over his own proletarian novel, *The Land of Plenty*.[17]

THE LAND OF PLENTY

The Land of Plenty is widely regarded as one of the major achievements of the proletarian movement. It is by far Cantwell's most important contribution to literary politics in that it is not only a fine radical novel but also perfectly illustrates his ideas about political literature. As an extension of his critical attitudes on proletarian fiction, the novel takes as its central problem one endemic to the genre: connecting the micropolitical level of workers' daily lives to the macropolitical level of larger questions of capitalism and class struggle. Some proletarian authors solved this problem through explicitly didactic interventions (though this occurs less commonly than is generally charged). These could range from the situationally credible and subtle to what one might call the "communist ex machina" approach—the plot device that Cantwell called "communist magicians," in which a radical organizer-agitator appears suddenly to offer Marxist conversion through a rabble-rousing speech. Cantwell uses this approach to a certain extent, but with subtlety, through the character Vin Garl, a Finnish worker and former member of the IWW who serves as the voice of labor history and organizational experience in *The Land of Plenty*. Garl clearly reflects the particular history of the Northwest in which Finnish socialists and Wobblies played a central role.

Cantwell's narrative offers both rich naturalistic detail on the psychology of class as worked out in a particular work site, and an overarching radical allegory addressing the larger politics of capitalism in the 1930s. Although this allegory (sometimes subtle, sometimes blatant) might be considered a mere "frill" on top of the naturalism, in working the allegorical vein he was, whether consciously or not, contributing to a long tradition of working-class literature extending back through Jack London and Rebecca Harding Davis to the dime novels of the nineteenth century, in which allegory was a key method of conveying class-conscious political analysis.[18]

Drawing its raw materials from Cantwell's four years of laboring at Harbor Plywood and his younger years of living in mill towns, *The Land of Plenty* is a detailed account of activity in a veneer wood factory and of the workers and bosses whose lives revolve around it. The novel depicts the conditions and events that precipitate a strike as seen through the eyes of a diverse group of characters representing various personality types, political positions, and class interests. Part I, "Power and Light," traces the events leading up to the strike, as viewed by workers and management. Part II, "The Education of a Worker," continues developing the strike as seen by numerous characters, but concentrates somewhat more centrally on one sensitive young working-class adolescent who is forced to come to terms with the class conflict touched off by the walkout.

The novel is constructed via twenty-three chapters, each labeled with the name of a character and (de)centered in the point of view of that character. I say "decentered" because each character is carefully constructed in relation to other characters such that the reader sees them at once as individual and as *social* beings; they are sufficiently individualized to seem like "real" human beings, but never to the point where they lose their value as social types and members of larger classes. Each chapter consists of a mixture of dialogue and free indirect discourse, thus reinforcing a sense of character as emerging socially.

The novel begins with the factory suddenly plunged into darkness by a power failure during the night shift. Details of the blackout are handled in naturalistic fashion, but images of darkness and light also form the overarching symbolic structure of the Marxian allegory. Set in 1929 on and around Independence Day, the blackout allegorizes the "power failure" of capitalism known as the Great Crash. Workers literally struggling to restore power have to do so amid the incompetence of the managerial class. Winters, an American Indian sawyer representing the strong presence of Native people in the Northwest, proves the most militant of the workers by seizing first a flashlight and later commandeering the boss's car to use its power and lights to help an injured worker. I have called the allegory Marxist, but more precisely it seems closest to the anarcho-syndicalist ideology of the IWW who, unlike the Communist Party USA, stressed the ability of workers to organize independently to create One Big Union to run an economy without bosses.

The blackout forms the center of the novel's early action and is viewed by the various characters in succession. First comes Carl Belcher (shades of Shakespeare's buffoon Sir Toby Belch), a former "efficiency expert" turned inefficient supervisor. Being *in* the factory but not *of* it, Carl stumbles about blindly and rather comically in the dark while attempting to devise a way of blaming the power failure on Hagen, the most senior "old hand" at the mill, whose prestige among his fellow workers Carl and the plant manager, MacMahon, fear. Carl is accompanied in his stumblings by his sycophantic assistant, Morley (feminized as "Molly" by the workers). Discussion between Morley and Belcher focuses on the struggle to control the pattern of blame with regard to the economic loss brought about by the outage. Hagen's section of the narrative, which immediately follows, continues this intricate dance as the older man seeks witnesses among his fellow workers regarding his whereabouts despite the darkness, in order to protect himself from the blame he knows Carl will try to inflict. But soon Hagen's concerns shift away from self-interest, when it is discovered that a "hoist man" has been crushed by a huge log set loose by equipment failure due to the blackout.

In contrast to the foreman Belcher and the plant manager MacMahon, both of whom eventually fall through a hole in the floor and become lost in the swampy, chemical-waste-ridden tide flats beneath the plant, Hagen and the other workers, "knowing the floors around their machines as they know their own homes" (14), move swiftly and efficiently through the dark factory in an attempt to rescue the hoist man. The narrative makes it clear that the workers are quite capable of running the factory alone—indeed, that they must protect it against the incompetent representatives of management. On the allegorical plane, this conveys the point that they are qualified to seize the means of production, and the prolonged situational irony of the foreman's and manager's inaction set against the quick actions of the workers suggests that the power failure of capitalism can only be set aright by the workers.

At a more naturalistic level, the temporary stoppage serves to foreground the structural conditions that make labor organizing difficult, as only such a break gives the workers time to think and talk among themselves about the layoffs, speed-ups, and wage cuts with which they had recently been burdened. In the Hagen sections of the novel and in those centered on Winters, the sawyer, these central characters have a series of encounters with small groups of their co-workers, gradually and cautiously building solidarity. These discussions are structured as concentric circles, moving out from the main characters to other named but "minor" worker characters, and then farther out to anonymous workers acting as a kind of chorus: *"Listen,* a voice said, *Just say the word and I'll walk out"* (117). The italics (in the original) reveal a different, abstract dimension, functioning as a hint of collective forces and the mass voice found in some "collective novels" in the proletarian genre.

Cantwell builds a sense of complicated class consciousness by contrasting an awareness of alienation (both alienating physical conditions and workers' alienation from the fruits of their labor) with a counterbalancing pride in work. Winters most fully embodies these contradictions. A "half-breed," he also represents the racial and ethnic contradictions inextricably entwined with class issues in the region. He realizes that in this factory, as in others where he had worked before, workers are being driven to inhuman lengths to meet a rush order. Just before the lights went out, he was himself a pure embodiment of industrial alienation:

> The Indian's face was set and his eyes were half-closed under the bright hanging light. The effort to keep up with the racing saws drove everything else out of his mind . . . ; there was nothing left for him now but the straight edge against which he lined the panels and the rolls that drew them in. Gradually his features emptied of life, only his swiftly moving hands and his intent eyes revealing the spirit in him. (39)

In addition to driving the workers too hard, the new foreman was robbing them of their pride in their work. Alert to minute nuances of sight and sound in the factory (17), the mill hands sensed that Carl was ruining *their* factory. In the context of *Land of Plenty* such knowledge is not an end in itself but a prerequisite part of a larger consciousness of class and the possibility of radical transformation. It becomes a utopian prefiguration of unalienated labor emerging when the workers work for themselves as the owners of the means of production.

Class-consciousness is always built in relatively small increments rather than through dramatic conversions. Winters, for example, building on his anger at Belcher, makes a discovery more profound than the mere incompetence of one supervisor as, in the darkness, a vision of his own entire life, touched off by thoughts of his dying wife, passes before him: "his memory would give him nothing but images of misery and terror until it seemed he had lived all his life on the scene of some vast wreck that had strewn the world with its victims; now he remembered the 'accidents' in the logging camps and the mills where he had worked, the ruined bodies of cripples, the loggers whose intestines were ruptured and torn from weights they pulled and the mad pace of their labors." (174). It becomes clear to Winters that these "accidents" were not accidents at all but the direct result of a profit-driven system that pushed machines and workers alike beyond their capacities.

When Belcher eventually finds an excuse to fire Winters, Hagen protests and is fired with him. The rest of the crew, sensing the injustice of the firings, force the boss, through mostly silent intimations of violence, to overrule Carl and rehire the workers. Thus Part I ends with the pride of the workers restored by their resistance to the supervisor and the plant manager: "They were proud; they were excited; some of the kids began yelling as they ran toward the factory. They had their first sure knowledge of their strength" (204). The title for Part I, "Power and Light," now shifts meaning to represent not power and light lost in the blackout but power and light gained through solidarity.

Part II, "The Education of a Worker," traces the parallel emergence of a strike and the gradual development of class consciousness in young Johnny Hagen, son of the "old hand." On a symbol-laden Independence Day in 1929, the day after the power failure, Johnny joins his father, Winters, a few other workers, and Vin Garl, who gives the workers their only knowledge of strike tactics (there is no union organized in the plant), in an informal gathering to discuss tactics in the event that Carl attempts once more to fire some members of the night shift (as he is rumored to be contemplating). When Garl begins to outline a plan of action, one of the workers asks him, "You a union man?"

> "Me? What union is there for a man working where I work?"
> "Wobbly?"
> "I used to carry a red [IWW membership] card during the War.... was in that fighting at Everett and after Centralia it got so hot for me I had to beat it to Canada.... But there's nothing left of them now."

> Johnny looked around at the men gathered in the yard. The harshness of the Finn's voice repelled him and he searched the faces of the men, trying to see some approval or disapproval in their responses to his words.
>
> "They didn't die out," Vin Garl said abruptly. "They were wiped out." He said wiped out with a curious intensity, his mouth closing over the words as though he were biting into them.
>
> Sorenson said cautiously, "We don't want to get everybody thinking we're a bunch of Reds."
>
> Vin Garl started to answer him. Then he nodded. (262–63)

This nuanced silence suggests Garl's savvy sense that Sorenson, who represents the most cautious faction of workers, is not ready for a further lesson in labor history that might redefine what being a "bunch of Reds" means.

Following this exchange, the workers begin to dispute the merits of the moderate American Federation of Labor, and Johnny leaves because arguing "got on his nerves." Johnny is at first repelled by the harshness of those with whom he would have had to throw in his lot and is caught up in the ethnic tension that has historically been a bane of the U.S. labor movement. He thinks of Vin Garl and his friend Waino, both Finns, as "foreigners sticking together and living on the wrong side of the river instead of like ordinary citizens" (263), and he resents their potentially dangerous interference in his (work)life. But then he remembers a ghastly story told to him by an older worker, a story about a kid not much older than Johnny who had had both his legs crushed off in an "accident" brought on by a speed-up. Johnny begins a slow, groping process that leads him to realize that violence, in its various forms, was constantly being directed against workers and that their own harshness was a necessary but inadequate defense against it.

As Johnny walks away from the scene of the strategy session, he also begins to understand the gulf that separates him from Walt Conner, representative of a tempting middle-class life. Conner, like Cantwell himself, had been forced by economic circumstance to quit college after a year. Initially, Johnny is attracted to Walt's talk about fraternities and campus life. As he and Walt talk during the blackout, Johnny begins to dream of the "ivy-covered halls, the long slopes of green lawn, the beautiful coeds, each with her own sports roadster, giving herself so gaily and passionately with a true F. Scott Fitzgerald abandon" (109). But he soon realizes that Walt was merely toying with him and using him to gain a chance to take advantage of Marie, a young Polish worker whom Walt assumes by her ethnic and class origins to be a "chippie"—a loose woman or whore.

This relationship between the two young men functions structurally in the novel, but it also suggests an element of autobiographical displacement, an allegory of Cantwell's own split consciousness. In *Laugh and Lie Down*, he had revealed considerable ambivalence toward his experience as a factory laborer. The autobiographical protagonist felt the factory in which he labored to be a more vital environment than the college he had been forced to leave, but he also felt shame at having to wear workers' overalls and had ambitions to own the factory one day. But as the radical movement, with its celebration of the heroic working class, grew all around him, the young Cantwell sloughed off most of this ambivalence and began to recreate himself as the gruff proletarian remembered by some of his colleagues. The satiric reference to gay "F. Scott Fitzgerald abandon" in the novel is one of several such allusions that suggest a kind of intertextual commentary on the Fitzgeraldesque dimensions of the author's earlier novel. As such, "Walt" serves as a condensed trope both for the discourse of a "decaying middle class," as found in much Communist polemic of the time, and for the literary embodiment of that decline in much "this side of paradise" fiction (117).

When Walt eventually betrays Johnny, a more directly relevant kind of "decadence" is revealed and another part of the latter's education begins. Johnny learns not only generally to distrust promises coming from the middle class but, when Walt becomes Carl's new assistant, to understand something about the functioning of class in the factory. When Johnny sees Walt riding in the foreman's car,

> something he had not understood before became clear to him. Somehow he had thought that people worked and rose in the world. In one swift glance at Walt riding important in Carl's car the picture was reversed and now in the depth of his bitterness he saw Walt rising in the world, yes, but rising in the way that a corpse rises when it has lain for a long time under water, rising and rotting as it was pushed out by the strong cold currents at the bottom. (304)

Johnny has begun to identify himself with the "strong cold currents at the bottom" who have nothing in common with the Walt Conners of the world. Cantwell certainly portrays the middle class in a highly unfavorable light, but later in the novel Walt has some minor awakenings of his own when he sees the forces of reaction frame his old friend Winters for murder and sees the disgusting nature of those for whom he works (339, 344–46). His responses remain ambivalent but at least hold out the possibility of his identifying with those "below" rather than "above" him.

When the night shift returns to work the evening after the blackout, they learn that Hagen, Winters, and twenty other workers have been fired. Spontaneous shouts of "Come on out!" arise from the night shift crew, and as word spreads inside the factory, the day shift shut off their machines to join their fellow workers: the strike begins. Earlier many of the workers had scornfully eyed the cheap display of the town's Independence Day parade, but now a real independence has been declared, and the workers are extremely excited.

As Johnny watches the police protect the scabs and sees how anxious they are to bust the heads of pickets, as he reads the accounts of the strike in the local paper and compares it to what he *knows,* a sense of the wider significance of all that is happening begins to dawn on him. Some day, he imagines, "it would happen again. Some day all the people would come out of [all] the factories, singing in the streets" (301). Slowly, he realizes that the battle is part of a much larger war, and as the importance of the strike becomes clear to him, he loses his distaste for "harsh" arguments.

During one of these arguments, Winters and Vin Garl, both now effectively without family, take the most militant stand, while Sorenson pushes for reconciliation. As Johnny's father, pressed as he is by financial burdens, begins to lean toward Sorenson's side, Johnny's own militancy is sparked, and the class struggle is symbolically passed on to another generation. The climax of the strike and the novel, comes during a violent rainstorm. A large group of pickets, thinking they have been granted permission to do so by the police, rush into the factory to seek shelter. The scabs, misunderstanding the intentions of the strikers, panic and rush to seek the protection of the police. The police, "with habitual and unimaginative roughness they are trained to employ," and "grunting . . . like speechless animals," push the scabs back into the crowd of strikers, unable to distinguish one contingent from the other. Suddenly the police, "so far off their native grounds," panic, shooting a scab (321).

In the ensuing melee the elder Hagen quickly reaches the main switchboard and, in an evocative turn on the blackout at the opening of the story, shuts off the lights to give the workers the protection of darkness, just as more shots are fired. He has transformed the accident of empowering "disempowerment" into an active, conscious process. As the scabs and police retreat from the workers' home ground, the strikers discover that, in effect, they have captured the factory.

But the strikers' triumph is short-lived. The workers occupy the mill overnight, but by dawn they find themselves surrounded by a cordon of police. Behind the police, a large crowd of townspeople, some sympathetic to the strike, others hostile, moves restlessly. After waiting all morning for the owner to arrive to begin negotiations, Johnny's father and another worker venture outside the factory to reconnoiter, and perhaps try to open up negotiations. As they do so, a fight breaks out in the crowd and again shots are fired. In the resulting pandemonium Johnny's girlfriend is viciously smashed by a policeman's club, but Johnny and Vin Garl manage to escape through the floor of the factory into the bushes on the tide flats beneath the mill—the same bushes in which Carl and MacMahon had become hopelessly lost earlier in the novel now offer the workers a refuge out of sight of the rampaging police (365–66).

As Johnny, Vin Garl, and another worker await nightfall so that they may escape undetected, Johnny learns that his father has been shot. His "education" has been completed, and the novel ends abruptly.

> The rain fell hard, drenching them while they waited, not like rain but like some new and terrible weapon of their enemies. Johnny tried to crowd under the driftwood and Vin Garl put his hand on his shoulder. "Come on, son," he said gently, "don't cry," and they sat there listening, . . . their faces dark with misery and anger, listening and waiting for the darkness to come like a friend and set them free. (369)

Darkness has by now revealed itself at the allegorical level as a metaphor for the failing power of capitalism, and thus the novel ends with the strike defeated but also with unspoken portents of the eventual defeat of brutalizing capitalists.

While the novel clearly centers on class issues, gender and race are handled with nuance and respect, and are never totally subsumed under vague class consciousness. Cantwell represents in several places in the novel the tension noted in his nonfictional portrait of Aberdeen between "the Americans" and various ethnic and racial groups, including Indians, Finns, and Poles and indicates degrees of difference among these "minorities." He also handles gender issues well, raising questions about what we would now call the "sexual harassment" visited on the women in the factory. He is also careful to note that the working-class "girls" are treated with far less respect (assumed to be "chippies") than the middle-class women, though all suffer from harassment. I have concentrated here on the issue of class in the novel because class still seems a relatively neglected dimension in our literary histories, despite some excellent recent work.[19] But *The Land of Plenty* and other works from the 1930s should remind readers that "intersectional analysis" (seeing connections among class, race, gender, sexuality, and other forces) is not the recent invention some believe it to be.

This complex analysis is made possible in large measure because class consciousness is handled not as a foregone conclusion but is studied in minute detail. As his critical essays make clear, Cantwell viewed literature as a means of exploring social complexities, not merely representing already known views. His strategy is clearly to slant his text in sympathy with the working class, but that does not mean he presumes to know precisely what they should do in a given situation. The text bears careful witness to the particularities of local conditions and local levels of organization without ignoring larger structures (the level of regional detail starts before the novel even opens, with a page of statistics from the Northwest timber industry).

The main radical character, Vin Garl, not only accurately reflects both the history of Finnish radicalism in the Northwest and the important regional legacy of the IWW but also assures that no "communist magician" comes in to save the day. But when the eastern capitalist plant owner, Digby, declares that the strike must be the work of Communists, the party is ironically invoked (338). The complex message here seems to be both that Communists get the blame or credit for the efforts of countless rank-and-file workers and that in turn those workers may in fact be building a more egalitarian future whether they identify with the party or not. This is very much the independent spirit of much of northwestern radicalism, in the past and in the present.

FROM THE CULTURAL FRONT TO ANTI-COMMUNIST CRUSADE

It is a clear reflection of the literary-political culture of the 1930s that *The Land of Plenty* received almost exclusively positive reviews, not only from leftist publications but from mainstream and even conservative ones. This is not surprising when one considers that this was the era that cultural historian Michael Denning has dubbed the "Age of the CIO" (referring to the Congress of Industrial Organizations, then the emerging force of the labor movement in the United States). In his magisterial work on 1930s culture, *The Cultural Front* (1996), Denning notes that a rich new, ethnically diverse working class culture was a major sociopolitical force in the Depression era and continued to be of great influence well into the 1950s.[20] Cantwell's was one of the clearest and strongest voices of this labor-centered independent literary left, and to a large extent this era of American history succeeded in achieving what he claimed a couple of years after the novel's publication to be his goal: to help "give working people a sense of their own dignity" and power. In this regard, the review of *The Land of Plenty* that he most prized came not from New York intellectuals, but from workers at his old factory. A mill hand at Harbor Plywood sent a detailed analysis of the novel, and said the men and women on the job loved it and were amazed at Cantwell's precise memory of the factory.[21]

Cantwell continued to be part of the leftist "cultural front" on into the later 1930s, with plans for a third novel about the San Francisco General Strike of 1934, one of the signal events of the era, and one that he had witnessed firsthand and written about for the *New Republic* and other journals. In *The Cultural Front*, Denning distinguishes between two main types of literary leftism: the "politics of affiliation" and "aesthetic ideologies." The former refers to activities like joining literary and cultural groups, signing petitions and pamphlets, or lending one's name to organizational letterheads. In this regard, Cantwell made a number of important public gestures of this kind, including signing a pamphlet endorsing the Communist Party candidates in the election of 1934, supporting the literary radical John Reed Club, and posting a number of letters to the editors of various publications in support of radical causes. But Cantwell's far more important work was his development of a radical aesthetic ideology as part of what I call "critical fellow-traveling." He became a central figure in developing, through both his criticism and his fiction, an independent Marxist cultural position that generally supported the goals of the Communist Party USA but was quite critical of the party's prescriptive criticism (as seen often in its newspaper, *Daily Worker,* and its literary journal, *New Masses*) and reductive ideas about instrumental literature. Along with colleagues like Edmund Wilson, Newton Arvin, James T. Farrell, and John Dos Passos, among others, he developed a position arguing, and in fiction demonstrating, that aesthetic quality need not and should not be sacrificed to radical political ideology.

No doubt the strangest of Cantwell's literary endeavors in the latter half of the 1930s was his commission to ghost write an autobiography of progressive capitalist E. A. Filene, founder of the Filene's department store chain. Cantwell was recruited by aging muckraker Lincoln Steffens at a promised rate of pay impossible for a young writer with a growing family to refuse. Cantwell saw the project as an opportunity to examine the class enemy at close range and to prove that capitalism could not be reformed from within. What he observed, and how he was treated by a millionaire philanthropist oblivious to his ghost writer's poverty, stirred Cantwell to anger and led him to write an "autobiography" Filene could only hate, and to draft on the side what amounted to a nonfiction novel about his troubled encounter with a self-deluded representative of the capitalist class.

It was while Cantwell was in Carmel, California in the spring of 1934 to work with Steffens on the Filene manuscript that longshoremen set off the San Francisco General Strike, one of the most dramatic labor struggles in U.S. history. Many on the left thought it presaged a revolutionary uprising. Fearing just that, federal, state, and private forces viciously attacked the strikers and their sympathizers, including Steffens and the visiting Cantwell, whose high profile, pro-labor reporting for *New Republic* made him a target. Vigilantes, mostly from the Carmel branch of the American Legion, physically threatened Steffens, Cantwell, Langston Hughes, and other leftist notables present in the town. Fearing for his life, no doubt with memories of what the American Legion had done to IWW revolutionaries two decades earlier, Cantwell and his wife were forced in to hiding in nearby Oakland.

Steffens, who had served as Cantwell's mediator with Filene, died not long after Cantwell's Carmel visit. Neither the ghost-written autobiography nor the nonfiction novel ever saw print. Cantwell also never succeeded in turning the events of the San Francisco strike and its aftermath into his third novel.[22] Financial pressures of a family now including three young children drove him into his first steady job, working for Henry Luce's then new magazine, *Time*. Over the last couple of years of the decade, both his sense of literary vocation and his political bearings weakened. His years at *Time* led to a "nervous breakdown" at the end of the 1930s, amid too much personal and political confusion, including a rightward drift and involvement with famed Communist spy turned anti-Communist fanatic, Whittaker Chambers.[23] His later writing career was spent mostly writing on safely nonpolitical topics, including years as an editor at *Sports Illustrated*, where he could write about his Northwest-bred love of the outdoors. He made plans for a *roman à clef* about the wild ideological swings of the period between the 1930s and the 1950s, and it is clear from outlines and partial drafts among his papers that he believed his association with Chambers had largely ruined his life, isolating him from his former leftist colleagues and tying him to fanatical anti-Communists. But once again nothing came of his efforts to return to fiction writing. One of his last published writings (he died in 1978) was a combined memoir, history, and travelogue, *The Hidden Northwest* (1972), from which the long history of the region's radicalism is almost wholly absent.[24] In this, he unfortunately contributed to the enforced invisibility of much of the everyday radicalism of ordinary working Americans that this present book, so many years later, is intended to help remedy.

DISRUPTED LEGACIES

About the time of Cantwell's death, a ten year-old boy from his hometown of Aberdeen was beginning to explore the literary-musical stylings that would make him a founding figure of grunge rock. Kurt Cobain grew up a working-class kid in an Aberdeen that remained little changed from the early twentieth century: it was still a rough and tumble, working-class town with few upward routes in its class structures. It is a sign of Cobain's time, and our current time, that his much heralded social anger is almost never analyzed in class terms, but only through the cliché of youthful rebellion. Cobain may have never developed class consciousness in any Marxist sense, but working-class experience shaped him in a myriad of ways.[25] The failure of Cobain and millions like him to identify as working-class, however, reflects setbacks to the labor movement over the last decades of the twentieth century. Driven largely by successful efforts to use racism as a divisive force, setting white workers against workers of color, the right wing's determined attacks on union power and cooptation of social issues to divide and conquer has led to an inability among most people to think coherently about the role of class in the everyday affairs of the United States. For this reason and many others, recovering the legacy of the cultural front era, in not only literary but more importantly in political terms, is a vital endeavor today.

I began this chapter by invoking the names of two early-twentieth-century Northwest radicals, John Reed and Anna Louise Strong, who moved out from the region to play prominent roles on the world stage. Let me end by briefly mentioning an event at the end of the twentieth century that brought the world stage to the Northwest. In November 1999 the World Trade Organization held its international convention in Seattle. The ensuing "Battle in Seattle" at last linked a long history of northwestern progressive activism to a worldwide movement opposing "corporate globalization." Students from the University of Washington, Evergreen College, and Washington State University, anarchist collectives from Eugene and Portland, Oregon, and a host of northwestern labor organizations joined thousands of activists from all over the globe in disrupting the convention, thus emboldening Global South WTO representatives at the summit to reject proposals biased toward corporate capitalists. Particularly impressive was the alliance between labor activists and environmentalists that gave the lie to the notion that the interests of labor and environmentalism are at cross-purposes. IWW "timber wolves" would have been proud of their descendants, even if too few of the latter knew that they were indeed descendants. So too would the critical fellow-traveling Robert Cantwell of the 1930s, whose wish to give working-class

Americans a central place in U.S. literary and cultural history remains as yet incompletely realized.[26]

One of the things that this collection of essays on radical regionalism of the 1930s should help us to recognize is that in every area of America there is a tradition of progressive struggle and progressive cultural activity that needs to be better known in order to enrich historical knowledge and inspire future action. Only by understanding that historical foundation can we move forward toward better strategies for achieving social justice and cultural representations that reflect the true depth and variety of this nation's people.

NOTES

1. This chapter is based upon extensive archival research in the Robert Cantwell Papers, housed in the Knight Library at the University of Oregon, Eugene (see also note 11 below), and draws from a work in progress, T. V. Reed, "Critical Fellow-Traveling: Robert Cantwell, Thirties Radicalism, and the Reworking of American Literature." Per Seyersted's *Robert Cantwell: An American Thirties Radical Writer and His Apostasy* (Oslo: Novus Press, 2004), while an exhaustively researched and useful biography is also, unfortunately, theoretically and interpretively thin, neither sympathetic to nor comprehending of Cantwell's complicated aesthetic and political positions in the 1930s. A quick overview of Cantwell's literary and journalistic work can be found in the pamphlet by Merrill Lewis, *Robert Cantwell* (Boise: Boise State University Press, 1985).

2. See Douglas Wixson, *Worker-Writer in America: Jack Conroy and the Tradition of Midwestern Literary Radicalism, 1898–1990* (Chicago: University of Illinois Press, 1994).

3. For more on the history of northwestern radical politics see Jeffery Johnson, *"They Are All Red Out Here": Socialist Politics in the Pacific Northwest, 1895–1925* (Norman: University of Oklahoma Press, 2008).

4. "Communism in Washington State," http://depts.washington.edu/labhist/cpproject/index.shtml (accessed 9/15/11).

5. In the early twenty-first century, in what may or may not be an example of Marx's famous claim that tragic history repeats itself as farce, a revived IWW union organized the workers of Washington state's most (in)famous retailer, Starbucks.

6. The best resources on IWW culture are *Rebel Voices: An I.W.W. Anthology*, ed. Joyce L. Kornbluh (Ann Arbor: University of Michigan Press, 1964), and Salvatore Salerno, *Red November, Black November: Culture and Community in the Industrial Workers of the World* (Albany: State University of New York Press, 1989).

7. On the Paterson Strike Pageant, see http://historymatters.gmu.edu/d/5649/ (accessed 9/15/11).

8. Louis Colman, *Lumber* (New York: Little, Brown, 1931); Clara Weatherwax, *Marching! Marching!* (New York: John Day, 1935).

9. Cantwell, "A Town and Its Novels," *New Republic*, February 19, 1936.

10. Class discord in a Washington mill town in the early twentieth century is brilliantly portrayed in Norman Clark's classic study, *Mill Town: A Social History of Everett, Washington* (Seattle: University of Washington Press, 1970).

11. As stated in note 1, these and other details about Cantwell's life cited here are drawn primarily from the Cantwell papers at the University of Oregon library. An online guide to the collection can be found at http://nwda-db.wsulibs.wsu.edu/findaid/ark:/80444/xv41731 (accessed 9/15/11).

12. For materials on the general strike, see http://depts.washington.edu/labhist/strike/ (accessed 5/1/2010).

13. "Hills Around Centralia," in *Proletarian Literature in the United States: An Anthology*. ed. Granville Hicks et al. (New York: International, 1935), 39–57.

14. Robert Cantwell, *Laugh and Lie Down* (New York: Farrar & Rinehart, 1931), ix.

15. Edmund Wilson, *The American Jitters* (New York: Scribners, 1932), 297.

16. Cantwell, "Can You Hear Their Voices," *New Republic*, October 18, 1933), 286.

17. Robert Cantwell, *The Land of Plenty* (New York: Farrar & Rinehart, 1934). All subsequent quotations are from this text and the page numbers are indicated in parentheses.

18. On the dime novel as allegory and as a site of working-class struggle see Michael Denning, *Mechanic Accents* (New York: Verso, 1987).

19. Two excellent recent anthologies, *Literature, Class and Culture*, ed. Paul Lauter and Anne Fitzgerald (NewYork: Longman, 2000), and *American Working-Class Literature*, ed. Janet Zandy and Nicholas Coles (NewYork: Oxford University Press, 2006), survey the rich array of class-conscious literature in the United States and provide bibliographies on some of the best criticism on this topic.

20. Denning, *The Cultural Front* (New York: Verso, 1996).

21. See William Deitz to Cantwell, n.d., included in letter from Calvin Fixx, November 4, 1934, Cantwell papers.

22. It is unclear how much of a draft he ever actually produced; no part of the manuscript has survived. It is clear that his ideas about the novel continued to shift, often confusingly, during the latter part of the 1930s. An "Outline" found in the Cantwell papers suggests that his ideas grew ever more grand, as he shifted focus from the strike itself to a wider terrain of the mid-to-late 1930s.

23. During his underground career Chambers sometimes used the alias Lloyd Cantwell, a fact that contributed a good deal of confusion to the 10,000-page FBI file on Cantwell that Cantwell himself obtained under the Freedom of Information Act in the 1970s. The FBI, with their usual perspicacity, utterly confused Cantwell's and Chambers's activities.

24. *The Hidden Northwest* (Philadelphia: Lippincott, 1972).

25. On Cobain's early life in a largely unchanged working-class Aberdeen see Mikal Gilmore, "The Road to Nowhere," *Rolling Stone* no. 683, June 2, 1994, 44–46, 53.

26. On the WTO action see T. V. Reed, *The Art of Protest: Culture and Activism from the Civil Rights Movement to the Streets of Seattle* (Minneapolis: University of Minnesota Press, 2005). For a rich set of resources including specifically regional contributions to the Battle of Seattle, see "The WTO History Project," http://depts.washington.edu/wtohist/ (accessed 9/15/2011).

PART IV
CALIFORNIA

Utopian and radical visions have defined California from the sixteenth century to the present. More than any other part of the American West and the New World in general, California has been seen as the ultimate Promised Land, the final Garden of Eden planted on the Pacific, and a focal point for utopian dreams and radical dissent. A place where grand hopes often meet with bitter disappointment, California has been a seedbed of radical thought and action; it has aroused people who, in Robert Hine's words, after finding "their promised land several cuts below the promise," have transformed their outrage into "a challenge, like the raised anarchist's fist, the fires of hope, the recurring symbols of basic change."[1]

The dynamics of disillusionment—of hopes dashed and dreams soured—are intensified by geography. Although the agrarian frontier presumably ended on the Great Plains in the 1890s, California's symbolic position at the continent's end deepens its significance as the final stop of westward movement and the last gasp of the American Dream. As described in greater detail in this book's final chapters, every personal failure seems magnified amid this inspiring natural landscape so full of promise, this land of last chances set against the Pacific. Joan Didion's notion that California is where "the mind is troubled by some buried but ineradicable suspicion that things had better work here, because here, beneath that immense bleached sky, is where we run out of continent" lurks in the consciousness of this Pacific-facing region and gives radical protest there a sharp and poignant edge.[2]

As in other western regions, radicalism peaked in California in the late nineteenth and early twentieth centuries and paved the way for the more self-conscious left-wing regionalism of the Depression decade. Described by Carey McWilliams as "the hidden spring" of "a deeply rooted indigenous radicalism that has been consistently 'socialist' and 'utopian,'" a generation of California writers and social critics coming to public consciousness by the 1880s created an enduring body of regionally inspired protest literature.[3]

Henry George's penetrating critique of economic inequality and land speculation in *Poverty and Progress* (1879); Josiah Royce's brave account of the state's racist and imperialist past in *California: A Study of American Character* (1886); Edwin Markham's indignant, widely read poem "The Man with the Hoe" (1898); Frank Norris's naturalistic portrayal of the Southern Pacific Railroad's brutal economic stranglehold and the 1880 Mussel Slough tragedy in *The Octopus: A Story of California* (1901); the brief success of socialist utopias, among them Burnette G. Haskell's Kaweah Colony (1885–90) and Job Harriman's Llano Del Rio commune (1914–18); the biting socialist novels and muckraking journalism of Jack London and Lincoln Steffens—all are examples of this earlier legacy of California-rooted radicalism.

Building upon this protest tradition and responding to the Dust Bowl inmigration and waves of strikes across California's fields, factories, and waterfronts, a younger generation of Marxist, proletarian, and generally left-leaning writers produced important social criticism during the 1930s and early 1940s. Often provoking the ire of large-scale agricultural and industrial interests, California's radical and progressive regionalists included social scientists, documentarians, poets, novelists, journalists, folksingers, and screenwriters. John Steinbeck, Paul Taylor, Dorothea Lange, Kenneth Rexroth, Tillie Olsen, Archie Green, and William Saroyan were some of the regional writers from the Bay Area and the Central Valley, and Carey McWilliams, Louis Adamic, Carlos Bulosan, John Fante, Alexander Saxton, and Oklahoma transplants Woody Guthrie, Will Rogers, and Sanora Babb were among those based in Los Angeles and Southern California.

Four talented writers embodied central features of this radical impulse. Novelist John Steinbeck (1902–68) and journalist and social critic Carey McWilliams (1905–80) were the most prominent and provocative members of this constellation of California writers, while the relatively obscure novelist and screenwriter John Sanford (1905–2003) and the Filipino immigrant novelist and essayist Carlos Bulosan (1911–56) created complex visions of racial, economic, and environmental injustice taking place in regional and transnational settings.

A longtime Communist Party member, Sanford wrote in relative isolation for seven decades, leaving behind twenty-three defiantly radical novels, histories, and memoirs that are only beginning to be appreciated. Jack Mearns's lucidly written chapter follows Sanford's career from his formative years in New York City in the 1920s and early 1930s to his move to California in 1936 and involvement in the Hollywood cell of the Communist Party in the late 1930s and early 1940s, and thence to the panoramic visions of American history he published in the 1970s, 1980s and 1990s. Sanford used regionally focused novels and historical narratives to "scourge the powers that be and to inspire the oppressed toward demanding political and social change." His uncompromising effort to "hector and shame America" into living up to its egalitarian potential, his multiple roots in New York and California, his tumultuous relationship with Nathanael West and the radical screenwriting community in Hollywood—these and other aspects of Sanford's life and work give him a distinctive voice among western regionalists on the left.

Unlike Sanford, who lived into his late nineties and issued indictments from a secure and relatively privileged position, Carlos Bulosan died in meager circumstances in his mid-forties after a difficult life as a working-class writer, union organizer, and labor educator. Stephen Mexal's chapter traces the evolution of Bulosan's distinctive version of radical regionalism shaped by his immigrant experience. Arriving in California from the Philippines in 1930 at the age of nineteen, Bulosan grappled with the complex relationship between place and politics and the tensions between regional, national, and global identities throughout his career. Like J. Frank Dobie and Américo Paredes in Texas and Mexico, Joe Howard in Montana and Canada, and Angie Debo later in her career, Bulosan envisioned his region's multiethnic culture in an international context. As Mexal demonstrates, Bulosan's politically charged writing linked the local and the global, merging a hard-won affection for California's land and folk with a wider transnational sensibility. Moving beyond doctrinaire Marxism, Mexal argues that Bulosan forged a "transnational liberalism of the left"— a form of radical leftism yoked to place yet directed outward "toward multiethnic tolerance, economic justice, and global egalitarianism."

While Bulosan and Sanford wrote in relative obscurity throughout their lives, Steinbeck and McWilliams had soared to national prominence by the eve of World War II. Both writers had herculean bursts of creativity in the mid- to late 1930s that culminated in a powerful and widely read works of regionalism and social protest. Published within months of each other in 1939, Steinbeck's *The Grapes of Wrath* and McWilliams's *Factories in the Field* sparked critical firestorms, and both books endure as radical regional classics. Yet even more than McWilliams's passionate exposé, Steinbeck's monumental novel is, according to David Wrobel, "the most significant single work of the regional revival of the interwar years, one that illuminated both the most positive and negative manifestations of regionalism." In his highly perceptive chapter on Steinbeck's three "years of greatness" from 1936 to 1939, Wrobel explains, among other things, how the author's intimate identity with his native Salinas Valley and heightening outrage at the brutal exploitation of working-class Californians lie at the heart of his iconic masterpiece. Underscoring both the racial limitations of Steinbeck's vision as well as his unparalleled ability to stir the national conscience, Wrobel provides an admirably balanced portrait of our most significant radical regionalist. In addition to achieving the remarkable task of being "at once both revolutionary and intensely American," *The Grapes of Wrath* continues to remind us of social and environmental ills that still plague California and the nation as a whole.

My concluding chapter examines McWilliams's education as a radical regionalist over a twenty-year period, from his arrival in Los Angeles in 1922 to his masterful work on labor and race relations cresting in the early 1940s. Like Conroy and Le Sueur in the Midwest and Botkin in the Great Plains, he was a pivotal force and one-man clearinghouse for the growth of left-wing regionalism in his region and throughout the nation. Acutely aware of the reactionary side of regionalism and one of its sharpest and earliest critics at the very beginning of the 1930s, he had forged a forward-looking, pluralistic form of regionalism in a series of influential books by the 1940s. More than any other regionalist, with the possible exceptions of Bulosan and Paredes, he was keenly aware of the interaction of race and region. Drawing on his work as a labor lawyer, journalist, and civil rights activist, he fearlessly revealed the dark recesses of California's past and present and promoted a farsighted vision of the state as the nation's racial frontier and multicultural meeting ground.

NOTES

1. Robert V. Hine, *California Utopianism: Contemplations of Eden* (San Francisco: Boyd & Fraser, 1981), 7.
2. Joan Didion, *Slouching toward Bethlehem* (New York: Dell Publishing, 1968), 172.
3. Carey McWilliams, *California: The Great Exception* (New York: Current Books, 1949), 189.

John Sanford. Courtesy of Jack Mearns.

CHAPTER TWELVE

John Sanford's Radical Regionalism

THE UNIVERSAL OF THE PARTICULAR

Jack Mearns

John Sanford was born Julian Shapiro in Harlem, in New York City, in 1904; he died in 2003 in Santa Barbara, California. That one sentence speaks volumes about the journey that was Sanford's life. Along the way, he was part of several of the important social movements of the twentieth century: he was a member of the wave of Jewish immigration escaping Russian pogroms; he was employed as a screenwriter in Hollywood during the golden age of the studio system; he became a member of the Hollywood cell of the Communist Party; and he was called before the House Committee on Un-American Activities (HUAC), where he refused to name names and was blacklisted.[1]

Sanford was the author of twenty-three books, including novels, personal interpretations of American history, and multiple volumes of autobiography and memoir. His writing style embraced modernism in its most radical form. The most challenging of his books have been compared to James Joyce's for their complexity and formal innovation. As Sanford's artistic radicalism grew, so too did the political radicalism of his topics. His books display an unstinting belief that the promise of America was somehow broken and that only revolution could restore its potential. He viewed his writing as a weapon with which to scourge the powers that be and to inspire the oppressed toward demanding political and social change.

Sanford came to his radical beliefs rather late in life. He himself was never clear about the source of his transformation. Alan Wald has noted that Sanford was not a deep thinker politically: "His was not a textbook Marxism, but a Marxism of a general character . . . an identification with an underdog against the oppressor." Although Sanford's affiliation with the

Hollywood wing of the Communist Party brought him into contact with deeper Marxist thinkers, like John Howard Lawson, he was not influenced by theorizing. In fact as a writer, Sanford rarely planned. He did not make outlines; he honed his work as he wrote and did little editing once a book was finished. Most simply put, both politically and stylistically, Sanford wrote from his gut, not from his head.[2]

This lack of an agenda in his work—other than the abstract aims of pushing the boundaries of style and trenchantly depicting America's social ills—begs the question of whether Sanford can truly be classified as a regionalist. Unlike many of the writers covered in this book, Sanford did not identify himself as a regionalist. In fact, he did not identify himself with any artistic movement, and he stubbornly resisted all attempts to influence his work, whether from editors at publishing houses or from Communist Party officials.

Far from being connected with a specific region, Sanford strove to become as universally American an author as he could be. This ambition is summed up in the dust jacket copy for his second novel, *The Old Man's Place* (1935), in which he states his intention to write a "book as American as [Mathew] Brady's pictures." Still, place was immensely important to Sanford's work. Rather than writing about the universal as a whole, he seemed to feel that the universal would arise from finely detailed focus on the smallest of scales. The best example of this approach is his trio of novels set in Warrensburg, a tiny town in the Adirondacks of New York state. In them Sanford sought to depict the entire scope of America as embodied by that mountain hamlet. Later in his career this impulse emerged again in his creative interpretations of American history. In the vast scope of his five volumes, Sanford chronicled the often-lamentable history of the United States through short vignettes, each portraying a moment in time. These works are mosaics of fine detail that, when viewed from afar, resolve into a panorama of America. At the end of his career Sanford evolved into a California regionalist, his autobiographical work vividly summoning forth his adopted home.[3]

Thus for most of his life Sanford did not wed himself to a particular region. Rather, he used region as a way of evoking the entire country. In doing so he found himself inadvertently aligned with the sympathies of American regionalism in its earliest and purest form.

SANFORD'S REGIONALISM

Benjamin Spencer has traced the roots of regionalism in American literature to its initial origins and aims. As far back as Henry Wadsworth Longfellow in the early nineteenth century, American writers were striving to create a distinctly American literature imbued with the unique geography and climate of the United States. But the vastness of the American continent prescribed that such an ambition must be rooted in region: topography, weather, and local customs varied tremendously from one area of the country to another. Travel was arduous, long-distance communication difficult. People typically spent their entire lives in the vicinity of their place of birth.[4]

Trying broadly to capture America would thus result only in a shallow abstraction, for it was impossible, Spenser explains, to encompass the "unembraceable diversity of the national life." The only way to capture the spirit of America was by evoking deeply the character of a particular region. To truly depict the whole one must bring to life the distinct local color of one of its parts. As early as 1839 the *Southern Rose* had stated: "When we do create an original literature, it will not be general but sectional in its character." After the Civil War the belief was that "the Great American Novel must be a composite of regional novels."[5]

A national American literature would thus arise out of the aggregated local literatures of America's regions—a unity springing organically from well-realized particulars. For "human nature is everywhere the same, and the faithful portrayal of an obscure provincial contains the universal story." In addition, the growing view by the end of the nineteenth century was that America would be more authentically captured in stories of the common person, rather than the rarified literature of New England that had long been revered as the apotheosis of American letters. In the twentieth century William Carlos Williams was an important proponent of American regionalism, as well as a mentor to the aspiring writer Sanford. Williams wrote: "One has to learn what the meaning of the local is, for universal purposes. The local is the only thing that is universal."[6]

An important impetus toward regionalism was the economic crisis of the Great Depression. Michael Steiner identifies three central themes of twentieth-century regionalism: "a search for . . . the indigenous or the primal basic America, a desire for a stable communal identity, and a reverence for the past—especially the memories that could bring a sense of order and certainty to a tumultuous present." These represented "an overriding impulse: the need for a sense of place amid the stress and dislocation of the depression." Thus, Sanford's ambition to craft a book as American as Brady's photographs by depicting the life of a tiny mountain town is consistent with the aims of American literature from its inception. Though not by plan, Sanford instinctively grasped that the best way to address national themes was through an intimate focus on life at the local level that transcends mere local color, such that "a local scene or character if painted faithfully becomes universal."[7]

JULIAN SHAPIRO I: THE MAKING OF A REGIONALIST

What motivates writers toward regionalism? Lucy Lippard has written, "The lure of the local . . . is the psychological component of the need to belong somewhere, one antidote to prevailing alienation . . . that undertone of modern life that connects it to the past we know so little." Robert Coles has written, "It is utterly part of our nature to want roots, to need roots, to struggle for roots, for a sense of linking the desire to possess the past with the need for a sense of place." And Steiner has suggested, "Persons who found themselves adrift sought the certainty of place." For many, the immense economic and social upheavals of the Great Depression ushered in a need to shore up a sense of belonging through finding and embracing one's roots. For Sanford this need can be traced farther back, into the early years of his childhood. Themes both personal and social shaped the boy into the man who would become a radical regionalist writer.[8]

Sanford was born Yonkel Lev Shapiro in 1904. His father was a Jewish immigrant who had fled Eastern Europe; his mother was born in the slums of Manhattan's Lower East Side to immigrant parents. In stark contrast, Sanford was born in Harlem, then a newly settled, fashionable Jewish enclave. A sign of the Shapiros' hopes for their son was their Americanizing of the Yiddish Yonkel Lev to Julian Lawrence. The boy's earliest years were privileged, with a mother who doted on him, and his father who prospered as a lawyer for the burgeoning Jewish building and real estate trades. But outside the world of Jewish immigrants, young Julian experienced anti-Semitism that left him feeling an outsider. When his mother's heart began to fail, all income went toward futile attempts to restore her health. Near destitution, they were constantly on the move, from one rooming house or cheap hotel to the next.

Finally, when Sanford was ten, his mother died. Her death would have a profound and life-long impact. Penniless, the Shapiro family had little choice but to move into the apartment of Sanford's maternal grandparents. According to Jewish tradition, as the oldest son, Julian began a year of mourning, during which he said *Kaddish*, the prayer for the dead, three times a day. He wore a black armband and was forbidden all enjoyment. He recalled feeling cut off from all other children, who had mothers.

After World War I Sanford's father's finances rebounded, and he remarried, moving out of the grandparents' apartment. But Julian refused to accompany the father. Though Sanford remained with his grandparents, he clearly did not feel at home, as evidenced by his running away several times. A sense of homelessness, alienation, and loss would shape Sanford's perspective as an author; the lure of a place to belong would be a powerful draw. Another crucial way his mother's death affected Sanford was the havoc it wreaked on his education. The child who had initially excelled in his studies did not even graduate from high school, after he was caught cheating on an English test his final term. Over the next two years, Sanford would attend three different colleges and spend less than a semester at Fordham Law School.

Finally, in 1924 Sanford returned to Fordham, where he completed a degree. During his time at Fordham, a chance encounter radically altered the path of Sanford's life. In 1925, on a New Jersey golf course, Sanford was playing by himself when he came upon another lone golfer, whom he recognized as a childhood Harlem acquaintance, Nathan Weinstein. It turned out that Weinstein was now going by the name Nathanael West. Sanford bragged that he was attending law school. But West's answer stunned him: "I'm writing a book."[9]

Since his mother's death, it had been as if Sanford's education were frozen in time. But following the golf course meeting, Sanford and West became frequent companions, with West spending hours lecturing the unschooled

Sanford on literature and the arts. Suddenly, after years of intellectual aridity, Sanford once more felt inspired to learn. He began a crash course in reading, being introduced to modernists like Joyce and Hemingway. One book that would have life-long resonance was William Carlos Williams's *In the American Grain* (1925), a collection of historical vignettes.[10]

JULIAN SHAPIRO II:
THE MAKING OF A RADICAL

Although it is relatively easy to trace the roots of John Sanford's regionalism to the alienation, privation, and loss he experienced during childhood, it is harder to find the source of his radicalism. Sanford himself, later in life, felt unable to identify the forces that pushed him politically leftward. Even in the worst of the rooming-house days, he was not exposed to the squalor of the Lower East Side tenements that a contemporary like Henry Roth endured. One likely inspiration was Sanford's maternal Uncle Dave, who had broken with Sanford's grandfather and joined the merchant marines. Perhaps in part to goad his capitalist father, Dave had become a leftist admirer of Eugene Debs. Dave's free-spirited influence was in the air during Sanford's adolescence.[11]

The trial and executions of Sacco and Vanzetti were a watershed, and often a conversion, experience for many radicals. By the summer of 1927, Sanford had graduated law school. He recalled being with a group of friends, some of whom had gathered around a radio; he heard one say, "Well, they burned 'em." "Burned who?" Sanford asked—and his friends reacted with utter disbelief that he did not know. Yet Sanford always maintained that, even though he had been a law student, and even though the case was one of the great *causes célèbres* of the 1920s, he had not heard of Sacco and Vanzetti until the night of their deaths. His embarrassment and shame about this incident would propel his radical turn as a writer, and the two Italians would remain important subjects of his work throughout his career.[12]

Still, it was years later, after he had moved to California, that Sanford found himself drawn to leftist concerns. After he joined the Hollywood cell of the Communist Party, his work became progressively more radical. Looking back, he claimed he was unable to explain his radicalization.

Clearly, leftist sentiments were in the air, so much so that by 1942 a magazine poll reported that a full quarter of the American population "favored socialism." Labor strife, such as the Loray Mill strike in Gastonia, North Carolina, in 1929, was avidly followed in the national press. And Sanford's first summer in California, 1937, "was the most violent in the history of American workers." Leftism was on the rise across America. And more specifically, the Hollywood that Sanford arrived in was in the midst of a unionizing trend, of which the screenwriters were at the forefront. Thus, Sanford found himself in an environment in which forces both social and professional, though perhaps imperceptible to him, swept him toward the left.[13]

JULIAN SHAPIRO III: THE MAKING OF A WRITER

Nathanael West's comment on the New Jersey golf course that he was writing a book opened up new vistas for Sanford. Though he continued with his legal studies, the law had lost its luster. He lived in two separate worlds: that of Fordham and that of literature and the arts. When he graduated and passed the bar exam, he joined his father's practice but pursued his new profession diffidently. The stock market crash of 1929 and its aftermath ate away at their business. By then, he had begun to publish brief sketches in literary "little magazines." Soon his short stories appeared in the premiere little magazines of the day, including *The New Review, Pagany,* and *Contact,* a journal edited by Williams and West.

Sanford and West spent the summer of 1931 in a rented hunting cabin in the Adirondacks, where the two hunted, fished, and wrote. Near the village of Warrensburg, Viele Pond was six miles into the woods by dirt road. West worked on his second novel, *Miss Lonelyhearts* (1933), and Sanford completed a draft of his first, *The Water Wheel* (1933). This summer in the woods would be an essential experience for Sanford, pushing him toward regionalism. Many of his short stories, and his next three novels, were set in the Warrensburg area. In addition, the native New Yorker's communion with nature would awaken a deep connection with the land that paralleled other regionalists'. West, in contrast, used this summer as the source for but a single chapter in *Miss Lonelyhearts*.[14]

After returning from the country in the fall, Sanford wrote a draft of a new novel, based on a story told him by the owner of Viele Pond, about a trio of World War I soldiers whose return brings chaos to the countryside. By 1933, when Sanford's first novel was published, he and West had quarreled. They would not see each other for several years, until they met in Hollywood, where both were employed as screenwriters. *The Water Wheel*, the only book published under his birth name, is highly autobiographical. Its main character, John Sanford, feels alienated in his social milieu of intellectual New York. The book's experimental style and content were unlike any of the work that followed. But the author's lifelong obsession with historical themes was presaged by the protagonist's musings about Philip Nolan (the Man without a Country) and in quotations from Robert Juet's *Discovery of the Hudson River* (1609), to which Sanford would return much later for the titles of his autobiography.

Early in 1935 Sanford's second novel, *The Old Man's Place*, about the trio of veterans' reign of terror, was taken by Albert and Charles Boni. Influenced by West's example and hoping to boost sales by avoiding an anti-Semitic reaction to his name, Julian Shapiro took as a pseudonym John B. Sanford, the name of his *Water Wheel* protagonist. In late August of 1936, on the basis of *The Old Man's Place*, Paramount Studios offered Sanford a contract as a screenwriter, making $350 a week. At the age of thirty-two he moved to Hollywood, where he finally had a paying job. Soon it would become clear that Sanford's talent for novel writing did not translate to writing for the screen, for none of his scripts was produced, and after a year he was unemployed. Fortunately, in a Paramount hallway Sanford had met Marguerite Roberts, who was becoming one of the more successful writers in the business. "Maggie" Roberts was literally born in a tarpaper shack on the plains of Nebraska, a world away from Sanford's Manhattan. Sanford and Roberts soon became a couple, and the out-of-work Sanford wrote his next novel in the back yard of Roberts's San Fernando Valley home.

THE WARRENSBURG TRILOGY

Sanford set his second, third, and fourth novels in the Adirondack town of Warrensburg, near Viele Pond. Through this trilogy, one can trace the arc of Sanford's development into a radical regionalist, as each successive book bores more deeply into the core of American life and values. Although a native of New York City, Sanford had experienced important childhood interludes in nature. He would draw on these, as well as the sense of place he had absorbed during his summer with West, to project a deep and loving evocation of the land.

The Water Wheel was resolutely a modernist novel, whose stream-of-conscious narration and wordplay owed much to Joyce. In *The Old Man's Place* (1935), though, Sanford was determined to create a book as accessible as it was American. Though devoid of social commentary, it did probe the violence at the core of the American psyche, a theme that would dominate the rest of Sanford's career. In *The Old Man's Place* a trio of veterans of World War I return to one of the men's family farm; the result is mayhem. The characters are grotesques—a common type in the literature of the day—who resemble the rustics that brought Erskine Caldwell critical and popular success.[15]

Sanford had begun his next novel, *Seventy Times Seven* (1939), while he was still living in New York. After his failed attempt at screenwriting, he took up the manuscript again, while he flirted with the Communist Party. The new novel shows some influence of his political evolution, yet it is not explicitly radical. *Seventy Times Seven* did, however, achieve what *The Old Man's Place* had failed to. It portrayed small-town American violence as deeply ingrained in the American character and as springing from a history of violence, in particular slavery and whites' mistreatment of Indians, which had begun with North America's discovery. This portrayal was fostered by the inclusion, mid-narrative, of a blank verse passage nearly twenty pages long—a collage of historical episodes. The interpolation of historical material in his fiction would become Sanford's signature.[16]

Seventy Times Seven, although not explicitly intended by Sanford as such, can be classified as a regionalist novel. In it, particularly in its blank verse passage, one can see the regionalist credo that "something of value disappeared with the colonization of America," that contemporary America was still paying the wages of this original sin. For many, the past represented a consoling sanctuary juxtaposed with the uncertainties and dislocation of the present. As Raymond Williams wrote, "The idea of an ordered and happier past set against the disturbance and disorder of the present [can] cover and evade the actual and bitter contradictions of the time." Far from being consoled by the past, though, Sanford was haunted by it. He mourned Americans as spoilers of a pristine and pure, idyllic wilderness; he used sense of place to tear away any cover, to prevent evasion, and to force people to confront the "contradictions of the time."[17]

Many writers and intellectuals in the 1930s saw regionalism as a positive force that would inspire; Sanford's regionalism, in contrast, was deeply paradoxical. On the one hand he intended his writing to be a catalyst for political transformation, a positive force toward change. Yet on the other hand his use of region was largely negative, revealing the dark undercurrents of American society. Unlike John Steinbeck, Carey McWilliams, and other California regionalists, Sanford did not suggest solutions to social problems. One of his enduring heroes was the abolitionist John Brown, whose rashness Sanford echoed. He saw his role as that of agitator, provocateur. His novels were like bombs: once he had lit the fuse and tossed them, his job was done. He left if to others to reassemble the pieces.[18]

The People from Heaven (1943) was Sanford's first overtly political book, begun after he had joined the Communist Party late in 1939. In it, the social fabric of tiny Warrensburg is torn by the arrival of a nameless black woman, who is raped and later shoots her white assailant. The characters can be considered, to use Michael Denning's term, "proletarian grotesques [who represent] an attempt to wrench us out of the repose and distance of the 'aesthetic.'" Sanford again wove historical material into the novel by inserting episodes from U.S. history between chapters of the narrative. In doing so he intended to lay bare America's legacy of racial hatred and violence.[19]

When *The People from Heaven* appeared, at the height of a wave of racial unrest including race riots across the country, its art came so close to being a literal weapon that even the Communist Party attempted to prevent Sanford from publishing the novel, seeing it as a too-radical call to violence in response to violence. The Communists branded it "anti-social," fearing it would inspire blacks to revolt, a premature uprising doomed to failure. Sanford, however, rejected any attempt by party functionaries to influence the content of his book, which "express[ed] an anger and empathy that preceded and transcended any formal adherence to 'party line.'" The book's style was as radical as its content. In writing such a novel Sanford seemed to throw down a gauntlet, daring the reader to understand. Such a challenge sometimes provoked bitter reaction from critics. The *New York Times*, for example, pilloried the book under the heading

"Assorted White Trash" as "entirely too abstract for the purposes of fiction," and the *Philadelphia Inquirer* found it to be "one of the most unconventional works of fiction since James Joyce's *Ulysses*."[20]

The People from Heaven reveals the contradictory impulses that underlay Sanford's regionalism. He was torn between a desire to seek refuge in place, at the same time that he rejected the possibility of such refuge by stripping the facade away from the illusion of place. Unlike many other regionalists, he drew little comfort from the past, finding few heroic figures to inspire the present. According to Wald, "Undergirding the whole novel is a powerful examination of the historical roots of the ugly racism lying beneath the superficial harmony of a rural community" that represents the entire American nation.[21]

The trajectory of Sanford's more and more doctrinaire writing can be contrasted with the books of his former friend and mentor, West. While for Sanford art was a weapon, aimed at inspiring readers to action to rectify society's ills, in West's work there is no moral or moral compass. West's authorial voice is distant and uninvolved; he does not urge an end to suffering and in fact seems to take gratification in the pain of his characters. Robert M. Coates described West's characters as "cavort[ing] in ... an emotional and spiritual vacuum."[22] And West himself once wrote to Edmund Wilson, "There is nothing to root for in my books and what is even worse, no rooters." W. H. Auden went further, writing with distaste, "A high percentage of the [characters] are cripples, and the only kind of personal relation is the sado-masochistic." People do not connect, do not relate to each other. Yet this situation is not portrayed as a cause for alarm.[23]

Neither are people connected to the land. For West, the summer at Viele Pond resulted merely in set dressing for one chapter in *Miss Lonelyhearts*. Later, when the two authors had separately moved to California, they both set novels there. While Sanford's embraced the geography of his new home, West's final work, *The Day of the Locust* (1939), betrays a continued detachment from place. Elizabeth Hardwick has written, "In West's fiction, there is landscape, but not of trees, grassy plains, sunsets on the horizon. His landscape is houses, rooms, bars, and their contents." West was an anti-regionalist, depicting the banished who are dislocated and disconnected from a sense of place, lost in a superficial landscape that is all artifice; he did so without intention to inspire.[24]

Sanford initially refused to read *The Day of the Locust*, writing a scathing letter to a mutual friend from their New York days: "I haven't read West's book because I simply can't tolerate the man. It's the God's honest truth that he's the only human being on the face of the earth that I really detest. . . . There's nothing in the world that he stands for on the same footing that I do." Echoing Auden's assessment, Sanford added that West's fiction was full of characters who were crushed and crippled by life, whom West sadistically depicted with the "brutality of the occasional vindictive bully—who is yellow." He continued:

> No man that I've ever known has less pity for the insulted and injured, less nobility in the face of a life that constantly tends toward making man seem ridiculous. It is a bad thing that life makes some spines look like a corkscrew; it is a contemptible thing that one of the lucky ones jeers at the result; and in [West's] literature there's always some hunchback who has to pay double, once to life and once to Mister West.[25]

West's ridicule of the common man flew in the face of Sanford's political and social convictions. Yet after West's death in a 1940 car crash, Sanford dedicated *The People from Heaven* to his former friend, whose "I'm writing a book" had changed his life.

JOHN SANFORD IN HOLLYWOOD: THE MAKING OF A CALIFORNIAN

After Sanford's arrival in Hollywood in 1936 California would remain his home for more than sixty-five years. He came at a time when motion picture studios were at the forefront of popular culture: by 1937 Americans spent three-quarters of their leisure dollars on movies. Sanford's life was miraculously transformed. He went from fecklessly scrounging change from his father's pocket to being able to afford a new wardrobe and automobile, and to send money back East to support his family. The actress Joan Crawford frequently invited him to dine at her home, and he briefly dated the starlet Jean Muir. He met fellow screenwriter Roberts, whom he would marry in 1939.[26]

Sanford had traded New York City for the wide-open, sunny spaces of Los Angeles; he had left behind the privations of the Depression for a glamorous life flush with cash. At the same time, he found himself inexplicably drawn to the plight of the less fortunate. He wrote an original, unproduced script about a strike at a factory called *Sit Down and Fight*. Sanford and Roberts's social life soon revolved around the Communist Party, but party members told Sanford that Roberts, as an outsider, represented a threat. She would either have to join the party or be excluded from its events. Roberts, of a liberal mind but apolitical, chose to join, saying, "I want to be with you." Sanford knew Maggie's joining exposed her to danger, but he did not stop her. It is as though he felt, if he truly believed in the cause, he should be willing to risk everything for it, including his wife.

Sanford's life in Los Angeles was one of dramatic contradictions. His writing became more and more radical. In addition to his novels, he contributed to *Black & White* and *The Clipper*, on whose editorial board he served with, among others, Carey McWilliams and Sanora Babb. He taught courses on the novel with Guy Endore at the party's People's Education Center in Hollywood. During World War II he wrote the screenplay for "The Battle of Russia," an army training film in the *Why We Fight* series, for Frank Capra's company in the Army Signal Corps. Yet Sanford's nonwriting life was clearly distinct from the revolutionary zeal of his creative work.[27]

Aside from a brief period in 1941 during which he teamed with Roberts at MGM, Sanford had no income. Roberts was becoming one of the most highly regarded and best-paid screenwriters in the business. She preferred Sanford to stay at home where he could write "our" books. During the war Roberts purchased four acres of land in Encino in the San Fernando Valley. In addition to fruit orchards and pens for a variety of fowl, there were stables for the racehorses Roberts bred and trained. Sanford's daily life was one of wealth and leisure. Aside from the content of his writing and financial contributions to progressive causes, his outward life—like many affluent party screenwriters'—was not that of a radical. He did not organize labor, did not walk picket lines, did not actively protest mistreatment of minorities, had not volunteered to fight in Spain. Many working screenwriters appeared to regard him, with a mix of envy and contempt, as a kept man.[28]

Roberts would always refer to the Encino period as the couple's "best years." But these years would come to an end in 1951, when Sanford and Roberts were called to hearings before the House Un-American Activities Committee (HUAC). Roberts had left the party years earlier, disenchanted with the pettiness she saw among its members. However, if she admitted former membership at the hearings, she would be obligated to name her associates, something she found abhorrent. Both Sanford and Roberts took the Fifth Amendment and were blacklisted. This effectively put an end to Roberts's career, forcing the Sanfords to sell their beloved Encino home. After a disillusioning and fruitless attempt to find work in Europe, the couple returned to an internal exile in the United States. In 1957 they bought a house in Santa Barbara, where they would live until their deaths—Roberts in 1989 and Sanford in 2003.

SANFORD'S HISTORICAL AND AUTOBIOGRAPHICAL WORK

From *Seventy Times Seven* on, Sanford's fiction had always contained historical elements. The most ambitious of these novels was *A Man without Shoes* (1951), his follow-up to *The People from Heaven*. In it, Sanford tried both to tell the story of all Americans through the life of one man and to depict the whole canvas of America through its history and geography—from New York to the West—once again capturing the regionalist aim of portraying the universal through detailed depiction of the particular. Sacco and Vanzetti's trial was an important theme. But *A Man without Shoes* ultimately failed as a work of fiction, as Sanford's politics overwhelmed the narrative. He used his characters to deliver diatribes to the reader, including pages of the protagonist's recounting the contents of lectures on Marxist economics he attends.[29]

Revealing his clear embrace of California as his home, Sanford set his next three novels there. In particular, *The Land That Touches Mine* (1953) vividly evokes the topography of his adopted state. The novel opens with a haunting depiction of the Northern California coastline. And much of the book takes place during summer in the desert town of El Centro, whose unrelenting heat oppresses the characters. But Sanford's fiction continued to be undermined by the political message he strained to convey. By 1967 he had exhausted the novel as a mode of expression.[30]

At Roberts's suggestion Sanford set out to write a book entirely comprising the historical vignettes that had been interludes in his novels. The result was so unconventional that publishers rejected it more than 250 times. *A More Goodly Country* (1975) represented the panoply of America—from the voyage of Columbus to the development of the atomic bomb—and it allowed Sanford to transcend the limitations imposed on him by the novel form. Varying his narrative voice to match his diverse subjects, he could now instruct by parable, allegory, and brief dramatic monologue. Eric Foner has asserted, "Sanford possesses qualities unusual even among [professional historians]: an eye for the telling detail or incident that opens up an entire world of meaning, an ability to plumb the inner thoughts and emotions of figures in the past and a genuine concern for society's outcasts and underdogs." The *Los Angeles Times* hailed *A More Goodly Country* as a masterpiece.[31]

Sanford followed up with three more volumes of personal interpretations of America, all conveying his sympathy for the powerless in society. His essential message continued to be the corruption that European colonization had brought to America's shores. Some of his most compelling pieces were focused purely on the natural calamity Americans had wrought, such as the decimation of the bison or the extinction of the passenger pigeon. At the age of eighty Sanford was at the top of his form. His writing sizzled with accusations of the inhumanity visited on the unfortunate, in the name of religion and profit, upon which America's power and wealth were built.

At an age when most writers are retired or dead, Sanford still had half his body of work ahead of him. He next embarked on a retelling of his and Maggie's lives, which would amount to nine books, including a five-volume autobiography. The draw of the elderly Sanford's regionalist sensibilities can be seen in these books' intent "to flee the uncertainties of the present for the assurance of the past and to cling to memory as a possession that cannot be lost." In particular, Sanford realized that his was the only consciousness that still held the life of his beloved Maggie. He was keenly aware that "his death meant not only the passing of [an] individual but also the complete loss of a host of memories." He dedicated himself to preserving his memories of people and times long gone.[32]

As with Sanford's historical books, his autobiography was structured into brief vignettes. Told with remarkable vividness and punctuated with historical pieces that reflect the social and political climate of the time, "the color of the air," these books present a life reimagined and dramatized. Merging his literary preoccupations, these volumes wed Sanford's life with the history of the United States. His final book, *A Palace of Silver* (2003), appeared a month before his death. It is a memoir of the bleak years after Maggie died. The book is a revealing portrait of the devastation of old age: the loneliness, the physical decline.

FROM THE PARTICULAR TO THE UNIVERSAL— A MORE PERFECT UNION

John Sanford did not publish his first book until 1933, when he was twenty-eight years old. But despite his late start he had a remarkably long career. His final book appeared seventy years later, shortly before his death at age ninety-eight. Sanford began as a short story writer and novelist preoccupied with history. Eventually his obsession with history overshadowed his fiction, and—though he had no formal training as a historian—he began a series of personal reflections on America. His early work drew critical acclaim, yet he spent most of his career toiling in obscurity.

Though not by conscious design, Sanford clearly embraced preoccupations and traditions that brought him into the fold of radical regionalists. Although Sanford is not associated with just a single region, he assiduously used close depiction of the landscape, dialect, and customs of particular locales to bring to life themes he saw as broadly representing America as a whole. His Warrensburg trilogy evokes the radical touchstones of Depression-era regionalism by embodying small-town America as the bequest of European colonization. Much later, his autobiography brought vividly to life the New York City of the first decades of the twentieth century, as well as Hollywood of the 1930s and 1940s, including the climate of dread surrounding the HUAC hearings and the blacklist. Throughout it all, a vivid sense of place infused his work.

During most of his career Sanford's work embraced a radical political view. Though in his personal life he gave little evidence of these beliefs, his writing scintillates with a vehement devotion to exposing America's economic and political wrongs. He knew these themes—a withering rebuke of the values in which Americans are raised to believe—would likely drive away the broader audience. Yet he refused to temper his indignation and mute his reforming vision. He sacrificed popular success in the hopes that his voluminous presentation of America's wrongs would help turn the country in a more egalitarian direction. Sanford dedicated the most blistering of his historical books, *The Winters of That Country*, "To a more perfect union." That was the goal he set for himself as a writer: to hector and shame America into becoming more of what it has the potential to be.

NOTES

1. For more extended biographical treatments, see Jack Mearns, "The Complex Legacy of John Sanford." *Firsts* 14, no. 1 (2004): 40–51; *John Sanford: An Annotated Bibliography* (New Castle, Del.: Oak Knoll Press, 2008); and "John Sanford: Lawyer and Writer," *Legal Studies Forum*, 34, no. 1 (2010): 317–32. In addition to Sanford's writings, biographical information is derived from my extensive interviews with him over the twelve-year period 1991–2003.

2. Alan M. Wald, "Introduction," in John Sanford, *The People from Heaven* (1943; reprinted, Urbana: University of Illinois Press, 1995), xx.

3. The Warrensburg trilogy comprises *The Old Man's Place* (New York: Boni, 1935), *Seventy Times Seven* (New York: Knopf, 1939), and *The People from Heaven* (New York: Harcourt, Brace, 1943). The historical books are *A More Goodly Country* (New York: Horizon, 1975), *View from This Wilderness* (Santa Barbara, Calif.: Capra, 1977), *To Feed Their Hopes* (Urbana: University of Illinois Press, 1980), *The Winters of That Country* (Santa Barbara, Calif.: Black Sparrow, 1984), and *Intruders in Paradise* (Urbana: University of Illinois Press, 1997).

4. Benjamin T. Spencer, "Regionalism in American Literature," in *Regionalism in America*, ed. Merrill Jensen (Madison: University of Wisconsin Press, 1951).

5. "Untraceable diversity": Spencer, "Regionalism in American Literature," 253. "Sectional in character": *Southern Rose* 8 (August 3, 1839): 398, cited in Spencer, 223. "A composite": William Allen White, quoted in Howard W. Odum and Harry E. Moore, *American Regionalism: A Cultural-historical Approach to National Integration* (New York: Henry Holt, 1939), 168, cited in Spencer, 229.

6. Spencer, "Regionalism in American Literature," 233. "What the meaning of local is": William Carlos Williams, *A Novelette and Other Prose* (Toulon, France: To Publishers, 1932), 117, cited in Spencer, 244. Sanford wrote about his relationship with Williams in *William Carlos Williams/John Sanford: A Correspondence* (Santa Barbara, Calif.: Oyster Press, 1984).

7. Michael Steiner, "Regionalism in the Great Depression," *Geographical Record* 73 (October 1983), 432–33. "A local scene . . . painted faithfully": Hamlin Garland, *Literary News* 9 (August 1888): 237, cited in Spencer, "Regionalism in American Literature," 235.

8. Lucy R. Lippard, *The Lure of the Local: Senses of Place in a Mulitcentered Society* (New York: New Press, 1997), 7. Robert Coles, *Migrants, Sharecroppers, Mountaineers* (Boston: Little, Brown, 1969), 116, cited in Steiner, "Regionalism in the Great Depression,"

444. Steiner, "Regionalism," 442. Michael Denning, *The Cultural Front* (New York: Verso, 1997).

9. Six years later this would be published as West's *Dream Life of Balso Snell* (New York: Contact Editions, 1931).

10. William Carlos Williams, *In the American Grain* (New York: Boni, 1925).

11. Stephen G. Kellman, *Redemption: The Life of Henry Roth* (New York: W. W. Norton, 2005).

12. Denning, *The Cultural Front*, 59.

13. Denning, *The Cultural Front*, 4, 19, 23.

14. Nathanael West, *Miss Lonelyhearts* (New York: Liveright, 1933); Julian L. Shapiro, *The Water Wheel* (Ithaca, N.Y.: Dragon Press, 1933).

15. Denning, *The Cultural Front*, 123. See, e.g., Erskine Caldwell, *Tobacco Road* (New York: Scribners, 1932).

16. John Sanford, *Seventy Times Seven*. The passage in blank verse appears on pages 148–66.

17. "Something of value": Lewis Mumford, *The Golden Day: A Study in American Experience and Culture* (New York: Boni & Liveright, 1926), cited in Robert L. Dorman, *Revolt of the Provinces: The Regionalist Movement in America, 1920–1945* (Chapel Hill: University of North Carolina Press, 1993), 6; Steiner, "Regionalism in the Great Depression," 434–35; Raymond Williams, *The Country and the City* (New York: Oxford University Press, 1973), 45; cited in Steiner, "Regionalism," 437.

18. David Wrobel, "John Steinbeck's Layers of Regionalism and Social Protest in the 'Years of Greatness.'" Michael Steiner, "Carey McWilliams, California, and the Education of a Radical Regionalist," this volume.

19. *The People from Heaven* would be reissued by the leftist Liberty Book Club in 1947; Denning, *The Cultural Front*, 123.

20. Denning, *The Cultural Front*; Wald, "Introduction," xxx; Alan M. Wald, *Trinity of Passion* (Chapel Hill: University of North Carolina Press, 2007), 189–90. Denning wrote, "Writers and artists of the modernist generation attempted to reconstruct modernism, to tie their formal experimentation to a new social and historical vision, to invent a new 'social modernism,' a 'revolutionary symbolism.'" *The People from Heaven* could be the exception that proves this rule; *The Cultural Front*, 61-62.

21. Craig J. Calhoun, "The Radicalism of Tradition: Community Strength or Venerable Disguise and Borrowed Language." *American Journal of Sociology* 88 (1983): 888; Wald, "Introduction," xxiv.

22. Robert M. Coates, "Messiah of the Lonely Hearts," *New Yorker*, April 15, 1933, 59.

23. West and Auden, quoted in Elizabeth Hardwick, "Funny as a Crutch," *New York Review of Books*, November 6, 2003, 24.

24. Nathanael West, *The Day of the Locust* (New York: Random House, 1939). Hardwick, "Funny as a Crutch."

25. John Sanford, letter to Naomi ("Nonie") Greenstein, August 2, 1939, Sanford archives, Howard Gotlieb Archival Research Center, Boston University Library.

26. Denning, *The Cultural Front*, 41.

27. Later, Capra's loyalty to America was questioned in part due to the favorable presentation of the Soviet Union in this film. Joseph McBride, *Frank Capra: The Catastrophe of Success* (New York: Simon & Schuster, 1992), 462.

28. Sanford and Roberts co-wrote the Clark Gable/Lana Turner comedic western, *Honky Tonk* (MGM, 1941).

29. John Sanford, *A Man without Shoes* (Los Angeles, Calif.: Plantin Press, 1951). After Sanford was unable to place this patently Marxist book, he chose to self-publish.

30. John Sanford, *The Land That Touches Mine* (New York: Doubleday, 1953), *Every Island Fled Away* (New York: Norton, 1964), *The $300 Man* (Englewood Cliffs, N.J.: Prentice-Hall, 1967).

31. Eric Foner, "Native Son," *Los Angeles Times Book Review,* October 19, 1997, 8. Robert Kirsch, "Possessed by American Mosaic," *Los Angeles Times,* October 30, 1975.

32. The autobiography, subtitled *Scenes from the Life of an American Jew*, comprised *The Color of the Air* (Santa Barbara, Calif.: Black Sparrow, 1985), *The Waters of Darkness* (Black Sparrow, 1986), *A Very Good Land to Fall With* (Black Sparrow, 1987), *A Walk in the Fire* (Black Sparrow, 1987), and *The Season, It Was Winter* (Santa Rosa, Calif.: Black Sparrow, 1991). There followed four volumes of memoir: *Maggie: A Love Story* (Fort Lee, N.J.: Barricade Books, 1993), *The View from Mt. Morris* (New York: Barricade, 1994), *We Have a Little Sister* (Santa Barbara, Calif.: Capra, 1995), and *A Palace of Silver* (Capra, 2003). Steiner, "Regionalism in the Great Depression," 444–45.

Carlos Bulosan. Courtesy of University of Washington Libraries, Special Collections (neg. no. UW 26563).

CHAPTER THIRTEEN

Toward a Transnational Liberalism of the Left

POSITIVE LIBERTIES AND THE WEST IN

CARLOS BULOSAN'S "AMERICA"

Stephen J. Mexal

LIBERTY AND "FREEDOM FROM WANT"

In early 1941, nearly a year before the United States would enter the Second World War, Franklin Delano Roosevelt used his State of the Union address to advance a new and emphatically global vision of liberal rights. He announced that America would now "seek to make secure" a new sort of transnational liberty, and that he looked forward to a "world founded upon four essential human freedoms."[1] The first two of these freedoms would have been familiar to Americans of all political persuasions, as their focus—"freedom of speech" and "freedom of every person to worship"—echoed the First Amendment of the U.S. Constitution, with the key distinction that these new freedoms sought to expand those rights to "everywhere in the world."[2] The third and fourth freedoms, though, delineated a sweeping expansion of the way liberty had traditionally been understood in the United States. "The third freedom," Roosevelt intoned, "is freedom from want—which, translated into world terms, means economic understandings which will secure to every nation a healthy peacetime life for its inhabitants—everywhere in the world."[3] The fourth freedom was "freedom from fear," which, "translated into world terms, means a worldwide reduction of armaments."[4] These final two freedoms, despite their seeming lack of controversy, in fact represented a significant reconsideration of American liberal practice.

Widely viewed as a moral defense of classical liberalism, Roosevelt's Four Freedoms captured the imagination of wartime America. As Ramón Saldívar put it, the speech turned the New Deal "outward on the world in general."[5] The notion of unassailable global liberties offered a transcendental liberal justification for the impending war effort, and the Four Freedoms soon found their way into patriotic works by a number of artists, musicians, and writers, including cartoonist Walt Disney, folklorist Américo Paredes, and, most notably, painter Norman Rockwell.[6] In 1942 Rockwell produced a painting for each of Roosevelt's Four Freedoms. They were published in the *Saturday Evening Post* early in 1943, with each image accompanied by a short essay written by a notable author of the day.[7] To accompany *Freedom from Want*, the editors of the *Post* requested an essay from a nearly unknown writer named Carlos Bulosan.

Bulosan was born November 2, 1911, in Binalonan, in the province of Pangasinan, Philippines, and had immigrated to the United States in July 1930, near the start of the Depression.[8] Although he had published a few poems in literary journals and had briefly edited a regional labor magazine called *The New Tide* in the 1930s, in 1943 he was known on the national stage—if he was known at all—mostly for a slim book of poetry titled *Letter from America* and a *New Yorker* short story called "The Laughter of My Father," both of which were published in 1942. His most significant work, a fictionalized autobiography entitled *America Is in the Heart*, would not appear for another three years. These works, particularly *America Is in the Heart*, are obsessed with the seemingly paradoxical goals of both creating a sense of regional place and problematizing the idea of "America." In other words, Bulosan sought a regional political aesthetic at the same time that he tried to unsettle a conventionally national political identification. In this he can be seen as working toward what Michael Denning has identified as a "radical regionalism," one emerging from his sense of an "absence of culture, the lack of roots" in America.[9] Though this regionalist aesthetic would come into sharper focus with his autobiography, which did not appear until 1946, his essay "Freedom from Want" contains one of the earliest examples of his budding left liberalism.

Rockwell's painting *Freedom from Want* depicts a Thanksgiving dinner with nine white (and oddly disembodied) faces clustered around a table, grinning in gleeful anticipation. The turkey is enormous, filling half the horizontal space of the painting. With its bourgeois, aggressively Caucasian family celebrating a uniquely American holiday with more food than many non-American families see in a month, Rockwell's painting neatly strips Roosevelt's speech of its transnational racial and economic context, re-presenting it in the symbols of conservative Americana. As a result, its accompanying essay by the thirty-one-year-old Carlos Bulosan is all the more jarring.

From its first sentence, Bulosan's "Freedom from Want" is oppositional, lodging itself against the bourgeois readers of the *Post* as well as, presumably, the white middle-class comforts of Rockwell's painting. "If you want to know what we are," the essay begins, "look upon the farms or upon the hard pavements of the city. You usually see us working or waiting for work, and you think you know us, but our outward guise is more deceptive than our history."[10] The tension between a bourgeois "you" and a proletarian "us" is emphasized by the grammatical equation of flesh-and-blood existence with menial work. In order to know "what we are," Bulosan writes of his invisible underclass, using the first-person plural form of the verb "to be," one should look to "the farms." Existence becomes conflated with agricultural labor.

The promises of the western world's liberal democracies, he continues, have not been extended to all. This has not been simply an economic failure, but a political failure—a collapse of the entire notion of liberal rights. Real freedom cannot exist, he writes, without a breakdown between producing and consuming classes:

> Our march toward security and peace is the march of freedom.... It is the dignity of the individual to live in a society of free men, where the spirit of understanding and belief exist; of understanding that all men are equal; that all men, whatever their color, race, religion, or estate, should be given equal opportunity to serve themselves and each other according to their needs and abilities. But we are not really free unless we use what we produce. So long as the fruit of our labor is denied us, so long will want manifest itself in a world of slaves. It is only when we have plenty to eat—plenty of everything— that we begin to understand what freedom means.... It is only then that we become a growing part of democracy.... We recognize the

mainsprings of American democracy in our right to form unions and bargain through them collectively, our opportunity to sell our products at reasonable prices, and the privilege of our children to attend schools where they learn the truth about the world in which they live.[11]

While Bulosan reminds the *Post*'s readers that middle-class comforts are often bought on the backs of an invisible underclass, he also reframes Roosevelt's basic argument about freedom. An equitable society, for Bulosan, means particular kinds of liberties: "*opportunity to* sell," not just the absence of overt interference from selling. And significantly, he yokes collective bargaining to American liberal democracy. Liberalism, for Bulosan, should not only neutrally protect the rights of the individual, it should advance a specific kind of liberty for the working class.

In this essay and in others, Bulosan tends to present himself along two intersecting axes: place and politics. The political axis is chronological. Most scholars of his life and work recognize his radical politics and his affiliation with the left. Yet in much of his work he presents his political awakening as beginning with his immigration to America, progressing *through* Marxism, and finally arriving at a transnational liberalism. This transnational *telos* is echoed in the axis of place. He presents his sense of place as germinating in the Philippines, growing new roots in the material specifics of California, progressing *through* a vague identification with America as a whole, and culminating in the rejection of geopolitical identity in favor of an abstract transnationalism. In his own autobiographical narratives, in other words, he presents the final iteration of his selfhood as transnational and liberal. But in fact, as "Freedom from Want" suggests, the impulse toward political liberalism—and, more specifically, toward a particular type of left liberalism—was present much earlier. In that essay, he appropriates the language and purpose of Roosevelt's Freedoms, drawing connections between their promised new age of global liberalism and his own vision of what Isaiah Berlin has called "positive liberties."

To understand the particular brand of political liberalism that emerged from Bulosan's experiences in California and would come to shape his transnational orientation, it is useful to sketch out some key distinctions in liberalism. Although a vexed term in present-day usage, "liberalism" simply refers to a philosophy of government emphasizing the centrality of individual rights. Because of its conceptual roots in the works of Enlightenment thinkers like John Locke, most scholars argue that American liberal practice originally implied what Isaiah Berlin famously identified as "negative liberties." Negative liberty, Berlin wrote, can be defined by "the degree to which no man or body of men interferes with my activity," or "the area within which a man can act unobstructed by others."[12] By this line of thinking, freedom, American style, originally meant freedom *from* governmental and social interference. Berlin contrasted negative liberal rights with positive liberties, which expand liberalism beyond a freedom *from* interference to encompass a freedom *to* achieve certain ends. Unlike negative liberties, which suggest an absence of governmental interference in the lives of individual actors, positive liberties imply a government that actively assists in the realization of particular social or individual goals.

Bulosan's "Freedom from Want" reimagines the negative liberties of classical American liberalism as the positive liberties of a new, and ultimately transnational, liberalism. Individuals in America, he writes, must be "given equal opportunity to serve themselves and each other according to their needs and abilities."[13] In more ways than one, this phrase echoes Marx's slogan "from each according to his abilities, to each according to his needs," and so the subversion here needs little explanation.[14] While ostensibly explaining the principles of "American democracy" expressed in Roosevelt's global negative liberties, Bulosan in fact offers a radical revision of American liberty, using the familiar (and even conservative) language of classical liberal democracy in order to align not only positive liberties but leftist thought with American liberal practice.

Anticipating a rhetorical maneuver he would return to many times throughout the 1940s and 1950s, Bulosan suggests, in one of the final paragraphs of "Freedom from Want," that the word "America" should be divorced from its physical referent. It should instead be viewed as a sort of rhetorical placeholder for a new, transnational egalitarian political consciousness. "The America we hope to see," he writes, "is not merely a physical but also a spiritual and an intellectual world."[15] America is here divorced from a tangible national locality and conceptually mapped onto the globe at large. This rejection of the nation-state is a persistent if seldom noticed theme in Bulosan's writing. In a letter in 1947 he recommends professing a national identification only insofar as that national identification helps others to move beyond national identifications. "There are things for us to do in America, in the name of our country," he writes, before immediately retracting the sentiment: "of course, though the word 'country' has become obsolete." However, he continues, words like "country" are "just the last residue of a nationalistic philosophy which we have acquired from our ancestors . . . but now the fight is for certain democratic principles, certain universal principles that belong to all mankind."[16]

The tension between the tangibility of California and the elusiveness of "America" is central in Bulosan's writing and his politics. Repeatedly in his work the historical specificity of the United States is ignored, and instead "America" comes to stand for a transnational liberalism that surpasses the economic and political borders of the nation. But this abstracted nation—and the radical, transnational liberalism that the word "America" eventually came to signify for him—was first rooted in the material reality of California. That is to say, if America becomes intangible, California and the West remain always immediate, always material. By cultivating an aesthetic appreciation of the land and labor of the far West and at the same time abandoning the "nationalistic philosophy" that has produced the nation, he looks forward to a global set of "democratic principles" that, as he suggests in "Freedom from Want," are in practice a set of positive liberties offering a leftist critique of classical American negative liberty.

WEST OF EVERYTHING

Many scholars have noted the significance of the Philippines in shaping Bulosan's politics and his career as a writer. Bulosan himself encouraged this interpretation at times, writing in 1955 that what "impelled" him to write was to "give a literate voice to the voiceless one hundred thousand Filipinos in the United States, Hawaii, and Alaska."[17] This is surely true, but it also ignores the myriad ways in which he sought to move *beyond* the nation as an arbiter of economic and political reality. And yet that is not to say that place was unimportant to him. One repeatedly overlooked aspect of his political sensibility is the central role that California played in his ability to imagine first Marxism, and later positive liberties, as compatible with American political practice.

By 1920 nearly four thousand Filipinos had immigrated to the American far West—California, Oregon, and Washington—and many more had gone to work on the sugar plantations in Hawaii. These numbers increased dramatically over the next decade. By 1930, when Bulosan arrived in Seattle, there were thirty thousand Filipino immigrants in California alone. Yet despite the presence of a large expatriate community, the lives of Filipinos in America were marked by economic, spatial, and political dislocation. By 1930, Carey McWilliams estimated, more than twenty thousand Filipinos worked as agricultural laborers in the West, another four thousand worked in fish canneries, and eleven thousand worked in hotels and restaurants.[18]

Migrant agricultural laborers had few rights regardless of nationality, and this disenfranchisement was exacerbated for the Filipinos, who were not even technically immigrants, legal or not. Until the Tydings-McDuffie Act of 1934 provided for the creation of a more independent Philippine commonwealth and formally recognized Filipinos in America as "aliens"—thus inventing the legal category of Filipino immigrant—Carlos Bulosan, like other Filipino residents of the U.S., occupied a legal and political gray area: not a citizen, not an immigrant, but a "colonial ward."[19]

Shortly after arriving in the United States in 1930, Bulosan began visiting farms and fields in California, meeting with radical labor organizers like Chris Mensalvas and occasionally working as an organizer himself. Though he may have started writing poetry as early as 1932, his local reputation as a writer began with the publication in 1934 of *The New Tide*, a small, bimonthly radical magazine.[20] The publication brought him into contact with William Carlos Williams, William Saroyan, Richard Wright, Carey McWilliams, and Sanora Babb. Even so, he would later minimize the significance of the magazine in shaping his political and authorial identity.[21] He seems to have considered it a juvenile relic of a still-forming political consciousness, and he never bothered to republish his work with the magazine or even to discuss it in greater detail. The clearest articulation of his political and regional identification would come in his later, more mainstream work.[22]

In his writing, he cultivates an aesthetic appreciation of the fields of California, yoking that appreciation to the cultivation of a particular liberal philosophy. In *America Is in the Heart* he writes that he briefly operated a "workers' school" because the "land had always been important" to him, and his "peasant heritage" seemed to demand that he teach field laborers of the "growth of democracy." To identify with the land and labor of the American West, by this logic, is to identify with liberal-democratic politics. In charting his changing relationship to the California landscape, he notes that at one point he had held a "desire to possess a plot of earth," but now, that material desire had been supplanted by an abstract wish to "*belong* to the land—perhaps to the whole world."[23] The yearning to subject the land is replaced by a yearning to be subjected *by* the land. In the former arrangement, individuals possess property unequally. But in the latter, economic distinctions between individuals are leveled in that they are possessed equally by the land itself. Bulosan's imagination of Californian soil inverts the classically liberal preference for individual property rights in favor of a transnational egalitarianism, a system in which individuals do not own plots of land that collectively compose nations, but are instead collectively subjects of "the whole world."

In 1952, several years after Bulosan had made his name as a writer, several Filipino union members in California found themselves facing deportation charges as a result of their "subversive" labor organization. The McCarran-Walter Act (technically known as the Immigration and Naturalization Act of 1952) reserved the right to deport naturalized immigrants for any speech or action deemed seditious, and union president Chris Mensalvas and others had been identified as "subversive" immigrants. To raise money and awareness for Mensalvas's legal defense fund, Bulosan decided to write not a pamphlet or an editorial, but a poem. That poem, "I Want the Wide American Earth," returned to a theme he had developed a decade earlier, in which the language of American democracy is employed in the name of transnational egalitarian justice.[24]

> Before the brave, before the proud builders and workers,
> I say I want the wide American earth
> For all the free.
> I want the wide American earth for my people,
> I want my beautiful land.
> I want it with my rippling strength and tenderness
> Of love and light and truth
> For all the free— (74–81)

Read one way, this passage is vaguely revolutionary, a rallying cry to conquer America "for my people." And yet earlier in the poem, Bulosan establishes that his verse is really directed toward "defenders of freedom, builders of peace," his "democratic brothers," and that the "beautiful land" he finds in the rhetorical "America" of the poem in fact composes the entire earth.[25] He couches his political goals within an appeal to the ethos of American liberalism, using words like "freedom," "democracy," and "America," with the ultimate effect of aligning his regional political goals—he wants, above all, for his friends to remain in California—with the larger signs and symbols of a mythic transnational polity. The same sort of nationalist rhetoric that enabled the exclusionary McCarran-Walter Act is here reappropriated, reinvested with aesthetic power, and finally deployed for transnationally liberal ends.[26]

Bulosan died in 1956, only a few years after writing this poem. He was ill virtually his entire life. From 1936 to 1938 he was hospitalized in Los Angeles for various ailments including tuberculosis; ultimately he died of viral pneumonia. And though he once said that "politico-economic ideas are embodied in all my writings," it is his self-proclaimed personal history" *America Is in the Heart* (1946) that in fact stands as the most pellucid example of the way his political and aesthetic sensibility was shaped by the economic geography of the American West.[27]

CALIFORNIA AND THE AMERICA OF *AMERICA IS IN THE HEART*

America Is in the Heart: A Personal History is not, as many scholars have demonstrated, much of a history at all, at least not in a particularly strict sense.[28] The book is instead best understood as a thinly fictionalized ethno-proletarian biography, the story of the Filipino immigrant workers as told through the eyes of one "Carlos Bulosan."

From the start, Bulosan intended the memoir as a political document. After the publication of "Freedom from Want" in the *Saturday Evening Post*, Philippines President Manuel Quezon, who was running a government in exile in Washington, D.C. while the Japanese occupied the Philippines, asked to meet with Bulosan. During the meeting he requested from Bulosan a "memorandum on the Filipinos on the West Coast."[29] Bulosan never fulfilled the request directly. Instead he wrote *America Is in the Heart*, a book that he hoped "would give [Quezon] all the materials he would need," for in writing "the life story of a common Filipino immigrant," Bulosan "would be presenting the whole story of the Filipinos in the United States."[30] Though Part I of *America Is in the Heart* tells the story of narrator Carlos/Allos's boyhood in the Philippines, fully two-thirds of the book concerns his time in the western United States.[31]

Bulosan depicts Allos's political and aesthetic awakening in California partly as a response to particular authors. Sometimes Allos is inspired by the formal qualities of a text, but more often he is impressed by the symbolic significance of a particular author. He reads Louis Adamic, Carey McWilliams, and John Fante and sees in "Fante's obscure background and racial origin," and in Adamic's status as a Slovenian immigrant, a "sense of kinship." He reads "the American Negro writer, Richard Wright," marvels at the "young" age of writer William Saroyan, the son of Armenian immigrants, and is astounded by Asian immigrant writers such as Yone Noguchi, who immigrated from Japan and was, "like myself," an "Oriental without education who had become a writer in America." Allos comes to think that all good writers are "moved by the same social force" and that they "reacted to the social dynamics of their time." His voracious reading slowly amplifies his radicalism. In one crucial scene he encounters a room stuffed with periodicals such as "*New Masses, Partisan Review, The New Republic, Left Front, Dynamo, Anvil*, and other Leftist publications, many of which sprung up and died in that one decade," and his political and artistic ambitions are fused.[32] From that point on, Allos comes to see his identities as a Filipino immigrant, a California resident, and a writer as intertwined and essentially political.

In other writing Bulosan fleshes out the literary and political biography that is somewhat subdued in *America Is in the Heart*. Like many of his peers he was at the time obsessed with "Marxist literature," and thought that "[in] the Soviet system we seemed to have found a workable system and a common belief which bound races and peoples together for a creative purpose," in contrast to the "decaying capitalist society" of America. The imaginative literature of America, though, he found wanting for political potency. "Dreiser, Anderson, Lewis, . . . Faulkner, Hemingway, Caldwell, Steinbeck" were all, in his opinion, merely "describing the disease" of America and not tracing its origins. And though John Steinbeck and Erskine Caldwell both influenced him in their ability to wed place to progressive politics while narrating the American scene, he dismissed them both as "writ[ing] in costume."³³ It seems he found fault with the fact that Steinbeck was not really *of* the itinerant agricultural laborers that often populated his novels.

Of course, Bulosan was not exactly one of those laborers, either. Despite scenes in *America Is in the Heart* that find Allos working in apple orchards and orange groves and vineyards, Bulosan himself was not strong enough for agricultural work.³⁴ It was his keen awareness of his own ethnic and national marginalization that produced his authorial identity, not some journalistic transcription of firsthand field experience. He saw himself as a member of a community of labor activists, not really as a member of a community of writers. (He once claimed, completely implausibly, not to have met any writers at all until after he had published his first three books.) Partly as a result, when in 1955 he recounted a few of his formative influences, he listed several unsurprising names: Honoré de Balzac, Maxim Gorky, Jack London, Pablo Neruda. As a young man, he adds, he was perhaps most influenced by "the Marxists in literary criticism." And yet he completes this list of influences by emphasizing place, not books or writers. His next sentence seems to disclaim criticism or literature or even radicalism as a formative influence: "If you have ever lived in one of the slums of the U.S., I know you would also be influenced by it. I lived in the slums of Los Angeles, and I never escaped its terrors, its soul-sickening atmosphere."³⁵

For Bulosan, there is no grammatical or conceptual transition between "the Marxists in literary criticism" and "the slums of Los Angeles." It is not that the political economy of Los Angeles confirms the essential correctness of Marxist analysis, it is rather that Marxism echoes the gut-level grasp of labor and capital that he had already apprehended by living in the Filipino ghettos of Los Angeles. The political and economic dislocation he associated with the urban spaces of California was fundamental to his radicalism—more important, even, than fellow left-leaning American writers or his much-prized "Marxist literature." For his emerging proletarian imaginary, the specifics of living as a Filipino "colonial ward" in the American far West mattered far more than the relative abstraction of dialectical materialism.

This basic dynamic, in which his political and authorial commitments become distilled from the mash of Californian geography and his own racial-economic dislocation, shows up repeatedly in his work. His narrative of his identification as a writer—which is simultaneously a narrative of his identification with the political left—begins not with books, but with work in California. "I was working at a fish cannery in San Pedro, California," he writes in a 1946 essay, until "my right hand was paralyzed; perhaps a relapse induced by the cold water where I washed the fish heads at the cannery."[36] He is fired from the cannery because his productivity slowed as a result of his injury, and, apparently out of fury, he starts to write. Bulosan takes pains to present his writing as a response to the exploitation of the Pinoy in the American West, both in a political sense (he was indignant at the labor injustices he suffered), as well as in a more pragmatic sense (he could not get another job; writing was his only option).[37] He presents his political and authorial emergence as entirely reactive. *If* the geography of California did not encompass such fertile earth and ocean, and *if* modern agricultural economies had not been able to benefit quite so much from a foreign-born and exploitable underclass, *then* his politics would not have been shaped in quite the same way and he would not, he leaves us to conclude, have turned to writing. The agricultural contours of the land ultimately shaped the political contours of his prose.

As a result, in *America Is in the Heart* he presents California as the site of the full flowering of his ethnic, authorial, and political consciousness. In the memoir the narrator's experience with California begins with a warning. A fellow Filipino warns the newly immigrated Allos that though "all roads go to California and all travelers wind up in Los Angeles," it is nonetheless "hard to be a Filipino in California." After detours in Seattle and the canneries in Alaska, Allos eventually arrives in California, and for a brief moment, it is the California of his dreams. Crossing the border from Nevada, he sees "a wide land of luxuriant vegetation and busy towns," looming above "a valley of grapes and sugar beets, all green and ready for the summer harvest." He goes to Stockton's Chinatown and begins to see and hear the familiar trappings of his people. He encounters "many Filipinos in magnificent suits," flush with money from picking asparagus. For a moment, this seems the California of myth and legend. It is a fertile, Edenic space, with an established community of Filipino expatriates who seemingly have already made their fortunes on this lush American land. Allos realizes that he is even walking on El Dorado Street. And though he idly wonders if he, like the *conquistadores*, is seeking "gold in the new land," the allusion to a history of conquest—an allusion perhaps serving as an understated reminder that Spain colonized the Philippines in 1565, thirty years after ships sent by Cortés claimed Baja California for Spain—passes without comment.[38] Possibly the reader, if not Allos, fantasizes briefly that this immigrant's narrative will be a story of social and financial mobility: a sort of reckoning, a return of the repressed.

Unsurprisingly, this prelapsarian California falls quickly. In a bar, as Allos watches, a Chinese man calmly "came out of a back room with a gun and shot a Filipino who was standing by a table."[39] Terrified, Allos bolts into the street and runs away. There he sees the Filipino Federation Building engulfed in flame, torched by Chinese gangsters as some sort of political retribution. For Allos the geography of urban California quickly becomes a geography of fear.

RADICAL LIBERALISM AND AESTHETIC POLITICS

Despite such disillusionment the fictionalized Allos and the real-life Bulosan are ultimately empowered by the hostility of the American West, not discouraged by it. In a letter written in 1947 Bulosan states that "out of the slums and kitchens of California, out of the fear and hatred," he "came out alive spiritually and intellectually." Similarly, by the close of *America Is in the Heart* Allos concludes that "no man—no one at all—could destroy my faith in America." He harvests this philosophical insight—a spiritual affirmation of a secular political faith—only because he has first cultivated the actual soil of California. Bulosan himself, by "digging my hands into the rich soil," was able to realize that the "American earth was like a huge heart unfolding warmly to receive me."[40] In other words, his intangible political faith in America sprouts from his physical interaction with the American earth. Unlike the picture he sketches of himself in the early 1930s—as a newly political activist, obsessed with "Marxist literature"—by the mid-1940s he increasingly describes himself as extracting left-liberal principles of justice and equality from a tangible sense of place. By 1946 it is his vision of the promise of American political economy, and not its actual practice, that drives his radicalism. The emergence of this rhetoric of faith, which echoes his 1947 proclamation that he has come "alive spiritually and intellectually" in California, seems linked in part to a burgeoning dissatisfaction with the provincialism and sectarianism of the radical left.

In one key scene in *America Is in the Heart* the Salinas headquarters of the Filipino Workers' Association is burned to the ground following a successful strike by lettuce pickers.[41] Jae H. Roe writes that this scene almost certainly refers to the historical Salinas lettuce strike of 1934, in which the Filipino Labor Union was joined by the largely white Vegetable Packers Association. This represented a rare moment of solidarity, because vegetable growers were typically able to pit the VPA against the FLU by playing on racial antagonisms.[42] Ultimately, though, growing white hostility toward ethnic labor unions led to increased anti-Filipino violence, and the white VPA distanced itself from the Filipino union. This failure of multiethnic labor solidarity, Roe argues, helped Bulosan "understand the necessity of conceptualizing that solidarity outside the 'sectarianism' of race and nationality, and within a global perspective of colonization and liberation."[43] For Bulosan, though, the failure of the lettuce strike also spoke to a more general difficulty with politics itself.

Before it is anything else, politics is first an aesthetic act. Before civic change can be realized in practice, it must first be imagined, put into language, put into narrative, and finally presented to the populace in such a way that the public is able imaginatively to enter into that narrative and envision an alternate social or economic vista. As historian F. R. Ankersmit has suggested, politics is "not part of the realm of facts or of values, but of aesthetics," and "only comes into being after and due to [aesthetic] representation."[44] But politics is not *only* an aesthetic act. It is also the unpleasant process of compromise and concession. Although Bulosan presents his younger self as driven to "Marxist literature" by the treatment of Filipinos in the fields and canneries of California, the transition from Marxism as an aesthetic event—that is, as a set of compelling images and stories—to the nuts-and-bolts realities of leftist political practice seems to have been problematic for him. He bemoans the fact that many of the "progressive" organizations he tried to work with in the 1930s too easily "dribbled into personal quarrels and selfish motives": "There were individuals who were saturated with the false values of capitalism and the insidiousness of their bourgeois prejudices poisoned their whole thinking. I became convinced that they could not liberate America from decay. And I became doubly convinced, as Hitler seized one country after another, that their prejudices must be challenged by a stronger faith in America."[45]

The practice of politics in California, with its parties and personalities and the pragmatics of negotiation, clearly rankled. If Bulosan's experiences in the California fields gave rise to a desire for political action, frustration with the difficulty of actually achieving that action in turn gave rise to an abstract, transnational political philosophy. So in much of his writing, he eschews the messiness of political praxis and instead appeals to a transcendental "faith in America." Yet this is clearly not a patriotism born of jingoistic religiosity. Instead, the word "America" comes to symbolize a new, transnational liberalism of the left.

Though Bulosan's rhetorical "America" was not necessarily yoked to the historical America, it was not necessarily divorced from that America, either. In a letter in 1940 Bulosan proudly asserted that he and his fellow Filipinos "like America. We want to live and die here."[46] This national identification, much like his leftist political commitments, was shaped by experiences of the Filipino immigrant laborers:

> Thousands of Filipinos, the major part of those in California, work in the fields. True, the farms are mostly corporation owned, but this cannot prevent a man who works close to the soil from feeling attached to that soil. Work in the fields is back-breaking, but the well-tended crops are green and beautiful. . . . Laboring in the fields becomes more than a means of earning a living. Field work is a part of the great American scene. Filipinos are a part of this scene. They are a part of America.[47]

This sense of regional and national identification initially seems paradoxical, even jarring. The back-breaking wage labor that produced Bulosan's radical opposition to American political and economic practice also, he claims, produced a deep affinity for and commitment to that same America.

This paradox is explained in part by his pervasive aestheticism. Perhaps because he was physically unable to work in the fields, both radical politics and manual labor became fundamentally aesthetic phenomena for him (when it was rhetorically convenient, at least). Though critics such as Susan Evangelista have classified *America Is in the Heart* as "essentially humanist and sentimental" and lacking the "Marxist idiom" present in some of his other writing, this somewhat misses the point.⁴⁸ Marxist ideals, for Bulosan, *were* humanistic. And like labor, they held aesthetic potential. So even though fieldwork is "back-breaking," because the resulting crops are "green and beautiful" labor becomes not only a political act but an act of aesthetic creation.

This connection is important because the political upshot of the aesthetic act seems, for Bulosan, to be the cultivation of an expansive liberalism. Fieldwork is "more than a means of making a living," it is a means of contributing in an aesthetically and materially meaningful way to the state of California. Filipino immigrants, he concludes, possess the inalienable political and economic freedoms of liberal selfhood, the same freedoms that he feels are a fundamental "part of America." But it is not enough to merely possess those liberties, or even to have them recognized. For Bulosan, freedom means an egalitarian system of accessing and exercising those liberties. His liberalism, then, is not a classical negative liberty but rather a new sort of global positive liberalism. Liberalism, by this logic, means a transnational equality of economic opportunity. Defining that positive egalitarianism as liberal and without borders—and yet still an integral "part of America"—is what drives both his politics and his aesthetics.

He ultimately dubs this liberal imaginary "America." Yet this sentiment is not an unalienated celebration of a literal nation. Bulosan was unswervingly focused on what he called "building a new America," not simply applauding the existing one.⁴⁹ This critical stance went hand in hand with his ambivalence over the practice of leftist politics—or, often, politics at all—if not the material outcome of those politics. Despite his clear commitment to Marxism in the abstract, by the 1940s he was often ambivalent about the possibility of translating what he saw as transcendent principles about justice and equality into political practice, and his early enthusiasm with the "Soviet system" had faded.⁵⁰ He became uneasy not only with the Communist Party, but also, it seems, with Marxism generally. Although communism would appear to lend itself to a polity predicated on positive liberties, for Bulosan, both communism and laissez-faire economic liberalism were ultimately conducive to inequality and were, as a result, systems of illiberal unfreedom.

Twice in *America Is in the Heart* Allos expresses wariness with communism in general and the Communist Party in particular. He professes a desire to be "sure that communism was what Filipinos needed," noting that "if it's communism our countrymen want, let them have it. I think that [allowing them the choice] is democracy." Trying to discern what "Filipinos needed," Allos takes a bus ride north, watching out the window as "familiar scenes" of "the color of green, the bitter taste of lemon peels, the yellow of ripe peels" all "evoked poetry in me."[51] For Allos, democracy is the definitive system of political rule. If communist principles are to be implemented, such change must proceed from the democratic process, because for him, liberal democracy is prior and superior to all other forms of government. Significantly, he seems to arrive at this sort of democratic foundationalism by observing the landscape of California. Landscape is transformed into literary aesthetics: to find beauty in the "yellow of ripe peels" is at once to have "poetry" evoked. And those literary aesthetics, in turn, reaffirm his political faith in liberal democracy. There is, then, a perceptible connection between the natural aesthetics of the far West and Allos's liberal anticommunism.

Though Allos deems the Communist Party ill-suited to the task of accomplishing what he feels are the most pressing social goals in America, he retains its basic egalitarian impulses and eventually seems to connect those impulses to a transnational liberalism devoted to positive liberties. Tellingly, he finds the party's egalitarianism embedded in the geography of California and the West:

> I can say now that communism among Filipinos had a false start. It was propagated by stupid little men, anti-Filipino. The principles for which the Party stood were nebulous and inspiring. . . . But the Communist Party had contributed something definite toward the awakening of Filipinos on the West Coast. Even though it had entirely forsaken them, a few of the more enlightened members gathered the carcass of their hope in socialism and tried to breathe a new life into it. . . . With this last hope, I looked toward the north once again. I wanted to run away from the stifling narrowness of Temple Street [Los Angeles]. There in the broad fields, under the wide skies, there in the wide world of grass, trees, and stars my mind would stir and radiate with a new light. I was obsessed with looking across vast lands and staring into the sky. In vast spaces I found a nameless relief from the smallness of my world in America.[52]

Even after rejecting the party as "anti-Filipino," Allos seeks to renew his faith in left politics by rejecting the "stifling narrowness" of Los Angeles and returning to the rural spaces of the central coast of California. Once more, leftism becomes yoked to place. In order to "breathe new life" into his faith in socialism, he hunts out the "broad fields," the "wide skies," and the "grass, trees, and stars" of the central coast. Here, he seeks to move beyond the party and its narrow rules while still retaining its "inspiring" elements, and wants to find in the aestheticism of the central coast an inclusive politics, a politics devoted to a freedom that exceeded the borders of the nation, that would transgress the smallness of his "world in America."

Yet again, though, Bulosan's poetry, politics, and pragmatism collide. Allos seems to reject the Communist Party because it was just that, a political party, forced to align itself with various constituencies, some of them "anti-Filipino," in order to achieve its goals. The reason he is able to renew his faith in "socialism"—tellingly, not "communism"—is that he forces himself to pretend that he is once again encountering that political philosophy in a budding state of pure aestheticism, out among the grass and the flowers and the wide open skies of the American West. For Bulosan, politics as philosophy is always beautiful, always in bloom. Politics as *politics*, however, is often corrupted, in a browning state of decay. This irony, whereby his politics is most perfect at the moment just before it actually becomes political, is captured by the controlling symbolic tautology of this passage, in which Allos seeks "relief" from the "smallness of [his] world in America" by looking for refuge in the "vast spaces" of the West. Or, put another way, he seeks to escape from the smallness of America into the vastness of America.

This contradiction ultimately resolves in the fact that even though his California is a tangible place of "grass, trees, and stars," Bulosan's "America" is finally not a material entity. The physical earth is more real than the nation-state. Much like his politics, this imagined global space he calls "America" is always embryonic, a social geography of economic and racial egalitarianism held in a state of perpetual abeyance. For him, writing the Californian West—transcribing the neocolonial exploitation of Los Angeles *and* the yawning, boundless liberty of the "vast spaces" of the undeveloped central coast—meant imagining a new America, one that would stand as a repudiation of the racism, nationalism, and economic injustice of the actual country. But imagining this new America also meant imagining a new politics: leaving behind classical negative liberties in favor of an egalitarian liberalism devoted to ensuring positive liberties. He ends up where he began: as a proponent of, as he put it in "Freedom from Want," a liberalism devoted to "opportunity *to*," not merely "freedom *from*."

As he did in "Freedom from Want," in *America Is in the Heart* Bulosan sought a government dedicated to ensuring a positive right to access, rather than merely a negative freedom from interference. He is, then, best understood as a radical democrat seeking to overturn the racial and economic inequality produced by an unchecked, laissez-faire classical liberalism. He also clearly saw this project as emerging from a unique regionalism that dissolved the materiality of California into the immateriality of "America." National politics thus become transnational, infusing key liberal principles into a new liberal order that would no longer be anchored to "merely a physical" place. In other words, by rejecting Communist Party parochialism and writing lovingly about California and the West, he begins to imagine a new, left liberalism that explodes the borders of the nation.

TOWARD A TRANSNATIONAL LIBERALISM OF THE LEFT

Bulosan seems not to have rejected radicalism; instead, he perceived himself as the vanguard of a new type of radicalism altogether. In a 1943 essay titled "Letter to a Filipino Woman" he linked "working toward a democratic society" to "the revolutionary march of the people toward a better life." And though he identifies this march as an essentially American revolution, it is also, he takes pains to clarify, a transnational struggle for a new type of egalitarian liberalism, one disconnected from borders of nation, race, and class:

> It is but fair to say that America is not a land of one race or one class of men. We are all America that have toiled and suffered and known oppression and defeat, from the first Indian that died in Manhattan to the last Filipino that bled to death in the foxholes of Bataan. America is not bound by geographical latitudes. America is not

merely a land or an institution.... America is the prophecy of a new society of men: of a system that knows no sorrow or strife or suffering.... America is also the nameless foreigner, the homeless refugee, the hungry boy begging for a job and the black body dangling from a tree.... All of us, from the first Adams to the last Bulosan, native born or alien, educated or illiterate—*We are America!* ... We will stand by America always, and renew the grand epic of democracy that *was* hers.... The common man is intuitively seeking the secret of fighting the war, because he is intuitively seeking the secret of fighting the peace. He is awakening to the necessity of a central democratic consciousness of universal freedom.[53]

With a few minor alterations, Bulosan would reuse this passage practically verbatim three years later as the emotional centerpiece of *America Is in the Heart*. In the passage, the aesthetic qualities of liberal democracy (signified in part by the way he describes a system of political rule with a literary term, as an "epic") create a particular type of transnational liberal selfhood. This "universal," "democratic consciousness" in turn markedly expands the institutional and political borders of America. This is not dissimilar to the rhetorical and political accomplishments of "Freedom from Want," in which the careful linguistic conservatism of Roosevelt's negative liberties are replaced, in Bulosan's essay, with an vision of egalitarian positive liberties that he identifies as essentially American. Bulosan's leftism is thus a curious beast, one invested in the imagination of a new system of transnational positive liberties called "America."

This, in the end, is perhaps the most radical thing about Carlos Bulosan. By seeking to rediscover a foundational political language in the material spaces of California, he reaches outward toward the world at large. He harks back to the traditional language of American liberal democracy—a language often used to marginalize the poor and the non-citizen—only to reclaim that language. In his writing, democracy, liberalism, and even "America" are halted in their too-easy slides into atomistic individualism, monopoly capitalism, and jingoistic nationalism. They are instead redirected toward multiethnic tolerance, economic justice, and global egalitarianism. This is an act of imagination, an act of aesthetics. In writing *his* American West, Bulosan cannily translates the traditional language of

American politics—a centrist liberal individualism of negative liberties—into a new, transnational liberalism of the left.

NOTES

1. Franklin D. Roosevelt, "State of the Union Address: January 6, 1941," in *State of the Union Addresses of Franklin D. Roosevelt* (Teddington, Middlesex: The Echo Library, 2007), 92.
2. Roosevelt, "State of the Union Address," 92–93.
3. Roosevelt, "State of the Union Address," 93.
4. Roosevelt, "State of the Union Address," 93.
5. Ramón Saldívar, *The Borderlands of Culture: Américo Paredes and the Transnational Imaginary* (Durham, N.C.: Duke University Press, 2006), 204.
6. For an excellent analysis of Paredes's poem "The Four Freedoms" (1941) see Saldívar, *The Borderlands of Culture*, 215–25; see also José Limón's chapter in this book.
7. Will Durant wrote the essay to accompany "Freedom of Worship," Stephen Vincent Benét handled "Freedom from Fear," and Booth Tarkington wrote "Freedom of Speech." These were established, name-brand authors, near or past the peak of their careers. Both Benét and Tarkington had already won Pulitzer prizes for their work and had published more than sixty books between them; Will Durant had at that point written eight works of philosophy and history and would later go on to win a Pulitzer and a Presidential Medal of Freedom.
8. There has been some confusion over Bulosan's date of birth. He himself claimed he was born November 24, 1913, among other dates, but Susan Evangelista notes that November 2, 1911 is the date given by his baptismal record and has been confirmed by his younger sister. Escolastica. E. San Juan, Jr., *Carlos Bulosan and the Imagination of the Class Struggle* (Quezon City: University of the Philippines Press, 1972), 2. Susan Evangelista, *Carlos Bulosan and His Poetry: A Biography and Anthology* (Seattle: University of Washington Press, 1985), 64.
9. Michael Denning, *The Cultural Front: The Laboring of American Culture in the Twentieth Century* (London: Verso, 1997), 133.
10. Carlos Bulosan, "Freedom from Want," *Saturday Evening Post* 215, no. 36 (March 6, 1943): 12.
11. Bulosan, "Freedom from Want," 12.
12. Isaiah Berlin, "Two Concepts of Liberty" (1958), in *Liberty*, ed. Henry Hardy (Oxford: Oxford University Press, 2002), 169.
13. Bulosan, "Freedom from Want," 12.
14. Karl Marx et. al., *Critique of the Gotha Programme* (1875; reprint, New York: International, 1938), 81.
15. Bulosan, "Freedom from Want," 12.
16. "Letter, March 12, 1947," in *On Becoming Filipino*, 175, 176.

17. "Autobiographical Sketch" (1955), in *On Becoming Filipino*, 216. Contrasting this depiction of a singular and unalterable national identity, Martin Joseph Ponce has argued that Bulosan should in fact be understood as a transnational subject, one who purposely addressed his fictionalized autobiography to the United States and the Philippines simultaneously. Ponce, "On Becoming Socially Articulate: Transnational Bulosan," *Journal of Asian American Studies* 8, no. 1 (2005): 52.

18. Carey McWilliams, *Brothers under the Skin* (1942; reprint, Boston: Little, Brown, 1964), 236–37. For these Filipinos, eking out a living prior to the crash of 1929 meant picking lettuce and strawberries in California in spring, moving north to Seattle and then Alaska to work in the canneries in the summer, then back to Washington to pick apples in the fall, and finally back to California to work as bellboys, bus boys, waiters, and dishwashers in the winter before starting the whole process over again. Evangelista, *Carlos Bulosan and His Poetry*, 3. As Cheryl Higashida notes, the "oxymoronic idea of 'nomad harvesters,' people who cannot settle on the very land that they cultivate, captures the contradictions within monopoly capitalism's penetration of California farming; the migrant fieldhands responsible for the crops' ripening are themselves doomed to rot." Higashida, "Re-Signed Subjects: Women, Work, and World in the Fiction of Carlos Bulosan and Hisaye Yamamoto," *Studies in the Literary Imagination* 37, no. 1 (2004): 40–41. For more on Filipino immigrants to California see H. Brett Melendy, *Asians in America: Filipinos, Koreans, and East Indians* (Boston: Twayne, 1977), 41–42.

19. For Bulosan, overcoming this sort of political and economic dislocation involved cultivating a sense of place rooted less in the specifics of national identity and more in the economic and political implications of labor. Later in life, in fact, he forswore the entire concept of national "roots." "I realized how foolish it was," he stated in a posthumously published essay, to try to "define roots in terms of places and persons," in part because "I would be as rootless in the Philippines as I was in America." His notion of place, as a result, is "not physical," but rather "intellectual and spiritual." In this sense, his awareness of his own political identity comes through the cultivation of an imaginative and aesthetic sense of place. And for him, the work of creating place through writing and reading occurred largely in the American West. Bulosan, "My Education," *Amerasia Journal* 6, no. 1 (1979): 113–19, reprinted in *On Becoming Filipino*, 129. For more on the ambiguous legal status of Bulosan and other pre-1934 Filipino immigrants see E. San Juan, Jr., "In Search of Filipino Writing: Reclaiming Whose 'America'?" in *The Ethnic Canon: Histories, Institutions, and Interventions*, ed. David Palumbo-Liu (Minneapolis: University of Minnesota Press, 1995), 220–22; and E. San Juan, Jr. "Carlos Bulosan, Filipino Writer-Activist: Between a Time of Terror and the Time of Revolution." *New Centennial Review* 8, no. 1 (2008) 105–106.

20. Evangelista, *Carlos Bulosan and His Poetry*, 10.

21. The *New Tide*, Bulosan wrote in 1946, "did not create a sensation," as it was "fumbling and immature." And though it "promised to grow into something important in the history of Filipino social awakening," it quickly "went out of existence," dying "a natural death." His willingness to dismiss the magazine (in his account, going from "The first issue of *The New Tide* was with the printers" to "Then it went out of existence" takes barely over a hundred words) is significant. In his book chronicling the lives of African-Americans during the Depression, *12 Million Black Voices* (1941), Richard Wright included a subtle allusion to Carlos Bulosan and his long-defunct magazine. "The seasons of the plantation

no longer dictate the lives of many of us; hundreds of thousands of us are moving into the sphere of conscious history," he wrote. "We are with the new tide. We stand at the crossroads." Carlos Bulosan, *America Is in the Heart* (1946; Seattle: University of Washington Press, 1973), 193. Richard Wright, *12 Million Black Voices* (1941; New York: Thunder's Mouth Press, 2000), 147. For an interpretation of Wright's possible influences on Bulosan see Oscar V. Campomanes and Todd S. Gernes, "Carlos Bulosan and the Act of Writing," *Philippine Studies* 40, no. 1 (1992): 77–78.

22. Bulosan did return to more straightforward leftist writing on occasion. Nearly twenty years after the dissolution of *New Tide* he edited the 1952 yearbook of the United Cannery, Agricultural, Packing and Allied Workers of America (UCAPAWA), International Longshore and Warehouse Union (ILWU) Local 37, and penned its opening editorial screed against "dangerous moves by certain branches of government," the "vicious lies of the capitalist press and yellow journalism," and the "war-mongering of big business." Making the occasional return to this sort of rabble-rousing leftist activism was enough to convince him (albeit in the absence of any available evidence) that he had been blacklisted from Hollywood during the McCarthy era. But in fact his most meaningful and lasting political affirmations are found in publications that announced themselves as largely aesthetic, and not explicitly radical, works. Evangelista, *Carlos Bulosan and His Poetry*, 21.

23. Bulosan, *America Is in the Heart*, 311, 273. Italics in original.

24. "I Want the Wide American Earth" (1952), in Evangelista, *Carlos Bulosan and His Poetry*, 88–91.

25. "I Want the Wide American Earth," lines 13–14, 78, 77.

26. Both those in favor of and those opposed to the McCarran-Walter Act sought to enlist the services of words like "freedom," "America," and "liberal" in their charge. One proponent argued that the Act "propose[d] a fundamental liberalization in our treatment of ex-totalitarians," a "redemptive" policy that made for a "more humane immigration procedure." See Mike Masaoka, "Letter to the Editor," *New York Times*, 27 April 1952, E8. Conversely, when President Truman vetoed the bill (a veto which was quickly overturned), he claimed the Act was "discriminatory," that it "violates the great political doctrine of the Declaration of Independence," and that it "denies the humanitarian creed inscribed beneath the Statue of Liberty." Senator Pat McCarran, obviously unwilling to cede the rhetorical battle over "America," immediately dubbed the quite-Constitutional veto "un-American." Quoted in Anthony Leviero, "President Vetoes Immigration Bill as Discriminatory," *New York Times*, 26 June 1952, A1, 14.

27. "Letter to Florentino B. Valeros, 8 April 1955," in *Sound of Falling Light: Letters in Exile*, ed. Delores S. Feria (Quezon City, 1960), 85.

28. Susan Evangelista has demonstrated that archival union records indicate that Bulosan never went to Alaska, yet in *America* he claims to have been "sold for five dollars" to "work in the fish canneries in Alaska." Evangelista, "Carlos Bulosan," in *Asian American Writers*, ed. Deborah L. Madsen (Detroit: Thomson-Gale, 2005), 11. See also Bulosan, *America Is in the Heart*, 101.

29. "Letter to Grace F. Cunningham, 1 August 1944," in *Sound of Falling Light*, 23.

30. Quoted in San Juan, "Carlos Bulosan, Filipino Writer-Activist," 109.

31. "Allos," the Greek word for "other," is the name of the narrator of *America Is in the Heart*, at least before that narrator comes to the United States and begins using his

"Christian name" of "Carlos," which is occasionally shortened to "Carl" when he begins writing for a radical newspaper. Bulosan, *America Is in the* Heart, 124, 182.

32. Bulosan, *America Is in the Heart*, 267, 71, 246, 265, 246, 266.
33. Bulosan, "My Education," 128–29.
34. Bulosan was a sickly young man and unable to do fieldwork; shortly after arriving in the United States he went to Los Angeles to live with his brother Aurelio and embarked, with Aurelio's support, on a period of self-education at the public library. Both Aurelio and a longtime friend, P. C. Morantte, testified that Bulosan was "simply not strong enough" for fieldwork. Evangelista, *Carlos Bulosan and His Poetry*, 9.
35. "The Writer as Worker" (1955), in *On Becoming Filipino*, 144.
36. "I Am Not a Laughing Man" (1946), in *On Becoming Filipino*, 138.
37. He continues by claiming, more than a little improbably, that after the publication of "Freedom from Want," what he had *really* wanted was to work in the asparagus fields in Stockton, but given that he "could not find a crew to work with because I was not fast enough," he was instead forced to write short stories for the *New Yorker*. "I Am Not a Laughing Man," 140.
38. *America Is in the Heart*, 112 ("all roads," hard to be a Filipino"), 115 ("wide land," "valley of grapes and sugar"), 116 ("magnificent suits," "gold in the new land").
39. *America Is in the Heart*, 116.
40. "Letter to Grace F. Cunningham, 24 September 1947," in *Sound of Falling Light*, 52. Bulosan, *America Is in the Heart*, 326.
41. Bulosan, *America Is in the Heart*, 194–95.
42. Jae H. Roe, "Revising the Sign of 'America': The Postcolonial Humanism of *America Is in the Heart*," *English Language and Literature* 49, no. 4 (2003): 913–14.
43. Roe, "Revising the Sign of 'America,'" 914.
44. F. R. Ankersmit, *Aesthetic Politics: Political Philosophy beyond Fact and Value* (Stanford, Calif.: Stanford University Press, 1996), 16, 47.
45. "My Education," 128.
46. "Letters to an American Woman, August 3, 1940," in *On Becoming Filipino*, 200.
47. "Letters to an American Woman, August 3, 1940," 201.
48. Evangelista, *Carlos Bulosan and His Poetry*, 22.
49. "Letter to a Filipino Woman" (1943), in *On Becoming Filipino*, 212.
50. "My Education," 129.
51. Bulosan, *America Is in the Heart*, 270.
52. Bulosan, *America Is in the Heart*, 293–94.
53. Bulosan, "Letter to a Filipino Woman," 212–13.

CHAPTER FOURTEEN

Regionalism and Social Protest during John Steinbeck's "Years of Greatness," 1936–1939

David Wrobel

> There are five layers in this book, a reader will find as many as he can and he won't find more than he has in himself.
> —Steinbeck to Pascal Covici, on the forthcoming
> *The Grapes of Wrath*, January 1939

THE YEARS OF GREATNESS AND DESPAIR

This chapter examines the published works and private correspondence of John Steinbeck (1902–1968) from 1936 to 1939, with special emphasis on the intersections of regionalism and social protest that characterize his most influential book, *The Grapes of Wrath* (1939). During this remarkably productive period—one that has been labeled "the years of greatness"—Steinbeck published his first strike novel, *In Dubious Battle* (1936); a series of newspaper articles on California migrant labor, "The Harvest Gypsies" (1936), for the leftist *San Francisco News*; the novella *Of Mice and Men* (1937); and a short story collection, *The Long Valley* (1938); all in addition to *The Grapes of Wrath*, which won the Pulitzer Prize in 1939.[1] The powerful film adaptation of *The Grapes of Wrath* was released in January of the following year.[2]

But the story of Steinbeck in the late 1930s is, of course, much more than a chronicle of a successful novelist whose work was adapted for the big screen. As Steinbeck scholar Robert DeMott asserts, *The Grapes of*

John Steinbeck. Courtesy of Special Collections and University Archives, Stanford University Libraries.

Wrath "both reflects history and creates history as it attempts to convey the reality of the labor situation."[3] And Steinbeck would say of his own efforts, "I'm trying to write history while it happens and I don't want to be wrong."[4] The novel was a clear catalyst for increased federal government attention to the plight of migrant labor. Moreover, his depiction of the migrants' living and working conditions received validation in the findings of Robert La Follette's Senate Civil Liberties Committee's investigation in

December 1939 and January 1940.⁵ The novel's legacy (not to mention its selling power) has lived on, for four generations now, as one of the most powerful and recognizable representations of the human tragedies and triumphs that accompanied the Great Depression. In the wake of witnessing the awful despair of migrant families, Steinbeck offered America a progressive vision as profound as that of fellow California leftist regionalist and activist Carey McWilliams (1905–1980), whose controversial study of migrant labor in the state, *Factories in the Field* (1939), was published shortly after Steinbeck's novel. The storm of protest that followed the publication of *The Grapes of Wrath* (and to which we will return), as California's growers' organizations sought to characterize the book as a pack of lies and its author as a Communist sympathizer or operative, underscores Steinbeck's centrality to any consideration of leftist regionalist thought in the Depression era.

REGIONAL JOURNEY TO A NOVEL

In exploring the multiple layers of regionalism and social protest in Steinbeck's writings in the "great years" 1936–39 we can understand how his vision for a more humane, more socially and morally responsible America became fully developed only when it intersected with his deep regionalist proclivities and concerns. The clash between California's thoroughly organized agribusiness interests, represented by the Associated Farmers and the California Citizens Association, and migrant workers and their supporters (including Steinbeck, McWilliams, and Eleanor Roosevelt) was at its core an economic one. Yet as is generally the case, that economic struggle became a cultural conflict, as well as a case study in the politics of regionalism, one that illustrates both the most positive and the most negative manifestations of people's deep attachment to place. In emphasizing the centrality of the politics of place to the migrants' struggle, Steinbeck created what is arguably the most significant single work of the regional revival of the interwar years, one that illuminated both the most positive and negative manifestations of regionalism.⁶

After his first novel, the uninspired *Cup of Gold* (1929), Steinbeck's early works—*The Pastures of Heaven* (1932), *To a God Unknown* (1933), and *Tortilla Flat* (1935)—all demonstrated his deep interest in place and helped establish him as an author of the California scene.[7] The ironically titled *The Pastures of Heaven*, like Sherwood Anderson's *Winesburg, Ohio* (1919), is comprised of a series of connected short stories, and like that earlier work illuminates the dark underside of what on the surface appears to be an idyllic place. *To a God Unknown* was the first of Steinbeck's works to deal with the topic of westward movement, and like *The Pastures of Heaven* it was a chronicle of failure and misfortune in California. The last of these three works, *Tortilla Flat*, a charming tale about the *paisanos* (men of mixed heritage) of Monterey, is considerably more upbeat than its predecessors and brought Steinbeck some modest financial reward.

There is a developing regional vision in these early works—place matters deeply—and some light social protest as well (in *Tortilla Flat*); but there is no real intersection of the two.[8] Indeed, underscoring his deep affinity for his native California soil, particularly the Salinas Valley and Monterey County, Steinbeck wrote to his publisher, Robert Ballou, late in 1932 (as he worked on *To a God Unknown*), distinguishing himself from the poet Robinson Jeffers, a Carmel resident and Pennsylvania transplant: "I know the god better than he does for I was born to it and my father was. Our bodies came from this soil—our bones came . . . from the limestone of our own mountains and our blood is distilled from the juices of this earth. I tell you now that my country—a hundred miles long and about fifty wide—is unique in this world."[9] There is a jealous quality to this early articulation of regional consciousness, an emphasis on primacy—a first in time, first in right sensibility—that does not seem to have been evident in Steinbeck's outlook a few years later but was at the heart of the anti-migrant attitudes in California that he began highlighting as early as 1936. However, the path to *The Grapes of Wrath*, with its powerful combination of regionalism and social protest, really began as Steinbeck made labor in the Depression the focus of his literary efforts. His 1936 publications, the strike novel *In Dubious Battle* and "The Harvest Gypsies" newspaper articles, are very different in form, tone, and approach, yet both were essential stages in the creation of a literary masterpiece a few years later.

In January 1935 Steinbeck wrote to his friend and fellow struggling writer George Albee about *In Dubious Battle* (then in manuscript form): "I have used a small strike in an orchard valley as the symbol of man's eternal, bitter warfare with himself." He added, "The book is brutal. I wanted to be merely a recording consciousness, judging nothing, simply putting down the thing." And, to that end, he explained, "I ended the book in the middle of a sentence. There is a cycle in the life of a man but there is no ending in the life of Man. I tried to indicate this by stopping on a high point, leaving out any conclusion" (*LL*, 98–99).[10] There is much in this gripping work that prefaces *The Grapes of Wrath*, but to examine those parallels requires a philosophical aside, involving the matter of causation.

Teleology is the study of final causes, the analysis of ultimate purpose or design as an explanation for natural phenomena, or human behavior. Teleological approaches emphasize cause and effect relationships that lead to clear conclusions or resolutions. Nonteleological approaches, on the other hand, focus simply on showing "what is," rather than passing judgment on what should, or could have been. *In Dubious Battle* was Steinbeck's first attempt at a nonteleological novel. He tried to be nonjudgmental and did not seek to provide a resolution to the problems he presented. It was also his first articulation, in novel form, of his "phalanx" or group-man theory. He had written in an unpublished 1934 essay, "Men are not individuals but units in the greater beast, the phalanx . . . [which] is not the sum of the natures of unit-men, but a new individual having emotions and ends of its own."[11]

Both the nonteleological approach and the phalanx theory would be more fully and effectively developed in *The Grapes of Wrath*. Moreover, *In Dubious Battle*, like the later novel, drew heavily on Steinbeck's personal experience with his subjects. In 1934 he interviewed labor leaders Cicil McKiddy and Carl Williams, key organizers of the 1933 strike by cotton workers in the San Joaquin Valley. He also began to spend time with migrant workers while preparing "The Harvest Gypsies" articles.[12] In addition to drawing inspiration from the cotton workers' strike, *In Dubious Battle* made direct reference to the San Francisco longshoremen's strike, which met with a violent police response on what became known as Bloody Thursday (July 5, 1934), when two protestors were killed and more than seventy wounded. As later, with *The Grapes of Wrath*, he was in a sense writing history as it happened. Also, like the later novel, *In Dubious Battle* was a novel that intentionally (and in quintessentially nonteleological fashion) closed with no clear resolution of the matters it addressed.

Another commonality between *In Dubious Battle* and *The Grapes of Wrath* can be found in the respective transitional moments of their appearance (the latter coinciding with the transition from the poverty of the

Depression years to the prosperity of the World War II era). Though it reached publication in early 1936, Steinbeck had started thinking about the book that would become *In Dubious Battle* as early as 1933. This was during the "third period" of the international Communist movement—when the emphasis of the Communist Party of the USA (CPUSA), mirroring Moscow's, was on promoting social revolution, as the time had seemingly arrived when capitalism was on the verge of collapse—and prior to the development of the Popular Front (1935–39), with its focus on cooperation of all elements on the left—from mild progressives to hard-core communists—against the rising forces of fascism. By the time *In Dubious Battle* was published, CPUSA, again in line with Moscow's directives, was calling for "collaboration with bourgeoisie . . . [and] extol[ling] the virtues of American democracy."[13] The ideological landscape had shifted massively in the time between the novel's conception and its appearance, even if American Communists' re-envisioning of their ideology as contributing to the progressive mainstream was not matched by a general public acceptance of them as part of that mainstream.

John Chamberlain, reviewing the book for the *New York Times*, proclaimed, "the publication of *In Dubious Battle* marks Mr. Steinbeck as the most versatile master of narrative now writing in the United States." He then added, "Call it fantasy if you like. Call it Communist propaganda, or call it subtle anti-Communist propaganda. The point is that *In Dubious Battle* is a wildly stirring story." Wilbur Needham in his *Los Angeles Times* review predicted that "neither radicals nor reactionaries will like the book, for they will never be sure just where Steinbeck stands."[14] Both reviewers were correct concerning the ambiguity of the novel's message, and Chamberlain was correct concerning its dramatic power.

From the opening pages, where a passionless and seemingly directionless Jim Nolan walks into a local Communist Party headquarters in San Jose, his father (a labor organizer) dead for three years and his mother just a month in the grave, and announces "I feel dead. Everything in the past is gone" (537), the novel takes on a frenetic pace.[15] Jim meets Mac, his mentor-to-be and the novel's other chief protagonist, and his apprenticeship in strike organizing begins. He and Mac travel to a California apple orchard where conditions for the migrant laborers and their families are deteriorating, and Mac immediately works to earn the trust of the community, even going so far as to help deliver a baby despite his absolute lack of expertise in the area of obstetrics. It quickly becomes clear that Mac is thoroughly committed to the principle that the party's revolutionary ends justify any means employed in the struggle. In the wake of the successful childbirth Mac callously remarks to Jim, "We've got to use whatever material comes to us. That was a lucky break. We simply had to take it. 'Course it was nice to help the girl, but hell, even if it killed her—we've got to use anything" (576). Mac uses people again and again in pursuit of the cause, and Jim, far from being repelled by Mac's approach, becomes the perfect apprentice. And then, as the strike moves toward its inevitably unsuccessful conclusion, after a series of graphically violent confrontations, Mac holds up Jim's dead body, its face blown completely away by gunfire, to the crowd of striking workers under the light of a lantern, and proclaims "Comrades! He didn't want nothing for himself—" (793).

Communists would have found little to aid their cause in the book, and the same can be said for California agribusiness interests. Steinbeck described movingly the desperate conditions faced by the workers and the violently oppressive actions of the organized large growers; but in showing so clearly the matching inhumanity of a methodically applied radical ideology wherein the ends always justify the means. he had created a work devoid of heroes, though certainly not one bereft of moral lessons. He had charted the anatomy of a strike, providing a comprehensive guide to the stages of organization, action, reaction, and accompanying ideologies, and the frightening mob mentality that resulted in acts of horrendous violence. But even more significantly he had begun to develop one of the foundational themes of *The Grapes of Wrath*. Half a century ago, Warren French explained that Steinbeck was calling in the book "for an end to man's inhumanity to man."[16]

Steinbeck would make that humanitarian call with considerably greater effectiveness in *The Grapes of Wrath* for many reasons, among them his heightened attention to place. In *Tortilla Flat* he had evoked the actual physical setting of the story; it was fundamentally a novel about place, as well as the inhabitants of that place. But *In Dubious Battle*, even with its occasional and evocative descriptions of landscapes and locations, is primarily a novel about ideology and human psychology. It is situated in California's apple country, but one might argue that it could take place anywhere. Yet there is one scene in the novel where Steinbeck explores the depth of human attachment to place, and it is one of the book's most powerful moments. Mac had convinced one of the smaller landowners, Mr. Anderson, to let the strikers camp on a few acres of his land, in return for picking his apple crop. But local vigilantes had then burned down Anderson's barn, destroying the crop and essentially ruining his livelihood. In the wake of the disaster, Anderson turns on Mac and the strikers and proclaims: "You bastards never owned nothing. You never planted trees an' seen 'em grow an' felt 'em with your hands. You never owned a thing, never went out an' touched your own apple trees with your hands. What do you know?" (783)

Steinbeck thus effectively highlighted the depth of the small growers' attachment to the land, and contrasted it with the strikers' lack of such heightened sensibilities as a consequence of their lack of proprietorship. Later, in *The Grapes of Wrath* he would explore the rise of corporate agribusiness and its disconnection from the land and concomitant inhumane power to evict people from it. But even more significantly, by the fall of 1936, as he turned his attention more fully to the conditions of California's migrant workers, one of his key observations was that large numbers of the newly arrived migrants from the southern plains had in fact owned their own land or had been long-term leaseholders.

BRUTAL HARVESTS AND SOCIAL VISIONS

"The Harvest Gypsies" series appeared in the *San Francisco News* between October 5 and 12, 1936. Tom Collins (1895 or 1897–1961), manager of the federal Resettlement Administration's Arvin Sanitary Camp for migratory laborers in Kern County (more familiarly known as the Weedpatch Camp) played an essential role in Steinbeck's education regarding the migrant labor situation.[17] Collins also worked closely during these same months (as Douglas Wixson points out in chapter 5, this volume) with Steinbeck's fellow radical regional novelist Sanora Babb. A character based on Collins appears in *The Grapes of Wrath,* and the novel was dedicated both to Collins and to Steinbeck's wife: "To Carol who willed it / To Tom who lived it." Steinbeck observed the tactful Collins at work enacting a program that enabled camp residents, who had suffered hunger and humiliation since arriving in the Golden State, to govern themselves and thus restore some of their pride and dignity. He also read Collins's detailed reports to the

Resettlement Administration's San Francisco office regarding migrant life and culture.[18]

Also vital to Steinbeck's understanding of the landscape of migratory labor was Eric Thomsen, regional director of the migrant camp program, who toured the San Joaquin Valley with the author in the fall of 1936. Although he never traveled with "Okie" migrants from the southern plains to California along Route 66, he did spend a great deal of time with migrant families from 1936 through 1938, learning about their labor conditions, values, diets, and speech patterns and using his own funds at times to help support them.

In the first of the seven pieces that comprised the newspaper series, he introduced California's new wave of migrants within the larger framework of regional reaction against newcomers: "[they] are needed, and they are hated," he wrote. "Arriving in a district they find the dislike always meted out by the resident to the foreigner, the outlander" (991–92).[19] But he then proceeded to distinguish these new arrivals from the Mexican and Filipino workers, recently deported and repatriated, whom they were displacing in the fields. These new workers, he emphasized, were agricultural migrants from Oklahoma, Kansas, Nebraska, and Texas, and were of English, German, and Scandinavian stock, "men who had worked hard on their own farms and had felt the pride of possessing and living in close touch with the land . . . resourceful and intelligent Americans. . . . They have weathered the thing, and they can weather much more for their blood is strong." Moreover, he explained, "they are not migrants by nature. They are gypsies by force of circumstance" (992–93).

Most significantly, he proclaimed (and in doing so articulated the sometimes lamentable intersections of race and regionalism): "It should be understood that with this race the old methods of repression, of starvation wages, of jailing, beating and intimidation are not going to work; these are American people" (994). This is an uncomfortable moment in the text for the modern reader, as Steinbeck privileges the newly arrived Euro-American migrants as less easily oppressed than their racially diverse precursors in the fields.[20] Yet it is worth pointing out that Steinbeck echoing Carey McWilliams's fierce indictment of California's "farm fascism" also emphasized the continuity in the brutal exploitation of migrant labor of all races by California's agribusiness interests.[21] By the sixth article for the *News* Steinbeck's position became much more direct: "The history of California's importation and treatment of foreign labor," he declared, "is a disgraceful picture of greed and cruelty," involving the previous repression of Chinese, Japanese, Mexican, and Filipino labor in the state (1015). In the seventh he averred that "the old methods of intimidation and starvation perfected against the foreign peons are now being used against the new white migrant workers. But," he predicted, "they will not be successful" (1018).

Was Steinbeck making a simple racialist point: that this new wave of white harvest gypsies would not be defeated by California agribusiness simply because, to use the language of the first of the "Harvest Gypsies" essays (and the title of the 1938 reprinting of the articles), "their blood is strong"? Or, was he making a more subtle point: that the campaign of California agribusiness and its supporters to oppress and dehumanize white migrant labor would not work because the very whiteness of the "Okies" made them visible to mainstream American society as victims in a way that their unfortunate forerunners in California's "factories in the fields" had not been? Perhaps he was consciously playing to the innate racial prejudice of his predominantly white audience to generate support for the new migrant workers.[22]

Certainly his work highlighted this victimization in ways that engendered deep empathy for his subjects. The second of the *News* articles, which chronicled the fortunes of three migrant "Okie" families in a typical California squatters' camp, each in a different stage of decline and despair, is surely one of the most moving and disquieting journalistic accounts of American poverty in the 1930s. The first family (husband, wife, and three children), formerly proprietors of fifty acres that "produced the tall corn of the middle west" (996), who once had had a bank balance of a thousand dollars to their name, had now been reduced to building a ten-by-ten-foot house with corrugated paper. But the first rain would turn the house into a "brown, pulpy mush," and this failed shelter combined with lack of good nutrition would subject the whole family to pneumonia (996). He emphasized that "there is still pride in this family" and that appropriate sanitary practices are still followed, because the father is "a newcomer and his spirit and decency and his sense of his own dignity have not been quite wiped out" (996–97).

The second family (husband, wife, and four children), former grocery store proprietors, now lives in a tattered, rotting tent; their sanitary standards are lower than the first family's, their diet less varied, and their number already reduced by one as a result—their four-year old boy has just died of malnutrition. "This is the middle class of the squatters' camp," Steinbeck reports, but "in a few months this family will slip down into the lower class. Dignity is all gone, and spirit has turned to sullen anger before it dies" (998). The third family (husband, wife, and three children) have tried to build a home from willow branches and weeds, paper, tin, and old carpet strips. They sleep on an old piece of carpet on the ground, folding it up over them. "The three year old child has a gunny sack tied about his middle for clothing. He has the swollen belly caused by malnutrition. . . . He will die in a very short time. The older children may survive" (998–99). The mother has experienced a series of stillbirths and infant deaths in recent years. The husband "has lost even the desire to talk" (999).

Steinbeck's point, as he describes what happens to men as their "children have sickened and died, after the loss of dignity and spirit have cut [them] down to a kind of subhumanity," is that "malnutrition is not infectious, nor is dysentery, which is almost the rule among the children" (999–1000). These are curable and correctible conditions, and the fact of their persistence is not attributable to the subhumanity of the parents or their "Okie" culture but to the meanness and inhumanity of California's organized agricultural interests. This much becomes crystal clear when he outlines the role of federal camps at Arvin and Marysville (in the fourth article in the series) in "restor[ing] the dignity and decency that had been kicked out of the migrants by their intolerable mode of life" (1006). He describes the government camps as thoroughly positive "experiments in natural and democratic self-government" that systematically "reduce the degenerating effect of the migrants' life" as effectively as California agribusinesses' oppressive labor system promoted those effects (1007–1008).

In addition to calling for an expansion of the Resettlement Administration's sanitary camp system for migrant workers, Steinbeck went much farther in the last of his *News* articles, advocating the allocation of state and federal lands for subsistence farms for migrant laborers: they could either lease the land at affordable rental rates or purchase it with long-term mortgages, in either case becoming able again to grow their own food to supplement their wages as crop pickers, and thus to escape the worst excesses of the current labor system.[23] The women and children would be able to tend the subsistence farms and enjoy the fruits of education and geographic stability—actually enjoy a sense of place—while only the employable men traveled to meet the seasonal demands of California agribusiness.

Steinbeck insisted, in the concluding article of "The Harvest Gypsies" series, that only the support of the federal government in guaranteeing farm workers' right to organize, and in prosecuting acts of "vigilante terrorism" sponsored by California agribusiness, could guarantee the peaceful future of the state. He called for the direct intervention of the U.S. Attorney General, because the nature and extent of violations of human dignity in the state had become so extreme: "And if the terrorism and reduction of human rights, the floggings, murder by deputies, kidnapings [sic] and refusal of trial by jury are necessary to our economic security, it is further submitted that California democracy is rapidly dwindling away. Fascistic methods are more numerous, more powerfully applied and more openly practiced than in any other place in the United States" (1022). Small wonder that California's agribusiness interests responded so negatively to Steinbeck's journalistic efforts in support of migrant laborers, or that even the progressive *San Francisco News* had developed strong reservations about printing his articles.[24]

Not surprisingly, Steinbeck's friends began to express concern for his safety. Responding to these fears, he would remark: "I am not important enough to kill and I'm too able to get publicity to risk the usual beating."[25] Such concerns only increased after publication of the enormously successful *Of Mice and Men* in March 1937. While not directly touching upon labor troubles or the suffering of migrant families, *Of Mice and Men* was set in the same region, on a ranch near Salinas, and revolved around George and Lennie's unattainable dream of owning a few acres and living "off the fatta the lan."[26] Of course, the dream of California as a promised land, where hard-working Dust Bowl refugees could eventually become landowners again, was at the heart of the big novel that Steinbeck was planning and began to discuss publicly by the end of 1937. Moreover, the theme of California as a paradise already lost was at the heart of his appealing story "The Leader of the People," which appeared in *The Long Valley* (1938). In the story Grandfather Tifflin, an old pioneer who earlier in life had led settlers across the plains and mountains to California, is now reduced to recounting his frontiering past to his grandson and lamenting that "there's no place to go.... Every place is taken" (204)—a harrowing reality that migrant families were then realizing.[27]

LAYERS OF REGIONALISM AND WRATH

Originally conceived under the title "The Oklahomans" and planned to have been about the indomitable spirit of California's newest migrants, the big book would eventually become something much more expansive, and tragic. Events on the ground shifted Steinbeck's direction. He would write to Elizabeth Otis in early February 1938 about the conditions in Visalia and Nipomo:

> I must go over into the interior valleys. There are about five thousand families starving to death over there, not just hungry but actually starving. The government is trying to feed them and get medical attention to them with the fascist group of utilities and banks and huge growers sabotaging the thing.... In one tent there are twenty people quarantined for smallpox and two of the women are to have babies in this tent this week.... I must get down there and see it and see if I can't do something to help knock these murderers on their heads. (*LL* 158)

He then implored Otis to keep the matter under wraps, "because when I have finished my job the jolly old associated farmers will be after my scalp again" (158).

A few weeks later he was in Visalia to witness the conditions firsthand and try and help the thousands of migrant families stranded by the floods. He wrote to Otis again in early March about what he had experienced:

> A short trip into the fields where the water is a foot deep in the tents and the children are up on the beds and there is no food and no fire, and the county has taken off all the nurses because "the problem is so great that we can't do anything about it." So they do nothing.... It is the most heartbreaking thing in the world.... I break myself every time I go out because the argument that one person's effort

can't really do anything doesn't seem to apply when you come on a bunch of starving children and you have a little money. . . . I want to put a tag of shame on the greedy bastards who are responsible for this. (*LL* 161–62)

Saddened and enraged by the nightmarish conditions in Visalia, he began his next attempt at a novel about the topic and completed a full draft of a scathing work titled "L'Affaire Lettuceberg." His correspondence reveals that the work focused more on the organized mistreatment of the migrants by the municipal leaders of Salinas and citizen vigilantes than it did on the suffering of the migrants themselves. But he recognized that "L'Affaire" was "a vicious book, a mean book," one that failed to capture the full drama, significance, and tragedy of the story he wanted to tell, and he destroyed the 70,000-word manuscript in mid- to late May. It was a cathartic exercise, and the multilayered masterpiece that he now began could not have been conceived and written without the detours of "The Oklahomans" and "L'Affaire."[28]

In late May 1938 Steinbeck began writing *The Grapes of Wrath*. Exactly five months later, on October 26, 1938, after a monumental effort, he wrote in his journal: "Finished this day—and I hope to God it's good."[29] Carol, his wife, came up with the title (in early September), drawing from the lyrics of "The Battle Hymn of the Republic," and Steinbeck insisted that the song (both the music and all the verses) appear on the inside front and back covers of the novel. He wrote to Pascal Covici on New Year's Day, 1939: "The fascist crowd will try to sabotage this book because it is revolutionary. They will try to give it the communist angle. However, the Battle Hymn is American and intensely so. Further, every American child learns it and then forgets the words. So if both words and music are there the book is keyed into the American scene from the beginning" (*LL* 174).

• • •

Steinbeck was right: the book would meet with intense opposition upon its publication. But what he had created was simply too powerful and relevant to suppress effectively. He had indeed created a novel that was at once both revolutionary and intensely American, and regional—because of his close attention to vernacular detail.[30] What is more, he had in the work somehow balanced the most extreme tragedy with a measure of hopefulness. This balance is evident in the book's controversial final scene, which has been misunderstood by some critics as overly sentimental. Speaking of Rose of Sharon's act of human kindness in another letter to Pascal Covici, Steinbeck refused to change the ending and dismissed any and all concerns about its appropriateness:

> I am sorry but I cannot change that ending.... if there is a symbol, it is a survival symbol not a love symbol, it must be an accident, it must be a stranger, and it must be quick.... The fact that the Joads don't know him, don't care about him, have no ties to him—that is the emphasis. The giving of the breast has no more sentiment than the giving of a piece of bread.... I am not writing a satisfactory story. I've done my damndest to rip a reader's nerves to rags. I don't want him to be satisfied. (*LL* 178–79)

Steinbeck added, in this revealing letter to his editor: "Throughout I've tried to make the reader participate in the actuality, what he takes from it will be scaled entirely on his own depth or hollowness. There are five layers in this book, a reader will find as many as he can and he won't find more than he has in himself" (178–79).

The novel is more than six hundred pages long and comprised of thirty chapters—sixteen of them interchapters (occupying about one-sixth of the novel's space) addressing on a macro-scale the migrant exodus from the Dust Bowl and experiences in the presumed promised land. The rest of the chapters are focused squarely on the experience of the Joad family. The book is also comprised of three sections, each devoted to a separate regional setting: the southern plains (chapters 1–11), the journey along Route 66 to California (chapters 12–18), and the Golden State (chapters 19–30). But the novel's power, as Steinbeck suggested, comes not from its sheer size or from its effective structure, but from the layers of connective tissue that enabled him to tell the story, on multiple levels.[31]

True to his suggestion that readers should be left to find the novel's layers for themselves, he did not delineate each level, though generations of Steinbeck scholars have since tried to. These layers might be equated, Louis D. Owens explains, to the various and increasing scales of experience that the work conveys, and which give it a universal significance beyond its time and place. Thus it can be viewed first as a novel about a single family (the Joads); second, as a study of a larger group of people and stream of migration (the Dust Bowl exodus—as conveyed in the interchapters); third, as a distinctly American saga; and, fourth and most broadly, as a story of humanity's struggle, as evidenced in voluminous biblical allusions throughout the novel.[32]

But Steinbeck may well have been alluding to something rather less direct and less obvious when he drew attention to the novel's layers. His attempt at a nonteleological approach had fallen short in the earlier work, *In Dubious Battle*, but in *The Grapes of Wrath* it threads almost seamlessly through the novel as he focuses squarely on conveying "what is" and largely avoids assigning direct blame to individuals or groups for the terrible circumstances the migrants face: "There ain't no sin and there ain't no virtue. There's just stuff people do," the preacher, Jim Casy tells Tom Joad (234).[33] This nonteleological layer was, from everything we can ascertain, thoroughly absent from "L'Affaire Lettuceberg" (which helps explain why Steinbeck destroyed that novel), but is a vitally important contributing factor to the richness of *The Grapes of Wrath* and one that clearly distinguishes it from the more direct advocacy politics that marked the genre of proletarian fiction in the 1930s.

Similarly central to the novel's message is a second layer, the transition from "I" to "we," as the Joads, from Ma and Rose of Sharon to Tom, eventually come to see themselves and their family unit as a part of something larger and more significant. The author's phalanx theory, described above, plays out most profoundly in Tom's farewell speech, in Rose of Sharon's humanitarian act that closes the novel (without bringing any resolution of the situation faced by the Joads, or the "Okies," or humanity more broadly), and in Ma Joad's moving "we're the people that live" speech (which brings the film adaptation to a close).[34]

The nonteleological layer—marked by Steinbeck's reluctance to pass definitive judgment on any of the involved parties, or to arrive at a tidy resolution of the complicated circumstances he has described—and the "I" to "we" layer—charting the path from unrestrained individualism to altruistic collective action—are complemented by a third, biblical, layer (Owens's fourth layer). This layer features the Exodus theme (Rose of Sharon's stillborn child placed in an old apple crate and floated down the river like Moses in the basket); and Jim Casey—initials JC—who dies and is born again in the newfound, other-centered consciousness of Tom Joad.

The novel, as DeMott reminds us, is replete with "Old and New Testament themes, parallels, analogies, allusions, and inversions."[35] The novel's fourth discernible layer might well be the regional layer, which in turn complements the biblical layer, with its emphasis on a people's exodus to the promised land and California's failure to live up to its own self-generated image.

While as good a candidate as any published in the twentieth century for the hallowed moniker The Great American Novel, *The Grapes of Wrath* is also, at its core, a book about the West, from the dried-out and dust-blown southern plains and consequent displacement of sharecroppers, tenants, and small landowners, to "highway 66 . . . the main migrant road . . . the long concrete path across the country . . . over the red lands and the gray lands, twisting up into the mountains, crossing the Divide and down into the bright and terrible desert, and across the desert to the mountains again, and into the rich California valleys" (334).

The novel's fifth layer has proven more elusive. Its matriarchal dimension could be a contender: Ma Joad becomes an increasingly powerful force throughout the narrative, and Rose of Sharon, through her selfless act, becomes a natural successor to Ma. Steinbeck's ecological awareness, also evident throughout the work, could conceivably constitute a layer: it is, at its core, a study of people in the natural environment, impacted by an absence of rain, and then cruelly, at the close of the novel, an overabundance—a flood. A case could also be made for "dignity," and its maintenance or perseverance in the face of all odds, as the fifth layer of the work. Moreover, the theme of dignity provides a deep continuity and transition from "The Harvest Gypsies" articles, which were concerned with the lamentable dissipation of dignity in the migrants, to *The Grapes of Wrath*, wherein the Weedpatch Camp serves a restorative function (regarding the migrants' dignity) and the indomitable spirit and dignity of the Joads proves impossible to break.[36]

Nonetheless, both the pervasive theme of dignity and the ecological dimension of the novel might both be subsumed within the aforementioned fourth, regional, layer. "Dignity" intersects with regional consciousness in some of the most profound moments in Steinbeck's epic, and it is in them that we find much of the novel's lasting power. Furthermore, when we look at the regionalist dimensions of the work we also find multiple layers. Indeed, just as *The Grapes of Wrath* manages to depict humanity at both its best and its worst—what people have been reduced to, and the good they can do in the face of those challenges (the ending is the most obvious case in point)—so it represents regionalism in both its most laudable and lamentable manifestations. It is to this fourth layer, in all its varied manifestations, that we now turn.[37]

Steinbeck began the novel with a description of the land: "To the red country and part of the gray country of Oklahoma, the last rains came gently, and they did not cut the scarred earth" (211), and then moved quickly to the matter of whether the men, under the watchful eyes of the women and children, would crack under the pressure of the worsening drought that was destroying that land. The theme of deep attachment to place, to the land itself, is the first of the novel's regional layers. In chapter 5, one of the early interchapters, Steinbeck recounts the scene as a tenant family is being thrown off the land it has occupied for generations:

> Grampa took up the land, and he had to kill Indians and drive them away. And pa was born here . . . it's our land. We measured it and broke it up. We were born on it, and we got killed on it, died on it. Even if it's no good, it's still ours. That's what makes it ours—being born on it, working it, dying on it. That makes ownership, not a paper with numbers on it.[38] (244)

This is no rose-scented regionalism, to be sure—Indians were killed and driven away for the land to be taken up—but it is a regionalism that somehow transcends land values; the land is useless, but it means too much to Muley Graves for him to leave it, and he will wander around it like an old graveyard ghost in the wake of his family's departure. This love of the land is contrasted with the tractor driver's disassociation from the land as he drives the machine that pulls the mechanical plow with its "twelve curved iron penes erected in the foundry, orgasms set by gears, raping methodically, raping without passion" (247). And in the wake of this industrialization of agricultural work, "men ate what they had not raised, had no connection with the bread. The land bore under iron, and under iron gradually died; for it was not loved or hated, it had no prayers or curses" (247). Indeed, Steinbeck wove this dichotomy—between the land as something that is in the blood and the soul and the memories of people (as well as land that holds the promise of the future, California) and land as a commodity in an ever-expanding corporate agribusiness system—throughout the novel.

We might call this a matter of "regionalism uprooted" as people try to hold onto their sense of place, even as they are evicted from the land. Steinbeck wrote in a later inter-chapter, "The houses were left vacant on the land, and the land was vacant because of this" (332). And sadly, for Grampa Joad, the very act of vacating the land he knew proved fatal. Commenting on Grampa's death, Al Joad says, "It's a goddamn shame. He been talkin' what he's gonna do, how he gonna squeeze grapes over his head an' let the juice run in his whiskers." But Casy responds, "He was foolin', all the time. I think he knowed it. An' Grampa didn't die tonight. He died the minute you took 'im off the place. . . . Oh, he was breathin' . . . but he was dead" (364).

But regional consciousness does not dissipate and disappear for everyone in the wake of migration from place. It is maintained on the road as migrants listen to each other's stories about the land, and these very stories make "the Western States nervous under the beginning change. Texas and Oklahoma, Kansas and Arkansas, New Mexico, Arizona, California." Steinbeck explained:

> One man, one family driven from the land; this rusty car creaking along the highway to the West. I lost my land, a single tractor took my land. I am alone and I am bewildered. And in the night one family camps in a ditch and another family pulls in and the tents come out. . . . For here "I lost my land" is changed; a cell is split and from its splitting grows the thing you hate—"We lost *our* land." (370)

Here the movement from "I" to "we," the phalanx theory, intersects with people's passion for place to ensure a restoration of regionalism. Farther along on the road, as evening falls in a makeshift migrant roadside camp, "the twenty families became one family, the children were the children of all. The loss of home became one loss, and the golden time in the West was one dream" (416).

That dream—the possibility for a restored regionalism—of course, comes into conflict with a stark reality when the Joads reach the California line and wade into the river. There they meet two men who are heading home to the Texas Panhandle, where "at leas' we can starve to death with folks we know." One of them explains, regarding California: "she's a nice country. But she was stole a long time ago" (428). It is during this encounter that the Joads hear the derisive term "Okie" for the first time: "Well, Okie use' ta mean you was from Oklahoma. Now it means you're a dirty son-of-a-bitch" (429). Then, as the Joads pull out of a gas station in Needles, preparing to cross the desert into California's agricultural heartland, one service-station attendant says to another: "Them goddamn Okies got no sense and no feeling. They ain't human. A human being wouldn't live like they do. A human being couldn't stand to be so dirty and miserable. They ain't a hell of a lot better than gorillas" (445).

With that comment from a total stranger with absolutely no investment in the Joads' or any other migrants' fortune or misfortune, we see the painful depths of a kind of regional consciousness we might label "regionalism through reaction."[39] That brand of regional identity forged in reaction to others manifests itself throughout the rest of the novel as landowners and local citizens continually dehumanize the migrants for their regional difference, their "Okie" background: "These goddamned Okies are dirty and ignorant. They're degenerate, sexual maniacs. These goddamned Okies are thieves. They'll steal anything. They've got no sense of property rights" (510).

Steinbeck crafted a story marked by multiple layers of regionalism, and one of the most powerful rejections of the reactionary brand of regionalism employed against the Dust Bowl migrants. Moreover, in highlighting this "regionalism through reaction," with its inhumane reliance on dehumanization as a modus operandi, Steinbeck showed the true nature of his efforts toward social protest in the novel. *The Grapes of Wrath* is not a proletarian novel, or even a particularly political one, for that matter. Rather, it is a novel about what human beings are capable of doing to each other, and for each other. This is the great power of the final scene, where Rose of Sharon, in the wake of the delivery of her stillborn child, offers her milk-laden breast to a dying man, a total stranger, to sustain his life; these are the harrowing depths to which California's migrants have been sunk, and the remarkable heights to which they have risen.

After the publication of the novel and the release of the movie, Steinbeck's literary representation of a contemporary scene literally "created history" as controversy raged over whether he had told the truth about the migrants. Enemies of the book and later the film engaged in actions that amounted to life imitating art imitating life as they sought to repress the literary representation of their own repression of migrant workers and their families. The politics of place were very much at the center of those efforts, too. Ruth Comfort Mitchell's critically unacclaimed novel *Of Human Kindness* was published in 1940 as an answer to *The Grapes of Wrath*. The author—actually a Los Gatos neighbor (certainly not a friend) of Steinbeck's—traced the history of a proud Anglo-Californian farm family and their travails in the face of the "Okie" migration. In August 1939, a few months after the publication of Steinbeck's novel, Mitchell spoke at a luncheon at the San Francisco Palace Hotel. The meeting was sponsored by a conservative women's organization, Pro America, which was determined to present a more positive picture of the state's treatment of migrant labor and thereby to discredit the work of Steinbeck, McWilliams, La Follette, and other critics of California agribusiness. She proclaimed to a thoroughly receptive crowd:

> We are the grandsons and daughters of the pioneers and Argonauts who crossed the plains on covered wagons and sailed around the Horn, and we deplore the changed thinking, the unsound, inflammatory, revolutionary thinking of great numbers of our people. In the old days California attracted the brave, the ambitious, the forceful, but of late years it has become a sort of Bird Refuge for cuckoos, for scolding jays. . . . for malcontents, subversive agitators and inciters to violence.[40]

Such expressions of reactionary regionalism enabled the self-defined "true Californians" to stand up and defend their homeland and be counted in opposition to the new arrivals who could never become true Californians. Mitchell's words were yet another incarnation of the age-old strategy of resort to selective memory of the past in the construction of reactionary regionalism—a sort of primacy in place that failed to acknowledge the displacement of other cultural groups generations earlier. Unlike Grandfather Tiflin's lament in "The Leader of the People," which recognized that an era had passed and was unrecoverable, Mitchell sought to use the past, selectively, in the interests of maintaining the status quo.

Steinbeck offered a more humane vision of place in *The Grapes of Wrath*, just as he had in "The Harvest Gypsies" articles published at the beginning of the "years of greatness." He also unearthed the ugly contours of the reactionary regionalism employed against the Dust Bowl migrants (and then against his own novelistic depiction of that process). In addition, his humane, apolitical vision for a progressive or enlightened regionalism, a vision of places shared by people who work the land, placed him decidedly on the left of the political-ideological spectrum in late-1930s California. He wrote in "The Harvest Gypsies" that the cost to the government of providing small plots of land, small houses, and schools for migrant families "would not be that much greater than the amount which is now spent for tear gas, machine guns and ammunition, and deputy sheriffs" (1020). That vision might still serve as a road map for a state whose history is haunted by the always inequitable and often inhumane realities of migrant labor systems and the reactionary regionalism they still inspire.

NOTES

Epigraph: *Steinbeck: A Life in Letters*, ed. Elaine Steinbeck and Robert Wallsten (New York: Viking Penguin, 1975; reprinted, Penguin Books, 1989), 178–79.

1. Tetsumaro Hayashi, ed., *John Steinbeck: The Years of Greatness, 1936–1939* (Tuscaloosa: University of Alabama Press, 1993). An expanded collection of "The Harvest Gypsies" was published in 1938 in pamphlet form as *Their Blood Is Strong*, by the Simon J. Lubin Society of California, to raise money for migrant workers. *In Dubious Battle* (1936), *Of Mice and Men* (1937), and the 1937 edition of *The Red Pony* were all published by New York–based publisher Covici-Friede.

In this chapter, unless otherwise stated, all quotations and citations of Steinbeck's works are taken from the collected editions published by The Library of America (New York): *John Steinbeck, Novels and Stories, 1932–1937* (1994), and *John Steinbeck, The Grapes of Wrath and Other Writings, 1936–1941* (1996), both volumes ed. Robert DeMott and Elaine A. Steinbeck. (Two further volumes cover later works not mentioned here.) And unless otherwise noted, all quoted correspondence is taken from *Steinbeck: A Life in Letters*, ed. E. Steinbeck and R. Wallsten, referred to as *LL* in brief citations.

2. Directed by John Ford and produced by Darryl Zanuck, the movie starred Henry Fonda and Jane Darwell as Tom and Ma Joad. It was nominated for seven Academy Awards and won two: John Ford for Best Director and Jane Darwell for Best Supporting Actress.

3. Robert DeMott with Brian Railsback, "Prospects for the Study of John Steinbeck," in *Resources for American Literary Study* 32 (June 2009): 9–47; quotation, 30.

4. Steinbeck to Elizabeth Otis, *LL* 162.

5. For more on the novel's impact on the political scene see Jackson Benson, *The True Adventures of John Steinbeck, Writer: A Biography* (New York: Viking, 1984), 418–23.

6. Robert Dorman has provided the most insightful study of this regional renaissance; see his *Revolt of the Provinces: The Regionalist Movement in America, 1920-1945* (Chapel Hill: University of North Carolina Press, 1993).

7. For more on Steinbeck and place see Susan F. Beegel, Susan Shillinglaw, and Wesley N. Tiffney, Jr., *Steinbeck and the Environment: Interdisciplinary Approaches* (Tuscaloosa: University of Alabama Press, 1997); and Kathleen Hicks, "'It Ain't Kin We? It's Will We?': John Steinbeck's Land Ethic in *The Grapes of Wrath*," in *The Grapes of Wrath: A Reconsideration*, ed. Michael J. Meyer (Amsterdam: Rodopi), 1:397-418.

8. The protagonists of *Tortilla Flat*, like "Mack and the boys" in *Cannery Row* (1945), a decade later, are determined in their efforts to remain outside of the conventional world of steady labor and attendant social respectability.

9. Steinbeck to Robert O. Ballou [early 1933], quoted in DeMott's chapter, "This Book Is My Life: Creating *The Grapes of Wrath*," in his book *Steinbeck's Typewriter: Essays on His Art* (Troy, N.Y.: Whitston, 1997), 146-205; quotation, 132.

10. Steinbeck to George Albee, January 15, 1935, *LL* 98-99.

11. Steinbeck, "Argument of Phalanx," unpublished essay, quoted in Robert DeMott, "Chronology," in Steinbeck, *Novels and Stories, 1932-1937,* 885.

12. DeMott, "Chronology," 885; see also Morris Dickstein, *Dancing in the Dark: A Cultural History of the Great Depression* (New York: Norton, 2009), 78.

13. For more on the phases of Communist Party USA activity see John Diggins, *The Rise and Fall of the American Left* (New York: Norton, 1992), quotation, 173-74.

14. John Chamberlain, "Books of the Times," *New York Times*, January 28, 1936, 17, reprinted in *John Steinbeck: The Contemporary Reviews*, ed. Joseph R. McElrath, Jr., Jesse S. Crisler, and Susan Shillinglaw (New York: Cambridge University Press, 1996), 53-54; Wilbur Needham, "California's Radicals," *Los Angeles Times*, February 2, 1936, 3:4, reprinted in *Steinbeck: Contemporary Reviews*, 59.

15. Cues for pagination are from *In Dubious Battle*, in *Novels and Stories, 1932-1937.*

16. Warren French, "Introduction," in *John Steinbeck* (New York, Twayne, 1961), xxvii. This work was one of the very first and remains one of the best critical studies of Steinbeck's works.

17. The Arvin Camp was one of fifteen such "demonstration" camps in California established by the Resettlement Administration and its successor organization, the Farm Security Administration. Twenty-five camps had been proposed for California, but conservative opposition in Congress and local opposition from the Associated Farmers and from local populations ensured that the camp system would only meet the needs of a small fraction of the state's migrant labor population.

18. For more on Collins's detailed weekly, sometimes bi-weekly reports see Benson, *True Adventures of John Steinbeck*, 342-46, and Benson's article "'To Tom Who Lived It': John Steinbeck and the Man from Weedpatch," *Journal of Modern Literature* 5 (April 1976): 151-210. Collins's reports provide the basis for Steinbeck's coverage of the Weedpatch Camp in the novel, and Collins would become a key consultant for the film adaptation of the novel.

19. Cues for pagination are from Steinbeck, *The Harvest Gypsies*, in *The Grapes of Wrath and Other Writings, 1936-1941.*

20. Charles Wollenberg addresses this racialist dimension of Steinbeck's thinking in his introduction to *The Harvest Gypsies*, xi–xii, and also reminds us (xii) that the new "Okie" migrants were actually less disposed to organizing against California agribusiness than Mexican and Filipino workers had been.

21. Carey McWilliams, *Factories in the Field: The Story of Migratory Farm Labor in California* (Boston: Little, Brown, 1939).

22. Kevin Hearle makes this suggestion in his essay "These Are American People: The Spectre of Eugenics in *Their Blood Is Strong* and *The Grapes of Wrath*," in *Beyond Boundaries: Rereading John Steinbeck*, ed. Susan Shillinglaw and Kevin Hearle (Tuscaloosa: University of Alabama Press, 2002), 243–54, esp. 248.

23. Company housing and stores are discussed in the third of the articles in *The Harvest Gypsies*, 1000–1005.

24. In a letter to George Albee in 1936 Steinbeck wrote: "the labor situation is so tense just now that the *News* is scared and won't print the series" (*LL* 132).

25. Steinbeck to George and Anne Albee, January 11, 1937 (*LL* 133).

26. *Of Mice and Men*, in *Novels and Stories, 1932–1937*, 797–878; quotation, 807. Candy, the old ranch hand in the novella, also buys into the dream of independent proprietorship.

27. Cue for pagination is from "The Leader of the People," in *The Grapes of Wrath and Other Writings, 1936–1941*.

28. Robert DeMott, "Introduction," in *John Steinbeck, Working Days: The Journals of "The Grapes of Wrath*," ed. Robert DeMott (New York: Viking Penguin, 1989), xxxix.

29. See *John Steinbeck: Working Days*, quotation, 93.

30. The exchange between the Joads and the Wilsons (from Kansas), whom they meet on the road, about the differences in regional speech patterns is an excellent example of Steinbeck's attention to this matter; see *The Grapes of Wrath* in *The Grapes of Wrath and Other Writings, 1936–1941*, 352.

31. For a useful discussion of the structure of the novel see the first major book-length work of Steinbeck criticism: Peter Lisca, *The Wide World of John Steinbeck* (New Brunswick, N.J.: Rutgers University Press, 1958), 144–77.

32. Louis D. Owens, *The Grapes of Wrath: Trouble in the Promised Land* (Boston: Twayne, 1989), 45. Notably, Owens identifies only four of Steinbeck's five layers.

33. Of course, the nonteleological thread does not weave its way through the novel with absolute seamlessness, as it is Jim Casy who, just prior to his death, clearly articulates the role of California's large growers in unethically setting wage levels to maximize profits and thereby consciously starving migrant families.

34. Ma Joad's speech in the movie draws on a passage from chapter 28 of the novel, p. 660.

35. Quotation from DeMott, "This Book Is My Life," 173. See Peter Lisca's good introduction to the novel's biblical layer in *The Wide World of John Steinbeck* (New Brunswick, N.J.: Rutgers University Press, 1958), 169–71; and four essays in Michael J. Meyer, ed., *The Grapes of Wrath: A Reconsideration*, 2 vols. (Amsterdam and New York: Rodopi, 2009): Christine Marie Hilger, "Sacred Path: Considering 'Road' as Religious Image in *The Grapes of Wrath*," 73–98; Kelly MacPhail, "'He's—a kind of man': Jim Casey's Spiritual Journey in the Grapes of Wrath," 99–127; A. Gilmore, "Biblical Wilderness in *The Grapes of Wrath*:

Steinbeck's Multi-layered Use of the Biblical Image," 129–47; and John Clark Pratt, "Religion in *The Grapes of Wrath*: A Reader's Guide," 149–59.

36. I am indebted to my western American history students for their insightful discussions of the novel's layers, and particularly to Rachel Rinn, for her attention to the "dignity layer."

37. I offer this exploration of a multifaceted fourth regional layer along with my admission of failure in the ongoing effort to delineate all five of Steinbeck's layers in the novel.

38. In the movie version it is Muley Graves who recites these lines in a series of flashbacks when in the company of Jim Casy and Tom Joad.

39. For more on how regional identity can form through opposition to outside forces see Clyde A. Milner II, "The View from Wisdom: Four Layers of Regional Identity," in *Under an Open Sky: Rethinking America's Western Past*, ed. William Cronon, George Miles, and Jay Gitlin (New York: Norton, 1992), 203–22; and David M. Wrobel, *Promised Lands: Promotion, Memory, and the Creation of the American West* (Lawrence: University Press of Kansas, 2001), 185–94.

40. This summary of Mitchell's novel and quotation from her speech are drawn from Rick Wartzman's coverage in *Obscene in the Extreme: The Burning and Banning of John Steinbeck's* The Grapes of Wrath (New York: Public Affairs, 2008), 41–48; quotation, 48.

Carey McWilliams. Courtesy of Will Connell, Jr.

CHAPTER FIFTEEN

Carey McWilliams, California, and the Education of a Radical Regionalist

Michael C. Steiner

In early September 1931 New York–based critic Edmund Wilson arrived in Los Angeles near the end of a cross-country tour as a roving reporter for *The New Republic*. During much of his brief stay in Southern California he was driven around the region by a twenty-six-year-old attorney, writer, and journalist, Carey McWilliams. Wilson's impressions of California, published the following year in *The American Jitters: A Year of the Slump*, were unrelievedly bleak: a series of sardonic send-ups lambasting the region's pasteboard architecture, shallow people, and religious quackery and ending with a grim portrait of San Diego as the nation's suicide capital and the "jumping-off place" for desperate migrants experiencing the bitter end of the American Dream.[1]

Nine years later, at the end of the Great Depression, Wilson's harsh view of the Golden State had softened slightly. In "The Boys in the Back Room" (1940), an essay on California writers, he recalled earlier remarks about the region by "a highly intelligent Los Angeles lawyer who had come to California from Colorado" and who had helped him to see Los Angeles as a "gigantic and vulgar" amusement center draining "the imaginative life of the State." But this 1940 diagnosis—influenced no doubt by that intelligent lawyer McWilliams—found a redeeming feature in California's cultural landscape. Describing the state's tradition of fiery left-wing protest, Wilson concluded that "the theme of class war" and "socialist diagnosis and the socialist hope" loomed larger in California than elsewhere in America. Arguing that "the labor cause has been dramatized with more impact by these writers of the Western coast than it has been, on the whole, in the East," he praised the "tradition of radical writing" that Californians like John Steinbeck and James M. Cain were "carrying on from Frank Norris, Jack London and Upton Sinclair." He traced this radical regional tradition to Henry George's crusade against the ruthless capitalist takeover of the state in the 1860s and 1870s and concluded, "California has since been the scene of some of the most naked and savage of America's labor wars. The McNamaras, Mooney and Billings, the Wobblies and Vigilantes, the battles of the longshoremen and the fruit-pickers, the San Francisco general strike—these are the names and events that have wrung blood and tears in the easy California climate."[2]

As Wilson realized, injustice seems to stand out more clearly in California than anywhere else in America. The haunting promise and beauty of the place inspire unrealistic hopes and angry protest. What might be called the fall from Eden theme—bitter disillusionment arising from dashed utopian dreams—has permeated California's history, and painful images of "blood and tears in the easy California climate" leapt to the national consciousness during the 1930s.[3] Commenting on California's volatile landscape on the eve of Sinclair's 1934 gubernatorial campaign, the editors of *The Nation* noted: "If ever a revolution was due, it was due in California. Nowhere has this battle between labor and capital been as wide spread and bitter, and the casualties so large ... nowhere has authority been so lawless and brazen; nowhere else has the brute force of capitalism been so openly used and displayed. . . . It was time for some sign of rebellion."[4]

Images of class conflict set against a breathtaking landscape, of trouble in paradise, riveted the nation's attention in the 1930s. A sense of flagrant injustice in a promised land now ripe for revolution has imbued a long-standing tradition of radical regionalism in California, and this expression peaked during the Great Depression. A host of artists and public intellectuals, including Dorothea Lange, Paul Taylor, Upton Sinclair, Lincoln Stephens, Woody Guthrie, Tillie Olsen, Nathanael West, Louis Adamic, and Will Rogers, called attention to glaring social and economic contradictions in the Golden State during this decade, but two fiery regionalists on the left loomed above them all.

Through their impassioned journalism and fiction, advocacy, and political organizing, John Steinbeck (1902–1968) and Carey McWilliams (1905–1980) expressed the deepest, most powerful and influential sense of place and protest in California during the 1930s. Intimately committed to the land and folk of California, both men were radicalized by events of the decade, and in bursts of creativity, peaking with the publication of *The Grapes of Wrath* and *Factories in the Field* within months of each other in 1939, Steinbeck and McWilliams sparked intense controversy and roused the national conscience with their enduring portrayals of injustice and want in a land of plenty. Although the two men never met, there are many parallels in their lives and their work that embody the best of left-wing and progressive regionalism. This chapter joins with chapter 14, David Wrobel's on Steinbeck's "Years of Greatness," to trace how each writer achieved that goal in the late 1930s and what their examples offer to readers and activists today.

AN AMERICAN PROPHET AND REGIONALIST ON THE LEFT

At first glance, regionalism seems a small part of McWilliams's varied career and monumental legacy. Usually remembered as the outspoken, long-term editor of the *Nation* and chronicler of California's quirky culture, he is now being celebrated for even more heroic feats. After years of relative eclipse, his star is on the rise as scholars rediscover his role as public intellectual, pioneer in race relations, precursor of the "new western" history, prescient environmentalist, and fearless advocate for civil rights. He is extolled as an inspiring "American prophet" in a recent insightful biography.[5] Fittingly described as "a sardonic Galahad, constant to the democratic grail," he is praised for his courageous defense of persecuted minorities, from unjustly condemned Mexican-American youths and relocated Japanese-Americans during World War II to blacklisted Communists and Civil Rights workers during the McCarthy and Nixon eras.[6]

Now honored as a patron saint of California history and acclaimed as a pioneer in grasping the dynamics of racism, the award-winning historian Kevin Starr has declared that "All efforts to understand California . . . are a series of footnotes to Carey McWilliams. . . . every writer on California becomes . . . a toiler in the vineyard that McWilliams first surveyed and planted." Asserting that "McWilliams is that rarest of chroniclers of a time and a place who gets more, rather than less, important with each passing decade," historian William Deverell simply concludes: "We are all his students." McWilliams was a versatile thinker and brilliant writer who could be both hilariously funny and fiercely outspoken, a champion for the underprivileged and a gadfly of the establishment. It is easy to understand how talk of McWilliams can, in Catherine Corman's words, quickly soar "into pure love-fest, ending with blanket endorsements."[7]

But love-fests and blanket endorsements do not cover every portion of his career. Scholars have not been so ready to celebrate his early years as a literary regionalist and contributor to the aesthetic regionalism that burgeoned during the interwar decades. His writing career was sparked in the mid-1920s by a Whitmanesque urge to trumpet the gaudy wonders of Los Angeles, his adopted city, over the rooftops of the world. Inspired by two seemingly antithetical mentors—Mary Austin and H. L. Mencken—young McWilliams began publishing zesty regionalist pieces in "little magazines" in the late 1920s. With their unlikely mixture of Austin's earth-bound mysticism and Mencken's smart-set cynicism, these youthful bohemian efforts seem to have little relation to the passionately engaged, politically charged masterpieces sparked, in his own words, by "the fires that burned so brightly—if briefly—in the best days of the 1930s."[8]

In a ten-year burst of Herculean productivity between 1939 and 1949, McWilliams wrote nine prophetic books devoted to searing public issues: *Factories in the Field* (1939), *Ill Fares the Land* (1942), *Brothers under the Skin* (1943), *Prejudice* (1944), *Japanese-Americans: Symbol of Racial Intolerance* (1944), *Southern California: An Island on the Land* (1946), *A Mask for Privilege: Anti-Semitism in America* (1948), *North from Mexico: The Spanish Speaking People of the United States* (1949), and *California: The Great Exception* (1949). These penetrating, impassioned works changed the American intellectual landscape. Written amid his frenzied public life as a crusading civil rights attorney and a progressive state official, all of which made him a lightning rod for right-wing fury, this spirited literary outpouring is rightly viewed as his major intellectual contribution from that era. Deeply probing yet widely accessible, imbued with a sense of injustice and ironic irreverence, these books stand as prose masterpieces. In many ways a potent blend of George Orwell, Studs Terkel, Howard Zinn, and Patricia Limerick at their best, they are a model of engaged radical writing, a continual wellspring of ideas and inspiration for contemporary historians, cultural critics, and public intellectuals.

In light of this monumental achievement McWilliams's early regionalist efforts might seem at cross-purposes with most of his career. As we have seen in many discussions through the chapters of this volume, the interwar upsurge in regionalism that helped launch McWilliams as a writer has often been dismissed as a narrow-minded, backward-yearning impulse during a national era of hard times. Whether chided as precious primitivists hiding from the world or indicted as dangerous fascists evoking the land and folk, western regionalists were pummeled from the center and the left of the political spectrum. Against this onslaught, it still seems treacherous for anyone on the left to be a regionalist.

Though he acknowledged regionalism's penchant for poisoning progressive ideals, McWilliams was nonetheless drawn to many of its values. Immersed in literary regionalism yet drawn to left-wing radicalism as the 1920s gave way to the Great Depression, he experienced the inner workings of what might be called the regional dilemma as profoundly as any public intellectual, then or now. Over a five-year period, from 1927 to 1932, he felt a tug-of-war between aesthetic and political commitments. He was torn between a sense of place that evoked focused literary expression and a passionate sense of injustice that compelled broad political action. The bright fires of the 1930s made literary regionalism—even the most sarcastic, bohemian versions—seem trivial. As one of his close friends put it, "the aesthetic hideaway was simply intolerable" during these cataclysmic years.[9]

Toward the end of his life McWilliams looked back over these pivotal years and his solution to the dilemma. "I got interested in this regional thing in part through Mary Austin," he recalled in a 1978 interview. "The Southern Agrarians were around and making noises.... And this was not quite like that, but it was the feeling that there should be more attention paid to western history, western writing.... It seemed ... as though this might develop into something important. It had the potential of that, but as the Depression deepened, regionalism was sort of pushed aside." "These literary interests swiftly receded as the Depression deepened," he wrote in his autobiography. "After 1932 I was writing almost exclusively about social issues, politics, and labor."[10]

Although McWilliams renounced literary regionalism in favor of left-wing activism early in his career, a deep-seated critical regionalism—a profound sense of the interaction of people and place and the need for social justice—remained the driving force and focal point of his best work. His magisterial books on California, the West, labor, and race relations are grounded in the immediate experiences of people in place—individuals and groups interacting in Los Angeles barrios and movie lots, San Joaquin Valley cotton fields and Orange County citrus groves, San Francisco's waterfront and Central Valley oil fields. This dynamic vision of everyday events and critical affection for the teeming land and life around him imparted a rare power and poignancy to his writing. By the late 1930s he had forged a distinctive radical-regional voice and became the most prominent spokesman for a national movement of alternative, pluralistic, and proletarian regionalism that found its strongest voices in California and the West.[11]

From his start in the mid-1920s as a bohemian aesthete debunking the vulgarity of mass culture, McWilliams had by the mid-1930s become a fierce champion of the downtrodden masses. By 1939, with *Factories in the Field* and its advocacy of statewide collectivization of all large-scale farms, he would be denounced by agribusiness as "Agricultural Pest No.1, worse than pear blight or boll weevil."[12] With that book's sweeping, passionate account of economic, racial, and environmental injustice, he found his radical regional voice. Championing civil rights and free speech and forging links between the abuse of nature and the mistreatment of minority groups, he directly inspired Cesar Chavez and other labor radicals of the mid- to late century and helped lay the groundwork for the countercultural and environmental movements of the 1960s and 70s that emerged from California. Drawing attention to capitalist exploitation of the land and of the Chinese, Japanese, Mexican, Filipino, and poor white migrants who worked it, he demonstrated the power of regionalism on the left for the 1930s and the present.[13]

How he achieved this radical regionalism and established his relationship to so many of the self-styled proletarian western regionalists featured in the present volume is but one chapter of an astonishingly active and productive life. In tracing the emergence of McWilliams's voice of regional dissent between 1922 and 1939 and evaluating its relevance for our own times, I now focus on crucial moments—conversions and epiphanies—that marked his evolution from an aesthetic to a politically charged regionalist.

THE EDUCATION OF RADICAL REGIONALIST

On March 18, 1922, seventeen-year-old Carey McWilliams arrived by train to Los Angeles from his home state of Colorado. He had just been expelled from the University of Denver after a disastrous St. Patrick's Day drinking spree, and this fall from grace had paralleled the collapse of his family's fortunes. His father, Jerry McWilliams, a prosperous rancher and state legislator from Steamboat Springs in northwestern Colorado, lost everything in the post–World War I agricultural depression, and when he died unexpectedly and penniless in 1921, Carey's mother and older brother moved to Los Angeles to restart their lives. Memories of a high-mountain, frontierlike childhood as well as of his father's destruction by indifferent economic forces would haunt him throughout his life and heighten his awareness of social injustice. But when he joined his mother and brother in Los Angeles in 1922, his mind soon became filled with more immediate impressions. In the 1920s, Southern California was bursting at the seams as the final gathering point for the western frontier. After his initial shock over the contrast between the panoramic beauty of his birthplace and the sprawling squalor of Los Angeles, young McWilliams embraced his new region with wonder-struck gusto.

His diary, begun on New Year's Day 1923 and continued through the 1970s, quickly filled with the high-spirited notes of an eighteen year old keenly sensitive to the exotic landscape and surging spectacle of his new place. Fittingly enough, the first two entries introduced themes that would occupy his life: the creation of regional identity and the dynamics of racial prejudice. The Rose Parade, he noted, "is a big advertising campaign . . . in such a superb setting, the Arroyo Seco Bridge hanging like a pattern of lace in the night!" And a few days later, after riding a streetcar back from his clerking job at the Los Angeles *Times*, he registered dismay at a blatant act of anti-Semitism.[14]

His first job, hunting down deadbeats who refused to pay their advertising bills to the *Times*, thrust him into the city's seamy underside. At the same time, courses he was taking at the University of Southern California (USC) introduced him to the region's literary cliques and budding intelligentsia. In nearly the same breath as describing streets swarming with "bums, drunks, fruiters and the scenes of God's creation," Carey also mentioned the joy of reading H. L. Mencken, Mary Austin, George Sterling, Robinson Jeffers, and Ambrose Bierce and of hearing Upton Sinclair speak to the USC Quill Club on literature and "the social revolution."[15] Within the space of a few weeks early in 1923, he first witnessed Sister Aimee Semple McPherson preaching at the Angelus Temple, expressed "the mad desire to laugh, to drink, to jazz around," and got "drunk as an idiot pauper" at the "Turkish Village,—danced with cabaret belle."[16]

A prolific wunderkind, who in Starr's words, "could type as fast as he could think and who thought faster than anyone," McWilliams began law school in 1926 even as he started running with his adopted city's first bohemian fast set.[17] He also began publishing scores of articles on literary regionalism in magazines across the country and launched his first book, a biography of Ambrose Bierce. The frenzied years between 1926 and 1929 marked the peak of his career as a literary rebel and self-conscious regionalist. A lively intellectual circle—described as a "sizzling sort of fellowship" including poet Hildegarde Flanner, architect Lloyd Wright, painter Kim Weber, book dealers Jake Zeitlin and Stanley Rose, writers Herbert Klein, John Fante, William Saroyan, and Louis Adamic—broadened his experience and expressive skills.[18] More distant literary mentors—Mencken, Austin, and Bierce—sharpened his fascination with capturing the quirks and varied textures of the American land and folk.

But most of all, the surging land and life of the region precipitated his creative genius. One of his earliest essays, simply titled "Los Angeles" and published in 1927, is imbued with a critical affection for the place. "Los Angeles is a harlot city—gaudy, flamboyant, richly scented, sensuous, noisy, jazzy," he wrote. "More and more the place takes on the aspect of a gigantic three-ring circus. . . . a mad world—a democratic brothel. . . . The very showiness of the place attracts, like an enormous scarlet beetle attracts or the huge amethyst ring of a bishop."[19] He soaked up the spirit of the place with boundless fervor, and twenty years later he would lovingly recall 1920s Los Angeles as "a great circus without a tent," where "ducks waddled along the streets with advertisements painted on their backs; six-foot-nine pituitary giants with sandwich board signs stalked the downtown streets; while thousands of people carrying Bibles in their hands and singing hymns marched in evangelical parades. With its peep shows, shooting galleries, curio shops, health lectures, and all-night movies, Main Street became a honky-tonk alley that never closed."[20]

And in one of the most powerful passages in American regional writing—a paragraph now etched in granite in the city's Pershing Square—McWilliams recounted how his exuberant if conflicted feelings about "this weirdly inflated village" changed one morning in 1929, after seven long years of exile "haunted by memories of a boyhood spent in the beautiful mountain parks, the timber-line country, of northwestern Colorado."

> I had spent an extremely active evening in Hollywood and had been deposited toward morning, by some kind soul, in a room at the Biltmore Hotel. Emerging next day from the hotel into the painfully bright sunlight, I started my rocky pilgrimage through Pershing Square to my office in a state of miserable decrepitude. In front of the hotel newsboys were shouting the headlines of the hour: an awful trunk-murder had just been committed; the district attorney had just been indicted for bribery; Aimee Semple McPherson had once again stood the town on its ear by some spectacular caper; a university of Southern California football star had been caught robbing a bank; a love-mart had been discovered in the Los Feliz Hills ... there was news about another prophet, fresh from the desert, who had predicted the doom of the city, a prediction for which I was morbidly grateful. In the center of the park I stopped to watch, a little self-conscious of my evening clothes, a typical Pershing Square divertissement: an aged and frowzy blonde, skirts held high above her knees, cheered by a crowd of grimacing and leering old goats, was singing a gospel hymn as she danced gaily around the fountain. Then it suddenly occurred to me that in all the world, there never was nor would there ever be another place like the City of the Angels. Here the American people were erupting, like lava from a volcano; here, indeed, was the place for me—a ringside seat at the circus.[21]

By creating equally loving descriptions of the region's dazzling natural landscape and of money-mad migrants mistreating it, McWilliams hoped that Southern Californians might someday learn to live up to the promise of their land and finally create the "great city on the Pacific, the most fantastic city in the world."[22] Written in 1946, this clear-eyed critical affection for a people and a place—this sardonic portrait of a weirdly wondrous region that deserves much more from the people who dwell in it—represents the zenith of his regional vision and stands as a hallmark of American regional writing.

McWilliams remembered his rocky pilgrimage across Pershing Square in 1929 as an epiphany and turning point in his sense of place and power as a writer. Yet it would take at least three more years after 1929—a period marked by an intensifying political consciousness and a widening geographical perspective—before he found his voice of radical regional dissent. By 1929 he had gained some fame as a regional tastemaker by publishing a host of articles on local color, folklore, and cultural regionalism throughout California and the West. Appearing in scores of magazines ranging from *Overland Monthly*, *The Frontier*, and *Southwest Review* to *The American Mercury*, *Harper's*, and *The Saturday Review of Literature*, many of these articles championed the clusters of writers and artists who proclaimed themselves "new regionalists" even as he mocked their nostalgic excesses. Deflating poisonous "myths of the West" that hover over the region "like a disembodied spirit murmuring strange incantations," he foreshadowed some work of the New Western historians by more than fifty years.[23]

Even such cynical regionalism would seem precious in light of the withering events of the 1930s. Even at its most biting moments, the critiques produced in his early cultural rebellion show little political content and suggest limited contact with the left. Yet his personal writing is sprinkled with seeds of doubt about the power of art to change what seemed to be an increasingly corrupt, unjust society. On August 23, 1927, the day Nicola Sacco and Bartolomeo Vanzetti were executed, twenty-two-year-old McWilliams interviewed Upton Sinclair in a dank cafeteria in Long Beach. He would later recall the sense of despair and deep anger toward the system that filled their conversation. A year later, in the summer of 1928, McWilliams and his close friend Louis Adamic, a Slovenian immigrant and writer, drove up the Pacific Coast from Los Angeles, each gathering writing material—McWilliams for his Bierce biography, Adamic for what would become *Laughing in the Jungle* (1932), his sprawling tragicomic treatment of the American scene. They stopped at Carmel to visit Robinson and Una Jeffers, and after walking the grounds of Tor House overlooking the rugged shoreline, both young writers were profoundly struck by Jeffers's bleak image of America as a "perishing Republic" and dark prophecy of a civilization-ending decade to come. For them, Jeffers's premonition marked a realization that the Lost Generation world of the 1920s was ending and would be "followed by a time of turbulence and upheaval."[24]

The year 1929 brought further political awakening and expansion of geographical interests. By July McWilliams was reading widely in the works of Lewis Mumford, Floyd Dell, Max Eastman, Waldo Frank, and Mike Gold and musing at length in his diary "about the nature of radicalism": "Isn't it just a welter of psychology—moods rather than ideals?" he wondered. "Or, to put it another way, radicals are born out of disgust with the world rather than from an intelligence as to what might be a better universe."[25] In October he traveled to New York City for the first time, beginning a complicated, life-long relationship with the place where he would ultimately live and work for the last thirty years of his life.

This first New York visit coincided with the stock market crash on October 29, 1929. But he was preoccupied with other things, especially with going through the galleys for his book on Bierce and with meeting as many of the city's radical intelligentsia as possible, through Adamic, who had just moved there. He enjoyed seeing Louis and his Greenwich Village dancer friend, Stella Sanders, and he was exuberant about the birth of his first book, but he was disillusioned with New York's intellectual scene, whose radicalism struck him as rootless, superficial, and infected with insufferable condescension toward anyone or anything west of the Hudson. He dismissed New York intellectuals who professed a Whitmanesque faith in "the redeeming efficacy of an indigenous culture" yet remained in "the dingy recesses of New York apartments" where they "prayed for the unregenerate hinterland."[26] The New York experience and train trip back home across the continent magnified his western pride and sense of place. Looking through train windows as he swept past Chicago, Kansas City, New Mexico, he dashed off rhapsodic prose poems remindful of Kerouac's work in a later era, to the great cities and sprawling immensity of the land. "The west, the west," he wondered, "what will come of the country here?"[27]

Back in Los Angeles, he began answering such questions about the West by intensifying his focus on the local scene and its vibrant cultural mix. He was also plagued by doubts about the social significance of his writing. In a journal entry, in nearly the same sentence as he noted the grotesque architecture along Wilshire Boulevard—"There is a great upwelling of puerile emotion and fancy; noisy, gaudy, blatant"—he also wondered about the larger importance of writing about such things: "Writers and artists should strive to be more in the foreground of events," he wrote. "They should write things that *do,*—that act. . . . To merely write is a decoration but of doubtful value. There is a certain pleasure in action and reaction."[28]

This deepening preoccupation with the regional spectacle combined with concern that he write things "that *do,*—that act" redoubled over the next year. Searching for meaning in the teeming, multiethnic city, he would write in his diary a two-page "Rhapsody on Entering the Arcade Building" with its kaleidoscope of "cafeterias, lunch counters and soda fountains, cheap haberdasher shops." In its wider setting the region comprised "a chimerical land," he concluded, "swift-changing, fluid, time-annihilating . . . such a raucous strip—and the great lands to the West."[29] "Frontier historians," he noted in a later entry, "should make a neat chapter out of Los Angeles, as the end of the trail." Anticipating the work of his friend Nathanael West in *Day of the Locust* (1939), he then noted, "Thousands coming here under such amazing conditions, it is not remarkable that confusion, and insanity, and great fear resulted."[30]

The urge to write radical, socially significant regionalism filled his chapbook *The New Regionalism in American Literature*, an essay of thirty-nine pages published late in 1930. A sweeping survey and stinging indictment of much of the regionalist movement, it also projected hope for a more critically engaged regionalism. Lambasting what Lewis Mumford, Bernard DeVoto, and Benjamin Botkin would decry as the besetting weakness of regionalism and its many backward-yearning enthusiasts, he complained that "the new regionalists reveal a typical modern tendency in their attempt to escape from the tumultuous present into a glamorous past. . . . In times so strenuous as ours, it is rather annoying to discover intelligent men devoting their talents to such tasks as listing the animals and plants in Oklahoma folk cures and noting, with infantile delight, the eroticisms in the folk-speech of taxi-drivers." The new regionalists, he argued, "have shown little interest in the proletarian heroes of the modern age." They "shun present problems with even greater dexterity" than the old local colorists, and they seemed to have only the most superficial connection to the land and life around them. "California, of course, has a poet for every realtor," he mocked. "Just how deep and abiding," he mocked, "is the infatuation of the regionalists for their land and its folk?"[31]

Despite such withering criticisms, this chapbook manifesto contained seeds for a more grounded, hard-hitting regionalism that anticipated calls for a "proletarian regionalism" by Constance Rourke, Meridel Le Sueur, and Benjamin Botkin.[32] In its most vigorous form, McWilliams stressed, regionalism gives the artist "familiarity with his environment," satisfies a thirst for community, and evokes critical affection for the land and life around him—a vibrant contrast to the intellectual sustenance of the typical eastern writer, trapped "in some cul-de-sac from which he emits faint and waspish denunciations of his native land."[33] He concluded that "despite its extravagant ambitions and occasional lapses in sense, regionalism has made Americans stand on their own legs," and beginning in 1930, he would forge a radical, politically charged regionalism that helped Americans understand the deeper workings of their strenuous times.[34]

His political education after 1930 was swift and dramatic. There is a world of difference, for example, between the flippant sarcasm of "Swell Letters in California," a send-up of sentimental art in 1930, and the fierce indignation of "Getting Rid of the Mexican," an angry account of Mexican deportations in 1933.[35] Of his shift from literary regionalist to labor journalist, he later recalled that "if anyone had said in 1929 when the Bierce book was published that a few years later I would be writing a book about farm labor in California, I would have said they were off their rockers.... But it all changed so fast."[36] Looking back, he concluded that "in the 1930s I became, and I have remained, an unreconstructed, unapologetic radical." More specifically, he explained, "I have never been a member of the Communist Party, but had I been accused of being a radical (western style), I would have readily pleaded guilty."[37]

Like Steinbeck, his contemporary, McWilliams was swept up in tidal waves of injustice and social ferment that reached their fiercest heights in California and the West. With its fervent strikes, migrations, and political extremism, California seemed at the center of things, and like Steinbeck, he found it impossible to ignore the upheaval and outrage surging around him. His respectable life as a lawyer for a blue-blood law firm and a part-time literary critic seemed pale and meaningless. "I'm quite discouraged about everything," he noted in his diary in August 1932. "I'm not pleased with my life, prospects, or achievements." Aroused by sweeping events and dissatisfied, even bored, with his personal and professional life, McWilliams turned his back on aesthetic regionalism and left his constraining marriage and lucrative Pasadena law practice in 1934 to devote himself to labor activism and legal advocacy for the working class.[38]

THE REGION AS COMMON GROUND AND RACIAL FRONTIER

The heightened political and racial awareness that filled McWilliams's diaries and letters between 1931 and 1934 represents the final stage in his growth as a radical regionalist. His expressive power seemed to soar with his rising social consciousness and decision to join ranks with the underdog—the submerged multitudes that Adamic would describe as "shadow America." Early in 1931 he discussed liberal politics with John Dewey and later drove Edmund Wilson around the region detecting signs of rebellion in the land. Through another friend, John Fante, a young Italian-American writer, he explored Bunker Hill's lower class and ethnic neighborhoods; he was introduced to the growing Filipino community in Los Angeles through emerging regionalist Carlos Bulosan. His long-standing attraction to the region's seething cultural landscapes extended into prisons, ethnic neighborhoods, fields, and factories. Doing legal work in a prison in 1932, he was struck by its mixed multitude—"Negroes laughing, Mexicans, whites." Visiting Boyle Heights on another legal errand, he noted, "You pass through the Japanese element.... Then you come to Mexican town. It is an amazing place ... a riotous disorder about everything."[39]

As early as 1932 his journal entries were peppered with distress about Mexican deportation, racial hate crimes, jobless friends pleading for money, and the brutal treatment of striking farm and factory workers across the state, often contrasting these struggles to California's stirring natural landscape. A scathing portrait of Depression-battered encampments in Riverside, for example, ends with the sight of "Temescal Canyon, the cottonwoods shimmering in the light," and a his litany of violent strikes sweeping the state concludes with a description of wildflowers "in riotous bloom."[40] His anger toward the system reached a crescendo in January 1934. "If the times don't change soon," he wrote, we'll be driven to desperate expedients.... You reach a point finally when you feel a responsibility to go out and bang tables, shout, and raise hell.... Here I am doling out help to a friend, and I have exactly $40.00 in the bank! The temptation at times is strong, to go out and *do something* for these people.... They are not to blame for being poor and jobless.... What they want is a set of ideas and a fight.[41]

This outburst marked a turning point. Beginning in 1934, he would devote himself to disturbing the established order; working as labor lawyer and investigative writer, he was willing to "bang tables, shout, and raise hell" to help underrepresented people fight for more equitable lives, to give Adamic's shadow America "a set of ideas and a fight." He began representing unions throughout the state—including Mexican-American citrus workers in Orange County in 1934 and 1936, potash miners in the Mojave Desert in 1935, rank-and-file studio hands in Hollywood in 1936, Filipino domestic workers in 1937. "No experience did more to shape my political point of view," he recalled, "than this brief engagement with labor. It pushed me beyond the liberalism of the period in the direction of a native American radicalism with which I could readily identify."[42]

In May 1935 he took a twelve-day back roads tour of the Sacramento Valley from Bakersfield to Salinas in a broken-down Dodge roadster with journalist Herbert Klein, who had just returned from Germany, reporting on the rise of Nazism. More than a year before Steinbeck's first tour of Central Valley migrant camps, McWilliams and Klein scoured the rural landscape, investigating labor relations and the rise of "farm fascism."[43] Their experiences interviewing agricultural workers of every race and ethnicity and witnessing their abject poverty and appalling working and living conditions culminated in a series of biting articles in 1936 that were rewritten and incorporated three years later into *Factories in the Field*. The 1935 tour was a deciding moment in his life. "Carey became a radical," Alice Greenfield McGrath recalled, "when he actually saw how migrant workers lived.... The sight of those people—that's what transformed Carey's life."[44]

In addition to writing a torrent of conscience-stirring articles and books, McWilliams threw himself into scores of political activities between 1934 and 1945, including campaigning for Upton Sinclair's ill-fated EPIC (End Poverty in California) run for governor in 1934, involvement in the Harry Bridges Defense Committee, intensive union organizing, headlining mass meetings and a national radio debate on the plight of migrant workers, defending victims of the 1943 Los Angeles Zoot Suit Riots and Japanese relocation, and serving four tumultuous years as the statewide director of the California Division of Immigration and Housing from 1938 through 1942.

By the mid 1940s, reflecting the racial ferment of war, he developed a farsighted vision of multicultural regionalism, of California and the West Coast as the national testing ground for an ethnoracially open democracy. In an essay originally entitled "The West Coast: Our Racial Frontier," he extolled the Pacific Coast and especially Los Angeles as the meeting place of four essential racial groups: White, Black, Asian, and Latino. Contrasting this four-way interaction to the black-white binary in much of the rest of the nation, he argued that "it is this basic difference in the pattern which serves to make the west coast our racial frontier. Here, in this one region, are represented important groupings of all the racial strains that have gone into the making of the American people."[45]

His positive image of the region as a multicultural seedbed where racial groups would develop complex patterns of fusion and separation is a tremendously fertile concept, one that built upon and moved beyond Adamic's pioneering work in ethnic pluralism during the same era. It is a vision that looks backward to Randolph Bourne's notion of a "Trans-National America" (1916) and forward to present-day concepts of the region as the framework of America's cultural diversity, as the "real geography" where groups of people interact in their daily lives, as, quite literally, the common ground where things—perhaps everything—takes place.[46]

McWilliams's vision of region as racial frontier and common ground had vast implications for regional theory. Two events in 1936 and 1937 signaled his firm commitment to a radical regionalism and reveal the roots of this multicultural perspective: his central role in the Western Writers' Congress in November 1936, and several impassioned letters written a year later, spotlight the final stages in his education as a radical regionalist on the left. In July 1936 he agreed to be the key Southern California organizer for a gathering of progressive and left-wing writers to be held four months later in San Francisco.[47] A regional offshoot of the first American Writers' Congress, held in New York City in April 1935, the Western Writers' Congress, like the Midwest Writers' Congress Meridel Le Sueur promoted at the same time in Chicago, was conceived as a forum to explore the relationship between western regional expression and left-wing protest. Part of the wider Anti-Fascist and Popular Front movements, the congress called upon "writers of America, particularly writers of the West, where the liberty-loving tradition of the pioneers is still fresh" to consider how their work could help workers and minorities in their struggle against the rising the "forces of reaction."[48]

From his office in the Arcade Building on Spring Street, McWilliams became a zealous promoter: calling local meetings, soliciting advice from organizers of the similar writers' congress in the Midwest, dashing off earnest invitations to all of the progressive writers and intellectuals he knew in Hollywood, academia, and elsewhere.[49] Some 250 writers from across the West attended the three-day congress, which opened at San Francisco's Scottish Rite Auditorium on November 13, 1936. A cross-section of speakers—including Harry Bridges, Upton Sinclair, Humphrey Cobb, Dorothy Parker, Donald Ogden Stewart, Ella Winter, Sara Field, William Saroyan, and Nathanael West—talked on topics ranging from labor and race relations to fascist and progressive trends in the film industry. The need for a radical western regionalism was an overarching theme.[50] San Francisco poet Kenneth Rexroth asserted, for example, that "insofar as we are poets, we are enemies to this society." Noting that "conditions for a regional renaissance are strong in the West today," he urged politically committed writers to reject blatant agitprop in favor of thoughtfully crafted art.[51]

McWilliams's speech to the congress, "The Writer and Civil Liberties," offered the most penetrating discussion of art and politics. Recounting his confrontations with "feudal despotism" and the brutal treatment of workers in company towns and factory farms throughout the state, he urged writers to go into the field to witness injustice and create art that would make a difference in the world. Scorning the notion of the "detached" artist, he evoked for his audience the socially engaged work of Thoreau, Dreiser, Dos Passos, and others. "Make no mistake," he declared. "Writers count; they are influential. And they must be convinced that in times such as these, even their silence, on occasion, is an influence which may cause further reaction."[52]

Two prominent Communist writers who could not attend gave ringing endorsements of proletarian regionalism in the West. Singing a paean to western literary mavericks Mark Twain and Jack London as rebellious antifascist archetypes, Mike Gold avowed: "I am a Western writer only by adoption . . . but I can feel the high beauty and terror and epic power of the region." Decrying the "spurious regionalism of the 'little' magazine" and "reactionary regionalism" of many southern and western writers, Meridel LeSueur called for a forward-looking "regionalism of class roots, class history." She enjoined progressive writers to nurture such consciousness in their own regions "to create stronger and richer roots for the growth of the creative personality, a wider and richer audience."[53]

McWilliams was in many ways the catalyst of this groundswell of left-wing proletarian regionalism in California and the West, and the final stage in his education as a radical regionalist occurred late in 1937, a year after the Western Writers' Congress. Early in October 1937 he wrote a remarkable letter to his close friend Louis Adamic, describing a momentous experience, an epiphany that he would reemphasize throughout his life. It had been nine years since their Carmel meeting with Robinson Jeffers that had been a harbinger of harsher, yet more electrifying, times. Adamic had dedicated his novel *Grandsons: A Story of American Lives* (1935) to McWilliams, who in turn had published a laudatory monograph, *Louis Adamic and Shadow America,* later that year. In this letter, however, McWilliams shifted direction and took his friend to task for being duped by the United Fruit Company into writing a book, *The House in Antigua* (1937), that could be read as a romanticized account of economic imperialism in Guatemala. Concerned that Adamic had lost his critical edge and fervor, McWilliams vehemently complained "there are no revolutionaries in America anymore! Don't you know that, following the new line, the Communists are defending the Constitution; draping themselves in the flag. etc. I confess that I'm somewhat intransigent, and that I like the old line better."[54]

After registering his disappointment with watered-down radicalism and the Popular Front, he recounted to Adamic what can only be termed a personal political epiphany. As a union lawyer, he had been asked to address 1,500 women walnut workers from a kaleidoscope of cultures gathered in a large hall in East Los Angeles. His words were translated into Armenian, Russian, Spanish, and Polish. "You should have been there," he wrote to Adamic, " to *feel* this thing: the excitement, the tension. And you should have watched some of those women as they got to their feet and tried to tell their experiences. . . . What profound meaning they conveyed! I felt, honestly, very weak, meaningless, and ineffectual." Many of the women held up fists that were swollen, bruised, and blackened from cracking walnuts by hand, and they complained that they would often slip on the scattered shells. A young, blond woman jumped up laughing, raced down the center aisle, bent over and lifted her skirt high to show McWilliams "a large black and blue mark right where you would expect it to be." The exuberant workers would applaud every time they heard the word "Organize!" "You felt stirred, profoundly stirred. . . . Such extraordinary faces!" he told his friend.[55]

This is the voice of radical regionalism at its best. If his revelation in Pershing Square in 1929 had expressed an astonishing love of place, his epiphany in 1937 among the East Los Angeles walnut workers illuminated his fervent urge for social justice. It was through such experiences in union halls, waterfronts, shops, and fields, in ethnic and working-class neighborhoods, among racial and ethnic groups of every type that McWilliams found the voice and vision that give *Factories in the Field* and the string of books that followed it their lasting power.

Factories opens with a recognition of the blunt contrast between sacred myths and profane realities in the Golden State. Beneath California's outwardly lovely landscapes and fabled romance lurks a "hidden history. . . . of untold human suffering," of terror and violence inflicted on the land and its people. Stretching from the era of Spanish rule to the present, McWilliams claims, the story of agriculture in California has been one of unending "theft, fraud, violence, and exploitation." The ongoing story of feudal and fascist rulers treating workers as beasts of the fields "is one of the ugliest chapters in the history of American industry." Asserting that in California "the mechanism of fascist control has been carried to further lengths than elsewhere in America," he dedicates his book to broadcasting the history and causes of this injustice and championing the rights of the 200,000 often homeless and starving migrant workers present throughout the state in 1939.[56]

His close attention to the Chinese, Japanese, East Indians, Armenians, Mexicans, Filipinos, and Dust Bowl migrants who made up this polyglot "army in tatters" is a vivid contrast to Steinbeck's all-white cast in *The Grapes of Wrath*. His sweeping claim that "before these workers can achieve a solution to the problems facing them, they will have to work a revolution in California landownership"—a revolution requiring the collectivization of corporate agriculture—may have been even more controversial than Steinbeck's evocation of a communal folk spirit among the oppressed.[57] With the publication of this brave book and those that followed it, McWilliams had achieved a forward-looking, pluralistic regionalism that inspires people today.

CONCLUSION

In 1965, fourteen years after leaving Los Angeles to become editor of the *Nation*, McWilliams looked back on his career from his vantage point in New York. Proudly asserting his regional credentials as the first person from west of the Mississippi—indeed the first person from west of the Bronx—to edit the hundred-year-old magazine, he then listed the most significant concerns of his life. "Somewhat in the order of their emergence," he wrote, "my special interests have been: organized labor and civil liberties, migratory farm labor, race relations, demagogic mass movement and, of course, all things related to California, its history, sociology, folkways, cults, population dynamics and politics—not to mention its coastline, mountain ranges, desert areas and lush valleys."[58]

A profound love for California—for its teeming culture, vibrant history, and matchless landscapes—was the driving force of his life as a writer and activist. A deep sense of place inspired his prose, and California provided a necessary foundation for observing the grounded experiences of social movements and people's lives. His best writing was informed by a hard-won love for the beauty and immense potential of the land itself, and his biographer concludes that "For McWilliams, the authority of the land, not the region's raffish society, was its chief source of hope."[59]

Often California's harshest critic, he could also be its strongest advocate. Keenly aware of the state's history of fiery protest, he drew support from California's "hidden spring" of "deeply-rooted indigenous radicalism which has been consistently 'socialist' and 'utopian' with the emphasis on social and racial equality."[60] For him, California was not only America's "racial frontier" and possible seedbed or common ground for a multiracial future, it was also a testing ground for pressing issues of migration, labor, civil rights, and the environment. Declaring that the state's population "includes every ethnic strain, every racial type, every social class," he stressed that "sequences that took decades to unfold elsewhere are often enacted here in a few years—you can see the process taking place before your eyes, as though in slow motion."[61]

Using California as a multicultural test case and drawing upon the state's socialist and utopian heritage, Carey McWilliams's radical regionalism serves as an example of a progressive pluralistic politics of place that might stir us today. His larger desire to forge "a program for a better America, a better civilization organically developed out of the soil and energy of this continent," could stand as a guiding principle for his time and ours.[62] Like many of the radical regionalists of his time, and many surveyed in this present volume, his ability to merge a deep-seated love of place with a passion for racial equality and social justice holds immense promise for the future.

NOTES

1. Edmund Wilson, *The American Jitters: A Year of the Slump* (1932; reprinted, Freeport, N.Y.: Books for Libraries Press, 1968). Chapters 12, 13, and especially 14, "The Jumping-Off Place," contain Wilson's 1931 comments on California.

2. Edmund Wilson, "The Boys in the Backroom" (1940), in Wilson's *Classics and Commercials: A Literary Chronicle of the Forties* (New York: Farrar, Strauss, 1950), 46, 47, 50–51.

3. See Don Mitchell, *The Lie of the Land: Migrant Workers and the California Landscape* (Minneapolis: University of Minnesota Press, 1996); Anne Loftis, *Witnesses to the Struggle: Imaging the 1930s California Labor Movement* (Reno: University of Nevada Press, 1998); and David Wyatt, *The Fall into Eden: Landscape and Imagination in California* (New York: Cambridge University Press, 1986).

4. "Upton Sinclair's Victory," *The Nation* 139 (September 12, 1934): 285–86.

5. Peter Richardson, *American Prophet: The Life and Work of Carey McWilliams* (Ann Arbor: University of Michigan Press, 2005).

6. See Daniel Geary, "Carey McWilliams and Anti-Fascism, 1934–1943," *Journal of American History* 89 (December 2003): 912–34, and Aaron Sachs, "Civil Rights in the Field: Carey McWilliams as a Public-Interest Historian and Social Ecologist," *Pacific Historical Review* 73 (May 2004): 215–48. The quotation is from Wilson Carey McWilliams's foreword to *Fool's Paradise: A Carey McWilliams Reader*, ed. Gray Brechin, (Berkeley, Calif.: Heyday Books, 2001), xvii.

7. Kevin Starr, "Carey McWilliams's California: The Light and the Dark," in *Reading California: Art, Image, and Identity, 1900–2000*, ed. Stephanie Bloom (Berkeley and Los Angeles: University of California Press, 2000), 15; William Deverell, "Privileging the Mission over the Mexican," in *Many Wests: Place, Culture, and Regional Identity*, ed. David Wrobel and Michael Steiner (Lawrence: University Press of Kansas, 1997), 235, 238; Catharine A. Corman, "Teaching—and Learning from—Carey McWilliams," *California History* 80 (Winter 2001–2002): 205.

8. In his "Steinbeck & the 1930s," 32-page typescript, Carey McWilliams Papers (Collection 1319), box 5, Department of Special Collections, Charles E. Young Research Library, University of California, Los Angeles.

9. Herbert Klein, personal interview, cited by Greg Critser in "The Political Rebellion of Carey McWilliams," *UCLA Historical Journal* 4 (1983): 37.

10. Carey McWilliams, "Honorable in All Things," transcript of an interview by Howard Gardener, July 10, 1978, McWilliams papers, Young Research Library; Carey McWilliams, *The Education of Carey McWilliams* (New York: Simon & Schuster, 1979), 66, 67.

11. On McWilliams and "proletarian regionalism" in California see Michael Denning, *The Cultural Front: The Laboring of American Culture in the Twentieth Century* (New York: Verso), 132–36, 226, 449–51.

12. He proudly cites the Associated Farmer's condemnation in *The Education of Carey McWilliams*, 77.

13. On McWilliams's pioneering work in environmental justice and his direct impact on Cesar Chavez see Sachs, "Civil Rights in the Field."

14. Date Book for 1923, entries for January 1 and January 5. The complete range of date books, 1923–70, is housed with the McWilliams papers, Young Research Library. Citations below supply only the dates of entries.

15. Date Book for 1923, entry for January 13; for the quotations, Date Book for 1924, entry for April 3.

16. Date Book for 1923, entries for January 28 through March 28.

17. Starr, "Carey McWilliams's California," 18.

18. Carey McWilliams, *Ambrose Bierce: A Biography* (New York: Boni, 1929). An insightful account of this radical Los Angeles subculture and McWilliams's central role in it is Daniel Hurewitz, *Bohemian Los Angeles and the Making of Modern Politics* (Berekley and Los Angeles: University of California Press, 2008). The quotation is from W. C. McWilliams's foreword to *Fool's Paradise*, xiii.

19. Carey McWilliams, "Los Angeles," *Overland Monthly and Out West Magazine* 85 (May 1927): 135, 136.

20. McWilliams, *Southern California: An Island on the Land* (New York: Duell, Sloan & Pearce, 1946), 133.

21. McWilliams, *Southern California*, 375–76.

22. McWilliams, *Southern California*, 377.

23. Carey McWilliams, "Myths of the West," *North American Review* 232 (November 1931): 432.

24. McWilliams, *Education of Carey McWilliams*, 50, 63. For another account of their 1928 meeting with Jeffers see Adamic, *My America, 1928–1938* (New York: Harper, 1938), 463–76.

25. Date Book for 1929, entry for July 9.

26. His disaffection with what he perceived be Adamic's newly gained, superficial New York radicalism shows in his Date Book for 1929, entries for October 19 and 30; his critique of New York condescension appears in "Localism in American Criticism: A Century and a Half of Controversy," *Southwest Review* 14 (July 1934): 426.

27. Date Book for 1929, entries for October 19, October 30, and what appears to be November 2.

28. Date Book for 1929, entry for December 12, emphasis underscored.
29. Date Book for 1930, entry for March 20.
30. Date Book for 1930, entries for March 20 and December 28.
31. McWilliams, *The New Regionalism in American Literature*, Chapbook no. 46. (Seattle: University of Washington Book Store, 1930), 23–24, 26, 10–11, 38–39.
32. Constance Rourke, "The Significance of Sections," *New Republic* 76 (September 20, 1933): 147–51; Meridel Le Sueur, "Proletarian Literature and the Middle West," in Henry Hart, ed. *American Writers' Congress* (New York: International, 1935), 135–38; Benjamin A. Botkin, "Regionalism and Culture," in Henry Hart, ed. *Writers in a Changing World* (New York: Equinox Cooperative Press, 1937), 140–57.
33. McWilliams, *The New Regionalism*, 35–36.
34. McWilliams, *The New Regionalism*, 32.
35. "Swell Letters in California," *American Mercury* 21 (September 1930): 42–47; "Getting Rid of the Mexican," *American Mercury* 28 (March 1933): 199–201.
36. "Honorable in All Things," McWilliams papers, Young Research Library.
37. McWilliams, *The Education of Carey McWilliams*, 320–21.
38. Date Book for 1932, entry for August 31. He touches upon this turning point in *The Education of Carey McWilliams*, 65–67, 85–86.
39. Carey McWilliams, *Louis Adamic & Shadow America* (Los Angeles: Whipple, 1935). Date Book for 1932, entries for March 2 and June 4.
40. Date Book for 1931, entry for October 24; Date Book for 1933, entry for October 13.
41. Date Book for 1934, entry for January 16, emphasis underscored. His personal life also hit rock bottom at this point. After separating from his wife and child late in 1934, he took a second train trip to New York and back and, brooding over his dissolving marriage asked, "How am I to be alive? Perhaps I am dead and dreamed this turgid dream.... Can I still go on living? And on what terms, and where?" Date Book for 1935, entry for March 12.
42. He outlines many of his labor-organizing activities in *The Education of Carey McWilliams*, 74–86; quotation, 85.
43. McWilliams, *The Education of Carey McWilliams*, 75.
44. Alice Greenfield McGrath, interviewed by Michael Steiner, Ventura, California, January 23, 2005. McGrath was McWilliams's close friend and associate for nearly thirty years, beginning in 1943, when he invited her, then a twenty-four-year-old social activist, to become the executive director of the Sleepy Lagoon Defense Committee.
45. The essay eventually appeared as "Critical Summary," in the special issue "Race Relations on the Pacific Coast," *Journal of Educational Psychology* 19 (November 1945): 194. Native Americans are absent from this spectrum, but they do feature in two of McWilliams's earlier books: *Factories in the Field* (1939) and *Brothers under the Skin* (Boston: Little Brown, & Co., 1943).
46. Randolph Bourne, "Trans-National America," *Atlantic* 118 (July 1916): 86–97. For a more recent version of McWilliams's image of the West and of region in general as multicultural cultural meeting ground see Patricia Nelson Limerick, "Region and Reason," in *All over the Map: Rethinking American Regions,* ed. Edward I. Ayers, et al. (Baltimore: The Johns Hopkins University Press, 1996), 83–104. The phrase and concept of "the real geography" comes from bioregionalist Barry Lopez's essay "Mapping the Real Geography," *Harper's Magazine*, November 1989, 19–24.

47. Barbara Chevalier to McWilliams, July 29, 1936, in "Material Relating to the Western Writers' Congress, 1936–1937," Carey McWilliams Papers, BANC MSS C-H 46, Bancroft Library, University of California, Berkeley.

48. "Call to a Congress of Western Writers," in "Material Relating to the Western Writers' Congress," McWilliams Papers, Bancroft Library.

49. Of particular interest is the exchange between McWilliams and Meridel Le Sueur in the summer and early fall of 1936 in which he asks her about the June 1936 Conference of Midwestern Writers held in Chicago, and she describes some of the proceedings, especially her opinions as well as Mike Gold's on the need for a proletarian regionalism: LeSueur to McWilliams, August 16; McWilliams to LeSueur, September 4 and again September 12; McWilliams to LeSueur, September 21, in "Materials Relating to the Western Writers' Conference," McWilliams papers, Bancroft Library.

50. Ella Winter, "Western Writers' Congress," *Pacific Weekly* 5 (November 30, 1936): 145–46.

51. Kenneth Rexroth, "The Function of Poetry and the Place of the Poet in Society," delivered at the 1936 Western Writers' Conference, in *World outside the Window: The Selected Essays of Kenneth Rexroth,* ed. Bradford Morrow (New York: New Directions, 1987), 6, 7.

52. "The Writer and Civil Liberties" was published in two issues of *Open Forum,* November 28, 1936, and December 28, 1936 (quotation, 3).

53. Mike Gold, "Why a Writers' Congress," *Pacific Weekly* 5 (November 9, 1936): 308; Meridel LeSueur, "Midwestern Writers' Conference," *Pacific Weekly* 5 (November 16, 1936): 320.

54. McWilliams to Adamic, October 3, 1937, McWilliams papers, Young Research Library.

55. McWilliams to Adamic, October 3, 1937. He also recalls the detail about the "large black and blue mark" in *The Education of Carey McWilliams,* 84.

56. McWilliams, *Factories in the Field: The Story of Migratory Farm Labor in California* (Boston: Little, Brown, 1939), 4, 6, 7.

57. *Factories in the Field,* 9, 324–25. For an account of the virulent response to Steinbeck's novel as well as to McWilliams's book and political activities see Rick Wartzman, *Obscene in the Extreme: The Burning and Banning of John Steinbeck's "The Grapes of Wrath"* (New York: Public Affairs, 2008).

58. "Personal Note," *Nation* 201 (September 1965): 25.

59. Richardson, *American Prophet,* 147.

60. McWilliams, *California: The Great Exception* (New York: Current Books, 1949), 189.

61. "Personal Note," 25.

62. McWilliams, *Louis Adamic,* 52.

Contributors

William Bevis is professor emeritus of English at the University of Montana, where he taught for nearly thirty years. He has published widely in the fields of regional theory and western American and Native American literature. His books include *Mind of Winter: Wallace Stevens, Meditation, and Literature* (University of Pittsburgh Press, 1988), *Ten Tough Trips: Montana Writers and the West* (University of Washington Press, 1990), *Borneo Log: The Struggle for Sarawak's Forests* (University of Washington Press, 1996), and a novel, *Shorty Harris, or The Price of Gold* (University of Oklahoma Press, 1999).

Bryna R. Campbell is a doctoral candidate and Lynne Cooper Harvey Fellow in American Culture Studies at Washington University in St. Louis, Missouri. A specialist on American art that engages issues of national and local identity, the 1930s, and political and social satire, she has recently helped curate an exhibition on Missouri radical painter Joe Jones and has given a number of guest lectures on midwestern regionalist art, radical art making in the 1930s, and the intersections between politics and aesthetics.

Robert L. Dorman is currently an associate professor of Library Science at Oklahoma City University and has taught American history at Harvard University, Brown University, the University of New Mexico, and the University of Oklahoma. He is the author of *Revolt of the Provinces: The Regionalist Movement in America, 1920–1945* (University of North Carolina Press, 1993) and *A Word for Nature: Four Pioneering Environmental Advocates, 1845–1913* (University of North Carolina Press, 1998). He was also a contributor to *The New Regionalism,* edited by Charles Reagan Wilson (University Press of Mississippi, 1998), and *Literature and Place, 1800–2000,* edited by Peter Brown and Michael Irwin (Peter Lang, 2006). His latest book is *Hell of a Vision: Regionalism and the Modern American West* (University of Arizona Press, 2012).

Jerrold Hirsch, Professor Emeritus of History at Truman State University, Kirksville, Missouri, is the author of *Portrait of America: A Cultural History of the Federal Writer's Project,* co-editor, with Tom Terrill, of *Such As Us: Southern Voices of the Thirties,* and co-editor, with Lawrence Rodgers, of *America's Folklorist: B. A. Botkin and American Culture.* He has written numerous journal articles and other contributions on the Federal Writer's Project, the history of American folklore studies, oral history, and disability history.

Sara Kosiba is an assistant professor of English at Troy University in Montgomery, Alabama. A specialist in midwestern literary regionalism, she is active in the Society for the Study of Midwestern Literature and an editorial board member of the *Dictionary of Midwestern Literature*, vol. 2. She has written about and published articles on Heartland writers as varied as Ernest Hemingway, Meridel Le Sueur, Dawn Powell, and August Derleth.

Shirley Leckie Reed, professor emerita of the University of Central Florida, is the author of *The Colonel's Lady on the Western Frontier: The Correspondence of Alice Kirk Grierson* (University of Nebraska Press, 1989), *Elizabeth Bacon Custer and the Making of a Myth* (University of Oklahoma Press, 1993), and *Angie Debo, Pioneering Historian* (University of Oklahoma Press, 2000). She co-authored, with William Leckie, *Unlikely Warriors: General Benjamin H. Grierson and His Family* (University of Oklahoma Press, 1998), and their collaboration resulted in his revised edition of *The Buffalo Soldiers: A Narrative of the Black Cavalry in the West* (University of Oklahoma Press, 2003). She has also co-edited, with Nancy Parezo, *Their Own Frontier: Women Intellectuals Re-Visioning the American West* (University of Nebraska Press, 2008).

Timothy Lehman is professor of history at Rocky Mountain College in Billings, Montana, where he teaches a variety of courses in western and environmental history. In addition to winning awards for his teaching, he has published articles on land reform, agricultural history, and wolves in the American West. His books include *Public Values, Private Lands: Federal Farmland Protection Policy, 1933–1985* (University of North Carolina Press, 1995) and *Bloodshed at Little Bighorn: Sitting Bull, Custer, and the Destinies of Nations* (The Johns Hopkins University Press, 2010), which was a finalist for the Great Plains Book Award and received the High Plains Book Award for Best Nonfiction.

José E. Limón is professor of English at the University of Notre Dame, where he also holds the Julian Samora Chair in Latino Studies and is Director of the Institute for Latino Studies. He has published in major scholarly journals and authored four books: *Mexican Ballads and Chicano Poems: History and Influence in Mexican-American Social Poetry* (University of California Press, 1992), *Dancing with the Devil: Society and Cultural Poetics in Mexican-American South Texas* (University of Wisconsin Press, 1994), *American Encounters: Greater Mexico, the United States, and the Erotics of Culture* (Beacon Press, 1998), and *Américo Paredes: Culture and Critique* (University of Texas Press, 2012). A new book, "Neither Friends, Nor Strangers: Mexicans and Anglos in the Literary Making of Texas," is in progress.

Jack Mearns is professor and chair of the Psychology Department at California State University, Fullerton. In addition to his work in clinical psychology, he is a scholar of mid-twentieth century cultural history. He is the literary executor for radical novelist John Sanford and is author of articles on Sanford and Robert M. Coates, as well as of a recent book, *John Sanford: An Annotated Bibliography* (Oak Knoll Press, 2008).

Stephen Mexal is assistant professor of English and comparative literature at California State University, Fullerton, and earned his Ph.D. from the University of Colorado, Boulder, in 2007. His teaching and research interests include critical theories of wilderness, the public sphere in the American Far West, race and critical race theory, urban space. masculinity studies, and hip-hop culture. His work has been published in *MELUS, English Language Notes, Studies in the Novel,* and the critical anthology *Eco-Man: New Perspectives on Masculinity and Nature* (University of Virginia Press, 2004). He is currently at work on a book-length project on liberalism and the discourse of wilderness in the nineteenth-century Western public sphere.

Julia Mickenberg is associate professor of American Studies at the University of Texas, Austin. She is the author of many articles on American radicalism, children's literature, and feminist radical protest. Her book *Learning from the Left: Children's Literature, the Cold War, and Radical Politics in the United States* (Oxford University Press, 2006) received prizes from the Society for the History of Children and Youth, the Children's Literature Association, the University of Texas Cooperative Society, and the Pacific Coast Branch of the American Historical Society. She is also co-editor, with Philip Nel, of *Tales for Little Rebels: A Collection of Radical Children's Literature* (New York University Press, 2008) and, with Lynne Vallone, of *The Oxford Handbook of Children's Literature* (2011). With support of a fellowship from the National Endowment for the Humanities, she is currently working on a manuscript entitled "The New Woman Tries on Red: Russia in the American Feminist Imagination, 1905–1945."

T. V. Reed is Buchannan Distinguished Professor of American Studies and English at Washington State University in Pullman. He has held Fulbright and Mellon fellowships and has been a visiting scholar at Rutgers University and at the Center for Cultural Studies of the University of California, Santa Cruz. His areas of research and teaching include interdisciplinary cultural theory, popular culture, digital culture, environmental justice, cultural studies, and the role of culture in social movements. His publications include *Fifteen Jugglers, Five Believers: Literary Politics and the Poetics of American Social Movements* (University of California Press, 1992) and *The Art of Protest: Culture and Activism from the Civil Rights Movement to the Streets of Seattle* (University of Minnesota Press, 2005). He is currently completing a book on 1930s proletarian novelist Robert Cantwell and another book on the social impact of new digital media. He is the web editor and manager of the matrix of sites culturalpolitics.net.

Michael C. Steiner is professor emeritus of American Studies at California State University, Fullerton, where since 1975 he has taught a wide range of courses on environmental history, folk culture, the built environment, regionalism, California, and the West. He has a won a national teaching and advising award from the American Studies Association in 2006, and has twice held a Distinguished Fulbright Chair (in Hungary in 1998–99 and in Poland in 2004). He has published prize-winning essays on Frederick Jackson Turner's sectional thesis and Walt Disney's Frontierland, and his books include three co-authored and co-edited volumes: *Region and*

Regionalism in the United States, with Clarence Mondale Steiner (Garland, 1988), *Mapping American Culture,* with Wayne Franklin (University of Iowa Press, 1995), and *Many Wests: Place, Culture, and Regional Identity,* with David Wrobel (University of Kansas, 1997).

Douglas Wixson is professor emeritus of English at the University of Missouri at Rolla and is currently a Visiting Research Scholar at the Harry Ransom Humanities Research Center at the University of Texas, Austin. A renowned expert on the American literary left, he has published scholarly articles on writers as varied as George Orwell, John Steinbeck, Thomas Hart Benton, Arna Bontemps, Paul Corey, Meridel Le Sueur, Williams Carlos Williams, Norman MacLoed, and Thornton Wilder. He has edited and written introductions to three of Jack Conroy's books; his own award-winning book *Worker-Writer in America: Jack Conroy and the Tradition of Midwestern Literary Radicalism* (University of Illinois Press, 1994) is widely cited. He has also published *On the Dirty Plate Trail: Remembering Dust Bowl Refugee Camps, 1938–1940* (University of Texas Press, 2007) and is working on a biography and social history, "From the Dry Lands: Sanora Babb, High Plains Novelist (1907–2005), Autoethnography and Literary Radicalism."

David Wrobel is Merrick Chair in Western American History at the University of Oklahoma. His books include *The End of American Exceptionalism: Frontier Anxiety from the Old West to the New Deal* (University Press of Kansas, 1993), *Promised Lands: Promotion, Memory and the Creation of the American West* (University Press of Kansas, 2002), and *Global West, American Frontier: Travelers' Accounts from the Nineteenth and Twentieth Centuries* (University of New Mexico Press, forthcoming 2013), as well as the co-edited volumes *Many Wests: Place, Culture, and Regional Identity,* with Michael Steiner (University Press of Kansas, 1997) and *Seeing and Being Seen: Tourism in the American West,* with Patrick Long and Earl Pomeroy (University Press of Kansas, 2001). He is currently working on two book projects: "The West and America, 1900–2000: A Regional History" (for Cambridge University Press) and "John Steinbeck's America." He co-edits two book series: The Modern American West (University of Arizona Press) and The Urban West (University of Nevada Press).

Index

References to illustrations appear in italic type.

Aberdeen, Wash., 255–56, 257, 269, 272–73
Abrahams, Roger, 143
ACA (American Contemporary Art) Gallery, New York City, 65, 73–76, 83n1, 85n35
Adamic, Louis, 312, 362, 363, 366, 368, 370
Addams, Jane, 21
Alexander, Steven, 74–77
Algren, Nelson, 21, 120, 130
Altgeld, John P., 21
America Is in the Heart (Bulosan): Allos as narrator of, 312, 325n31; Allos as worker in apple orchards, 313; Allos deems Communist party anti-Filipino, 319–21; Allos is warned about being a Filipino in California, 314; Allos on geography of fear, 315; Allos's first impression of California, 314–15; Allos's liberal anticommunism, 318–19; Allos's faith in America, 315; authors who inspire Allos, 312; and Bulosan's changing relationship to the California landscape, 309–10; as Bulosan's most significant work, 304; California as site for emergence of political consciousness, 314; fictionalized ethno-proletarian biography, 311, 325n28; and government dedicated to positive right to access, 321; life story of common Filipino immigrant, 312; Marxism critiqued in, 317–18; and Salinas lettuce strike of 1934, 316. *See also* Bulosan, Carlos
American Contemporary Art Gallery (ACA) in New York City, 65, 73–76, 83n1, 85n35

American Folkways series (Caldwell), 39–40
American Jitters, The (Wilson), 353
American Mercury (Mencken, ed.), 142
American play-party, 141
"American Way, The" (Le Sueur), 35–38; and call for regionalism, 37–38; "captains of industry" as villains, 36, 37; enduring questions raised in, 36–37; and failure of America's promise in Midwest, 36; and prairie woman image, 38; as tribute to Midwest, 38–39; and Whitman's civic call to arms, 35–36
American Writers' Congress: and Botkin, 135, 150, 151; and Herbst, 61; and Le Sueur's address of 1935, 22, 39, 42n1, 81, 82; and Le Sueur's promotion of Midwest chapter, 32
Anaconda Copper Mining Company, 212, 216
And Still the Waters Run (Debo), 173
Anvil, The (magazine): and Babb, 127; edited by Jack Conroy, 120; merger with *Partisan Review*, 32, 33–34; short-lived magazine for radical regionalism, 22
Appeal to Reason (Wayland), 87, 95, 124
Arts of the South (painting by Benton), 76
Arvin Sanitary Camp for migratory laborers, 125, 334–35, 337, 349n17
Auden, W. H., 293
Austin, Mary: critical response to, 7–8; on decentralization, 4; example of interwar regionalism, 155n13; on "feel of the purposeful earth," 6; interest in Indian cultures, 165; and McWilliams, 356, 357;

Austin, Mary (*continued*)
  mystical bond with Native Americans, 103

Babb, Alonzo (grandfather), 116, 118, 124
Babb, Anna Jeanette ("Jennie") Parks (Mrs. Walter Babb), 115, 116, 117–18, 119
Babb, Sanora, *110*; and affinity for Native Americans, 117; and Alonzo's influence on, 124; arrest of in refugee strike, 128; background of, 88, 89, 111–12; birth of, 116; chilly reception by publishers, 130; and CPUSA, 123; critical response to, 8–9; and death threats to, 128; early years of, 112; education of, 119; and experience with 1934 storm, 121–22; family life of, 116–19; FBI scrutiny of, 130; and Great Depression, 114; growing up in central High Plains, 113–14; and journalism career in Los Angeles, 120; and leftist friends of, 120; legacy of, 131; literary influences on, 112–13; literary radicalism of, 127; magazines contributed to, 127; marriage to Howe, 130; and "Okies," 126; and progressive causes of, 122–24; radical regionalist voice of, 112; rejection of refugee novel, 129; writing inspired by dysfunctional family, 118. *See also* Babb, Sanora, works of; High Plains as bioregion
Babb, Sanora, works of: *Cry of the Tinamou*, (short stories), 112; *Dark Earth and Other Stories*, 112; *Lost Traveler*, 112, 119, 129; "The Old One" (short story), 121; *Owl on Every Post*, 112, 119, 129; *Told in the Seed* (poems), 112. See also *Whose Names Are Unknown*
Babb, Walter (father), 116–17, 118, 119
Barber, Benjamin, 10
Baron, Herman, 74, 76
Beaver Men, The (Sandoz), 105
Benton, Thomas Hart, 23, 65, 66, 74–75, 82, 83
Berlin, Isaiah (British philosopher), 306–307

Bernhard, Andrew (Herbst's brother-in-law), 49
Bevis, William, 207, 229
Bingham, George Caleb, 76
Bioregionalism, 113, 247
Bizzell, William Bennett, 142, 146, 151–52, 153
Blivin, Bruce, 55
Blowout grass of Sand Hills, 93, 106
Bohrod, Aaron, 23, 67
Botkin, Benjamin A., *134*; as academic folklorist, 136; and American play-party, 141, 142; background of, 135–36; and Brandt, 142, 152, 153; on complementary approaches of regional and proletarian writers, 150–51; as controversial figure at OU, 153; and emergence of new classes, 143; and FBI file on, 152; and folklore and popular media, 145, 146; on *Folk-Say* and *Space*, 149; on his passion for beliefs, 152; and HUAC, 153; leftist leanings questioned by friends, 152; as leftist theorist of folklore *and* regionalism, 135; legacy of, 153–54; and Le Sueur, 150; and Living Lore units in FWP, 153; and Louise Pound, 135, 141, 153; manifesto of 1929, 137, 138–39; and Marxism, 141; McWilliams's response to *Folk-Say*, 144–45; National Folklore Editor of FWP, 152, 153; and new beginnings, 142; and New Regionalism, 4, 5; and Oklahoma as literary material, 141–42; and pessimism toward Oklahoma culture, 149; and regionalism, 29–30, 148; regard by leftist writers, 149–50; and rejection of legitimacy of radical regionalism, 151; relevance to regionalism ignored, 137; response to Bizzell's criticism, 151; and response to McWilliams, 145; types of regionalists identified by, 147–48; and University of Oklahoma, 88; on unwritten folk literature, 145. *See also* Botkin, Benjamin A., works of
Botkin, Benjamin A., works of: "Folk in Literature, The" (1929 manifesto), 137,

138–39; "Folklore and Culture," 152–53; "Regionalism and Culture," 150–51; "Regionalism: Cult or Culture?" 35; *Space* (magazine), 148–49; "We Talk about Regionalism—North, East, South, and West," 5, 147–48. *See also* Botkin, Benjamin A.; *Folk-Say* series
Bottle Dancer (painting), 79
Bourne, Randolph, 368
"Boys in the Back Room, The" (Wilson), 353
Brandt, Joseph: and Botkin, 142, 152, 153; and Debo, 171–73; as first director of OU Press, 142, 165; Lottinville as OU replacement for, 176; move to Princeton University Press, 173. *See also* Debo, Angie Elbertha
Bray, Kingsley M., on Sandoz, 106–107
Breadloaf Writers' Workshop, 218, 222
Brooks, Homer, 192–93
Brothers under the Skin (McWilliams), 356
Brown, Dee, 241
Brown, John, 87, 292
Brownell, Baker, 212, 219–20
Bryan, William Jennings, 87, 94
Bryant, Louise, 205
Bulosan, Carlos, 302; assertion that Filipinos "like America," 317; birth of, 304, 323n8; claim that writing is response to exploitation in American West, 314, 326n37; and Communist Party, 318; death of, 311; and disillusionment with progressive organizations, 316–17; editor of *New Tide*, 309, 324nn21–22; essay in contrast to Rockwell painting, 304–306; as Filipino immigrant in 1930, 309, 324n19; and Filipino president Quezon, 311; formative influences listed by, 313; as labor activist, 313; liberalism of, 318; and McCarran-Walter Act (1952), 310, 324n26; and McWilliams, 366; and Mensalvas's defense fund, 310–11; and negative vs. positive liberties, 307; obsession with Marxist literature, 312; and pervasive aestheticism, 317–18; and Philippines as influence on, 308–309, 324nn17–18; political liberalism of, 306–307; and political potency absent in American literature, 312–13; poor health of, 311, 313, 326n34; and rejection of nation-state as theme, 307–308; and Roosevelt's Four Freedoms speech, 303–304; and sense of place and politics, 304–306; slums of Los Angeles contributing to radicalism of, 313–14; and transnational liberalism of the left, 279, 306, 308, 321–23. *See also* Bulosan, Carlos, works of

Bulosan, Carlos, works of: "Freedom from Want" essay, 304–305, 323n7; "I Want the Wide American Earth," 304; "Laughter of My Father, The" (short story), 304; *Letter from America*, 304; "Letter to a Filipino Woman," 321–22. See also *America Is in the Heart*; Bulosan, Carlos; "Freedom from Want"
Bury My Heart at Wounded Knee (Brown), 241
Butte, Mont., 205, 216

Caldwell, Erskine, 39–40, 259, 291, 312
Calhoun, Craig ("Radicalism of Tradition"), 2, 27
California: focal point for utopian dreams and radical dissent, 277; potential for revolution in 1930s, 353–54; progressive regionalists of, 278; radicalism in, 277–78; and radical regionalism during Great Depression, 354; E. Wilson's bleak view of in 1931, 258–59, 353. *See also* Bulosan, Carlos; McWilliams, Carey; Sanford, John; Steinbeck, John
California (McWilliams), 356
Call for Revolution and Universal Brotherhood, A (mural by Orozco), 72
Calverton, V. F., 8, 29
Campbell, Bryna, 23, 65
Cantwell, Robert, 252; analysis of Aberdeen as producer of radical novelists, 255–56; background in Pacific Northwest, 253–54, 274n1; birth of, 256;

Cantwell, Robert (*continued*)
Communist Party candidates endorsed by, 271; death of, 272; family surrounded by cycles of boom and bust, 256–57; and father's death, 257; fiction-writing focused on Northwest, 254–55; ghost writer for Filene's autobiography, 271; and Henry James as literary master, 258; and IWW, 257; and Marxist influence of literary intellectuals, 259; move to New York in early years of Depression, 258–59; proletarian literary movement, support for, 259–60; as *Sports Illustrated* editor, 272; strong vice of labor-centered literary left, 270; threatened as strike sympathizer, 271–72; and *Time* magazine, 272; and unfulfilled plans for *roman à clef*, 272, 275n22; and Whittaker Chambers, 272, 275n23. See also Cantwell, Robert, works of
Cantwell, Robert, works of: *Hidden Northwest, The*, 272; "Hills around Centralia," 257; *Laugh and Lie Down*, 257–58. See also Cantwell, Robert; *Land of Plenty, The*
Capital City (Sandoz), 99–100, 102
Capra, Frank, 13, 295
Castle, The (Kafka), 99
Cather, Willa, 88, 112
Ceremony (Silko), 232
Cerf, Bennett, 128–29
Chadsey, George, 70, 72
Chambers, Whittaker, 272, 275n23
Chametzky, Jules, 31
Chase, Stuart, 214
Cheyenne Autumn (Sandoz), 104–105
Choctaw Indian research. See under Debo, Angie Elbertha
CIO (Congress of Industrial Organizations), 270
Clements, Frederick, and classic study of prairie grassland, 93, 214
Cobain, Kurt, 272–73
"Cold Night" (Paredes), 189
Collier, John, 165, 171, 175, 230, 234–35, 243

Collins, Tom: and Arvin Sanitary Camp for migratory laborers and relationship with Steinbeck, 334–35, 349n17; and Babb as assistant to, 111, 124–26, 127; background of, 125–26; FSA administrator, 111
Colman, Louis, 255
Coming Struggle for Power, The (Strachey), 99
Commonwealth College, Mena, Ark., 76–77
Communist Party of the USA (CPUSA), 13, 77–78, 122–23, 255, 292, 332–34. See also *New Masses* (CPUSA magazine)
Conroy, Jack: chilly reception by publishers, 130; critical response to, 8; editor of *The Anvil*, 120; and Joe Jones, 71–72; mentioned, 61, 147; and as proletarian regionalist, 22; and *Worker-Writer in America*, 30
Contempo (magazine), 120
Cooper, Alfred (grandfather), 159
Copland, Aaron, 13
"Corn Village" (Le Sueur) (short story), 35
Cowley, Malcolm, 22, 150, 259
Cow People (Dobie), 197, 199
CPUSA. See Communist Party of the USA
Crazy Horse (Bray), 106
Crazy Horse (Sandoz), 103–104
Creek Nation, Debo's research on, 173–74
Crèvecoeur, J. Hector St. John de, 230
Crichton, Kyle, 8
Critical regionalism, 6, 14, 17n12, 153
Cronon, William, 14
Crusaders (Le Sueur), 29, 41–42, 46n57
Cry of the Tinamou, The (Babb) (short stories), 112
Cultural Front, The (Denning), 270
Cup of Gold (Steinbeck), 329
Curry, John Steuart, 5, 23, 74

Dainotto, Roberto, 10, 140–41
Dale, Edward Everett: Debo's critique of, 163–64; as inspirational teacher, 160–61, 163; as kindred soul to Debo, 161; letters of introduction in D.C. for

Debo provided by, 164; misogyny of, 172; rejection of Debo instructorship by, 172; Turner as mentor to, 160; as Wardell's mentor, 172. *See also* Debo, Angie Elbertha

Dark Earth and Other Stories, The (Babb), 112

Davis, H. L., 205–206

Davis, Stephen L., 195, 196, 200–201

Dawes Commission: and Foreman, 164–65; high crime rates in Choctaw republic reported by, 166, 168, 180n37

Day of the Locust, The (West), 293, 364

Death of Jim Loney, The (Welch), 232

Debo, Angie Elbertha, *158*; actual story of Five Tribes uncovered by, 168–69; awards won by, 167, 176; background of, 158–59; birth of, 159; and Brandt, 171–73; and Choctaw Nation research by, 164–67, 179n27; and Creek Nation abuses uncovered by, 173–74; and Dale, 161, 163–64, 172; and Dawes Commission reports, 166, 168, 180n37; death of, 177; employment opportunities during WWII, 176, 182n79; epitaph of, 177; and gender injustice, 162–63, 167, 171–72; *Indians, Outlaws and Angie Debo* (PBS documentary), 177; legacy of, 177; and love of land, 159–60; and Meriam Report on Indian affairs, 164, 180n28; *Oklahoma: A Guide*, introduction by censored in, 174–75, 182n75; and Porter quotation, 174; prominent persons exposed as Indian exploiters, 170, 172; replaced at West Texas after earning Ph.D., 167; retirement of, 176–77, 183n82; and return to Marshall to write, 167–68; and "spirit of Oklahoma," 160, 167; and University of Chicago, 161–62; and West Texas State Teachers College, 163; and WPA work of, 174. *See also* Dale, Edward Everett; Debo, Angie Elbertha, works of

Debo, Angie Elbertha, works of: *History of the Indians of the United States*, 176; *Oklahoma: A Guide*, 174–75, 182n75; *Prairie City*, 175; *Rise and Fall of the Choctaw Republic*, 167; *Road to Disappearance*, 174; *And Still the Waters Run*, 173, 177; *Tulsa*, 175. *See also* Debo, Angie Elbertha

Debo, Edward (father), 159–60

Debo, Edwin (brother), 159

Debo, Lina Cooper (Mrs. Edward Debo) (mother), 159, 161–62, 170, 179n8

Debs, Eugene, 21, 60, 64, 124, 253, 288

Denning, Michael, 3, 12–13, 270, 292, 304. *See also* Proletarian regionalism

Desert Land Act (1877), 114

DeVoto, Bernard, 9, 218, 224–25

Dewey, John, 4, 15, 366

Dickstein, Morris, 12–13, 14

Disinherited, The (Conroy), 61

Dobie, J. Frank, *185*; anti-Roosevelt views in early 1930s, 194; background of, 88, 185–87; and Cambridge University, 196; death of, 197; education of, 188; and FBI file on, 196; firing by UT, 196; and HUAC, 196–97; and King Ranch, 200; and leftward political turn of, 194–96, 199; legacy of, 197; and Mexican Americans, 196; as "Mr. Texas," 189, 196; and new regionalism, 14; and Paredes, 90, 200–201; as perpetrator of racist histories, 201, 203n45; racial integration advocated by, 195, 200–201; and return to Texas roots, 197, 199; and southwestern Texas, 189; and teaching regional folk culture, 188–89; transnational dimension of, 187; and WWI, 188. *See also* Dobie, J. Frank, works of

Dobie, J. Frank, works of: *Cow People*, 197, 199; *Tongues of the Monte*, 196; *Voice of the Coyote, The*, 196. *See also* Dobie, J. Frank

Dorman, Robert, 88, 93, 170, 218–19

Dubuque Dial (magazine), 22

Dust Bowl: Babb's experience with 1934 dust storm, 121; and dispossessed farmers, 122. *See also* FSA (Farm

Dust Bowl (*continued*)
  Security Administration); Jones, Joe, and Dust Bowl themes; Steinbeck, John

Eliade, Mircea, 10
Ellison, Ralph, 88
Emerson, R. W., 148
Endore, Guy, 295
Erdrich, Louise, 232
Ethan Frome (Wharton), 246
Executioner Waits, The (Herbst), 48, 58–59
Exile's Return (Cowley), 22

Factories in the Field (McWilliams): articles on "farm fascism" incorporated into, 367; compared with *The Grapes of Wrath*, 279–80, 329, 355, 372; publication of, 356; radical regional voice found in, 358, 371–72
Fante, John, 120, 126, 312, 366
"Farmer Looks Ahead, The" (Herbst), 47
"Farmers Form a United Front, The" (Herbst), 47, 55–56
Farm Security Administration (FSA): and Babb, 111, 124, 128, 129, 131; founding and function of, 111, 124–25. *See also* Resettlement Administration
Farrell, James T., 61
Federal Theatre Project, 7, 122
Federal Writers' Project (FWP), 151, 152, 153
"Feet in the Grass Roots" (Herbst), 47, 52, 53, 54, 63n17
Ferber, Edna, 13
Fey, Harold, 232–33
Filene, E. A., 271
Fisher, Vardis, 8, 206
Fixx, Calvin, 258
Flanagan, Hallie, 6–7
"Folk in Literature, The" (1929 manifesto) (Botkin), 137, 138–39
Folk-Say series (Botkin): *Folk-Say* (1930), 145–46; *Folk-Say: A Regional Anthology* (1929), 142, 143–44; *Folk-Say: A Regional Miscellany* (1929–32), 140; *Folk-Say IV: The Land Is Ours* (1932), 146–47
Food, Inc. (Kenner) (film), 247

Ford, John, 13
Foreman, Grant, 164–65
Four Freedoms speech by Roosevelt, 303–304
Frankfurter, Felix, 12
"Freedom from Want" (Bulosan): early example of Bulosan's liberalism, 304–305, 306; negative liberties replaced with positive ones, 307, 308, 322; and opportunity, 321; and President Quezon, 311–12
Freedom from Want (Rockwell), 304–305, 323n7
Frontier, The (magazine), 206, 234, 362
FSA. *See* Farm Security Administration
FWP. *See* Federal Writers' Project

Garza, Catarino, 187
George Washington Gómez (Paredes) (novel), 190–91, 192, 200
Geronimo: The Man, His Time, and His Place (Debo), 176
"Getting Rid of the Mexican" (McWilliams), 365
Gold, Mike, 50
Grandsons (Adamic), 370
Grapes of Wrath, The (Steinbeck): biblical themes of, 342–43; candidate for "Great American Novel," 343; compared with Babb's writings, 127, 131; construction of, 341; and controversy after publication, 340–41, 346–47, 355; critique of agribusiness in, 334; dedications of, 334; film adaptation, 327, 348n2; and *In Dubious Battle*, 331–32; layers of, 341–42; legacy of, 329; and Ma Joad's speech, 342, 350n34; matriarchal dimension of, 343; and Mitchell, 347; and multiple layers of regionalism, 346; nonteleological approach in, 342, 350n33; "Okie" as derisive term, 346; path to writing of, 330–31; published before Babb's novel, 129; Pulitzer prize winner, 327; as radical regional classic, 280; and regional consciousness continues in wake of migration, 345–46;

and regional dimensions of, 343–45; and regional revival in interwar years, 327, 329; and title selection, 340; and vernacular detail, 340, 350n30; writing of, 340
Graves, Maurice, 205
Great Depression: in central High Plains, 114; and distinctive radical-regional voice, 358; and impetus toward regionalism, 4, 21, 285–86; and Joe Jones, 65–67; regionalism pushed aside in, 357
Great Plains, The (Webb), 214
Great Plains and Texas: and plains tradition of radical agitation, 88–90; volatile political history of, 87–88. *See also* Botkin, Benjamin A.; Debo, Angie Elbertha; Dobie, J. Frank; Paredes, Américo; Sandoz, Mari
Green, Archie, 1, 11
Green, Elizabeth. *See under* Jones, Joe
Guthrie, A. B., 224, 234
Guthrie, Woody, 13, 88, 111, 278

"Hammon and the Beans, The" (Paredes), 189
"Harvest Gypsies, The" series (Steinbeck), 335, 350n20: advocates state and federal lands for subsistence farms for migrants, 337–38, 348, 350n23; and California's treatment of foreign labor, 335–36; and intervention of U.S. Attorney General called for, 338; migrant workers, Steinbeck's experience with, 331; new wave of migrants introduced in, 335; publication of in *San Francisco News*, 327, 334; role of federal camps outlined in, 350n23; victimization of immigrants highlighted in, 336–37
Haywood, William "Big Bill," 205
Healey, Dorothy, 128
Heidegger, Martin, 10
Henri, Robert, 106–107
Herbst, Josephine, 48, 51, 63n8; on "Americanism," 50; autobiographical nature of work, 48, 58; contempt shown for Iowa's literary life, 51–52; distance as aid to appreciation of roots, 52–53; farmers' struggles continuing concern of, 53–55; on farmers' visions of new social order, 55; farm life highlighted in notes of, 57–58; legacy of, 47, 61, 62, 63n1; marriage to Herrmann, 50; and midwestern writers, 61; path to revolutionary politics of, 22–23; radical circles of, 50, 61; radicalism of, 49–50; report on striking farmers in Sioux City, 52; rural background of, 49. *See also* Herbst, Josephine, works of; Trexler/Wendel trilogy
Herbst, Josephine, works of: *Executioner Waits, The*, 48, 58–59; "Farmer Looks Ahead, The," 47; "Farmers Form a United Front, The," 47, 55–56; "Feet in the Grass Roots," 47, 52, 53, 54, 63n17; "Iowa Takes to Literature," 51; *Pity Is Not Enough*, 48, 58–59; *Rope of Gold*, 48, 59–60. *See also* Herbst, Josephine
Herrmann, John (Herbst's husband), 50
Hicks, Granville, 29, 149
Hicks, John, 88, 97
Hidden Northwest, The (Cantwell), 272
High Plains as bioregion, 113: adaptation of farming to arid land, 114–15; allotment from land laws inadequate, 114; and disruptions of Great Depression, 114; financial resources exhausted by farmers, 115; and overuse of Ogallala aquifer for irrigation, 116; sense of loss reflected in Babb's writings, 114
Hill, Joe, 254
"Hills around Centralia" (Cantwell), 257
Hine, Robert V., 3, 277
Hinterland (magazine), 22, 32, 61, 127
Hirsch, Jerrold, 44, 89, 127
History of the Indians of the United States (Debo), 176
Hollywood inquisition, 130. *See also* HUAC; McCarthy era
Homestead Act (1862), 114
Honey in the Horn (Davis), 205–206

House Committee on Un-American Activities (HUAC): and Botkin, 153; and Dobie, 196–97; and Hollywood inquisition, 130; and Le Sueur, 26, 41, 46n57, 153; and Sanford, 283, 296
House in Antigua, The (Adamic), 370
House Made of Dawn (Momaday), 232, 241
Howard, Josephine (mother), 210–11
Howard, Joseph Kinsey, 206, *208*; and Anaconda Copper Mining Company, 212, 216; antipathy toward city of Butte, Mont., 216; and appreciation for labor unions, 211; and articles championing underdog in national magazines, 211–12; background of, 210; and bond with mother in fatherless home, 211; charged with overdramatization in *Montana*, 217; and compassion for dispossessed, 211, 216; congressional testimony of, 219; criticized as troublemaker, 221; and DeVoto, 218; early death of, 222, 224; as globalist of transnational frontier, 207, 224; and grassland morality tale, 213–14; and Guggenheim Fellowship, 222; legacy of, 218–19, 224–25; and Métis people, 206–207, 210, 223–24; and Montana Study with Brownell, 212, 219–21; Powell as source for protests, 215–16; reception of *Montana*, 212–13; as spokesperson for regional culture, 222; and suggested alternatives to predatory capitalism, 216–17; writing career pursued after *Montana*, 218; and "wrong side up" story, 209–10. *See also* Howard, Joseph Kinsey, works of
Howard, Joseph Kinsey, works of: *Montana*, 206, 212–14, 217–18; *Montana Margins*, 222; "Prophet without Honor," 215; *Strange Empire*, 206, 210, 222–25. *See also* Howard, Joseph Kinsey
Howe, James Wong (Babb's husband), 130
HUAC. *See* House Committee on Un-American Activities
Hugo, Richard, 234
Hurston, Zora Neale, 147

Ill Fares the Land (McWilliams), 356
Immigration and Naturalization Act of 1952, 310
Indian Removal (Foreman), 164–65
Indians, Outlaws and Angie Debo (PBS documentary), 177
Indians and Other Americans (McNickle and Fey), 232
Indian Tribes of the United States (McNickle), 235
In Dubious Battle (Steinbeck): based on 1934 strikes in California, 125, 331; first strike novel, 327; nonteleological approach of, 342; opening of, 332–33; reviews indicate ambiguity toward CPUSA, 332; scene showing depth of human attachment to place, 333–34; Steinbeck on, 330–31; themes of *The Grapes of Wrath* developed in, 333
Industrial Workers of the World. *See* IWW
Interwar regionalism, 4–9, 12–14, 27
"Iowa Takes to Literature" (Herbst), 51
Iowa Writers' Project (WPA), 32, 40–41
"I Want the Wide American Earth" (Bulosan), 304
IWW (Industrial Workers of the World): and Cantwell, 257; in Midwest, 31; in Northern West, 205; in Pacific Northwest, 274n5; in Sioux City, Iowa, 49; in Washington State, 254

Janson, H. W., 9
Japanese Americans (McWilliams), 356
Jeffers, Robinson, 362–63
Jihad vs. McWorld (Barber), 9–10
John Reed Club, 21, 271
Johnson, Dorothy, 234
Jolly Flatboatmen in Port, The (Bingham), 76
Jones, Joe, 66; anti-lynching theme of, 77–79; background of, 67–68; Benton and Wood contrasted with, 23, 66–67, 75, 82; and Chadsey, 70, 72; as Communist Party member, 67, 69–70, 77–78; and Conroy, 71–72; and Elizabeth Green,

68, 69, 70, 73, 80, 84n9; and formal modernism, 68–69; and frustration over mural controversy, 72; Le Sueur's writing parallels, 82–83; and mural commission at Mena, Ark., college, 73, 76–78; and New Hats organization, 68, 84n10; and political activism in New York, 72–73; as proletarian artist of Midwest, 23, 65–66; as radical regionalist, 67; and Resettlement Administration, 65; reviews of work, 75–76; in social context of Great Depression, 67, 79; *Social Protest in Old St. Louis*, 69–72; and solo exhibition at ACA Gallery in NYC (1935), 65, 74–76, 83n1, 85n35; and Unemployed Art Class, 69–72, 74. *See also* Jones, Joe, and Dust Bowl themes; Jones, Joe, works of

Jones, Joe, and Dust Bowl themes: and Communism, 78, 82; first involvement in Dust Bowl problems (1936), 79–80; and Guggenheim Fellowship to record Dust Bowl effects, 80; imagery tied to working-class background of, 82; and Le Sueur's description of the Midwest, 81–82; narrative of dislocation, 81

Jones, Joe, works of: *Landscape* (painting), 68, 83n6; *Lynching* (painting), 78; *Midwestern Landscape* (painting), 81; Old Courthouse mural, 78, 81; *Roustabouts* (painting), 75–76, 82; *Social Protest in Old St. Louis* (mural), 69–72; *Windmill and Two Bulls* (painting), 81. *See also* Jones, Joe

Joplin, Janice, 249

Kafka, Franz, 99
Kazin, Alfred, 6, 60
Kazin, Michael, 2
Kemmis, Dan, 247
King Ranch (Texas), 186, 200
Kinkaid Land Act, 95, 98
Klein, Herbert, 367
Kosiba, Sara, 22–23, 47
Kramer, Dale, 32

Land of Plenty, The (Cantwell): abrupt ending of, 23, 268–69; autobiographical elements of, 207, 261, 265–66; class, gender, and race issues in, 263–64, 267, 269; and Great Crash of 1929, 261–62; F. Scott Fitzgerald, references to, 266; and industrial alienation, 263; IWW "wipeout" in, 264–65; Johnny's distrust of middle class in, 266–67; major achievement of proletarian movement, 207, 260; message of, 269–70; naturalism of, 261–62; northwestern radicalism evident in, 269; positive reviews of, 270; pride of workers who resist supervisor, 264; strike and police protection of scabs, 267–68, 268; strike tactics explained to workers, 264; structure of, 261, 262–63; style of, 260. *See also* Cantwell, Robert

Landscape (Jones) (painting), 68, 83n6
Land That Touches Mine, The (Sanford), 296
Lange, Dorothea, 5, 7, 13, 278, 354
Langer, Elinor (Herbst biographer), 49, 50, 55
Laugh and Lie Down (Cantwell), 257–58
Laughing in the Jungle (Adamic), 362
"Laughter of My Father, The" (Bulosan), 304
Leach, Neal, 10
"Leader of the People, The" (Steinbeck), 338–39, 347
League of American Writers, 25, 32, 61, 152
Leckie Reed, Shirley A., 90, 157
Left Front (magazine), 22, 312
Legacy of D'Arcy McNickle, The (Purdy), 229
Lehman, Tim, 206–207, 209
Le Sueur, Meridel, 24; address to American Writers' Conference (1935), 22, 39, 42n1, 81–82, 83; assessment of by others, 8, 26; and Babb, 120; blacklisted by HUAC, 26, 41, 46n57; call for "regionalism of class roots," 370; chilly reception by publishers, 130; as Communist, 26–27;

Le Sueur, Meridel (*continued*)
cornfield as recurring motif of, 24, 35; feminist perspective of, 25–26, 34, 45n31; and idealized prairie woman, 38; and interest in Botkin's work, 149, 150; and Joe Jones's work, 82–83; and McWilliams, 368–69; and Midwestern literary radicals, 30–31; Midwestern roots of, 31–32, 36, 42; and *Midwest* magazine, 29, 33–34, 35; and Midwest Writers' Conference, 32; and radical regionalism, 6, 7, 22, 25–26, 42, 43n3; on rise of working class, 7; vision of, 39; writing career of, 29. *See also* Le Sueur, Meridel, works of

Le Sueur, Meridel, works of: *Crusaders*, 29, 41–42, 46n57; "On Proletarian Literature in the Middle West" (1935 speech), 25, 39, 42n1, 81, 83; "Proletarian Literature and the Middle West," 150; *Salute to Spring*, 35; "Salute to Spring" (short story), 61–62; *Worker Writers*, 41–42. *See also* "American Way, The"; Le Sueur, Meridel; *North Star Country*

Letter from America (Bulosan), 304

Letters from an American Farmer (Crèvecoeur), 230

"Letter to a Filipino Woman" (Bulosan), 321–22

Limerick, Patricia, 14–15, 356

Limón, José, 90, 184

Lincoln, Abraham, 21, 29, 38, 211

Lippard, Lucy, 286

Little Red Songbook, The, 254

Local color movement, 144, 246, 285–86, 364–65

"Locavore" movement, 247–48

Lomax, John, 148

Lone Star (Sayles) (film), 14

Long Valley, The (Steinbeck), 327, 338

Lost Traveler, The (Babb), 112, 119, 129

Lottinville, Savoie, 176, 177

Louis Adamic and Shadow America (McWilliams), 370

Love Song to the Plains (Sandoz), 105

Luce, Henry, 259, 272

Luhan, Mabel Dodge, 165

Lynching (painting by Jones), 78

"Macaria's Daughter" (Paredes), 189

Man at the Crossroads (mural by Rivera), 72

Man without Shoes, A (Sanford), 296

Marching! Marching! (Weatherwax), 255

Marx, Karl, 9, 69, 240, 259

Marxism, in 1930s: Americanized version in Midwest, 30–31; and Herbst, 49–50; and Howard, 211; in New York during Depression, 258–59; and Paredes, 189–90, 198, 199; and regionalism, 27–28, 141

Mask for Privilege, A (McWilliams), 356

Massey, Doreen, 10

Mathews, John Joseph, 165

May, Lary, 12–13

McCarran-Walter Act (1952), 310, 324n26

McCarthy era, 26, 123, 130, 384

McGrath, Alice Greenfield, 367

McNickle, D'Arcy, 207, 241, 228; attention given after death, 229; background of, 233–34; and Bureau of Indian Affairs, 230, 234; and centrality of place, 232; co-founder of National Congress of American Indians, 235; on Collier, 243; coming home stressed by, 231; complex vision of, 206; and crash of 2008, 242; and dedication of The D'Arcy McNickle Library, 248; father of Native American novel, 233; and "leaving" plots, 230–31, 232; and life between two cultures, 234; and Merriam, 234; Native American fiction pioneer, 229; radical analysis of liberal capitalism by, 241, 242; radical revisions made to earlier work by, 242–43; and tribalism, 232; and University of Montana, 234; writings, 1926–36, 241. *See also* McNickle, D'Arcy, works of; Tribalism, regionalism, and the new localism in the age of ecology

McNickle, D'Arcy, works of: *Indians and Other Americans*, 232; *Indian Tribes of the United States*, 235; "Six Beautiful in

INDEX

Paris," 241; "Snowfall," 241; *Surrounded, The*, 231–32, 234, 241; *They Came Here First*, 242–43. *See also* McNickle, D'Arcy; *Wind from an Enemy Sky*

McNickle, William (father), 233

McWilliams, Carey, 352; and Babb, 120; and biography of Ambrose Bierce, 360, 362, 363, 365; and Botkin, 144–45; and Bulosan, 312; and California as nation's racial frontier, 280, 372–73; as catalyst of left-wing proletarian regionalism in the West, 370; and chapbook manifesto indicting regionalist movement, 364–65; and cynical regionalism in 1930s, 362; and discouragement with personal and professional life, 365–66; early writing career of, 356; editor of the *Nation*, 355, 372; and first New York experience, 363; and growth as radical regionalist, 363, 366; as labor lawyer and investigative writer, 366–67; literary output, 1939–49, 356; and Los Angeles epiphany, 360–61; move to California in 1922, 359; and New Regionalism, 4, 6; and personal political epiphany to Adamic, 370–71; political activities, 367–68; preoccupation with regional spectacle, 364; as "prolific wunderkind," 360; and promise of progressive pluralistic politics, 373; rediscovered as public intellectual, 355–56; and regional dilemma of, 357; as regional tastemaker, 362; shift from literary regionalist to labor journalist, 365; social significance of work questioned by, 363–64; speech to congress on art and politics, 369; and tour of Sacramento Valley, 367; vision of multicultural regionalism developed by, 368; and Nathanael West, 364; and Western Writers' Congress, 368–69. *See also* McWilliams, Carey, works of

McWilliams, Carey, works of: *Anti-Semitism in America*, 356; *Brothers under the Skin*, 356; *California: The Great Exception*, 356; "Getting Rid of the Mexican," 356; *Ill Fares the Land*, 356; *Japanese Americans*, 356; *Louis Adamic and Shadow America*, 370, 373n62; *Mask for Privilege, A*, 356; *New Regionalism in American Literature, The* (chapbook), 144, 364; *North from Mexico*, 356; "Personal Note," 372–73; *Prejudice*, 356; *Southern California*, 356, 360, 361; *Spanish Speaking People of the United States*, 356; "Swell Letters in California," 365; "The Writer and Civil Liberties," 369. *See also Factories in the Field*; McWilliams, Carey

McWilliams, Jerry (father), 359

Mearns, Jack, 279, 283

Melby, Ernest, 219–20

Mencken, H. L., 141–42, 356

Mensalvas, Chris, 310

Meriam, Lewis, 179n27

Merriam, Harold Guy, 206, 234, 248

Métis people, 206–207, 210, 223–24

Mexal, Stephen, 279, 303

"Mexico-Texan, The" (poem by Paredes), 189

Mickenberg, Julia, 22, 25

Midland, The (magazine), 120, 121, 127, 147

Midwest (magazine): Le Sueur as editor, 29, 33–34, 35, 39; and Midwest Federation, 32; as voice of progressive regionalism, 21–22, 31, 32–33, 44n22

Midwest: idealized pastoral image of, 53, 63n17; and midwestern literary radicals, 30–32, 44n22; overview, 21–23. *See also* Herbst, Josephine; Jones, Joe; Le Sueur, Meridel

Midwestern Landscape (painting by Jones), 81

Midwest Federation of Arts and Professions, 32

Midwest Writers' Conference, 32

Mind and Society, The (Pareto), 99

Miss Lonelyhearts (West), 289, 293

Mitchell, Ruth Comfort, 347

Momaday, N. Scott, 232, 241

Montana (Howard), 206, 212–14, 217–18

Montana Margins (Howard), 222

More Goodly Country, A (Sanford), 297

Moveable Feast, A (Hemingway), 52
Mumford, Lewis, 18n17; and Botkin, 89, 136, 148; on neurotic defeat of regionalism, 7–8; on universality of regional culture, 15; work read by McWilliams, 363

Nash, Gerald, 11
Nation, Carrie, 87
Nelson, Cary, 27
New localism, 246–48
New Masses (CPUSA magazine), 8, 22, 26, 55, 71, 127, 255
New Negro Renaissance, 140
New Regionalism in American Literature, The (chapbook, McWilliams), 144, 364
New Tide, The (Bulosan, ed.), 309
New Western History, 5, 11, 14–15, 17n12
Noguch, Yone, 312
Northern West, 272–74; turbulent labor history of, 205–207. *See also* Cantwell, Robert; Howard, Joseph Kinsey; McNickle, D'Arcy
North from Mexico (McWilliams), 356
North Star Country (Le Sueur): folk history of Upper Midwest, 22; as legacy of WPA Writers' Project, 40, 41, 46n52; and Midwest as cradle of democracy, 40–41; publication of, 29, 39–40

Odum, Howard, 89, 136, 244
Of Human Kindness (Mitchell), 347
Of Mice and Men (Steinbeck), 126, 327, 338
Oklahoma: A Guide to the Sooner State (Debo and Oskison, eds.), 174–75, 182n75
Old Courthouse mural (Jones), 78, 81. See also *Social Protest in Old St. Louis*
Old Jules (Sandoz), 93, 97, 102, 105–106. *See also* Sandoz, Jules
Old Man's Place, The (Sanford), 284, 290
"Old One, The" (Babb) (short story), 121
Olsen, Tillie, 13, 120, 130, 278, 354
Olson, Floyd B., 21
Orozco, José Clemente, 72

Otis, Elizabeth, 339
Owl on Every Post, An (Babb), 112

Palace of Silver, A (Sanford), 298
Paredes, Américo, *186*; background of, 88, 187; bohemian lifestyle of, 189; and Chicano student movement, 198–99; and Dobie, 90, 200–201; early radical politics, 192; as English professor at UT, 197; and folk culture as specialty, 197–98; Marxism in work, 189–90, 198, 199; military service in WWII, 193–94; and new regionalism, 14, 90; postwar career in Asia, 194, 199; transnational dimension of, 187. *See also* Paredes, Américo, works of
Paredes, Américo, works of: "Cold Night," 189; *George Washington Gómez*, 190–91, 192, 200; "The Hammon and the Beans," 189; *"With His Pistol in His Hand,"* 198, 200; "Macaria's Daughter," 189; "The Mexico-Texan" (poem), 189; "Rebeca," 190; "Revenge," 189. *See also* Paredes, Américo
Parenteau, Isador (McNickle's grandfather), 233
Pareto, Vilfredo, 99, 100
Parker, Dorothy, 229, 243
Partisan Review (magazine), 32, 33–34, 120
Pastures of Heaven, The (Steinbeck), 329, 330
Paterson Strike Pageant, 254
Paz, Octavio, 193
People from Heaven, The (Sanford), 292–93
Phillips, Frank, 164, 179n27
Pity Is Not Enough (Herbst), 48, 58–59
Political History of the Cherokees, 1838–1907 (Wardell), 171
Pollan, Michael, 247
Popular Front movement: and Botkin, 147, 150; and Communist Party approval of American folk material, 8; and cooperation among all leftist elements, 332; McWilliams's disappointment with, 370; and struggle against fascism in late 1930s, 120; U.S. incarnation of, 28–29;

and Western Writers' Congress (1936), 368–69
Porter, Pleasant (Creek leader), 174
Pound, Louise, 88, 97, 135, 141, 153
Powell, John Wesley, 114, 215, 217, 218
Prairie City (Debo), 175
Prejudice (McWilliams), 356
Princeton University Press, 173
"Proletarian Literature and the Middle West" (Le Sueur), 7, 25, 150
Proletarian regionalism: Cantwell's support for, 259–60; complementary approaches of regional and proletarian writers, 150–51; "egalitarian dreamers," profound impact of on American society, 3; and proletarian regionalist magazines, 22; McWilliams as catalyst of in the West, 370; and writers' and artists' rediscovery of home regions, 13; and Constance Rourke, 12–13. See also *America Is in the Heart*; Denning, Michael; *Land of Plenty, The*; "Proletarian Literature and the Middle West"; Regionalism
"Prophet without Honor" (Howard), 215
Purdy, John, 229

Quezon, Manuel, 311

"Radicalism of Tradition" (Calhoun), 2, 3, 27
Rainey, Homer, firing of at UT, 195
Ransom, John Crowe, as representative regionalist, 6, 7
"Rebeca" (Paredes), 190
Rebel Poet, The (magazine, ed. Conroy), 22, 147
Red Rock, Okla. Terr., 116–17
Reed, John, 205, 254, 273
Reed, T. V., 207, 253
"Region, Power, Place" (Bevis), 229
Regionalism: defined, 2, 3–4, 12, 209, 243; emergence of, 5–6; examples of in 1930s, 7; Frankfurter on, 12; and Great Depression, 4; and Marxism, 27–28; opposing viewpoints on, 1–2; and politics, 5; and regionalists as

fascists, 11–12; roots of, 285–86. *See also* Proletarian regionalism; Western regionalism
"Regionalism and Culture" (Botkin), 150–51
"Regionalism: Cult or Culture?" (Botkin), 35
Report on the Lands of the Arid Region (Powell), 215
Resettlement Administration (RA; later FSA): and Tom Collins, 124–28, 334–35; established in 1935, 111; and Joe Jones, 65, 79–81; Steinbeck calls for expansion of, 337. *See also* Farm Security Administration
"Revenge" (Paredes), 189
Rexroth, Kenneth, 13, 278, 369
Rich Land, Poor Land (Chase), 214
Riel, Louis, 207, 223–24
Rise and Fall of the Choctaw Republic, The (Debo), 167
Rivera, Diego, 72
Road to Disappearance, The (Debo), 174
Roberts, Marguerite ("Maggie"). *See* Sanford, Marguerite ("Maggie") Roberts
Rockwell, Norman, 304
Rogers, Will, 13, 88, 177, 278
Roosevelt, Franklin Delano, 193; abhorred by oil establishment, 195; and Dobie's opposition to in early 1930s, 194, 195–96; and Four Freedoms speech of 1941, 303–304; Paredes's criticism of Four Freedoms speech, 192, 193; and regional principles, 5
Rope of Gold (Herbst), 48, 59–60
Rourke, Constance, 12–13, 29, 147, 365
Roustabouts (painting by Jones), 75–76, 82
Royce, Josiah, 16
Rushdie, Salman, 10

Saldívar, Ramón: in praise of Paredes's poems, 192; on Roosevelt's Four Freedoms, 304
Salinas lettuce strike of 1934, 316
Salute to Spring (Le Sueur), 35
"Salute to Spring" (Le Sueur), 61–62

Sánchez, George I., 192–93
Sandoz, Jules (father): adaptability to land of, 94–95; and brutality of, 95–96; death of, 96; redemption of in *Old Jules*, 102, 105–106. See also *Old Jules*
Sandoz, Mari, 92; as agrarian, 106; background of, 88–90, 93–94; blinded in one eye in blizzard, 96; and *Cheyenne Autumn*, 104–105; childhood influences on, 95–96; *Crazy Horse*, writing of as therapeutic, 103–104; death of, 105; death threats received by, 102; and "guyascutus" theme of, 100, 102; and Kafka's *Castle*, 99; marriage of, 96; *Mein Kampf* as inspiration for, 98; mentors of, 97; and Native Americans, 103–104; pessimistic worldview of, 94, 99, 105; and regionalist social democracy in works of, 101, 103; Ida Tarbell as personal inspiration, 102; urban lifestyle as salvation for, 101–102. See also Sandoz, Mari, works of
Sandoz, Mari, works of: *Beaver Men, The*, 105; *Capital City*, 99–100, 102; *Cheyenne Autumn*, 104–105; *Crazy Horse*, 103–104; *Love Song to the Plains*, 105; *Old Jules*, 93, 97, 102, 105–106; *Slogum House*, 97–98; *Son of the Gamblin' Man*, 97, 106–107; *Tom-Walker, The*, 100–101, 102. See also Sandoz, Mari
Sanford, John, 279, 282, 283, 298–99; autobiography, 297; background of, 283; born Julian Shapiro, 286; blacklisted by HUAC, 283, 296; classification as regionalist questioned, 284; as Communist Party member, 279, 283, 288–89, 292; compared with Joyce, 293; and death of mother, 287; education of, 287–88; evolution as California regionalist, 284; and Hollywood, 294–96; law career, 289; and People's Education Center, 295; positive reviews of, 297; radicalization of, 288–89; regionalism as paradoxical, 292; and Maggie Roberts, 290, 294–95; and roots of regionalism, 285–86; "Sanford" as pseudonym, 290; and Warrensburg (N.Y.) trilogy, 284, 286, 290–94, 299n3; work contrasted with that of West, 293. See also Sanford, John, works of; Sanford, Marguerite ("Maggie") Roberts; West, Nathanael
Sanford, John, works of: *Land That Touches Mine, The*, 296; *Man without Shoes, A*, 296; *More Goodly Country, A*, 297; *Old Man's Place, The*, 284, 290; *Palace of Silver, A*, 298; *People from Heaven, The*, 292–93; *Seventy Times Seven*, 291; *Water Wheel, The*, 289, 290, 291; *Winters of That Country, The*, 299. See also Sanford, John
Sanford, Marguerite ("Maggie") Roberts (Mrs. John Sanford), 290, 293, 294–95, 296, 298
San Francisco General Strike, 271–72
Satanic Verses (Rushdie), 10
Saturday Evening Post, 212, 304, 311
Saxton, Alexander, 278
Sayles, John, 14
Schivelbusch, Wolfgang, 11
Scholsser, Eric, 247
Schumacher, E. F., 246
Science and Society: A Marxian Quarterly, 152–53
Scott, William, 51
Seattle World Trade Organization convention, 273–74
Seventy Times Seven (Sanford), 291
Shapiro, Julian. See Sanford, John
Shaw, Edward, 177
Sheffy, Lester Fields, 163
Shortridge, James R., 53
"Significance of the Frontier in American History" (Turner), 161
Silko, Leslie Marmon, 232
Simpson, Jeremiah "Sockless Jerry," 87
Sinclair, Upton, 11, 354, 360, 362, 367, 369
Siqueros, Alfaro David, 23
"Six Beautiful in Paris" (McNickle), 241
Slogum House (Sandoz), 97–98
Small Is Beautiful (Schumacher), 246
Smith, Henry Nash, 1, 11

"Snowfall" (McNickle), 241
Snyder, Gary, 247
Social History of Missouri (mural by Benton), 82
Social Protest in Old St. Louis (mural by Jones), 69–72. *See also* Old Courthouse mural (Jones)
Sollors, Werner, 10
Son of the Gamblin' Man (Sandoz), 97, 106–107
Southern Agrarians, 3, 8, 150, 357
Southern California (McWilliams), 356, 360, 361
Southern California Country (McWilliams), 40
Space (magazine, ed. Botkin), 148–49
Spanish Speaking People of the United States (McWilliams), 356
Steffens, Lincoln, 271–72, 278
Stegner, Wallace, 218
Steinbeck, John, 328; affinity for his native California, 330; Babb's notes on Dust Bowl refugees given to, 126; Babb's work rivals that of, 89, 127, 130–31; concern for safety after "The Harvest Gypsies," 338; on controversial ending of *The Grapes of Wrath*, 341; early works of, 329–330; and FSA, 111, 125; and history, 327–28; on *In Dubious Battle*, 330–31; and "L'Affaire Lettuceberg" aborted, 340; as radical regionalist, 280; on revolutionary character of *The Grapes of Wrath*, 340; on Visalia conditions, 40; and vision for more humane America, 329, 348; writing of *The Grapes of Wrath*, 340. *See also* Steinbeck, John, works of
Steinbeck, John, works of: *Cup of Gold*, 329; "Leader of the People, The," 338–39, 347; *Long Valley, The*, 327, 338; *Of Mice and Men*, 126, 327, 338; *Pastures of Heaven, The*, 329, 330; *Their Blood Was Strong*, 125; *To a God Unknown*, 329, 330; *Tortilla Flat*, 329, 330, 349n8. *See also Grapes of Wrath, The*; "Harvest Gypsies"; *In Dubious Battle*; Steinbeck, John

Steiner, Michael C. (editor): on California, 277–81; on Carey McWilliams, 353–76; on Great Depression, 114; on Great Plains and Texas, 87–91; on Midwest, 21–23; on Northern West, 205–207; on regions as places where "primal cultures" can offset a top-heavy machine civilization, 244; on themes of twentieth-century regionalism, 285–86; on turn to regionalism in 1930s and 1940s, 184
Strachey, John, 99, 100
Strange Empire (Howard), 206, 210, 222–25
Strong, Anna Louise, 205, 254, 273
Struggle for Negro Rights (art exhibition, 1935), 73
Suckow, Ruth, 6, 21
Surrounded, The (McNickle), 231–32, 234, 241
"Swell Letters in California" (McWilliams), 365

Taft-Hartley Act (1947), 123
Taylor, Paul, 13, 278, 354
Taylor Grazing Act, 216
Teleology, defined, 331
Tenayuca, Emma, 192–93
Ten Days That Shook the World (Reed), 254
Ten Tough Trips (Bevis), 229
Tester, Jon, 248
Texas Rangers, 200
Texas Rangers, The (Webb), 8
Their Blood Was Strong (Steinbeck), 125
They Came Here First (McNickle), 242–43
To a God Unknown (Steinbeck), 329, 330
Told in the Seed (poems by Babb), 112
Tom-Walker, The (Sandoz), 100–101, 102
Tongues of the Monte (Dobie), 196
Toole, K. Ross, 217
Tortilla Flat (Steinbeck), 329, 330, 349n8
Trexler/Wendel trilogy (Herbst): Book 1, *Pity Is Not Enough*, 48, 58–59; Book 2, *The Executioner Waits*, 48, 59; Book 3, *Rope of Gold*, 48, 59–60; Herbst's

Trexler/Wendel trilogy (*continued*)
reflections on, 61; Kazin review of *Rope in New York Herald Tribune*, 60
Tribalism, regionalism, and the new localism in the age of ecology: and food reformers, 247; and freedom of choice, 249; and irrelevancy of "place," 244; and liberal capitalism as center, 243–44; and liquidity linked to liberalism, 248; and localism as regionalism, 246–47; and "locavore" movement, 248; and McNickle, 246; and opposition of ecology and postmodernism, 245; "region" redefined by rise of ecology, 244–45; regions defined, 243; sustainability as key, 246; and tribalism, 245–46; and voice of regionalists, 244. *See also* McNickle, D'Arcy
Tugwell, Rexford, 80
Tulsa (Debo), 175
Turnbull, James, 23, 67
Turner, Frederick Jackson: Dale's mentor, 160–61, 163, 168; on darker edge to plains tradition in 1890s, 87–88, 97, 99; frontier thesis of, 97; and *North Star Country*, 40; as progressive historian, 21; on "rights of man," 30; and sectionalism, 4, 16
Tydings-McDuffie Act of 1934, 309

University of Oklahoma Press: Brandt as first director of, 142, 165; and Civilization of the American Indian Series, 165; Debo dissertation published by, 167; and Debo's fear of retaliation against, 172–73; as leading publisher of Indian history, 171; and Lottinville, 176; and publication of *Road to Disappearance*, 174; and Shaw, 177

Vaquero of the Brush Country, A (Dobie), 187, 189
Voice of the Coyote, The (Dobie), 196

Wa'Kon-tah (Mathews), 165
Wallace, Henry, 21, 29, 196

Wardell, Morris, 171–73
Washington state: as Cantwell's home state, 206, 207, 253, 257–58; and emergence of regionalist painters, 205; and IWW, 254, 274n5; and labor radicalism, 253–54; as timber country, 256
Water Wheel, The (Sanford), 289, 290, 291
Wayland, Julius, 87, 124
Weatherwax, Clara, 255
Webb, Walter Prescott, 6, 8, 90, 114, 115, 214
Welch, James, 232, 234
West, Nathanael: as anti-regionalist, 293; and *Day of the Locust*, 293, 364; death of, 294; as inspiration for Sanford, 287–88, 289; and McWilliams, 364; and McWilliams's writers' congress in San Francisco, 369; and *Miss Lonelyhearts*, 293; and Sanford, 279, 294; Sanford contrasted with, 293. *See also* Sanford, John
"West Coast: Our Racial Frontier, The" (McWilliams), 368
Western regionalism: condemnation of American regionalists, 7–8, 10–12, 29; contemporary attacks on, 9–10; Dickstein on, 13–14; Limerick on, 14–15; May on, 13; opposing viewpoints on, 1–2; Williams on, 14
Western Writers' Conference, 368–70
"We Talk about Regionalism—North, East, South, and West" (Botkin), 5, 147–48
White, Richard, 14, 247
Whitman, Walt: call to arms, 35–36, 45n36; call to "study out the land," 6, 16, 18n15; history as seen by, 38
Whose Names Are Unknown (Babb), 131; Babb's radical regionalist voice expressed in, 112; and publication delayed, 89, 128–29; publication of in 2004, 130; source of title, 126
Williams, William Appleman, 14
Wilson, Edmund, 258–59, 271, 293, 353–54, 366

Wind from an Enemy Sky (McNickle), 235–37: "Bad Medicine" of liberal capitalists rejected in, 207; critique of, 237–40; most political of McNickle's works, 235; Adam Pell as advocate for Indians, 229–30, 235–37, 240, 242–43, 247; published posthumously, 229; and radical analysis of liberal capitalism, 240–41; rewriting of by McNickle, 242; "Snowfall" as seed story for, 241; and tribalism, 230, 232

Windmill and Two Bulls (Jones) (painting), 81

Winter in the Blood (Welch), 232

Winters of That Country, The (Sanford), 299

Wirth, Louis, 8

"*With His Pistol in His Hand*" (Paredes), 198, 200

Wixson, Douglas, 22, 30–31, 89, 111, 147, 151

Wobblies. *See* IWW

"Woman's Influence on the French Revolution" (Dale), 172

Wood, Grant: contrasted with Jones, 23, 66, 75, 82, 83; critical response to, 8; regionalist imagery of, 5; as self-proclaimed regionalist, 6

Word Ways (Purdy), 229

Worker-Writer in America (Wixson), 22, 30–31, 147

Worker Writers (Le Sueur), 41–42

World Trade Organization convention (Seattle), 273–74

Worster, Donald, 14, 247

WPA (Works Progress Administration), 174–75

"Writer and Civil Liberties, The" (McWilliams), 369

Wrobel, David, 280, 355

Wynn, Dudley, 8

Zelinsky, Wilbur, 31

www.ingramcontent.com/pod-product-compliance
Lightning Source LLC
Chambersburg PA
CBHW022057150426
43195CB00008B/169